Toronto Maple Leafs
Diary of a Dynasty 1957–1967

Toronto Maple Leafs
Diary of a Dynasty 1957–1967

Kevin Shea
with Paul Patskou
Roly Harris and Paul Bruno

Firefly Books

A FIREFLY BOOK

Published by Firefly Books Ltd. 2010

Copyright © 2010 Firefly Books Ltd.

Text copyright © 2010 Kevin Shea with Paul Patskou, Roly Harris and Paul Bruno

Photographs copyright © 2010 individual photographers as credited

First printing

Publisher Cataloging-in-Publication Data (U.S.)

Shea, Kevin.

   Toronto Maple Leafs : diary of a dynasty, 1957-1967 / Kevin Shea with Paul Patskou, Roly Harris and Paul Bruno.

[   ] p. : photos. ;   cm.

Includes bibliographical references and index.

Summary: This book chronicles the seasons when the Toronto Maple Leafs skyrocketed from last place in the NHL to become the powerhouse team of the decade.

ISBN-13: 978-1-55407-636-9 (pbk.)

ISBN-10: 1-55407-636-6 (pbk.)

1. Toronto Maple Leafs (Hockey team) -- History. I. Patskou, Paul. II. Harris, Roly. III. Bruno, Paul. IV. Title.

796.962/ 64/ 09713541 dc22   GV848.T6S543   2010

Library and Archives Canada Cataloguing in Publication

Shea, Kevin, 1956-

   Toronto Maple Leafs : diary of a dynasty, 1957-1967 / Kevin Shea with Paul Patskou, Roly Harris and Paul Bruno.

Includes bibliographical references and index.

ISBN-13: 978-1-55407-636-9 (pbk.)

ISBN-10: 1-55407-636-6 (pbk.)

   1. Toronto Maple Leafs (Hockey team)--History.

I. Patskou, Paul II. Roly, Harris, 1947- III. Bruno, Paul, 1959- IV. Title.

GV848.T6S54 2010   796.962'6409713541

C2010-901870-2

Published in the United States by

Firefly Books (U.S.) Inc.

P.O. Box 1338, Ellicott Station

Buffalo, New York 14205

Published in Canada by

Firefly Books Ltd.

66 Leek Crescent

Richmond Hill, Ontario L4B 1H1

Cover and interior design: opushouse.com

Formatting: opushouse.com

The publisher gratefully acknowledges the financial support for our publishing program by the Government of Canada through the Canada Book Fund as administered by the Department of Canadian Heritage.

Printed in China

Front cover photo: Toronto Maple Leafs captain George Armstrong victorious with the Stanley Cup after beating the Detroit Red Wings in the 1964 final. (Lee Balterman/Sports Illustrated/Getty Images).

Back cover: The 1964 team. (Graphic Artists/Hockey Hall of Fame) Spine: The Stanley Cup. (Graphic Artists/Hockey Hall of Fame) Recurring image, interior: Leafs sitting on the boards. (Imperial Oil-Turofsky/HHOF).

*We dedicate this book to all Maple Leafs' fans who
steadfastly hold out hope of one day soon experiencing a
Stanley Cup championship to add to the memories
of those relived on these pages.*

CONTENTS

FOREWORD
BY JOHNNY BOWER

I started playing hockey when I was around ten years old. I don't know why I became a goaltender. Maybe it's because I wasn't a very good skater.

I ended up with the Cleveland Barons of the American Hockey League in 1945. There, Bun Cook, our coach, really worked with me on my angles. I came to really like Cleveland. On November 3, 1948, I married Nancy in Cleveland. With the Barons, we won the Calder Cup in 1948, 1951 and 1953.

Rumours started to circulate that the New York Rangers were interested in me. I started to get excited. I had wondered while I played in the minors if I'd ever get a chance at the NHL. Yet, when the trade was made, I had mixed emotions. I didn't know whether I wanted to go or not because of my age. I was going to be twenty-nine, and I thought about retiring. But I joined the team. It was in New York that I learned the poke check. Former Rangers' goalie Charlie Rayner taught me how to execute what became my signature move. We had some tough times in New York — the team struggled and didn't make the playoffs while I was there, but one great thing that happened for us in New York was that Nancy and I became parents for the first time.

I was up and down between the Rangers and the minors. In 1955–56, playing with the Providence Reds, we beat my old team, the Cleveland Barons, to win the Calder Cup. It was my fourth AHL championship.

I returned to the Barons in 1957–58. I really liked it in Cleveland, and even though there were offers to return to the NHL, I refused to go. I had no desire to leave Cleveland. But the Toronto Maple Leafs weren't going to take no for an answer, and selected me from the Barons in the Intra-League Draft. I really didn't want to go.

The Leafs hadn't made the playoffs the previous two seasons and hadn't won a playoff series since they had won the Stanley Cup in 1951. I made the team, and it was the best thing that happened to my hockey career. I figured I'd be in Toronto for a couple of years, but ended up playing with them until 1970.

When we won the Stanley Cup in 1962, my son threw his arms around me and said, "Daddy's just won the Allan Stanley Cup!" It was very exciting for all of us!

Once you win one Cup, you want to keep going. But when you win the Stanley Cup, everybody else wants to beat you. We managed to win three in a row. Then, to everybody's surprise, we beat the Canadiens in 1967 and won the fourth Stanley Cup of that decade. During our surprising run, I think deep down that everybody in that Maple Leafs' dressing room knew we were part of something special and were enjoying a ride together that most of us would never take again as teammates. The NHL was going to double in size to start the 1967–68 season, and with so many players on our team over the age of thirty we knew that many of us would be moving on at the end of the season. We all figured it was our last year to be Leafs. That's why we worked our hearts out to beat Chicago and Montreal.

When the Maple Leafs won the Stanley Cup in 1967, I grabbed two bottles of champagne left in the dressing room, hid them behind my bench, then took them home. My wife Nancy marked on the label, "Do not open until the Leafs next win the Stanley Cup."

Nancy and I celebrated our fiftieth wedding anniversary on November 3, 1998, and we had a party at the house. I thought, "What can I do to make this a special occasion?" Then I remembered the champagne. I got one of the bottles, took the wire off and pressed on the cork. Usually, when you open a bottle of champagne, it makes a big popping sound and then a stream of champagne flows out. Not this time. Three-quarters of the bottle was empty; it had evaporated. It didn't taste too good, but I've still got the other bottle. That one's full, I checked. We're saving that one until the Toronto Maple Leafs again win the Stanley Cup.

Johnny Bower

INTRODUCTION

Standing at centre ice, I glance around at the empty Maple Leaf Gardens. Gone are the Stanley Cup banners, as well as the banners honouring Ace Bailey and Bill Barilko. Gone, too, are the boards, the players' benches and the penalty box. Many of the seats have been removed — some sold, some stored — but surprising to me is how many seats remain.

What isn't gone, of course, are the memories.

From the dusty concrete floor, I look up to where my grey season seats were once located.

When I moved to Toronto in 1984, the first thing I did was drive to Maple Leaf Gardens and simply sit in my car, across the street on Carlton, and gaze at the building. There, after years of being a Toronto Maple Leafs' fan, I was finally seeing the historic home of my hockey team.

From the time of my first hazy memories, my Dad had my brother and me seated beside him, each clutching a small cup of ginger ale and picking away at a handful of potato chips while watching the Toronto Maple Leafs on *Hockey Night in Canada* on Channel 9 in Windsor, every Saturday, without fail.

I don't recall that Dad ever mentioned having a favourite player, but he liked all the Leafs — Mahovlich, Keon, Horton, Bower. My Mom, who flitted between the TV screen and ironing (on Saturday night!), took a less passionate view of the game but still was fascinated by the boys in blue and white. And for such a sweet and gentle soul, we were warned to call her if a fight broke out. Inevitably, she'd race up the stairs on hearing "Fight! Fight!," seldom in time to see the combatants in action. But it was a great part of our family Saturday nights.

Although I was young, I watched and remember every one of the Stanley Cup championships won by the Maple Leafs during the 1960s. The Stanley Cup finals were special events that called for a gathering of the extended family. My Mom, Dad, brother Dale and I would gather at the my grandparents' home — at one time, my grandfather's grocery store — to watch the Maple Leafs claim the Stanley Cup on *Hockey Night in Canada*.

My brother and I have loved the Toronto Maple Leafs from our earliest memories. I'm convinced hockey team allegiance is generational — more nature than nurture. By instilling a love of the Maple Leafs in my brother and me, my father gave his boys an incredible inheritance.

Hockey Night in Canada was a ritual for most Canadian families each Saturday. Throughout English Canada, the Toronto Maple Leafs were embraced as Canada's team. Today, to be a Toronto Maple Leafs' fan is one of the world's great paradoxes. A city mad about hockey sells out every game, has a twenty-year waiting list for season tickets and celebrates each victory like it's the Stanley Cup final. And yet the franchise hasn't won a championship since 1967.

For Leafs' fans, the decade from 1957 to 1967 is a revered and hallowed era. During that period, the team went from worst to first, and enjoyed the spoils of a dynasty that earned Stanley Cup victories in 1962, 1963, 1964 and 1967. It's been more than forty years since that dynasty ended, and the era is still regarded as the zenith of the Leafs' franchise. From those teams come an extraordinary number of Hall of Famers: fourteen players and two builders. Names like Johnny Bower, Tim Horton, Dave Keon and Frank Mahovlich are regarded as icons in Canadian sporting annals.

When I moved to Toronto, I was informed that tickets to watch the Leafs at Maple Leaf Gardens were absolutely impossible to get, so never made the effort to find any. Astonishingly, I received a pair of Leafs tickets for Christmas from my girlfriend in 1984. I cried in disbelief. "How did you get these?" I stammered. "Walked up to the box office," she said, shrugging.

That game fuelled my desire to attend every Leafs game possible. I called Maple Leaf Gardens, enquiring about season tickets. "There's a twenty-year wait," I was told, but I figured by then, I'd be in a position in my career that I could afford them, so added my name to the list. That summer, my mailbox held what I consider one of the most wonderful — and luckiest — pieces of mail that I ever received. I ripped open the envelope from Maple Leaf Gardens and read that I had become a season ticket subscriber for the 1985–86 season. My seats were greys, section 96 up in the north end.

From that vantage point I watched my Toronto Maple Leafs, for better and often worse. I watched Wendel's NHL debut and his eventful career unfold before my eyes, the end of the Harold Ballard era, and Gilmour's glory years. And, of course, I was there for the final game at Maple Leaf Gardens on February 13, 1999.

I saw beer appear and the troughs disappear. I saw more bad games than good. And I loved every single moment I spent in Maple Leaf Gardens.

Now, here I stand, on the same spot where so many historic events transpired: the first-ever game at the Gardens, November 12, 1931; the Maple Leafs' first Stanley Cup win on April 9, 1932; Kenny Doraty's goal in the Gardens' longest game on April 3, 1933; the Ace Bailey All-Star Game of February 14, 1934; the improbable Stanley Cup win of April 18, 1942; tragic Leafs' hero Bill Barilko's dramatic final goal on April 21, 1951; and three of the four Stanley Cup championship wins of the 1960s.

Taking a moment to catch my breath and soak up the memories a little longer, I squeezed my eyes tightly shut and envisioned George Armstrong accepting the Stanley Cup on behalf of his Maple Leaf teammates, right there on the very spot on which I stood.

Hockey is my religion, and I am in my church.

Kevin Shea
February 2010

1

How the Team Became a Dynasty

So, how did this dynasty come to be? And why?

Complex questions with equally complex answers.

On February 14, 1927, local sportsman Conn Smythe, who had been unceremoniously turfed from his role as the inaugural general manager of the New York Rangers, used his severance to help purchase the floundering Toronto St. Patricks. Three days later, the team debuted as the Toronto Maple Leafs.

Smythe took enormous pride in his team, and even more in its accomplishments. As the de facto general manager, he presided over Toronto Maple Leafs' Stanley Cup wins in 1932, 1942, 1945, 1947, 1948, 1949 and 1951.

Conn had a succession plan in place that would see his son, Stafford, eventually take over the Toronto Maple Leafs. "Sometimes, I think back to the first time Stafford and I talked seriously about his future in my business," Conn wrote in his autobiography, *If You Can't Beat 'Em in the Alley*, referring to a time in the 1930s when Stafford was a teenager. "I want to work for you, Dad," Stafford said.

The story moves forward twenty years. "After one particularly good year in the middle-1950s, I gave him a Cadillac," continued Conn. "As soon as he got the car, he wanted the seat I was sitting in (as owner of the Leafs). One day, when we were arguing some policy matter, he said in exasperation, 'I should be running this place!' I said, 'I'm not retiring! What the hell have you ever done that I should turn everything over to you?'"

Conn encouraged Stafford to create a hockey committee that would serve as a sounding board on decisions. The younger Smythe did just that in March 1957, and under his chairmanship, Stafford brought in jeweller Jack Amell; John Bassett, Sr., publisher of the *Toronto Telegram* and future owner of CFTO-TV; stockbroker George Gardiner; Bill Hatch, vice president of McLaren's Food Products; alcohol importer George Mara; and, briefly, Ian Johnston, a lawyer. Each of the members was a successful entrepreneur in his thirties or early forties. That changed when fifty-four-year-old Harold Ballard, manager of the Toronto Marlboros junior hockey club, was added to fill a vacancy left by Ian Johnston's departure. "Good men in many ways," commented Conn in his book, "But it just seemed that once the bunch of them got together, a certain amount of good sense went out the window." He added, "The press was quick to scoff, giving them the nickname of the 'Silver Seven,' having something to do with the idea that many had been born with silver spoons in their mouths."

The Silver Seven hockey committee met weekly, discussing the team's situation, and frequently travelled with the Leafs on the road. Sportswriters questioned the viability of the committee, as the group's carousing was legendary, and a not-so-well-kept secret.

In November 1961, Conn was ready to sell his shares in Maple Leaf Gardens. "Stafford and I talked for three days over various aspects of the deal, and finally reached an agreement," wrote Conn. "At the time, I thought I was selling only to him, and [he] gave me the assurance that the honesty and class I had tried to bring to the place would continue. A few days later, when he told me he was selling part of my shares to Ballard and Bassett, I exploded. 'That's a lousy deal! That's the worst business mistake you could ever make! You have the whole pot and now you're going to get a third instead, so that every time this place makes a million dollars, you're going to give two-thirds away!'"

Stafford didn't have the finances to buy the Gardens' shares on his own, but Harold Ballard believed he could raise the $2 million required to purchase the shares. The two spent several nights poring over the Maple Leaf Gardens' financial records to analyze how successful the organization could be. When Stafford went to his job at the gravel pit, Ballard went to work on the manager at his branch of the Bank of Nova Scotia. After some negotiations, Ballard asked Stafford to meet him at the bank; the loan had been approved and there were papers that needed to be signed. Ballard then insisted that John Bassett Sr. be included, in spite of Stafford's belief that the two could make the purchase on their own. Together, the three arranged the financing to offer Conn $2.3 million, or approximately $40 per share (the shares were trading at $33 each at the time), giving them almost 60 percent of the team and Maple Leaf Gardens. Each of the three partners would own approximately 20 percent of the shares.

On November 23, 1961, the deal was consummated, begrudgingly by Conn, who tendered his resignation as president and managing director. Bassett's *Toronto Telegram* broke the story with a front-page headline that blurted: "Change of Control for The Gardens." Conn was rewarded with a retiring salary of $15,000 per year for life, an office, secretary, car, driver and seats to home games. He was also retained as a member of the board of directors, a position from which he resigned in March 1966.

Chief scout Squib Walker helped construct the previous Maple Leafs' dynasty, and at that time, he stated that his top five priorities in evaluating hockey prospects were "skating ability, puck-handling, heart, hockey sense and, a distant fifth, size." Howie Meeker recalled that "Squib and his scouts rated the hockey skills of the prospects, but they also added verbal and written information about the boy's parents — they talked with the clergy, school principals, bank managers — anyone and everyone who could help determine which lads had the best breeding. Hockey ability, many times, took second to breeding in Connie [Smythe]'s mind." The scouts looked for this "breeding" on behalf of the elder Smythe.

Walker's successor, Bob Davidson, learned his lessons well, and under the tutelage of Conn Smythe became notable as one of the finest judges of hockey talent in NHL history. While the Smythes and Imlach get much of the credit for building the dynasty of the 1960s, the unheralded Davidson also had his fingerprints all over the roster. "The nucleus of that club really was a vision of Bob Davidson's, who built that strong club," stated Frank Mahovlich. Davidson's uncanny ability to secure much of the finest junior talent in the country was nothing short of incredible.

With Stafford Smythe, Davidson established a feeder system that found talented players in their early teens and placed the boys within the Leafs organization, nurturing the best prospects so that they progressed upwards through a system that would eventually see them play Junior B with the Weston Dukes, Junior A with the Toronto Marlboros and then turn professional, with a chance to play with the parent Maple Leafs. Among the Marlies who progressed through this system to the Leafs were Bob Baun, Carl Brewer, Billy Harris and Bob Pulford.

"With the Marlies, they wanted to develop a strong organization, so you knew that you were going to get good coaching," explained Billy Harris. "That is just so important for young hockey players early in their careers. The pluses of playing for an organization like the Marlboros is the fact that you get lots of playing time plus, at a very early age, you are positively influenced by the NHL club. If you're thirteen or fourteen years old and you're practising in the Gardens, you can't help but wonder what it would be like playing professional with the Leafs six or seven years down the road. Another thing is that, as a thirteen- or fourteen-year-old, we could get into the Gardens to see all the Leaf games. We didn't have seats but we could stand in the blues or greys. It was a great organization to be with and they treated us well."

Mahovlich mentioned another stream of talent that provided outstanding prospects for the Leafs. "There was a group from St. Mike's

[St. Michael's College] that came up. Dickie Duff, myself, Davey Keon, Timmy Horton." The creative Davidson had, at his fingertips, the most incredible scouting staff ever assembled — and it was free. "You had every priest in Canada keeping an eye on the best hockey players in his parish with thoughts of sending them to St. Michael's," remembered Father William O'Brien, former archivist at the private boys' school.

The Marlboros and the Majors were exceptionally strong. The Marlies, with squads that included several future Maple Leafs, captured the Memorial Cup in 1955, 1956 and 1964. The St. Michael's Majors won the junior championship in 1961, and then left the Ontario Hockey Association in a battle over length of schedule, long road trips hampering school studies, and the aggressiveness exhibited in the league at that time.

There were only 120 jobs in the NHL during the "Original Six Era," and Toronto mined its vast resources to find the finest talent for its roster. "We were successful as minor hockey players, so the reinforcement and the confidence would already be there," mentioned Dick Duff. "Guys like Brewer, Mahovlich and myself, just to name a few, didn't even play the last year of juniors. We went directly to the Leafs, and from the Leafs we never missed a beat. So we were quite aware of the circumstances when we came to Toronto. We knew they were only interested in about three guys on a yearly basis. They built the competitive feeling right into their own farm system. There would be sixteen players from St. Mike's and sixteen more from the Toronto Marlboros all looking to play in the NHL. And both of those teams had a Junior B team, so we're talking about a minimum of sixty-four players of junior age in the Leafs' system. Only one or two guys would come out of that system, so only the best guys would get there, no matter what team they came from. Timmy Horton played on the St. Mike's team and they finished last, and he's one of the guys who made it to the Leafs because he was the whole team the year he was there. It was pretty obvious what Toronto wanted — they wanted talented players who had a certain amount of ability and there had to be a competitive toughness factor built into that."

While a terrific feeder system was locking up some of the finest young talent in Canada, once Punch Imlach joined the Maple Leafs he infused the roster with veterans to create an exceptional club. "There was a nucleus of about five or six players — Dickie Duff, Bobby Pulford, Bob Baun, Carl Brewer and myself — who had great success in junior," suggested Mahovlich. "Then Punch came and added a few older fellows like Johnny Bower, Bert Olmstead, Red Kelly and Allan Stanley. The mixture of age with the youth really gelled. The group just fit together. It was Punch Imlach's vision, and he built a very strong club."

"It was a character team," suggested Carl Brewer. "All of us, whether it was from St. Mike's or the Marlboros, had come up with a championship feeling and felt that we would be successful. We expected to win and we expected to be successful. That was groomed into us, whether it was St. Mike's or the Marlboros. Teams were sponsored, so we belonged to the Leafs from the time we were twelve years of age. The dressing room was healthy and it was confident."

Imlach's reclamation projects were not only veterans, but often were unheralded players who played their hearts out when given another chance in the NHL. Johnny Bower, Bert Olmstead and Allan Stanley were well-known veterans, but Gerry Ehman and Larry Regan, for example, were relatively unknown, yet played valuable roles with the Leafs during the transition from also-rans to front-runners. "That was one of my advantages," explained Imlach. "I knew everybody in the Quebec League and I knew everybody in the AHL [American Hockey League], so I had a pretty good feel for a player. And they were better than I had [with the Leafs at the time]." Ehman played one game with Boston and six with the Red Wings, but had been a fixture in the minors, had played under Imlach with the Quebec Aces of the Quebec Hockey League (QHL), and had been a high-scoring forward for Imlach's Springfield Indians in 1957–58. Regan had shuffled through the minors before landing a starting role in Boston in 1956–57, winning the Calder Trophy as rookie of the year. Imlach had known him from his tenure with the Quebec Aces as well as from his time in the Bruins' system.

Allan Stanley, one of the valuable early additions to the dynasty, reflected on the team's experience. "Imlach was the first one who I saw come out and publicly say that he doesn't care how old a player is. If he produces, he plays for him. He was true and blue to that statement, and he went along with the old guard there. He believed in the combination of youth and experience, and for him it worked out really super."

"We had a really good mixture of young guys, guys who had spent four of five years in the league, and then we had other guys who had been in the league ten or twelve years, so it was a good mixture and everybody contributed," explained Dave Keon. "Nobody was jealous of anybody else's contribution. We were all working to one end and that was to win the Cup. Everybody was happy to do anything that could be done to enhance our chances."

During the previous Maple Leaf dynasty from 1947 to 1951, the team was built around great goaltending in Turk Broda and strength at centre — they didn't come much better than Syl Apps, Ted Kennedy and Max Bentley. Punch Imlach used the same formula in creating his teams. He had Johnny Bower in goal and great strength down the middle. "We had tremendous centremen," said the coach. "We had Pulford, Kelly and Keon. Hinky [Billy Harris] could have been a starter on any other team. He was a great little hockey player. He was an excellent skater and he had manoeuvrability. Unfortunately, when that team started to win hockey games, you just couldn't beat one of those three guys out."

With a talent-laden roster and good team chemistry, Imlach discarded the highly defensive game that his predecessors in Toronto had established and allowed the players more autonomy on the ice, as long as they played responsibly and within his rules. "Up until Imlach came along, they wanted everybody to be just up and down defensively," recalled Dick Duff. "To Punch's credit, I think he sensed that these young guys were gifted junior players and said, 'Let's not put the clamps on these guys. Let Mahovlich go with the puck. Let Keon go with the puck and let Duff do what he wants to do. Let them be artists out there.' He kept the game simple." Imlach's main role was as a motivator. "If you can keep the guys up for the game, it's great," suggested Duff. "The good players generally do it themselves."

So how did the Toronto Maple Leafs of the 1960s become a dynasty? It was an incredible blend of foresight in discovering and nurturing prospects combined with defying prevailing hockey logic by making shrewd trades that infused the roster with veteran talent. The core of the team had great character, and was infused with a competitive instinct that worked in tandem with the innate talent. But along with those traits were the addition of two less strategic requirements: timing and kismet.

2

1957–58: Disappointment and Despair

The 1950s all but passed by the Toronto Maple Leafs.

The previous dynasty — four Stanley Cup championships in five years (1947, 1948, 1949 and 1951) — ended with the Stanley Cup winning goal, scored in overtime, by tragic Leafs' hero Bill Barilko.

In 1951–52, Toronto finished third but was eliminated in four straight games by the Detroit Red Wings. The following season, 1952–53, the Leafs missed the playoffs altogether, finishing fifth and prompting coach Joe Primeau, who led the team to the Stanley Cup in 1951, to leave hockey and concentrate on his building-block business.

The team earned a third-place finish in 1953–54, but again, Detroit eliminated the Leafs in the semi-final in five games. Another third-place finish in 1954–55 once again led to Toronto being swept in the semi-final by the Red Wings, who went on to win the Stanley Cup both years. In 1955–56, the Maple Leafs finished well back in fourth, and again, didn't survive playoff competition at the hands of the Red Wings, losing in five games. King Clancy was behind the bench for Toronto during those three seasons.

It should be noted that Conn Smythe made several questionable deals during this decade, contributing to Toronto's descent out of playoff competition. While fans never know the entire reasoning behind trades, it certainly appeared that Smythe was panicking in an attempt to bring his Maple Leafs back to respectability. Fleming Mackell was traded to Boston for Jim Morrison in January 1952, and in his first season with Boston, scored twenty-seven goals and was named to the NHL's First All-Star Team. Smythe sent Cal Gardner, Ray Hannigan, Gus Mortson and Al Rollins to Chicago for Harry Lumley in September of that year. While Lumley was an All-Star for Toronto, the price was extremely high. Fern Flaman was returned to Boston for Dave Creighton in July 1954 and earned All-Star recognition in three subsequent seasons, later being named captain in a career that led to the Hall of Fame. That same month, the Major's long feud with Danny Lewicki ended when he sold the winger to the Rangers, who then turned into a twenty-nine-goal scorer and a Second Team All-Star in his first season with New York.

In 1956–57, Howie Meeker, a popular former Leafs' winger, was hired to coach the team. The Maple Leafs were lacking in both talent and excitement, which was ironic, as the team's slogan that year was "Rock 'n' roll with Howie Meeker and his Crew Cuts" (a nod to the burgeoning musical style and a band called the Crew Cuts, who had a hit at the time titled "Sh-Boom."). And to make matters worse, there was total confusion in the management. Although Conn Smythe held the title of general manager through the decades, it was Hap Day who actually managed the team. Under Day's regime, the Toronto Maple Leafs played a stifling defensive brand of hockey that had been enormously successful through the late 1940s and into the early 1950s, but without adequate talent, had failed miserably through the late 1950s.

No matter who was behind the bench, Conn Smythe never relinquished his command on the team. "Sure, the coaches ran the practices and made most of the speeches at the pep rallies," said Meeker. "We helped put the defence pairs together, the forward lines together and suggested changes when things weren't working. But in those days, it was Conn Smythe who really controlled the team." The Conn Smythe fonds at the

Archives of Ontario include a number of notes sent to Leafs' coaches indicating who should play. The notes always ended stating that these were "suggestions," but the message was clear. Added Meeker, "I'll give Smythe credit as a motivator, as an organizer and a judge of personalities. He had a fair eye for talent, but compared to Hap Day, what he knew about playing the game of hockey you could write on the head of a pin."

With the Leafs having been eliminated from the playoffs, between periods of the March 23, 1957, contest between Toronto and Detroit, Smythe mused that the current Leafs' system was out of date, and let the press corps know that Hap Day was going to be asked if he was still available to manage the team. That single sentence caused a tsunami of controversy. Day was livid at the inference that he might not be with the team after thirty years. Back in Toronto, he met privately with Smythe and resigned after having been undermined so publicly.

Day had joined the franchise in 1924–25, predating even the change of name from the St. Pats to the Maple Leafs in 1927. A star defenceman and the first captain of the Leafs, Day was hired as coach in 1940–41 and stayed in that position until the spring of 1950, guiding Toronto to five Stanley Cup championships during his tenure. Until his resignation, he was assistant general manager by title, but actually served as the team's GM.

The final game of the 1956–57 season heralded a new era for the Toronto Maple Leafs. A fifth-place finish that season precipitated necessary alterations to the lineup of the team. Coach Howie Meeker and Conn Smythe discussed how the team needed substantial changes. Meeker suggested that the team wasn't strong enough in goal, that the defence needed upgrading, and that there was no offence beyond the team's first line.

Stafford Smythe, as chairman of the Silver Seven hockey committee, declared, "It's time we put a little enjoyment back in the game for the players." Emphasis was placed on youth, and the Leafs employed many players stocked on the two Ontario junior affiliates, the Marlboros and the St. Michael's Majors, as the building blocks of the future. The foundation of the team would be built around veteran defenceman Tim Horton, third-year Leaf Dick Duff, sophomore netminder Ed Chadwick and rookie Frank Mahovlich, all alumni of St. Michael's Majors. The Marlboros had provided George Armstrong, second-year forward Bob Pulford and defenceman Bob Baun, as well as rookie Billy Harris, all of whom would play large parts in the pending dynasty.

Conn Smythe was spending more and more of his winters in Florida, and his son Stafford was being groomed to take over the team, getting more involved in the day-to-day hockey operations. The Smythe tandem countered Hap Day's defensive system with a squad that attacked and scored goals. The careers of two veteran Maple Leafs' captains also came to a conclusion. Ted Kennedy's comeback bid had been largely unsuccessful. He had retired following the 1954–55 season, but returned for the latter half of the 1956–57 season. Kennedy sat out the final three games of that season so that the Leafs could get a look at a junior phenom named Frank Mahovlich, who was summoned for a three-game trial wearing number 26. The tenure of another former Leafs' captain, Jimmy Thomson, also came to an end because of his role in helping form a players' association.

Off-ice activities shaded much of the 1957–58 season, very strongly impacting the Toronto Maple Leafs. The fledgling players' association had been initiated by Ted Lindsay of the Detroit Red Wings during the 1956 NHL All-Star Game in Montreal. At the time, NHL teams owned players through their entire career, dictating salaries and benefits and lording the fear of demotion to the minors as an incentive for players to fall in line. While team owners were getting wealthier, with sold-out arenas game after game, players were earning a pittance and most needed to take on summer jobs during the off-season. Few players had anything more than a high-school education; in fact, most had left school before graduating so they could pursue a career playing hockey, so life after retirement was anything but secured. "It was a dictatorship during the six-team league," stated Lindsay. "They'd say, 'Jump,' and you'd say, 'How high and how many times?' Every player in that six-team league, all he wanted to do was play hockey. That was our livelihood — we never argued the point. They gave us our contracts. They said, 'Take it, that's all you're going to get.'"

"Terrible Ted," disliked yet respected as a competitor throughout the league, was able to recruit a handful of opponents to discuss basics for players such as minimum salary levels and a properly funded pension. "I'm not Einstein by any means, but I'm also not stupid," he said. "I wanted to show the owners that we wanted to negotiate something, but we weren't demanding to run the league. I wanted to be able to get a voice. If the laws we have today would have been in place back then, all the owners and managers would have been in jail. It was like slavery back then."

Secretly, the players met and decided to form an association. "The guys were all from small towns, and they had interpretations of what the word 'union' meant," Lindsay explained. "They didn't like the word 'union.' The lawyers kept saying, 'Fellas, you're going to have to have a union.' I kept saying, 'We can do it with an association. The guys don't want a union.'"

Towards the end of the 1956–57 season, the association found its legs. Support was all but unanimous. "We had the meeting and everybody joined but Ted Kennedy (who was retiring for good at the end of the season)," said Lindsay. "He didn't believe in it, which was fine. No one condemned him for that. Mr. Smythe believed in loyalty to country and your team. When Mr. Smythe found out about the association and found out that Ted Kennedy had not informed him that we had formed the association, Mr. Smythe figured that he was disloyal. In fact, that was so far from the truth. I feel very strongly that that cost Ted Kennedy a lifetime job with the Toronto Maple Leafs."

When the club owners learned of the plans to form an association, they were incensed. Intense pressure was applied to break the association. Howie Meeker recalled that the Smythes set out to destroy it, ordering solicitor and Maple Leaf Gardens' board member Ian Johnston to do everything possible to bring about its downfall. Meanwhile, in Detroit, GM Jack Adams made good on his threats to do anything he could to scuttle the association. Said Lindsay, "Finally, I got traded to Chicago with Glenn Hall [in July 1957] and so was Jimmy Thomson from Toronto."

Jimmy Thomson had been ordered not to join the team for the final four games of the 1956–57 season. Along with the pending youth movement, Thomson had earned a spot in Conn Smythe's doghouse by taking an active role in the creation of the players' association. In August 1957, prior to the next season, the long-serving Leafs' defenceman was shuffled off to the Chicago Black Hawks, which had become the outcast franchise of the NHL at that time. Thomson had captained the Leafs' squad from the start of the season until January 12, 1957, when Ted Kennedy came out of retirement to play, and Teeder also resumed the captaincy he had held from 1948–49 to 1954–55. Curiously, Thomson's rights reverted back to the Leafs for the 1958–59 season (he ended up retiring and never did return to play with the Leafs), so it was, in fact, a one-year sentence imposed on the All-Star defenceman by Smythe.

The association heads took the concerns of the players to the NHL team owners on September 23, 1957, but were dismissed. The owners claimed they could not negotiate because the four U.S. teams fell under the auspices of a national labour relations board in New York, while Toronto and Montreal operated under Canadian law. "Then, as more pressure was added, the guys started to realize that we had to have a union," stated Lindsay. "We were an international sport so we had to certify in Canada and we had to certify in the United States. We picked Toronto as the place to certify in Canada. We picked Detroit in the U.S."

The day before the November 6 vote in Toronto, Conn Smythe, Ian Johnston and Clarence Campbell called a command performance meeting of the Leafs — no media allowed — and attempted to intimidate the players by demanding that they vote on the union issue that moment, but the team refused.

The next day, prior to the certification vote, Milton Mound, one of the lawyers for the association, accused Smythe and Campbell of bullying the Leafs' players and using "unfair labour practices." "It's embarrassing to see three grown men trying to intimidate these young boys," stated Mound, referring to the NHL president and the two Smythes. "We want the clubs to agree on a minimum salary and on working conditions. We're also concerned with the proper allocation of television revenue. Some of it should be used for players' pensions and other benefits." It was also suggested that the Toronto players wanted a clause in their contracts that would make them free agents after five years.

According to *The Globe*, "With increasing bitterness on both sides, it is the good name of hockey that will suffer before the rapidly widening chasm in owner-player relations is healed. It will take a modern Solomon to bring both parties together, as there is no indication that either side is ready to back down."

In spite of threats and objections, the November 6, 1957, certification vote, led by Tod Sloan, along with Dick Duff and Sid Smith, Toronto's representatives with the association, was passed unanimously by the Maple Leafs.

While coaching the Leafs the previous season, Howie Meeker knew that something was being planned, but chose to keep his inkling to himself. As a former player, he agreed that the players had a need to organize, and respected their courage. "Many times in the last forty years I have had reason to be proud of my association with the players of the Toronto Maple Leafs, but never more than to the eighteen gentlemen who withstood the challenge of ownership, who put the game and the players before individuals persecution," wrote Howie Meeker in *Golly Gee — It's Me!*

But a subsequent vote in Detroit saw two of the Red Wings break rank and decide not to support the formation of an association. With Lindsay gone, Gordie Howe and Red Kelly led the Detroit players away from the players' association. The dissension formed a crack that proved to be the ultimate demise of the players' best-laid plans. On February 5, 1958, a conference of owners and player representatives was held in Palm Beach, Florida. All six team owners refused to recognize the players' association, which lost its bid for recognition as a result. Nevertheless, because of the players' actions, the National Hockey League owners agreed to increase the minimum salary to $7,000, to limit the number of exhibition games played, to increase pension benefits, to increase hospitalization benefits and to increase the playoff pool.

Although the players' association did not fly at that point, by 1967 it took hold and stuck, with the formation of a unified collection of players that has served its membership very well through the years. The National Hockey League Players' Association of today was built upon the blood and sacrifices made by Ted Lindsay and his colleagues, including Maple Leafs Jimmy Thomson and Tod Sloan, who were martyred for their intentions.

Conn Smythe appointed George Armstrong as the new team captain beginning with the 1957–58 season. "I would have made him captain before, but had left it to the hockey committee and Hap, who had chosen Thomson instead," admitted Smythe. "I told Armstrong before he signed that I wanted one-hundred-percent loyalty to the Maple Leafs from him."

Smythe followed that announcement by inviting Howie Meeker to his office and offering him the vacant general manager's position. Howie said he needed time to consider the proposal. Having been a member of Parliament from 1951 to 1953, Meeker didn't really need the stress. In his heart, he knew that he should decline, a decision supported by his wife, Grace. But a phone call to ex-GM Day changed his mind. "Take the job," he was told. "There are only six jobs like it in the world, and since Conn will sell Maple Leaf Gardens to Stafford, you won't last long (neither Meeker nor Stafford Smythe had any use for the other). "Get your name on a three-year deal, read and learn. You'll learn more about NHL hockey operations in a year than you will in five years anywhere else."

The thirty-two-year-old Meeker accepted the position on May 13, 1957, and for the next six months, worked without a contract. At his hiring, Smythe and Meeker agreed that Howie would relinquish his coaching duties. In his autobiography, Conn Smythe later stated, "All theory and no practice was Meeker's trouble. If he had a team made up of 'Rocket' Richard and four more like him, he couldn't win."

Howie was pleased that Billy Reay, the former star of the Montreal Canadiens and coach of the Rochester Americans, an American Hockey League team jointly sponsored by the Canadiens and the Leafs, had been hired to replace him as coach. "I gladly left the coaching problem in his hands," said the GM. "I don't think I would have had any influence anyway."

In one of his first duties, Meeker signed junior phenom Frank Mahovlich to a contract, but was chastised by Conn Smythe for offering too much money. Correspondence sent to Smythe by Meeker through the summer suggested several players available for acquisition, including Allan Stanley from Boston and Johnny Bucyk from Detroit. These letters went largely ignored, although Stafford Smythe, through King Clancy, did assure Meeker that the team's future was secure because of the development plan he had nurtured through the two Toronto-based junior clubs, the Toronto Marlboros and St. Michael's Majors.

Before training camp opened, Meeker attended an NHL-sponsored symposium that involved the NHL, AHL and QSHL (Quebec Senior Hockey League). He left, having been impressed with a minor league executive named Punch Imlach. "I think Stafford Smythe left the meeting with that same feeling and had already tagged him as a replacement for Howie Meeker," said Howie.

During that fall's training camp, held in Sudbury, Stafford Smythe asked Meeker to join him in his office, and confronted his general manager regarding the minimal efforts to improve the team. Meeker responded, "Stafford, I asked for direction, for permission to trade for players on three different occasions and you totally ignored my correspondence." The discussion grew heated, and according to Meeker's autobiography, Smythe pressed his hands on Meeker's chest and pushed him. Howie reared back and punched Smythe, then left the office.

Howie Meeker was fired by Conn Smythe (although it was certainly Stafford's decision) on October 4, just four days before the start of the 1957–58 season. Maple Leaf Gardens issued a statement: "It has been decided at a meeting of the hockey committee that, in the best interests of the club, Howie Meeker is immediately discharged from his duties, for obvious reasons of inexperience and incapability with the new set-up."

"Meeker didn't have the experience needed for that kind of a job and needs to learn more about it," admitted Stafford Smythe. "That would be no handicap if this were a team where everything was cut and dried, but with so much to be done, we had to take action right away." Meeker agreed to stay on, at full salary, working with publicity director Spiff Evans, and goes down as one of the only NHL general managers to never have managed his team in a regular season game.

The general manager's position was filled by a consortium of Stafford Smythe, assistant general manager King Clancy, coach Billy Reay and head scout Bob Davidson.

Hawks Shut Out Leafs in Season Opener
Tuesday, October 8, 1957

The season seemed destined to be a disaster. Management was in disarray, and that trickled down to the team itself. The introduction of rookie Frank Mahovlich, who had played three games the previous season, gave promise of things to come, but it was clear that 1957–58 was going to be a challenging campaign. It started out with a 1–0 loss to the Black Hawks in the season opener in Chicago.

Leafs Dumped by Detroit in Home Opener
Saturday, October 12, 1957

The initial *Hockey Night in Canada* broadcast of the season featured some revolutionary features in the evolution of televising sports. From November 1, 1952, when the first English-language *Hockey Night in Canada* broadcast had gone to air (the French-language version had debuted on October 11, 1952), viewers watched the game from a high angle that gave an overview perspective of the game. Towards the end of the 1956–57 season, the show began to experiment with other camera angles, testing various vantage points within Maple Leaf Gardens during selected NHL contests as well as minor hockey games. Beginning with this home opener, a 5–3 loss to the Detroit Red Wings, the camera angle moved lower, and to this day remains the principal camera view on the broadcast of hockey games.

The intermissions on *Hockey Night in Canada* also changed with this initial home game of the season. From the program's debut, the intermission (usually only the one intermission was shown, as the program signed on well after the start of the game) utilized a discussion format called the "Hot Stove League" featuring former Leafs Syl Apps and Harold Cotton. At this season-opening broadcast, however, this format was abandoned in favour of live interviews conducted by *Globe and Mail* hockey writer Scott Young. Filmed features were also being used by this point.

Rocket and Pocket Rocket Sock It to Toronto
Thursday, October 17, 1957
The Richard brothers single-handedly crushed the Maple Leafs when Montreal trounced Toronto 9–3. Younger brother Henri scored 3 goals and added 3 assists, and older brother Maurice scored twice, bringing his regular season career total to 499.

Hat Tricks and Shutout Blitz Boston
Saturday, October 19, 1957
The peripatetic Leafs rebounded beautifully two nights after being swarmed by the Canadiens when Ed Chadwick shut out the Bruins 7–0. Brian Cullen and Billy Harris both fired three goals past beleaguered Don Simmons in the Boston goal.

Hawks Steal Point from Toronto as Mortson Salutes Smythe
Saturday, November 2, 1957
A goal by Eddie Litzenberger with twenty-seven seconds left in the contest stole a win from the Maple Leafs, giving the Chicago Black Hawks a 3–3 tie. Moreover, Pete Conacher's debut with the Leafs in the same rink where his father, Charlie, once electrified crowds, and Bobby Hull's *Hockey Night in Canada* debut were both overshadowed by another incident during the contest.

At this time, the Maple Leafs' players were mere days away from a certification vote that would be a critical point in the acceptance of a National Hockey League Players' Association. The very idea incensed Conn Smythe, and the bad blood spilled out onto the ice. During the third period, Chicago's Gus Mortson, a former Stanley Cup champion with the Leafs, was called for holding. While sitting in the penalty box, Mortson blasted referee Gaye Stewart, a former teammate. Smythe, who usually watched the team from his box in the greens (cheekily referred to by the Leafs' players as "Berchtesgaden") was seated behind the penalty box during this game. He leaned in towards Mortson and said, "Why don't you tell Lewis and Mound [the association's New York lawyers] about it?" Mortson responded by shaking his fist at Smythe, then, leaping to his feet, he saluted "The Major." He then thumbed his nose at the Gardens' president. The entire incident was televised by *Hockey Night in Canada,* with Foster Hewitt providing running commentary.

After the contest, Mortson chatted with his coach, Tommy Ivan, about how to handle the incident with Smythe. They decided that Gus should apologize to Smythe, and the two met, but failed to make peace. "We had a nice friendly conversation," said Mortson, laughing. "Covered ten years in two minutes."

Big Game from Big M
Sunday, December 1, 1957
Frank Mahovlich was living up to the hype that surrounded him. On the first of December, Mahovlich, who was playing centre that season, scored his first career hat trick in a 7–2 win over the Black Hawks. The Big M would enjoy another three-goal performance on Christmas night as his Leafs edged Montreal 5–4.

Bad Blood Boils Over in Leafs 3–1 Trumping of Chicago
Saturday, February 22, 1958
The bitter feelings between Toronto and Chicago had already been firmly established. During Toronto's 3–1 win over the Hawks, *Hockey Night in Canada* cameras picked up an incredible fight between Mortson and Toronto's Bob Pulford in the corridor between the teams' dressing rooms, which were located across the hall from each other.

Canadiens Set Record in Win Over Leafs
Thursday, March 20, 1958
With the season having slipped away long before, Toronto was outscored by Montreal 7–4, and in doing so, the Canadiens established an NHL record for team scoring. The Habs' 243 goals eclipsed the previous record of 236 scored by the Red Wings in 1951.

The frustration of a torturous season saw the Maple Leafs go winless in the season's final nine games, dropping them haplessly into a last-place finish. The most perplexing thing was that the team was utterly quixotic. On October 17, Toronto was whipped 9–3 by the Montreal Canadiens and in the very next game, the Leafs manhandled the Boston Bruins by a 7–0 score. They could occasionally score in bunches — they pummelled the New York Rangers 7–1 on January 25 and hammered the Red Wings 9–2 on February 1 — yet took their lumps in equal measure. They were shut out 7–0 at the hands of the Bruins on March 9 and blanked 7–0 by the Rangers on March 22. On certain nights, they looked like they were unstoppable. On others, they simply didn't have the talent to compete.

Billy Reay, whose debut as an NHL coach was anything but auspicious, endured a very challenging season. While Dick Duff led the team in scoring with a fine season of twenty-six goals and forty-nine points, another Dickie, Montreal's Moore, was the NHL scoring leader with thirty-six goals and eighty-four points. Frank Mahovlich edged Bobby Hull as the NHL's best rookie, winning the Calder Memorial Trophy, but there was little else in the way of good news for the Leafs.

For the first time in franchise history, the team finished sixth in the six-team NHL. The franchise was at its lowest ebb.

1957–58 Regular Season Standings						
FINISH	TEAM	GAMES	WINS	LOSSES	TIES	POINTS
1	Montreal Canadiens	70	43	17	10	96
2	New York Rangers	70	32	25	13	77
3	Detroit Red Wings	70	29	29	12	70
4	Boston Bruins	70	27	28	15	69
5	Chicago Black Hawks	70	24	39	7	55
6	Toronto Maple Leafs	70	21	38	11	53

Regular Season Netminding

RK		PLAYER	GP	MIN	W	L	T
1	1	Ed Chadwick	70	4200	21	38	11
		TEAM TOTALS	70	4200	30	26	14

1957–58 Regular Season Scoring

RK	NUMBER	PLAYER	GP	G	A	PTS	PIM
1	17	Dick Duff	65	26	23	49	79
2	15	Billy Harris	68	16	28	44	32
3	18	Brian Cullen	67	20	23	43	29
4	10	George Armstrong	59	17	25	42	93
5	19	Barry Cullen	70	16	25	41	37
6	12	Ron Stewart	70	15	24	39	51
7	11	Tod Sloan	59	13	25	38	58
8	27	Frank Mahovlich	67	20	16	36	67
9	20	Bob Pulford	70	14	17	31	48
10	7	Tim Horton	53	6	20	26	39
11	26	Gary Aldcorn	59	10	14	24	12
12	3	Jim Morrison	70	3	21	24	62
13	14	Rudy Migay	48	7	14	21	18
14	8	Paul Masnick	41	2	9	11	14
15	21	Bobby Baun	67	1	9	10	91
16	2	Marc Reaume	68	1	7	8	49
17	16	Gerry James	15	3	2	5	61
18	8	Sid Smith	12	2	1	3	2
19	16	Pete Conacher	5	0	1	1	5
20	22	Earl Balfour	1	0	0	0	0
21	24	Carl Brewer	2	0	0	0	0
22	1	Ed Chadwick	70	0	0	0	0
23	22	Ken Girard	3	0	0	0	0
24	24	Al MacNeil	13	0	0	0	9
25	11	Bob Nevin	4	0	0	0	0
26	26	Noel Price	1	0	0	0	5
		TEAM TOTALS	70	1127	192	304	496

SLAPSHOTS AND SNAPSHOTS
HOCKEY NIGHT IN CANADA — BEFORE AND AFTER

The inaugural television broadcast of *Hockey Night in Canada* aired on November 1, 1952, at 9:30 p.m., with play-by-play by Foster Hewitt picked up in the middle of the second period. It wasn't until the 1956–57 season, when the actual start of the game moved from 8:30 to 8:00 p.m., that telecasts signed on at 9:00. Then, it wasn't until the 1963–64 season that *Hockey Night in Canada* signed on at 8:30, with the action joined in progress late in the first period. By the start of the 1968–69 season, the entire game was finally made available to hockey fans at the new TV start time of 8:00 p.m.

On occasion, fans were surprised to be able to watch some extra action. Viewers tuning in on November 30, 1963, saw that the start of the game had been delayed due to the poor ice conditions at Maple Leaf Gardens. This was the era that preceded colour television, but there was no mistaking the brown ice on which the players were attempting to play. The rodeo, booked at Maple Leaf Gardens until the night before that Leafs' game, had left its mark on the ice surface, and the start of the game was delayed so that the ice could be cleaned more thoroughly.

So why did *Hockey Night in Canada* not broadcast games in their entirety? There are two schools of thought. On one hand, the Smythes believed that broadcasting a full game would erode their attendance at games. But the broadcaster played a role, too. By sacrificing popular network shows, they might jeopardize viewership and revenue for their station.

Fans, who had waited all week to watch their televised hockey game, grew familiar with the closing themes of the television shows that directly preceded *Hockey Night in Canada*. These are some of the popular shows that aired just before the games in the era of the Maple Leafs' dynasty:

October 13, 1956 – *Holiday Ranch*
October 12, 1957 – *Holiday Ranch* and *The Perry Como Show*
October 11, 1958 – *The Perry Como Show* and *Perry Mason*

October 10, 1959 – *Wanted: Dead or Alive* and *Sea Hunt*

October 8, 1960 – *The Aquanauts* and *Perry Mason*

October 14, 1961 – *Red River Jamboree* and *Perry Mason*

October 13, 1962 – *Red River Jamboree* and *The Jackie Gleason Show*

October 12, 1963 – *The Beverly Hillbillies, The Saint* and *The Jackie Gleason Show*

October 17, 1964 – *The Beverly Hillbillies, The Saint* and *The Jackie Gleason Show*

October 23, 1965 – *The Beverly Hillbillies* and *The Jackie Gleason Show*

October 22, 1966 – *The Beverly Hillbillies, Tarzan* and *The Jackie Gleason Show*

October 14, 1967 – *The Beverly Hillbillies, High Chaparral* and *The Jackie Gleason Show*

Following each *Hockey Night in Canada* broadcast between 1956 and 1966, many fans chose to watch *The Juliette Show*. Over an instrumental version of "Love and Marriage," the announcer welcomed viewers with, "Now, let's meet and greet your pet, Juliette!" Juliette, who never used her married surname (Cavazzi), was a permanent fixture on Canadian television. CBC Archives described *The Juliette Show*'s successful formula as follows: "A typical program would include Juliette, always showing off an exquisite new dress, performing several solo musical numbers and several with one of her male escorts and singers." The show was as much a Saturday night tradition as *Hockey Night in Canada*.

3

1958–59: The Miracle Finish

The Original Six nomenclature, while in fact erroneous (the National Hockey League was created in 1917 with the Montreal Canadiens, the Montreal Wanderers, the Ottawa Senators and the Toronto Arenas), depicted what many regard as the glory years of the league, lasting from 1942–43 until the conclusion of the 1966–67 season. And during that twenty-five-year period, several dynasties emerged. The Detroit Red Wings finished first eight of nine seasons beginning in 1948–49, winning the Stanley Cup four times in that period. The Montreal Canadiens dominated the NHL with a record five consecutive Stanley Cup championships beginning in 1955–56. The Toronto Maple Leafs won the Stanley Cup six times in the ten seasons between 1941–42 and 1950–51, although the rosters of the championships in 1942 and 1945 differed greatly from the team that won the Stanley Cup in 1947, 1948, 1949 and 1951. And legend, as we know, reminds us that the Maple Leafs enjoyed a second dynasty in the 1960s, winning the Stanley Cup four times.

But in 1958–59, it would have been difficult to predict such success was ahead. The Maple Leafs had missed the playoffs two springs in succession, and the moribund team was floundering again.

The Montreal Canadiens, winners of the Stanley Cup in three successive springs, were so deep in talent that they were able to allow their prospects time to really develop and then earn a spot in the NHL lineup. They had a formidable roster that included Jacques Plante in goal and a blue-line corps of Doug Harvey, Tom Johnson, Jean-Guy Talbot and Bob Turner. The Richard brothers, Beliveau, Geoffrion and Moore were tough to dislodge from their forward berths, but Ralph Backstrom finally got his shot that season. Bert Olmstead, deemed expendable, was lost to Toronto in the Intra-League Draft.

The New York Rangers finished second in 1957–58, but were ousted in the semi-final, leading to great disappointment within the franchise. The team added several players they believed would bolster their roster, including Eddie Shack from the OHA's Guelph Biltmores. Jim Bartlett was promoted from the AHL Providence Reds. With Gump Worsley in net, Lou Fontinato, Bill Gadsby, Jack Hanna and Harry Howell on defence and a forward contingent that included Andy Bathgate, Andy Hebenton, Camille Henry and Dean Prentice, the Rangers felt quite satisfied with their chances going forward.

Jack Adams, general manager of the Detroit Red Wings, cleaned house in spite of a third-place finish the previous year. He wisely kept a nucleus of netminder Terry Sawchuk, defencemen Red Kelly and Marcel Pronovost and forwards Alex Delvecchio, Gordie Howe and Norm Ullman, but swept much of the roster clean beyond that. Gone were several veterans, replaced by Gerry Ehman in a trade with Springfield and prospects Charlie Burns and Len Lunde.

The Boston Bruins surprised everyone (but themselves) by scratching their way to the Stanley Cup final the prior spring, ultimately losing to the Canadiens' juggernaut in five games. Ageing Harry Lumley continued his solid play in goal, paired with youngster Don Simmons. The blue-line contingent, consisting of Bob Armstrong, Leo Boivin, Fern Flaman, Larry Hillman, Doug Mohns and newly acquired Jim Morrison, was going to be tough to penetrate. Up front, the "Uke Line" of Johnny Bucyk, Bronco Horvath and Vic Stasiuk paced their attack, joined by Leo Labine, Fleming Mackell, Don McKenney and Jerry Toppazzini. Jean-Guy Gendron joined the Bruins from New York.

Chicago Black Hawks seemed to have the team of the future, although they hoped that the future would arrive sooner than later. After years of desperation, the team had nurtured a very strong lineup. Glenn Hall was superb in goal, and the defence, led by Pierre Pilote and Elmer Vasko, had been shored up with the acquisition of Al Arbour from Detroit, Jack Evans from the Rangers and Dollard St. Laurent from Montreal. Bobby Hull, Ted Lindsay, Ed Litzenberger, Ron Murphy and Eric Nesterenko comprised the strength up front, with Johnny McKenzie looking as though he was ready to step into the Hawks' lineup full time. As punishment for his role in the aborted Players' Association, Toronto sold Tod Sloan to Chicago. The Hawks also picked up Earl Balfour from Toronto in the draft.

After his dismal debut, Billy Reay knew that drastic changes were necessary in order to change the fortunes of the team. He knew the Leafs needed help in goal. "Goalkeeping in hockey is like pitching in baseball," he said. "If you haven't got it, you've got nothing at all."

Without an official general manager in place, the Leafs worked through the summer at convincing veteran minor league goaltender Johnny Bower to join the Leafs. Bower had been buried in the New York Rangers' system, and at thirty-three years of age, seemed unlikely to return to the NHL. Happy in Cleveland with the American Hockey League Barons, Bower had turned aside previous overtures from both Toronto and Boston to sign and re-enter the ranks of NHLers. But on June 3, 1958, Toronto selected Bower from Cleveland in the Intra-League Draft. "I really didn't want to go," admitted Johnny. Convinced by Jim Hendy, the Barons' owner, that he should give Toronto a shot, Bower acquiesced and decided to report to the Maple Leafs, but only after negotiating a two-year "irrevocable" contract at $10,000 per year plus moving expenses. "Bower will give us a big lift in goal," Billy Reay told the *Toronto Daily Star*.

At the start of the 1958–59 season, Reay planned to platoon Bower with current Leafs' netminder Ed Chadwick, because the one-goalie system in the NHL was quickly coming to an end. The Stanley Cup champion Montreal Canadiens had enjoyed some success by inserting Charlie Hodge into occasional games to keep Jacques Plante fresh for the playoffs. The Boston Bruins had split their goaltending duties between Harry Lumley and Don Simmons, while the New York Rangers had enjoyed success in net with Gump Worsley and Marcel Paille through the 1957–58 season.

Reay also recognized that the team's youth would benefit from some veterans being inserted into the lineup.

Prior to the NHL Entry Draft of juniors, which was introduced in 1963, players were contracted to teams by way of the C-Form, a document that indentured a player to a team by the simple exchange of a minimal amount of money and a signature on the contract. But that didn't preclude wild wheeling and dealing between clubs.

An Intra-League Draft existed at that time. Toronto, finishing last, would have first selection from the group of players not protected by their respective teams. In the act of rebuilding, the Leafs salivated over the prospect of stealing a discard and turning that player into a valuable piece of the playoff-bound puzzle.

Five of the six teams declined to select a player in the first round of the draft. When the Montreal Canadiens plucked Danny Lewicki from the New York Rangers' list, they dropped Bert Olmstead from their protected list. Reay was incredulous. He and Olmstead had enjoyed success together playing as teammates with the Montreal Canadiens. Olmstead was a skilled playmaker, unequalled in winning battles in the corner. He simply knew how to win. The Leafs, choosing next, immediately claimed Olmstead. He would go on to play an important role in the transformation of the Toronto Maple Leafs.

There was a little-known stipulation tied to Toronto's acquisition of Olmstead. The Leafs had to agree on a particular executive setup in Rochester of the American Hockey League, a team that the Leafs and Habs co-sponsored, in spite of their lengthy disdain for each other.

During that summer, Bert Olmstead got himself into legal trouble and was convicted of "grievous assault" on a West Vancouver mining executive following a trapshooting competition. At the banquet, the man apparently ridiculed Olmstead, who proceeded to attempt to flush the man's head down the toilet. Stafford Smythe, acting general manager, and Coach Reay simply hoped that Olmstead would get out of jail in time for training camp. NHL president Clarence Campbell said it wasn't hockey-related, and therefore did not assess any punishment. Olmstead was released on $1,000 bail and went home to Saskatchewan to harvest his crop. Later, instead of jail time, he was assessed a large fine and paid the damages; it is likely that the Leafs may have offered some "assistance." When Conn Smythe was informed of Olmstead's incident, he said, "That's the type of fighter we need on this team!"

Meeker's earlier assertion that the Maple Leafs' executives were interested in Punch Imlach had been correct. Stafford Smythe had indeed been impressed with Imlach, who was without a job that summer. Imlach had been coach and general manager of the Springfield Indians of the American Hockey League, a team owned by eccentric Hall of Famer Eddie Shore, and had guided the team to the Calder Cup final. But Shore decided to end his agreement to have the Indians affiliated with the Boston Bruins, leaving Imlach without a job. The Bruins had offered Punch a position as a trouble-shooter for the organization, including overseeing the farm system, but Imlach was not overly enthused. At the behest of the Bruins, he attended the annual hockey meetings held in Montreal in June 1958. While there, he was approached by Harold Ballard of the Leafs and told that Stafford Smythe wished to speak with him. After getting permission from Walter Brown, the Bruins' president, Smythe offered Imlach a position similar to the one Boston had offered.

Imlach declined the offer, telling Stafford, "You have no general manager. I want that job, or at least the opportunity of getting it." Smythe continued to pursue, finally agreeing to give Imlach the position of assistant general manager with the opportunity to prove himself and earn the position of general manager.

The hockey committee got involved at this point, with noted concern about whether Imlach could work with Billy Reay as a coach. "I said I wouldn't have any trouble with Reay," Imlach noted in his autobiography. "I didn't want anything to do with coaching the hockey team. I was hired to get players and be responsible for how the hockey club made out, not to interfere with Reay as coach in his own dressing room or behind the bench."

George "Punch" Imlach was hired by the Toronto Maple Leafs in August 1958.

Imlach had been a fine hockey player. As a junior, he starred with Ed Wildey's Toronto Young Rangers from 1935–36 to 1937–38, then played senior hockey with the Toronto Goodyears (1938–39 to 1939–40) and Toronto Marlboros (1940–41). In a game against Windsor, Imlach was on the receiving end of a fierce bodycheck that left him dazed. The *Toronto Telegram* described him as appearing "punch drunk" after the hit, and the nickname "Punchy" stuck. Not long afterwards, the tag became "Punch," and for the rest of his life, to all but his wife, Dodo, he was Punch Imlach.

After enlisting in the army in the Second World War, Imlach coached an army hockey team in Cornwall, Ontario. He returned to hockey after being discharged, joining the Quebec Aces, where he remained from 1945–46 to 1956–57, taking the reins as coach and general manager and later, part owner of the QSHL club, helping groom Jean Beliveau for an NHL career. In 1957–58, Imlach was hired by the Boston Bruins as general manager of the AHL's Springfield Indians, and before the season had concluded, also took on the task of head coach, but mercurial team owner Eddie Shore took back control of the team.

"We were very successful last year," a smirking Smythe told a gathering of reporters at the announcement of Imlach's hiring. "Although it was our first under the Silver Seven setup, we got to the bottom of the league for the first time in history. I guarantee that we won't do any worse this year."

The Toronto Maple Leafs held their training camp once again in Peterborough, and the team stayed at the Empress Hotel. However, early indications were that Reay and Imlach were not getting along.

"Nobody really knew what to expect," suggested Bob Baun. "Everybody knew this funny little guy was walking around the halls and nobody really knew what his job was." Bob Haggert, the Leafs' young trainer, agreed. "When Imlach arrived, we knew very little about him. But, from the moment he arrived, it took him maybe two weeks to assess the team. He saw, on one side, that we had this great pool of terrific players who had played for the Marlboros and St. Mike's, and they were so good. So he started to fill in the blanks." Through the next few months, Imlach shored up the team by picking up a number of veteran players to mesh with his eager young squad. "There was a theory that Imlach absolutely destroyed. The theory was that if you were thirty or thirty-one, you were finished," continued Haggert. "Punch changed the way you manage your hockey team. There is no better product than experience."

On October 8, just prior to the opening game of the 1958–59 regular season, Imlach plucked Allan Stanley from the Boston Bruins for Jim Morrison and cash. Stanley, a veteran, was expected to add stability to a defence that featured Bob Baun, rookie Carl Brewer, Tim Horton, Steve Kraftcheck, Noel Price and Marc Reaume.

"I didn't think that I'd ever play for Toronto," reminisced Stanley. "I always wanted to play for Toronto because they were always my team when I was a kid."

Little did anyone realize at the time, but the acquisition of Allan Stanley gave Toronto a defensive quartet that would anchor the blue line and serve as the foundation of the team for several years. As the Montreal Canadiens' dynasty of the 1970s was built on the bedrock of "the Big Three" (Guy Lapointe, Larry Robinson and Serge Savard), so too was the Toronto dynasty anchored by an equally strong defence corps of Bob Baun, Carl Brewer, Tim Horton and Allan Stanley. "As a goalie, you're only as good as your defencemen," said Johnny Bower, saluting the quartet. "I believe, to this day, that the reason I am in the Hall of Fame is because of that foursome."

Carl Brewer still retained a year of junior eligibility when he was offered a five-game tryout with the Leafs at the conclusion of training camp. He was so impressive that, following those five games, Brewer was signed to a professional contract by the Maple Leafs. The negotiation was just the first of his run-ins with Punch Imlach, who handled the dealings. While Brewer's father implored him to simply sign, Carl insisted on a signing bonus equal to the $4,500 granted to his former junior teammate, Bob Nevin. Imlach offered $1,600. Finally, after the youngster refused to sign, Imlach surrendered a signing bonus of $4,000 and offered a two-year contract. "Nothing of rubber or flesh passes him; he can hit hard, clear the pass accurately and skate and manoeuvre exceptionally well," wrote the *Toronto Telegram* of Brewer that fall. Johnny Bower, in his autobiography *China Wall,* added, "He was a great competitor. He wanted to win. He didn't know what the words 'to lose' meant. He was good at moving the puck. He really helped me a great deal moving some of those guys [from in front of the net]. Carl wasn't afraid to block shots for me, either. I had the best seat in the house to watch Carl!"

The plan was that each defensive pairing would have one rusher and one defensive blue liner. Hard-hitting Bobby Baun was going into his third year with the Leafs. At first, Imlach paired Baun with Tim Horton, placing Brewer and Steve Kraftcheck together and using Marc Reaume as a fifth defenceman. But later, Punch experimented with putting Horton and Allan Stanley together and placed rushing Carl Brewer with the steadying Baun, and something clicked. "On the ice, we complemented each other," stated Baun.

With Tim Horton and Allan Stanley, optics were that Horton had the offensive gifts while Stanley balanced the two defensively. In fact, like the pair of Baun and Brewer, both Horton and Stanley were very responsible in both halves of the rink.

"Tim was always a good hockey player," suggested George Armstrong. "But he really became a great player when he and Al started playing together."

Allan Stanley concurred. "We just seemed to fit right in. After a while, we knew every move the other one would make in any situation. It's not often that you play with somebody and are able to have that kind of confidence in him. We were like brothers off the ice, too. Tim and I used to talk a lot. We'd talk hockey and we just seemed to click." Horton and Stanley were paired on the Leafs' blue line for ten years.

Sloan Exacts Revenge on Leafs in Season Opener
Saturday, October 11, 1958
Readying for the opening game of the 1958–59 season, the Toronto Maple Leafs were prepared to put memories of their miserable 1957–58 season behind them. The first game of a new season is always an exciting event — a blank canvas for the teams and anticipation from the fans. *The Hockey News* had predicted that Toronto would endure a second straight sixth-place finish. On October 11, the Maple Leafs opened their season being challenged by the Chicago Black Hawks at Maple Leaf Gardens.

Viewers of *Hockey Night in Canada*, joining the game in progress at 9:00 p.m., missed seeing the Leafs' long-serving employee, Hap Day, conduct the ceremonial faceoff. Day had been a player, coach and assistant general manager with the Leafs.

As the televised portion of the game began, Foster Hewitt announced the score and the scorers, and then made an announcement of his own. "This season, the play-by-play for radio and TV, I'm very proud to say, will be handled by my son, Bill Hewitt. After thirty years of network play-by-play broadcasting, my efforts will be to interject highlights and comments during the course of the play. So, now here is your new play-by-play commentator, Bill Hewitt."

Astute viewers noted modest changes as they watched the opening night broadcast. The Maple Leafs were sporting sweaters with laces for the first time, and for the first time in the history of Maple Leaf Gardens, there was Plexiglas along the boards.

The Leafs dropped a 3–1 decision to Chicago, with Tod Sloan enjoying a two-goal game in his return to Maple Leaf Gardens. Sloan was determined to show up the Leafs after the way he felt he had been treated. In his post-game comments, Foster Hewitt mentioned that it was the same old story that occurs when a former player comes back to haunt his old team, as Sloan had done. Bobby Hull scored the other Chicago goal, with Steve Kraftcheck replying for the Maple Leafs. The Three Stars were Sloan and Danny Lewicki of the Hawks and new Leaf Bert Olmstead.

Bert Olmstead had been part of three successive Stanley Cup championships with Montreal, and was angry that the team had let him go to Toronto in the draft. "I felt absolutely rotten," he admitted. "I played about twenty games with torn knee ligaments. I knew in the afternoon of my last game that I wasn't going to be there the next year. They offered me a job in the organization and said, 'You can coach any team that you want, except the big team. The medical report is so bad that you won't skate again, ever.' I said, 'I don't believe that, and I don't want to coach.' I asked Toe Blake, 'Who do you think is an up-and-coming team?' He said, 'Chicago,' and I said, 'I won't go to Chicago, but I'll go to Toronto.' In June, I was in Toronto.

"When I first came to Toronto, they had a bad hockey team," Bert recalled. "They had to make changes and they made changes. Every change that Imlach made was a good change. We ended up with a bunch of good people in the dressing room, but they'd never won anything."

Trainer Bob Haggert was there to greet Bert when he arrived. "Olmstead was a very unique person," he said. "He came from a winning team in Montreal. As far as I was concerned, he was a bona fide leader and the biggest inspiration on that team. He was a player who, when he spoke, you listened, and by God, you'd better pay attention. He took three days to size up everybody and from then on, he got on everybody's case. He told everyone, 'You can be better hockey players!' He took no nonsense from anybody."

Haggert admired what Olmstead contributed to that Maple Leafs team. "He was probably the most prepared player, game in and game out, of any player I've ever met in my life. When he came to a game, he was ready to play and he knew exactly what had to be done. He was the undisputed leader of that team. His positive attitude (and veteran experience) made him a club-house leader."

But not everyone was as enamoured of the veteran Olmstead. "He was an interesting phenomenon," remarked Carl Brewer. "He was respected because he had come from the Montreal Canadiens. They expected Bert to be a leader on the Toronto Maple Leaf hockey club. I didn't really get along with him nor could I stand his act. He probably didn't like my act either. What amazed me was how the younger players, guys who were older than me, worshipped Bert Olmstead. I thought, 'This is insane! This guy is rather miserable.' We had a lot of verbal jousts. No, we didn't get along at all. Some would call him intense. I called him surly."

Bruins Drop Game and Jaws
Saturday, October 18, 1958
Hockey Night in Canada viewers witnessed the Maple Leafs' first victory of the season, a raucous 3–2 win over the Boston Bruins. Ron Stewart scored twice for Toronto and Carl Brewer picked up his first NHL goal.

During the contest, Boston lost both Bronco Horvath and Doug Mohns to broken jaws, and general manager Lynn Patrick claimed that illegal elbow pads worn by the Leafs were the cause of the injuries.

This issue had crept up during the playoffs in the spring of 1958. Montreal coach Toe Blake claimed that the Red Wings were using elbow pads akin to brass knuckles. At the semi-annual meeting held September 19, the NHL passed legislation that outlawed the old, hard elbow pads, insisting that proper padding be used to eliminate injuries. Yet, in the NHL All-Star Game played just before commencement of the 1958–59 campaign, Montreal's "Boom Boom" Geoffrion was injured when elbowed by Red Kelly, playing on the NHL All-Star squad. Incensed, Blake sent the team's trainer into the dressing room of the All-Stars, where Aubut found many of the players still using the older, and therefore illegal, elbow pads.

Following their complaint to Clarence Campbell, the NHL president instructed his referee-in-chief, Carl Voss, to travel to each of the six NHL cities to inspect equipment, specifically the elbow pads being used. After the two Bruins' stars both had their jaws broken in the first week of the NHL season, Campbell admitted that Voss had scrutinized the equipment in every NHL city but Toronto, so the NHL president could not say with certainty that the Maple Leafs were guilty.

Allan Stanley, playing against his former teammates, was selected as the game's first Star. Jerry Toppazzini, who scored both Bruins' goals, was the second Star and Ron Stewart was Star number three.

Bower Earns First Shutout in Blue and White
Saturday, October 25, 1958
Following a six-day rest, Toronto showed up ready to play on *Hockey Night in Canada*, with Johnny Bower earning his first shutout as a Maple Leaf in a 3–0 blanking of the Red Wings. Dick Duff, Bob Pulford and Brian Cullen potted the goals.

During the second-period intermission, viewers watched National Hockey League President Clarence Campbell present Leafs' star Frank Mahovlich with the Calder Memorial Trophy as the league's best rookie in 1957–58. As Campbell stepped onto the ice surface, accompanied by captains Gordie Howe on one side and George Armstrong on the other, the crowd booed heartily. With public address announcer Red Barber making the announcement, the NHL president simply handed the trophy to Mahovlich. On the broadcast, Foster Hewitt added that Bobby Hull of the Black Hawks had been the runner-up to "The Big M."

Imlach Names Untouchables
Saturday, November 8, 1958
Toronto sought revenge from the Boston Bruins, who had shut out the Leafs 2–0 the previous Sunday at the Boston Garden. In Toronto for the Saturday night tilt, the Maple Leafs collected two goals from Billy Harris and singles from George Armstrong, Brian Cullen and Bob Pulford as they thumped the Bruins 5–3. Leo Boivin, Jim Morrison and Don McKenney replied for Boston.

Punch Imlach appeared during the intermission segment on *Hockey Night in Canada* and explained his role of assistant general manager, stating, "Well, actually, there is no general manager so the duties of the manager are falling on me, so I have to assume all the duties of a manager of a hockey club." Asked if there is anyone he wouldn't consider trading, Punch replied, "Well, they're all expendable except three that we shouldn't deal. That would be Mahulavich [Imlach never did pronounce Mahovlich's name correctly], Brewer and Pulford."

"I didn't realize he was doing that because everybody else was pronouncing it different ways," said The Big M. "It's a difficult name to say, but people tried. The press tried to make something out of it, but I don't believe there was anything personal. From day one, that never bothered me."

Drastic Times Call for Drastic Measures
Friday, November 28, 1958

"As the first weeks of that season wore on, one thing got plainer and plainer," recalled Imlach in his memoirs. "The Leafs just weren't playing for Billy Reay." After the Detroit game, the Silver Seven hockey committee called Imlach in and asked him to fine each of the players. Punch talked them out of it but called each player individually into a room where he and Billy Reay explained that when the fans weren't satisfied neither was management. Imlach threatened to fine each Leaf $200 if they didn't collect at least one point in upcoming road games against Boston (November 16) and New York (November 19).

Toronto tied Boston 4–4 but was stomped on by the New York Rangers 7–4. Dismayed with the performance of their team, the Silver Seven met again with Imlach. They discussed firing Reay and asked Punch for his thoughts. "I told them that the team obviously wasn't playing for Reay. I thought he wasn't tough enough on them, that he was trusting them to do things and they were letting him down." But Punch now held the cards. "They asked me what I would do about it. I said I wasn't the general manager; I was only the assistant general manager. That's when they decided to make me the general manager, to be fully responsible for making the rules for the hockey club and for seeing that coach and players alike stuck to them."

With the team mired in last place, on November 21 the announcement was made to the media that Punch Imlach had been handed the reins of the Toronto Maple Leafs and was now the team's general manager. Imlach was quoted as saying that there were things that were wrong with the club and they would be fixed. "I'd rather be shot for a lion than a lamb," he told *The Globe and Mail*. The Toronto Maple Leafs had lost ten, tied one and won just five in the first sixteen games of the season.

Under the Imlach regime, Toronto tied the Rangers, and then played to a draw with the Black Hawks, but on November 26 they were again booed off the ice in a 5–2 loss to the Red Wings at Maple Leaf Gardens. The next night, playing the Wings in Detroit, the Red Wings edged the Leafs 3–2.

On November 28, Imlach made his decision. He met with Conn Smythe and told "the old man" that he was going to relieve Billy Reay of his coaching duties. "Well, if that's the way it is," responded Smythe.

As the team assembled in the dressing room for their 4:00 p.m. practice, Punch strode into the room. "Never mind practising today," he said, stopping the players in their tracks. "I've had to relieve Billy Reay as coach." Each player was called into the nearby medical room, told to bring his items as he would not be returning to the dressing room after his chat with Imlach. The GM asked each one, "Will you play hockey for me?" To a man, each promised Imlach that he would play for him. Knowing that Olmstead was close to Reay as former teammates, Imlach was particularly concerned about his veteran forward, but was assured that he would play as diligently for Imlach as he had for any coach.

Johnny Bower recalled, "I got along really good with Billy [Reay]. I remember him coming to me once and he said, 'John, this is a really important game for me. They're putting the pressure on me because we're losing and if we lose this game, I've got a feeling I might go.' I was very sorry to hear that. They did let him go."

Carl Brewer, in a later Leafs TV interview, stated, "I really liked Billy Reay. I liked what he did and I liked what he had to say."

Bob Pulford was later asked about the coaching change and commented, "When we were in midget hockey and played badly, the coach would really give us heck. Sometimes. I think we still need to be treated that way."

Imlach changed the texture of the team, immediately loosening the restrictions that Reay had placed on the players. "Imlach knows what he wants and has a knack of getting his ideas across to the player," Tim Horton told the *Toronto Daily Star*. "Now, I don't worry about making mistakes. I know Punch will pull me off the ice, correct the error and send me back into action. There's no danger of being shunted to the end of the bench without being told why."

Billy Reay had instructed Horton to pass the puck as soon as he got it in the Leafs' zone. "I like to carry that puck, have a good look before I pass it," Horton said. "Imlach instructed me to do so. Now, I'm looking forward to every shift on the ice instead of worrying about the possibility of making mistakes."

Added Frank Mahovlich, "When Punch came to Toronto in fifty-eight, it was a real boost. Everyone started playing ten or fifteen percent better than they ever had before. I thought he was good for the first three or four years. He got the most out of everybody and turned things around."

Imlach stepped behind the bench as the interim coach until he could find a replacement for Reay. "He doesn't have to consult me about hiring someone, although he probably would," suggested Stafford Smythe. Even Bert Olmstead, who had been close to Reay, recognized that something had had to happen. Punch appointed Olmstead as an assistant coach. Although he relinquished that role a few weeks later because he wasn't being consulted on team moves, the veteran's experience and leadership were important for the team's growth.

It was interesting timing for Imlach to fire Reay — most of the sports reporters were in Vancouver covering the Grey Cup at the time.

Imlach and Olmstead Predict Playoffs for Leafs

Saturday, November 29, 1958

Viewers of *Hockey Night in Canada* saw the debut of Punch Imlach as interim coach of the Toronto Maple Leafs. The team played well, but was downed 2–1. Kenny Wharram and Pierre Pilote tallied for Chicago, with Billy Harris scoring for the Leafs. The Three Stars were Pilote, Allan Stanley and Hawks' netminder Glenn Hall.

In the second intermission, Foster Hewitt spoke with Bert Olmstead about being named assistant coach. "My duties aren't too severe as yet," admitted Olmstead. "I believe the main responsibility that I have to look after this year is to run practices and the team when George Imlach is not available. He is the general manager and has taken on extra duties of coach. He has his hands full." Asked whether the Leafs had the talent to compete, Olmstead stated emphatically, "Yes, I have no doubts in my mind that we should be able to hit that fourth spot."

Bert was clearly drinking Imlach's Kool-Aid. "Right then, I started to say, as often as anybody would listen, that we were going to get off the floor, that we were going to make it into one of the first four places in the league — be one of the teams that would play for the Stanley Cup," Imlach declared in his autobiography. "I talked loud and long. I did it on purpose. Somebody had to give that team the idea that they could win. Somebody had to stand up for them in public. I tried to do that."

Leafs Unbeaten in Six since Imlach Replaced Reay

Saturday, December 13, 1958

Unbeaten in five games, Toronto was down 4–3 late in the game against the Rangers. New York's fourth goal had been a cheap one at Bower's expense. "I went up and down the bench behind the players," recalled Punch. "I said, 'Your goalkeeper is a horse's ass if you don't get that goal back. This is a team, and you don't want anybody on it to be a horse's ass. So get it back!'" With ninety seconds left in the game, Imlach pulled Bower for an extra attacker and Dick Duff replied with the tying goal at 18:38. With that tie, Toronto had gone unbeaten in six games. That night, Billy Harris, Red Sullivan and Dick Duff were named the game's Three Stars.

Imlach's Son Surprises with Reveal of Favourite Player
Saturday, December 20, 1958

The winning streak came to an end as quickly as it had begun. Boston doubled Toronto 6–3 on December 14 and Montreal dumped the Leafs 4–1 on the 18th. The *Hockey Night in Canada* broadcast on December 20 featured the Maple Leafs at home to the Boston Bruins. The game concluded in a 2–2 tie, with Armstrong and Stewart scoring for Toronto and Jean-Guy Gendron and Don McKenney for the Bruins.

With a nod to families on *Young Canada Hockey Night*, Foster Hewitt interviewed his grandson Bruce Hewitt and Punch Imlach's son Brent (who would briefly play for the Leafs several years later) during the second intermission. Foster asked five-year-old Bruce what he would say when a Maple Leaf scored a goal, and his grandson replied, "I say, 'He shoots and scores,' too!" Foster replied, "We'll have to put you to work one of these days. Your Dad [Bill Hewitt] was on the broadcast well over twenty years ago and he was eight at the time."

Hewitt then spoke to Brent Imlach and asked him about his favourite player. "I like Dickie Duff…and Jean Beliveau," replied the young Imlach, who had met Beliveau when his father coached the big centre with the Quebec Aces. Ironically, seven years later, Brent suited up for Toronto and was sent out by his father to take the opening faceoff against that same classy Montreal star.

Leafs Deal Detroit a Shutout as Imlach Makes Changes
Thursday, December 25, 1958

On Christmas Day, Ed Chadwick, playing his first game in five weeks, blanked the Detroit Red Wings 2–0. Punch Imlach explained how he rotated his goaltenders. "My idea of the whole thing is that the fellow who is playing the best at the time will continue to play. If Chadwick wins tonight, Bower will have to win his job back again. As it was, Bower was playing well and it had to wait until he had an injury to put Chadwick in to see what he could do. You don't change a winning club. If we're winning, we're going to stick with what we have. We have enough trouble winning as it is."

Two days before Christmas, Imlach made a deal to acquire hard-working Gerry Ehman. A long-time favourite of the Leafs' GM, the veteran forward arrived in Toronto from Hershey of the AHL in exchange for cash and the loan of Willie Marshall. Ehman had played for Imlach in Quebec in 1954–55 and scored forty goals under him in Springfield in 1957–58. In fact, hearing that Eddie Shore was impossible to play for, Ehman had originally quit hockey rather than report to the Springfield Indians. But after relenting, he blossomed under Shore, becoming an All-Star and earning another shot at the NHL. When the AHL's Indians split from the Bruins, Boston wanted to keep Ehman, but Eddie Shore's asking price was so steep that the Bruins declined. Shore then traded Ehman to Detroit, but Gerry was unable to crack the Red Wings' lineup and was sent to the Hershey Bears, Detroit's AHL affiliate. Punch Imlach struck a deal with Baz Bastien, the general manager of the Bears. "Buy Ehman from Detroit and I will give you Willie Marshall in return." Marshall had been unable to make the Leafs full time, but was a scoring sensation with the Pittsburgh Hornets. The deal was made and Toronto ended up with the unsung Ehman. "When we got him in that trade, nobody was very impressed," admitted Imlach. "I put him on right wing with Billy Harris at centre and Frank Mahovlich on left, and that was one hot scoring line."

Second Shutout in a Week is Christmas Gift for Chadwick
Wednesday, December 31, 1958
The Maple Leafs were pleased to see that the calendar was about to give them a fresh start. Toronto celebrated New Year's Eve by blanking the first-place Montreal Canadiens 2–0. Ed Chadwick earned the shutout, his third of the season and second of the week.

Imlach Confirms that Search for Coach is Over
Saturday, January 3, 1959
With a new year came a new lease on life for the Maple Leafs. Imlach, who still considered himself a temporary coach, was looking for the right

personality to coach his team. He had spoken to former New York Ranger Alf Pike, who was doing well coaching the Winnipeg Warriors of the Western Hockey League (WHL). But Winnipeg asked for players in return for the poaching of their coach, so Imlach, with few players to spare, declined hiring Pike. Two or three years earlier, Toronto's AHL club in Pittsburgh had been disbanded and Toronto lost a lot of the Hornet players in the draft. Toronto shared an AHL affiliate in Rochester with the Montreal Canadiens, but only had four or five players with the Americans. "After the Pike deal didn't work, I didn't look any more," admitted Imlach. "Especially when I knew that what the Leaf management really wanted was for me to keep on as coach."

That night, Eric Nesterenko and Earl Balfour scored for the Black Hawks, with Bob Pulford tallying for Toronto in a 2–1 Leafs' loss.

Leafs Pick Up Steam — and Regan
Saturday, January 10, 1959
It had been a productive week for the Maple Leafs. Toronto doubled New York 4–2 on January 4 and beat Detroit 3–1 on the seventh. That same day, Punch claimed Larry Regan on waivers from the Boston Bruins. "I'd had Larry in Quebec," said Imlach. "I knew what he could do. He's got a lot of go in him and was a hell of a stickhandler. He also had a pretty good gift for being a positive thinker."

On the *Hockey Night in Canada* broadcast of January 10, Toronto spanked Boston 4–1. George Armstrong connected twice and singles went to Dick Duff and Billy Harris. Johnny Bower was selected as the first star, Harris the second and Armstrong was the third star.

Bounced Leaf Coach Billy Reay Appears on *Hockey Night in Canada*
Saturday, January 24, 1959
What potentially could have been an awkward moment turned out to be a very good interview as Billy Reay, in his first television appearance since his firing, was interviewed regarding international hockey. After being dumped by Toronto, Reay had been named manager of the Belleville

McFarlands, who brought home the gold medal representing Canada at the World Championship in Prague, Czechoslovakia.

That night, the Bruins beat Toronto 3–1, with Doug Mohns, Carl Brewer and Bronco Horvath selected as the Three Stars.

Viewers Get a Glimpse into the Future
Saturday, February 28, 1959

On the last day of February, Toronto hosted the Detroit Red Wings. The second intermission featured the trainers of the two teams — Lefty Wilson for Detroit and Bob Haggert for the Maple Leafs — who traded stories with announcer Wes McKnight. Holding up a clear goalie mask created by Delbert Louch from St. Mary's, Ontario, Wilson, who had played three NHL games in goal as an emergency substitute, explained that the Red Wings insist that their goaltenders wear masks in practice. Haggert replied that in Toronto, the decision is optional.

Terry Sawchuk, who wouldn't start wearing a mask in games until 1962, earned the first star on the night, backstopping the Wings to a 4–2 victory. Frank Mahovlich was the second star and Gordie Howe was the third. Leaf-killer Red Kelly scored two goals in the game, including an empty-netter late in the third.

Bruins Forced to Use a Student in Goal
Saturday, March 7, 1959

While travelling by train from Boston to Toronto, Bruins' goalkeeper Harry Lumley ate a shrimp cocktail that made him deathly ill. Lumley arrived in Toronto and the Leafs' team doctor, Hugh Smythe (Stafford's brother), immediately was summoned. Dr. Smythe administered medication but told the Bruins' management that he doubted that Lumley would be strong enough to play that evening. The Bruins' management contacted Punch Imlach. In the NHL, the home team was responsible for supplying a spare goaltender in the case of an emergency. Imlach contacted Don Keenan, a twenty-year-old mechanical engineering student at the University Toronto who had practised with the St. Michael's Majors but had not played an actual game with them since an emergency the previous spring.

Keenan, who had been studying for an exam, showed up at Maple Leaf Gardens and was astounded to learn that he would indeed be starting for the Boston Bruins in a game broadcast on *Hockey Night in Canada* that evening.

Milt Schmidt, Boston's coach, repeatedly forgot the name of his netminder, but Keenan played surprisingly well. Toronto won by a 4–1 score, with two goals from Ron Stewart and singles by Gerry Ehman and Carl Brewer. Horvath connected for Boston. The Three Stars of the game were Bower, Ron Stewart and the young Boston goalie. Don Keenan stopped thirty-seven of forty-one in what was to be his only NHL game. Keenan, who knew many of the Leafs from his days with St. Mike's, later ribbed Imlach that he was the reason the Leafs made the playoffs that season.

Leafs Get a Sniff of Playoff Berth

Saturday, March 14, 1959

The Maple Leafs were seven points out of a playoff berth with just five games remaining to play. Any of the last three teams in the standings could steal the final playoff spot. The Detroit Red Wings were in sixth place, the Maple Leafs in fifth and the New York Rangers clung to fourth like a hungry dog to a soup bone.

The Rangers were showing signs of falling apart. Their coach, Phil Watson, was beginning to panic. A few weeks earlier, he had issued commandments for his wayward team: no drinking, no smoking in the dressing room and no gambling, and established an 11:30 p.m. curfew. Players caught breaking the rules faced a $100 fine. Then, following a 5–1 home loss to the powerful Canadiens, he kept his team on the ice, making them perform drills for an hour while the maintenance staff cleaned up the rink. As the losses mounted, more and more blame was heaped on goalie Gump Worsley, although he pointed his finger publicly at Lou Fontinato and Dean Prentice as well.

That weekend, Toronto played a home-and-home set against the Rangers. *The Globe and Mail* wrote, "A win for the Rangers in either game will send Leafs to the embalmers." The Leafs had to win both to stay in contention.

Imlach, the master motivator, found superb ammunition that morning. Curiously, the National Hockey League issued its playoff schedule, including contingency plans and dates, but nowhere was there any mention of the Toronto Maple Leafs. Imlach still clung to the fervent belief that his team was going to compete for the Stanley Cup. In the dressing room before the game, he slammed the league for their lack of faith and, in the words of King Clancy, told his charges that he wanted them to stick the schedule "where Paddy put the potato." To a man, the Leafs understood.

The *Hockey Night in Canada* viewers were treated to an intense contest that night. The spirited Leafs beat the Rangers in every way a team can be beaten. Johnny Bower shut the door and refused to allow a goal, while the forwards feasted on the Rangers. The final score was 5–0, with Mahovlich and Duff both contributing two-goal performances and Armstrong collecting the other. But during the third period, a brawl ensued, leading to many penalties, fines and injuries. The Leafs showed great character, standing up for each other. "Leapin' Lou" Fontinato had been on a mission. TV viewers watched as he crosschecked Regan violently into the glass, scrapped with the Leafs, who valiantly backed each other up in the brawl — a characteristic intrinsic to the formation of team spirit and their eventual success — and then engaged in a tussle with a spectator while in the penalty box, a fracas that emptied the benches.

"That should be quite a hockey game in Madison Square Garden tomorrow night," predicted Wes McKnight after the game. "There is no love lost between the Leafs and the Rangers, two teams battling it out for the fourth and last playoff position."

As it turned out, it was.

The home-and-home series took the Maple Leafs to Madison Square Garden on Sunday night. Down 6–5 late in the game, the Rangers pulled their goalie but came up empty, and Toronto hung on for the narrow victory. Bob Pulford scored the winning goal on a long shot that beat Gump Worsley, and George Armstrong recorded a hat trick in the game.

Those four points gained through the weekend catapulted Toronto over Detroit into fifth place, just three points behind the Rangers with three games left to play. The schedule didn't look as though it favoured Toronto: the remaining games were against Montreal, Chicago and Detroit. Worse yet, Toronto had never won more than two games in a row through the entire 1958–59 season.

During a team meeting at 11:00 a.m. on March 19, Imlach learned that Montreal's Jacques Plante had been given the night off after showing up at the rink with a face swollen with boils. Claude Pronovost, brother of Red Wings' defenceman Marcel, was designated to play goal for the Canadiens. The Rangers complained bitterly to NHL president Clarence Campbell, believing that Toronto was getting an unfair advantage, but the protesting was to no avail.

By the end of the second period, Pronovost had allowed five Toronto goals and was replaced to start the third period by Claude Cyr, who had spent the season with the Hull-Ottawa Canadiens of the Eastern Professional Hockey League (EPHL). Cyr earned his first and only NHL activity facing the Maple Leafs in that game and was solid, if unspectacular, allowing one goal as Toronto doubled Montreal 6–3. This put the Maple Leafs only one point behind the New York Rangers for the final playoff berth going into the final weekend of the season.

That evening, Boston beat the Rangers 5–3 in New York.

Detroit Ousted and Leafs One Point Back of Playoff Position
Saturday, March 21, 1959

In an afternoon contest, the Rangers faced off against Detroit while the anxious Leafs watched the game on the *CBS Game of the Week*. That evening, on *Hockey Night in Canada*, Toronto faced the Chicago Black Hawks.

During the second intermission, Foster Hewitt staged a panel to discuss the spring's playoff scenarios. With Hewitt were three former Maple Leafs Stanley Cup winners: King Clancy, "Baldy" Cotton and Joe Primeau. Primeau commented, "With their spirit and the way they are going, I think the Leafs have a good chance." Clancy added, "The way that Punch Imlach has been handling this club, he deserves to get in the playoffs."

That night, the surging Leafs, led by a two-goal effort from Frank Mahovlich, spanked the third-place Black Hawks 5–1 in an especially chippy contest. But New York kept pace. That afternoon, the Rangers had beaten Detroit 5–2, eliminating Detroit from playoff contention for the first time in twenty-one years. Going into the final day of the regular season, Toronto was still one point behind the New York Rangers for a playoff spot.

Exuding bravado, Imlach told each player to pack enough clothes for a week, because after they beat Detroit to slip into the playoffs, they'd be straight off to Boston for the semi-finals.

Imlach Clairvoyant as Regan's Productivity Pushes Leafs into Playoffs
Sunday, March 22, 1959

On that Sunday, the final day of the 1958–59 regular season, the New York Rangers were challenged by the Montreal Canadiens in a game that started at 7:00 p.m., while the Maple Leafs faced the Red Wings in Detroit, with that contest beginning at 8:00. "We're going to get that fourth playoff spot," Imlach assured Bob Haggert. "I'll tell you why we're going to win. The Canadiens are playing New York in Montreal tonight. There are two guys who play for the Montreal Canadiens, Jean Beliveau and Marcel Bonin, they played for me in Quebec City and they won't let me down."

By the time the puck dropped in Detroit, Montreal was ahead of the Rangers by a 2–1 count. But before the Leafs knew it, Norm Ullman and Marcel Pronovost had scored and Toronto was behind 2–0 to the Wings. Then, at 16:58 of the first period at the Olympia in Detroit, the public address announcer gave the fans a final score in the other game: Montreal, with youngster Charlie Hodge in goal, had defeated New York 4–2. That meant that a Leafs' win would propel them into fourth place and a playoff berth. Incidentally, Jean Beliveau had two goals and an assist and Marcel Bonin chipped in with an assist for Montreal, and their old pal Punch.

At the end of the first period, Imlach decided he had no need to talk to his team — they knew the task at hand. But Stafford Smythe saw his coach in the hallway and offered premature condolences. "Well, at least you had a good try," he said, "You have nothing to be ashamed of."

Imlach exploded, his balding head a red as a beet. "What the hell are you talking about?!? We've come too far to lose now!"

As the players approached the ice surface for commencement of the second period, captain George Armstrong told his coach, "Don't worry, Punch. We'll get it for you!"

Larry Regan knocked in Armstrong's rebound to close the gap, then Bob Baun scored his first goal of the season with a shot from the point. The score then seesawed, as Ullman put Detroit up 3–2 at 15:16, but less than two minutes later, Carl Brewer again evened the score. Regan scored his second goal just twenty-one seconds after Brewer (he had also assisted on Brewer's tally). Toronto was up 4–3 late in the second, and then Pronovost struck again, knotting the game at four-all.

Stafford Smythe left the arena and took a walk down to the Detroit River — he couldn't stand the pressure. Regan laughed, "Hey Stafford, when we win the Stanley Cup, will you come into the dressing room and give us just a little smile?"

Although Regan and Imlach had history together, it was not always warm and fuzzy between the two. At one point, Regan barked at Imlach, saying, "I've made you famous in every league you've worked!" Imlach's response? "Yeah, and you'd better make me famous in this league or you'll be unemployed!"

With the score tied 4–4 early in the third period, Larry Regan skated over to Dick Duff in the faceoff circle in the Toronto end. "You're going to get the winner," he said. "I'm going to give it to you." At the faceoff, Regan darted through the neutral zone with the puck. Cutting left at the Wings' blue line, Regan tucked the puck through Warren Godfrey's legs, then beat Red Kelly wide and found himself in the corner with the puck. Regan saw Duff flying into the slot and fed him the puck. Duff one-timed the puck as he received it at the edge of the crease and beat Terry Sawchuk to give Toronto a 5–4 lead. Billy Harris later added an insurance goal and the scoreboard told the tale: Toronto 6, Detroit 4. Regan had scored two goals and added two assists.

The Cinderella Toronto Maple Leafs were going to be one of four teams competing for the Stanley Cup!

Asked when he felt Toronto had won the game, Armstrong admitted, "When the game was over. I never had a feeling like this."

Imlach brought the Leafs back from the dead. "Imlach is not satisfied with one miracle a season," wrote *The Globe.* "He actually believes he can win the Stanley Cup and, at that precise moment, there isn't anybody who might even timidly suggest he is suffering from delusion. A few months ago, the repeated Imlach incantation that the Leafs would reach the playoffs was accepted sombrely and sceptically by disrespectful hockey writers. They studiously avoided looking at him during his embarrassing spells, trusting that it was only a temporary seizure and that he would recover." Even Conn Smythe was dubious about Imlach's predictions, asking whether the Leafs had hired "a mad man or a coach."

Bob Haggert recalled, "Winning in Detroit and making the playoffs convinced everybody in that room that we could win [the Stanley Cup]. In the game of hockey, winning is believing and believing is winning."

In an interview on Leafs TV, Carl Brewer reflected on the season. "We had been somewhat mediocre throughout the course of that season. Towards the end of the year, we were respectable and in the final game of the season, we finally got into the playoffs, which was really exciting for us. Punch Imlach, at that point in time, did a remarkable job."

"Many of us look back at that game as the night we started to turn things around," recalled Billy Harris.

Gump Worsley was made the scapegoat for the Rangers' collapse. His team lost six of their final seven games. But the parallel to New York's elimination was Toronto's ascension. The Maple Leafs won their final five games, scoring twenty-eight goals to their opponents' thirteen. Imlach's season-long bravado had inspired his team to reach beyond their perceived ability. "I haven't been connected with anyone that had more savvy or common sense insofar as hockey is concerned," stated King Clancy. "Getting Punch into the organization has to be one of the big highlights for Toronto. The Leafs got a marvellous coach and Punch took on a tough job when he elected to be manager as well. This is the test of a great man, and this is just what Imlach is."

Dickie Moore of the first-place Canadiens finished the season with ninety-six points — forty-one goals and fifty-five assists — to win the Art

Ross Trophy as the league's scoring champion. Montreal also had the Vezina Trophy winner in Jacques Plante, the Norris Trophy recipient in Tom Johnson and the Calder Trophy winner, Ralph Backstrom, who edged out Toronto's Carl Brewer. Andy Bathgate of the Rangers was chosen as the NHL's most valuable player. Detroit's Alex Delvecchio won the Lady Byng as the most gentlemanly player.

While first-place Montreal met the Chicago Black Hawks, third-place finishers during the regular season, Toronto faced the second-place Boston Bruins in the 1958–59 semi-final.

Throughout the season, the Leafs were never expected to make the playoffs. Even when Punch Imlach took over behind the bench, no one saw the move as an indicator that the team's fortunes would improve. But one man stood steadfast in his belief that Toronto would compete for the Stanley Cup. That man was Punch Imlach.

"He has the guts of a safecracker," stated the *Boston Daily Globe*.

"We'll win in six games," predicted Imlach. "The only reason it will go six games is that we want to end it in Toronto in front of our own fans because they've been so faithful to us." He added, "Then we'll take the Canadiens in seven, the last one in overtime. I've always been lucky in playoffs and I'm not changing now."

"They're a hungry team," admitted Milt Schmidt, coach of the Bruins. "They won their last five games to make the playoffs. They're bound to be cocky. Their coach is cocky. Punch gets his club to give one-hundred percent."

1958–59 Regular Season Standings						
FINISH	TEAM	GAMES	WINS	LOSSES	TIES	POINTS
1	Montreal Canadiens	70	39	18	13	91
2	Boston Bruins	70	32	29	9	73
3	Chicago Black Hawks	70	28	29	13	69
4	Toronto Maple Leafs	70	27	32	11	65
5	New York Rangers	70	26	32	12	64
6	Detroit Red Wings	70	25	37	8	58

1958–59 Regular Season Scoring

RK	NUMBER	PLAYER	POS	AGE	GP	G	A	PTS	PIM
1	9	Dick Duff	LW	22	69	29	24	53	73
2	15	Billy Harris	C	23	70	22	30	52	29
3	27	Frank Mahovlich	LW	21	63	22	27	49	94
4	16	Bert Olmstead	LW	32	70	10	31	41	74
5	20	Bob Pulford	LW	22	70	23	14	37	53
6	10	George Armstrong	RW	28	59	20	16	36	37
7	12	Ron Stewart	RW	26	70	21	13	34	23
8	7	Tim Horton	D	29	70	5	21	26	76
9	17	Gerry Ehman	RW	26	38	12	13	25	12
10	8	Larry Regan	RW	28	32	4	21	25	2
11	18	Carl Brewer	D	20	69	3	21	24	125
12	26	Allan Stanley	D	32	70	1	22	23	47
13	14	Brian Cullen	C	25	59	4	14	18	10
14	19	Barry Cullen	RW	23	40	6	8	14	17
15	22	Dave Creighton	C	28	34	3	9	12	4
16	21	Bob Baun	D	22	51	1	8	9	87
17	2	Marc Reaume	D	24	51	1	5	6	67
18	22	Gary Aldcorn	LW	23	5	0	3	3	2
19	11	Rudy Migay	C	30	19	1	1	2	4
20	4	Steve Kraftcheck	D	29	8	1	0	1	0
21	8	Willie Marshall	C	27	9	0	1	1	2
22	1	Johnny Bower	G	34	39	0	0	0	2
23	1	Ed Chadwick	G	25	31	0	0	0	0
24	11	Bob Nevin	RW	20	2	0	0	0	2
25	23	Noel Price	D	23	28	0	0	0	4
		TEAM TOTALS			70	189	302	491	846

Regular Season Netminding

RK		PLAYER	POS	AGE	GP	MIN	W	L	T
1	1	Johnny Bower	G	34	39	2340	15	17	7
2	1	Ed Chadwick	G	25	31	1860	12	15	4
		TEAM TOTALS			70	4200	27	32	11

Bruins' netminder Harry Lumley had been dismissed from Toronto following the 1955–56 season because Ed Chadwick had been groomed as the Leafs' goaltender of the future. The Leafs sold Lumley and Eric Nesterenko to the Chicago Black Hawks for $40,000. Relegated to the minors, Lumley found a home with the Buffalo Bisons, Chicago's AHL partner. Midway through the 1957–58 campaign, Boston's goalie, Don Simmons, suffered a dislocated shoulder and the Bruins, desperate for an experienced netminder and unable to acquire Johnny Bower from the Cleveland Barons of the AHL, purchased Lumley from the Hawks for $15,000. Lumley stepped into the crease and performed admirably in place of Simmons. But the hapless Simmons suffered an attack of appendicitis and was forced out of the lineup again, giving Lumley a further opportunity to shine. Going into the playoffs against Toronto, both Lumley and Simmons were available. The irony is that Lumley now had the opportunity to seek revenge on his former team.

The Boston Globe asked the Bruins' coach whether Johnny Bucyk would play after suffering a twelve-stitch cut to his mouth. "Why not," shrugged Schmidt. "He doesn't skate with his mouth!"

In the same regular season game against the Leafs in Toronto, both Doug Mohns and Bronco Horvath broke their jaws. To conclude the season, both wore protective helmets. "Mohns and Horvath requested months ago they be allowed to remove their masks, but acting on the advice of Dr. Ronald Adams, we refused to let them do so," said coach Milt Schmidt. Imlach stirred up the hornet's nest, claiming that the two were suffering from "stage fright." "The two guys who are scared are Mohns and Horvath. Else, why won't they take off those masks they're wearing? I asked Mr. [Clarence] Campbell about the masks and he said the doctor wanted them to continue wearing them. This armour gives them a false sense of security and belligerency," stated Imlach. "They don't need them. They're just afraid of getting hit!"

Curiously, a CBC spokesperson said it was "highly unlikely" that television programming would be altered to accommodate the semi-final between Toronto and Boston. Toronto's surprise playoff berth caught programmers off guard, and a ninety-minute musical, *Salad Days*, was scheduled for the same time as the opening game of the series.

Meanwhile, WGR-TV Buffalo had asked permission to broadcast the opening game of the semi-final between Toronto and the Bruins. Boston agreed, but Conn Smythe referred the Toronto decision to Foster Hewitt, who handled broadcast rights for the Maple Leafs. Hewitt declined, citing that Imperial Oil held territorial rights and, as they were sponsoring the radio broadcast, it would have been overshadowed by a television broadcast. They had no desire to sponsor both.

That first semi-final game was not televised. "It became apparent that the franchise could not be transferred without harming Imperial Oil's continuing association with the hockey telecast," stated a media release. "Rather than deprive viewers in this area of Thursday night's game [game two in the series], arrangements have been made to clear time on a Hamilton station." Responding to "a small but vocal minority," CBC arranged for CHCH Television in Hamilton, which had been broadcasting some *Hockey Night in Canada* games from Maple Leaf Gardens that season, to clear its evening programming to air the game beginning at 9:00 p.m. (the puck was scheduled to drop at 8:00). It was also announced that all subsequent play-off games in which the Leafs played would be broadcast by CBC.

Lumley Leads Bruins to Series-Opening Victory
Game One, Semi-Final – Tuesday, March 24, 1959

Earlier in the day, Imlach called for a practice at noon. "We're going to play four good periods — one at noon and three at night." Punch's reputation as a taskmaster wasn't far from the truth. "I figure if you are going to play a hockey game for an hour, you should probably practise for two hours. It's like a track coach who prepares his runners for a one-mile race by running them five or ten miles."

Harry Lumley was masterful in the Bruins' net, allowing only one goal in a 5–1 win in the opening game of the semi-final. "Although this was Harry's 70th playoff game, it is doubtful if the husky 32-year-old veteran ever gave a more impressive display of his netminding skills," wrote

The Boston Globe. Milt Schmidt, the Bruins' coach, commented, "Lumley was the big difference in this game."

Jerry Toppazzini, Leo Labine, Vic Stasiuk, Larry Leach and Don McKenney scored for Boston, with former Bruin Gerry Ehman supplying Toronto's only goal. In defence of the score, weighed so heavily in the Bruins' favour, Milt Schmidt stated, "I thought the Leafs played a solid, careful game. The score isn't indicative of the play."

Punch Imlach, behind Toronto's bench, suggested that that the loss was an anomaly. "The two kids on defence [Baun and Brewer] were a little nervous," he stated. "That's natural. They've never been in a Stanley Cup playoff before."

George Armstrong shrugged. "It just showed us that we aren't invincible."

The 5–1 loss was even more devastating for Toronto. Bert Olmstead went down with a charley horse after a hit by Leo Boivin in the second period and was replaced by bespectacled Gary Collins, who had spent the regular season with New Westminster of the Western Hockey League (WHL). Olmstead had been one of the Leafs' most dependable forwards through the team's late-season run for a playoff berth. "Broken bones, whatever you can name, they weren't as painful as this thing," grimaced Olmstead.

Bruins Up Two Games to None in 4–2 Win
Game Two, Semi-Final – Thursday, March 26, 1959
Jean-Guy Gendron, "looking like an escapee from a funeral parlour" according to *The Globe and Mail,* was suffering a case of the flu that had him doubtful to play in game two. Yet, the "rubber-legged" winger proved to be the hero in a 4–2 Boston win over Toronto. With the score tied 2–2 late in the third, Gendron scored what proved to be the winning goal at 15:59. Leo Labine added an empty net insurance marker to give the Bruins the win and a two-games-to-none lead in the rugged semi-final. Former Leaf Fleming Mackell scored twice for Boston. Dick Duff and Ron Stewart scored for the Maple Leafs.

Again, Harry Lumley shone for Boston, making several clutch saves in the third period. Lynn Patrick, Boston's general manager, commented on how well Lumley had played. "I don't think Lumley will ever play as well in goal again. Goalkeepers have games like that only once in a lifetime." Punch Imlach added, "Lumley beat us, there's no doubt about that."

The game featured a free-for-all that followed the final buzzer. Bob Pulford and Doug Mohns engaged in a stick duel, but the main feature shifted to a wrestling match between Bert Olmstead and Larry Hillman, who had waged an ongoing feud through the game.

"It was the impression of the Boston team that the score was an inaccurate portrayal of an extremely tough game," wrote *The Globe and Mail.* "With a few breaks, they insist, Leafs might have finished in front with a similar margin."

"I think it's going to be a long series," suggested Lynn Patrick. "And I wouldn't care to say right now who will win. One thing I'm sure about — even if we're leading the series three to zero — I won't feel confident, not with Imlach behind the Toronto bench."

Leafs Battle Back to Edge Bruins in Game Three

Game Three, Semi-Final – Saturday, March 28, 1959

Back in Toronto for game three, the Leafs earned a 3–2 victory in a *Hockey Night in Canada* broadcast on the full CBC network. Vic Stasiuk potted a pair of goals in a losing cause for the Bruins. Bob Pulford scored the first goal for Toronto. Gerry Ehman was the game's hero, scoring at 17:08 of the third to tie the contest, then scoring the deciding goal at 5:02 of overtime. A thunderous ovation greeted the Leafs' unsung hero, who was chosen by New York forward Andy Bathgate as the first star of the game. Lumley and Pulford were the second and third stars. Foster Hewitt called Toronto "the fightingest Leaf team in years."

"I've been hearing all year about what a tough bunch of players those Bruins are. What a laugh that is," said Punch Imlach. "If they're tough, it's about time they showed it. They haven't scared anybody yet."

The Globe wrote, "There was a frank, lumpy feeling in the Gardens that the Leafs would lose this one simply because Lumley, for most of the game, had proved to the satisfaction of local scientists that it is possible to be in two or three places at the same time."

Ehman's timely scoring can be attributable to turning the series around. Had Boston won, they'd have gained an almost insurmountable three-games-to-none lead, likely ending the Leafs' magical season right then, but with the game three victory, the momentum shifted in favour of Toronto.

Series Tied on Big M's Clutch OT Goal
Game Four, Semi-Final – Tuesday, March 31, 1959
Toronto's Larry Regan had suffered a broken hand and found it too sore to play, so Rudy Migay was summoned by Toronto from Rochester of the AHL. Migay skated with the so-called Black Aces — those players on hand to substitute for a regular in the case of an injury or slump. Gary Collins, Barry Cullen, Noel Price and Marc Reaume all worked out with Migay and goalkeeper Ed Chadwick. Bob Baun had a twisted ankle and Regan had a broken hand, so it was important to have the subs prepared to step into the lineup.

Although it was a different contest, game four concluded with the same result as game three, as Toronto again scored an overtime goal to defeat the Bruins 3–2 at Maple Leaf Gardens. Gerry Ehman scored in the first, while Brian Cullen gave Toronto its second goal in the third. Jerry Toppazzini and Bronco Horvath also scored in the third to send the game into overtime.

In sudden death, Jean-Guy Gendron was assessed a five-minute major for cross-checking Ehman. The Bruins were incensed with the call. "Ehman charged from one side of the ice to the other after Gendron," sputtered an exasperated Schmidt. "I thought at first that he was giving the penalty to Ehman for charging. When [referee Red Storey] finally decided on a major to Gendron, he should have chased Ehman too!"

Imlach's retort defended his forward. "Ehman isn't the charging type of player. He just came across the ice to check Gendron and he got it on the nose." Ehman's bloody nose had a little help, according to the Boston newspaper: "Ehman wasn't cut and he admitted later that he blew his nose pretty hard to help produce the blood that influenced Storey to give a major penalty."

During the subsequent power play, Frank Mahovlich lashed a twenty-foot backhander past Harry Lumley in the Boston net at 11:21 of the overtime period to win the contest and even the series between Toronto and Boston.

"Lumley, who had unveiled a new set of miracles for a shrieking mob throughout the game, was so distraught by Mahovlich's goal that he hammered his trusty stick on the top of the net and flung the fragments to the ice," reported *The Globe and Mail.* "Lumley has been around a long time, but I've never seen him play any better," suggested the Bruins' GM. "I've never seen him move so fast, and he really wants to win. He hates losing, especially to Toronto."

"It's too bad that the fine play of two great teams in a great hockey game should be ruined by one man," expressed Milt Schmidt, alluding not so subtly to referee Red Storey, who called the major on Gendron in overtime. That controversy paled in comparison to one that would follow later for Storey.

Perennial All-Star Gordie Howe selected Harry Lumley, Frank Mahovlich and Carl Brewer as the first, second and third stars of the contest.

Third Straight Victory Puts Leafs Ahead in Series
Game Five, Semi-Final – Thursday, April 2, 1959
Game five returned to the Boston Garden, with both teams having won two contests. Toronto dressed Rudy Migay in place of Larry Regan, while Doug Mohns did not dress for Boston due to a knee injury suffered in game four.

"Bower brilliant in Toronto net," screamed the sports section headline in *The Globe.* The Maple Leafs bounced the Bruins 4–1 to earn three consecutive victories, and led the series three games to two. Bert Olmstead, Dick Duff, Frank Mahovlich and Bob Pulford contributed goals for

Toronto, while Jerry Toppazzini added Boston's lone goal midway through the third with the game already out of reach for the Bruins. The Boston fans sent their team off the ice to a chorus of boos. Johnny Bower, who had been very solid but buried under an avalanche of plaudits for Boston's Harry Lumley, played a superb game for Toronto.

At 9:36 of the first period, Larry Leach earned a double minor for roughing, while Tim Horton was assessed a minor for charging. Two minutes later, Horton was back on the ice, but a minute after that, Leach was released from the penalty box. The exit was sixty seconds early, a mistake admitted by the timekeeper from Montreal's crew, who was working the game in Boston. The timekeeper notified referee Eddie Powers, who put Leach back in the box a minute later to serve the final sixty seconds of his sentence. Fortunately for the red-faced off-ice official, neither team scored during the mix-up.

The Three Stars of the game were Johnny Bower, Frank Mahovlich and Allan Stanley. Also notable was Gerry Ehman, who scored his fourth goal of the playoffs in the Toronto victory.

As the players slowly undressed after their victory, sucking on orange quarters to replace fluids, Harold Ballard entered the dressing room and asked for the club's attention. "I have an announcement to make," he said. "I'd like you to meet your new coach." Astonished, the players spun around to see who would be behind their bench. One chuckle became three, and soon the dressing room was convulsing with laughter. Punch Imlach walked in, removed his fedora and stood there, sporting a toupee. The Beatle wig had arrived at the hotel, from a fan.

Addressing the media afterwards, Imlach stated, "We can win [the series], but it's not going to be easy. Don't forget the Bruins were in front and we fought back. They can do the same thing."

Rebounding Bruins Edge Leafs to Tie Series

Game Six, Semi-Final – Saturday, April 4, 1959

The series returned to Toronto for game six, and Boston surprised the Leafs, outscoring them 5–4. Bronco Horvath scored at 12:56 of the third period to earn the win for the Bruins. Johnny Bucyk, who had gone scoreless through the first five playoff games, scored twice in the game after being told by Coach Schmidt that he was too defence-minded. Boston also counted markers from Toppazzini, McKenney and Horvath to win the game. Olmstead, Ehman and Mahovlich, with two, responded for Toronto.

Johnny Bower was hurt in a collision in the second period, but stayed to finish the game. By this time, the Bruins' roster was badly battered. Doug Mohns returned to the lineup in spite of injuries, and Bob Armstrong was battling a pulled groin muscle, as was Fern Flaman. Jim Morrison caught a Carl Brewer slapshot in the face, but returned later in the game after taking fifteen stitches above his upper lip. Jerry Toppazzini was playing with separated ribs. "It took a lot of courage for those fellows to continue," stated Milt Schmidt. "I know what it is to have injuries like that. As a player, I had them all and I appreciate the agony the player endures as he tries to keep playing."

Punch Imlach returned Rudy Migay to the Rochester Americans and re-inserted Larry Regan, broken hand and all, into the lineup between Dick Duff and George Armstrong. "[The hand] felt a thousand times better than when I tried to play in the fourth game," Regan announced. "I couldn't do anything."

The HEM Line (Harris-Ehman-Mahovlich) continued to shine for the Leafs, even in a losing cause. Both Ehman and Mahovlich scored in the third period. Red Sullivan of the Rangers selected Boston's Bronco Horvath as the game's first star, with Johnny Bucyk and Frank Mahovlich as the second and third stars.

Leafs Eliminate Bruins; Reach Stanley Cup Final for First Time Since 1951
Game Seven, Semi-Final – Tuesday, April 7, 1959

Red Storey was scheduled to referee the seventh and deciding game of the Toronto-Boston semi-final, but returned to his home in Montreal, stating that he had no intention of returning to the NHL after remarks made by league president Clarence Campbell that Storey "froze" when he failed to call two tripping penalties against the Canadiens late in the game in the other semi-final series, which had sparked an outpouring of anger from Chicago fans. Storey responded, "I walked the streets of Boston last night before making up my mind to quit. I've got no intentions of going back."

"I never criticized any of my officials publicly and I never would," stated Red Dutton, Campbell's predecessor. "When Campbell took over from me, I told him to back up his officials at all times. I just can't understand him. It's a terrible thing."

In a unique development, at the conclusion of game six between Toronto and Boston, *Hockey Night In Canada* used a new technical advancement to switch to Chicago in order to catch the end of the Hawks/Canadiens game. Revolutionary at the time, the achievement had happened to coincide with the infamous event, as viewers witnessed Chicago fans attacking referee Storey on the ice.

With referee Eddie Powers substituting for Storey, the deciding game was set for the Boston Garden. Several players from both teams limped into game seven. Bob Armstrong, Fern Flaman, Doug Mohns, Jim Morrison and Jerry Toppazzini were playing injured for the Bruins, while Larry Regan was nursing a broken hand for the Leafs. *The Boston Globe* cheekily stated, "The worst fracture of the series was Imlach's prediction that his team would win [the series] in six games." Milt Schmidt laughed in telling reporters, "I'm sorry we changed Punch's timetable. I hated to do it," he said, chuckling sarcastically.

The results were heralded by *The Globe and Mail*. "Toronto Maple Leafs, who consider accomplishing miracles as part of the day's work, catapulted their way into the Stanley Cup final tonight with a dramatic 3–2 win over the crippled Boston Bruins."

The Boston Globe stated, "[The game] had terrific speed, robust checking, clever passing and an almost superhuman effort by the players of both teams. And the suspense, to a roaring crowd of 13,909, was sometimes almost unbearable."

The teams were tied 1–1 at the end of the first period, with Toronto's goal scored by Larry Regan, complete with his broken hand in a cast, while Vic Stasiuk replied for the Bruins. Boston went ahead 2–1 by the end of the second on a goal by defence stalwart Leo Boivin. Bob Pulford tied the score in the third while Danny Polizani was serving netminder Harry Lumley's slashing minor.

Twenty-seven-year-old rookie Gerry Ehman scored what proved to be the winning goal at 17:27 of the third period, as the upstart Maple Leafs edged the heavily favoured Bruins to win the series and put Toronto in the Stanley Cup final for the first time since Bill Barilko and the boys won the championship in 1951. It was Ehman's sixth goal of the series, quite remarkable given that he scored but twelve for the Leafs during the regular season.

Ehman was familiar with Imlach's systems, and had a deceptively quick shot that he was able to release without benefit of a windup. Playing with Mahovlich and Harris on a line that clicked immediately, Ehman was enjoying his first NHL playoff series. He scored three important goals in the series against the Bruins, and while he played well in the final that year, he was not as effective against Montreal, yet ended the playoffs that spring with six goals and seven assists for thirteen points in twelve games. Had there been a Conn Smythe Trophy for most valuable playoff performer at that time (it wasn't introduced until 1965), there seems little doubt that Gerry Ehman would certainly have been considered a candidate.

In spite of the loss, Harry Lumley provided unfailingly superb netminding for Boston. In the second period, the game was held up for twenty-eight minutes while Lumley had a tooth removed and seven stitches added to his mouth after taking a Dickie Duff shot in the face. Lumley returned to great applause in what *The Boston Globe* called "one of the finest ovations ever given a professional athlete at the Garden." Asked to assess the pain in his mouth after taking seven stitches to the lip and breaking a tooth, Bruins' netminder Harry Lumley said, "The only pain I felt came from what I saw on the scoreboard!"

The devastating loss marked the final appearance in the playoffs until 1967–68 for the Boston Bruins.

Bert Olmstead made post-game comments that offered some sage soothsaying. "Three years from now, this Leafs team will be unbeatable because of the invaluable experience they'll pick up in playoffs. Only a few of these fine young players know what it is to be in the Stanley Cup playoffs, and they're learning valuable lessons now."

When pundits heard Imlach proclaim early in the season that the Toronto Maple Leafs would make the playoffs, even though they were mired in last place, they would just as easily have believed that you could boil the ocean. But all of a sudden, the bandwagon was overloaded with believers in Punch's Cinderella squad.

The first-place Montreal Canadiens were defending Stanley Cup champs, and heavily favoured to win again in the spring of 1959. In fact, the Canadiens had won Lord Stanley's legacy the three previous springs. Montreal was riding a juggernaut, finishing first with 91 points, 18 more than second-place Boston. The Canadiens had once again run ahead of the pack, scoring 258 goals and allowing just 158. In contrast, the fourth-place Maple Leafs had squeaked into the playoffs with 65 regular season points, scoring 189 goals and allowing 201.

The Canadiens' attack was led by scoring leader Dickie Moore (96 points), Jean Beliveau (91 points, including a league-best 45 goals) and Bernie Geoffrion, who finished sixth in scoring. By comparison, Dick Duff had led the Leafs in regular season scoring, finishing seventeenth in the league with 53 points. Billy Harris was one point behind his teammate. "I was playing extremely well for Punch. He had me playing with Mahovlich and Gerry Ehman," Harris recalled some years later. "At that time, I was playing quite a bit and my weight would fluctuate between one-fifty-eight and one-sixty-four, and Imlach wanted me up as close to one-hundred-and-seventy pounds as possible. Once every two weeks, he had a case of stout delivered to our house in East York. He wanted me to have a bottle of stout prior to every meal, hoping to put on some weight. The project was successful. I pretty well played between one-sixty-five and one-hundred-and-seventy pounds the last couple of years I played in the NHL. In fact, for a while, Bobby Haggert, our trainer, had to weigh me in before practice and if I wasn't one-sixty or more, I wasn't allowed to practise."

The Leafs preached that balance beats brilliance. "We have more good scorers than Montreal," stated the confident Imlach. Jean Beliveau, in fact, had fractured two vertebrae in the semi-final and it was uncertain whether he'd play in the final.

To shore up their lineup, the Maple Leafs summoned Pat Hannigan from New Westminster of the WHL, and Dave Creighton, Al MacNeil and Rudy Migay from the AHL Rochester Americans.

Habs Draw First Blood in Battle for Lord Stanley's Cup
Game One, Stanley Cup Final – Thursday, April 9, 1959
The opening game of the Stanley Cup final was a dull affair for fans seated in the Montreal Forum, as well as those watching on *Hockey Night in Canada*.

Henri Richard potted the first goal, tapping a Dickie Moore rebound behind Bower. Dick Duff evened the score on a breakaway. Billy Harris then deflected a point shot from Tim Horton to put Toronto up 2–1. Ralph Backstrom evened the score on a beautiful deke. Late in the second period, Andre Pronovost blasted a shot past Bower from thirty feet. But less than two minutes later, Ron Stewart tipped in a Carl Brewer shot to tie the game at 3.

Marcel Bonin, wearing a pair of Maurice Richard's old gloves for good luck, bounced a blooper past Bower for the winning goal at 11:59 of the third, and then Dickie Moore added an insurance marker later in the period to give the Canadiens a 5–3 victory and a one-win edge in the race to the Stanley Cup.

Montreal exploited the Leafs' mistakes to earn the win. "Imlach's men were sloppy in their own zone and it was failure to move the puck with authority that led to their undoing," wrote the *Toronto Daily Star*.

The game was not without its aggressive play. Ab McDonald suffered a charley horse and Boom Boom Geoffrion took a two-stitch cut on the top of his head. Maurice Richard made two brief appearances during the game, both on the power play, and was still a long way from 100 percent after having fractured his ankle on January 18. The Rocket was perturbed at getting so little ice time, and went out of his way to inform his coach that he was ready for a regular shift.

"This is going to be a long, tough series," prophesied Montreal coach Toe Blake. "It was close for fifty-five minutes." When asked about Imlach's prediction of the Leafs' victory, he said, "Predictions are for gypsies."

"This will be the easiest game the Canadiens will have against us," responded the Leafs' coach.

Gordie Howe selected the Three Stars and chose Marcel Bonin at one, Ralph Backstrom at two and Dick Duff at three.

Bonin had been demoted to Rochester, an AHL team shared, ironically, by both Toronto and Montreal, in December of that season. To do that, the Canadiens put him on waivers and any team could have claimed him for $15,000. No one put in a claim, however. Bonin, a fan favourite because of his exploits wrestling bears and chewing glass, was called back up to Montreal when Maurice Richard was injured. He ended up scoring seven goals in the Chicago series and three against Toronto that spring.

Leafs in Tough as Canadiens Take Second Game of Final

Game Two, Stanley Cup Final – Saturday, April 11, 1959

Commenting on the opening game loss, Stafford Smythe said, "They [the Leafs] are facing a mountain — the biggest one in hockey. They have to win four out of the next six from the best team in the world." Punch Imlach replied, "Don't worry about that. My guys are going to climb that mountain and win the Cup."

Playoff star Gerry Ehman sat out the morning practice after suffering a bruised instep from blocking a shot in the first game. The foot was X-rayed, but there were no broken bones.

The puck dropped at the Forum in Montreal, and it was all Canadiens all the time from that point on. Tom Johnson of the Habs scored the game's first goal on a power play, and Claude Provost scored both of Montreal's other goals, as the Canadiens beat Toronto 3–1 in game two. Ron Stewart counted Toronto's only goal.

"Besides figuring in the big goals, [Doug] Harvey drove the Leaf attackers frantic with his masterful defensive play," reported the *Toronto Daily Star.* "His puck control was the acme of perfection." Stafford Smythe concurred: "If we didn't have to cope with that Doug Harvey, the teams would be even. He beat us single-handed." Harvey set up the winning goals in both of the first two games of the final. "You can't make mental errors in the Stanley Cup," said Bert Olmstead. "Our guys let Harvey take them out to left field on that winning goal. He set up the Marcel Bonin winner in the first game the same way. Canadiens have grown fat for four seasons on such mistakes."

Frank Mahovlich suffered a charley horse when he was checked by Bob Turner. "Mahovlich will play because the Leafs wouldn't have a hope and a prayer without him," commented the *Daily Star.*

The Three Stars were Claude Provost, Doug Harvey and Johnny Bower.

Duff's Overtime Tally Pulls Toronto to Within a Game of Habs

Game Three, Stanley Cup Final – Tuesday, April 14, 1959

The final moved to Toronto for game three. Desperate to be competitive, the Leafs dressed Frank Mahovlich, in spite of his injury, and Larry Regan, sporting a cast on his broken hand, had it removed so he, too, could play.

Toronto scored the important first goal, with Billy Harris tallying at 16:29 with both teams a man short. Marcel Bonin evened the score at 17:31 with Carl Brewer serving a double minor. Bert Olmstead added to the Toronto total in the second, and Dickie Moore tied the game early in the third. With ten seconds remaining in regulation time, Ralph Backstrom scored a goal, but it was called back, as the linesman had blown his whistle, indicating that Jean-Guy Talbot had preceded Backstrom and the puck over the Leafs' blue line.

Tied 2–2, the contest went into overtime. At 10:06, Dick Duff crossed the blue line and fired a slapshot that beat Jacques Plante for the game-winning goal. "I slapped the puck as I hit [Tom] Johnson because I was too tired to use a wrist shot," Duff explained. "It hit Johnson's skate and changed direction just enough to fool Plante. I was actually sick from the heat of the building and the pace of the game when I went out for that shift. That was my last spurt and I had to make it good." Exhausted but excited, Duff added, "Some people have told me I've been slapping them too much lately. King Clancy told me to cut it out."

It was a triumph of desire over finesse. "That was a team effort," said Bert Olmstead. The Three Stars of the game, selected by Gordie Howe, were Dick Duff, Henri Richard and Bert Olmstead.

Commenting on the contest, Foster Hewitt said, "It was a very close, hard-fought game — the best one of the series, incidentally."

During the game, Tim Horton suffered a twelve-stitch cut above his right eyelid after taking Geoffrion's errant stick in the face. Boom Boom took himself out of the play to apologize to Horton, but there was no penalty on the play.

There was quite a history lesson for viewers of *Hockey Night in Canada.* Wes McKnight spoke to the members of the extraordinary Kid Line, catching up with Charlie Conacher, Joe Primeau and "Busher" Jackson, twenty-eight years after they gave the Toronto Maple Leafs their first Stanley Cup championship. A perturbed Conacher blasted Armstrong for missing the net on his shots. Later, Tom Foley spoke with two goaltending legends — Bill Durnan, former star of the Montreal Canadiens, and Percy LeSueur, who had guarded the goal for the Ottawa Silver Seven.

Montreal One Game Away from Cup in Spite of Mystery Goal
Game Four, Stanley Cup Final – Thursday, April 16, 1959
Hockey fans were stunned when they learned that The Rocket would not play in game four. He had been used very sparingly to that point, and seemed to be struggling.

To define how the teams and their coaches' styles differed, the Leafs underwent a tough forty-five-minute practice of skating and shooting on the morning of game four, while Toe Blake called off Montreal's practice after just ten minutes. "I believe you have to do a certain amount of hard work, regardless of how tough your previous game has been," said Imlach. "It's been very successful for me and I'll continue along that line."

It was a curious game, with Montreal on the winning side of a 3–2 score. The first two periods provided thrill after thrill, with the teams going end-to-end, but without scoring. All five goals in the game came during the third period, and the Canadiens scored their three goals in the space of six minutes.

Ab McDonald, sliced on the forehead by Bower's stick during that period, scored the first goal and set up the second. Ralph Backstrom scored what he called "the biggest goal I ever scored." The *Toronto Star* wrote, "Geoffrion stood out like a flaming beacon as he rallied his side on a number of occasions with fierce checking, effective puck-carrying and play-making." Johnny Bower could only shake his head after the game as he commented on the forty-foot bullet fired by Geoffrion that found the net between the Leafs' netminder and the post. "I just got a glimpse of the puck as it rocketed into the net," he said Bower. "They don't call him Boom Boom for nothing!" Toe Blake, the Montreal coach, said, "It was the best game Boomer's played since coming back from his injury." Frank Selke commented, "When we allowed Geoffrion to go to Florida near the end of the season, he promised us a dividend on the trip. I guess this was it!" Geoffrion was still bothered by abdominal pains and took medicine before each game.

Billy Harris scored Toronto's first goal. Frank Mahovlich, one of five forwards on the ice for the Leafs near the end of the game, pushed in a Gerry Ehman rebound at 18:36 of the third for the other Toronto goal.

The Maple Leafs scored a goal in game four that went undetected by game officials. Imlach claimed that a shot by George Armstrong entered the net and then exited through the netting. Game film later confirmed his claim. The Leafs' captain fired the puck, Plante kicked out his right leg and the net clearly bulged, but the puck ended up behind the net, and although the Leaf players stood with their arms raised, the play continued. Maurice Richard, doing colour commentary on French-language radio, said (in French), "The puck seemed to go right through the net!" The goal, which would have given Toronto a tie game, was not counted. "Not since Marilyn Bell beat Lake Ontario has the public become so steamed up about something that happened in sport," claimed the *Toronto Daily Star*. Carl Brewer recalled that one of the newspapers brought a crew in to examine the net and found a hole. "What apparently had happened was some players got pushed in [the crease area] and one of the skates sliced the cord and cut the net."

Choosing the Three Stars once again, Gordie Howe selected Bernie Geoffrion, Ab McDonald and Billy Harris.

In Spite of Valiant Effort by Leafs, Canadiens Capture Cup
Game Five, Stanley Cup Final – Saturday, April 18, 1959
Although the Canadiens were up three games to one, the Maple Leafs were not about to let their Cinderella story evaporate. "My guys win the do-or-die battles," said Imlach. "They did it in the final league game at Detroit

and they'll take the Canadiens in this all-or-nothing game at the Forum."

"My fellows have tremendous respect for those Leafs. They fight until the last second of every game, and are skating fools," said Toe Blake." We want to win this thing at home. We are confident, not cocky."

Sixty sportswriters covered game five in Montreal. What they saw was a dominant Canadiens' squad mount a seemingly insurmountable 5–1 lead in the first fifty minutes of the game. But, in the final ten minutes, Toronto rallied behind goals from Mahovlich and Olmstead. At 17:27, Imlach pulled Johnny Bower from the goal in favour of a sixth attacker. This "created the wildest finish in the history of the league," crowed *The Daily Star*.

Ralph Backstrom opened the scoring in the first period, with Mahovlich sitting out a crosschecking penalty. Before the period ended, Bernie Geoffrion and Tom Johnson had also scored for Montreal. Geoffrion and Bonin added Montreal goals in the second, with Bob Pulford collecting a goal for Toronto.

Then, in the third period, Imlach's team rallied. Mahovlich ripped a wrist shot from between the faceoff circles that eluded Plante at 12:07 to make the score 5–2. Bob Baun took a tripping penalty at 14:12, followed closely by a hooking penalty to Dickie Moore forty-seven seconds later. The Forum crowd called for The Rocket. Coach Blake tapped him on the shoulder, indicating he wanted him out for the next shift, but Richard simply shook his head no. Moments later, Ehman carried the puck into the Canadiens' zone and dropped a pass to Olmstead, who was knocked off balance but managed to spin around and put the puck past Plante at 16:19.

The Leafs never gave up. With Bower out of the net for the added skater, Toronto pressed. "That was one of the toughest few minutes I have ever had in this league," admitted Jacques Plante. But in front of 14,701 fans at the Forum, the Montreal Canadiens earned a 5–3 win and a new NHL record of four consecutive Stanley Cup championships.

Toe Blake said, "The tension this season was terrific. We were out to break the three-straight Cup record that we've shared with the Leafs. To me, this was my club's finest hour."

RK	NUMBER	PLAYER	POS	AGE	GP	G	A	PTS	PIM
1	17	Gerry Ehman	RW	26	12	6	7	13	8
2	27	Frank Mahovlich	LW	21	12	6	5	11	18
3	20	Bob Pulford	LW	22	12	4	4	8	8
4	9	Dick Duff	LW	22	12	4	3	7	8
5	15	Billy Harris	C	23	12	3	4	7	16
6	16	Bert Olmstead	LW	32	12	4	2	6	13
7	12	Ron Stewart	RW	26	12	3	3	6	6
8	18	Carl Brewer	D	20	12	0	6	6	40
9	10	George Armstrong	RW	28	12	0	4	4	10
10	7	Tim Horton	D	29	12	0	3	3	16
11	26	Allan Stanley	D	32	12	0	3	3	2
12	8	Larry Regan	RW	28	8	1	1	2	2
13	14	Brian Cullen	C	25	10	1	0	1	0
14	22	Dave Creighton	C	28	5	0	1	1	0
15	21	Bob Baun	D	22	12	0	0	0	24
16	1	Johnny Bower	G	34	12	0	0	0	0
17	24	Gary Collins	C	23	2	0	0	0	0
18	19	Barry Cullen	RW	23	2	0	0	0	0
19	11	Rudy Migay	C	30	2	0	0	0	0
20	23	Noel Price	D	23	5	0	0	0	2
21	2	Marc Reaume	D	24	10	0	0	0	0
		TEAM TOTALS			12	32	46	78	173

1958–59 Playoff Scoring

Stafford Smythe, noticeably proud of his team, stated, "I've never seen a finish like they staged with their goalie out in that last two minutes and thirty-three seconds. The fans walked out of this rink talking about that instead of Canadiens' fourth straight Stanley Cup." Imlach just shook his head. "If we'd had just a little bit of luck here or there, we might have made it all the way from last place to the Stanley Cup."

"If they'd had more like him, it might have been different," said Tom Johnson of former teammate Bert Olmstead. "It was a good season," Allan Stanley told a writer. "Too bad it couldn't have lasted longer." An exhausted Dick Duff said, "We learned a lot. Now we know what we have to do."

Playoff Netminding											
RK	NUMBER	PLAYER	POS	AGE	GP	MIN	W	L	GA	GAA	SO
1	1	Johnny Bower	G	34	12	746	5	7	38	3.06	0
		TEAM TOTAL			12	746	5	7	38	3.06	0

Gordie Howe, doing work on *Hockey Night in Canada*, dropped by the Montreal dressing room to congratulate the victors, as they slowly dressed and readied themselves for a victory celebration at the Queen Elizabeth Hotel.

Dickie Moore led the playoffs in scoring with seventeen points (five goals and twelve assists). Marcel Bonin scored ten goals to lead all playoff performers. Gerry Ehman, with thirteen points, was the Maple Leafs' leading playoff scorer the regular season.

As Stanley Cup champions, each member of the Montreal Canadiens earned $1,750, another $1,250 for defeating Chicago in the semi-final plus $1,000 for finishing first during the regular season. The Maple Leafs earned $2,150 each. For finishing fourth, they each collected $150, for defeating Boston in the semi-final, they earned $1,250, and each member added $750 as runners-up for the Stanley Cup.

In the dressing room, melancholy at the loss, team captain, George Armstrong, toasted the coach. "Here's to Punch Imlach, the man who got us off the floor and put playoff money in our pockets." Visibly moved, Imlach replied, "To hell with the Canadiens. Here's to MY champions — the gamest that ever strapped on a pair of skates."

Although his first Stanley Cup was still three years away, through his life, Tim Horton identified 1958–59's miracle run to the playoffs as the most fun he ever had playing hockey.

The Maple Leafs, originally intended to take the midnight train back to Toronto, were given a reprieve by Punch Imlach. "Blow off some steam," he told his team. "We'll stay overnight and take the train home tomorrow."

Bob Haggert told a story on Leafs TV. "When the players were leaving the dressing room, Bert Olmstead said to me, 'Be at this nightclub in

Montreal at two o'clock.' I said, 'Sure!' Bert was there with Doug Harvey and Tom Johnson, his two best friends on the Montreal Canadiens. Both Doug Harvey and Tom Johnson said the third period of this hockey game was the toughest period they had played all year. And both said there was no doubt in their minds that it was just a matter of time before we [the Leafs] won the Stanley Cup."

In his book, *Hockey is a Battle,* Imlach reflected back on 1958–59, stating, "That season is still the greatest thrill of my life."

SLAPSHOTS AND SNAPSHOTS

HOCKEY NIGHT IN CANADA — BROADCAST ADVANCES

Innovations on *Hockey Night in Canada* were common throughout the 1950s and 1960s, ranging from new camera angles to replays to colour broadcasts.

George Retzlaff, a thirty-year-old technical director from Winnipeg, was chosen to produce the Toronto broadcasts when they put *Hockey Night in Canada* on the air in 1952. And in Montreal, a former print journalist, twenty-four-year-old Gerald Renaud, was hired to pioneer hockey telecasts in French that first season. Both Retzlaff and Renaud felt it was imperative that the right camera angles be used, giving viewers at home the "best seat in the house." Both dismissed suggestions of extra high-angle cameras, also ignoring proposals to install cameras on both sides of the rink. Considering this was a new technology at the time, the telecasts produced via their television "production trucks" were seamless. Thirty years later, Ralph Mellanby, long-time executive producer of *Hockey Night in Canada*, maintained that many of the procedures pioneered by the two early producers were still in use because they simply could not be improved upon.

By the late 1950s, the show began experimenting with game coverage. After the final whistle of a playoff game in Toronto on April 4, 1959, the CBC network switched live to Chicago Stadium to join the Montreal/Chicago contest in progress. Danny Gallivan, who began calling the Montreal Canadiens' games in English in 1953, welcomed the Toronto audience as the second period was winding down. As it turned out, the third period of that game happened to be one of the most tumultuous in NHL history, with irate Chicago fans attacking referee Red Storey on the ice. It was the final game for the beleaguered referee, as he resigned after the game. This bonus coverage proved to be especially memorable for *Hockey Night in Canada*.

Foster Hewitt, who called the first Maple Leafs' game on television on November 1, 1952, continued television play-by-play until the end of the

1957–58 season. In the opening game of the next season (October 11, 1958), Foster introduced his son to the audience and announced that Bill would be taking over television play-by-play duties. Foster stayed on television for the next three seasons as the first Toronto colour commentator. At the start of the 1961–62 season, Foster switched back to radio-only, and Bill continued on television. By 1963–64, *Hockey Night in Canada* brought back the colour commentator by rotating various newspaper writers in the booth with the younger Hewitt. Then, for the 1965–66 season, Brian McFarlane became the regular colour commentator in the booth. In Montreal during the 1960s, Keith Dancy gave expert analysis in the booth alongside Danny Gallivan.

During the 1960s, there was no equivalent to Don Cherry on a "Coach's Corner"-type of intermission feature, nor was there a "Satellite Hot Stove," although the original "Hot Stove League" was a popular intermission feature on radio, and later television, until the end of the 1956–57 season.

Most viewers remember Ward Cornell as the host of the *Hockey Night in Canada* intermissions, but from 1957 to 1960, there was no regular host. Instead, a number of broadcast personalities took turns hosting programming between periods. Foster Hewitt, Scott Young, Tom Foley, Jack Wells, Wes McKnight, Doug Maxwell, Ted Reynolds and Johnny Esaw were some who filled the prestigious role before Cornell became the regular host.

During the 1958–59 season, intermissions consisted mainly of player interviews, with a few forays into interviewing others in the hockey world. In keeping in step with the times, "The Cisco Kid," complete with his western gear, was interviewed during the 1959 semi-final.

For the 1963–64 season, with the television start of 8:30 p.m, there were two intermissions to fill with content for the first time. Long-time radio personality Jack Dennett joined the broadcast crew with his "Hockey News Roundup." Memorable intermission guests included Prime Minister Lester

Pearson discussing his own hockey career and phenoms Bobby Orr and Wayne Carleton, who were interviewed while still playing junior hockey.

This format of interviews, highlights and features was prominent until the 1970s when "Showdown," a skills competition, was introduced and the early 1980s, when Don Cherry arrived on the scene.

Beginning with the opening match of 1959–60, Ed Fitkin became a regular on the intermissions, bringing viewers videotaped highlights of the first half of the game that had not been televised — an incredible innovation in broadcasting at the time. Another popular feature was the "Hockey Quiz," which featured comedian (and Maple Leafs' fan) Johnny Wayne, of Wayne and Shuster fame, as a participant.

Hockey Night in Canada technicians continued to tweak the broadcast, which led to two technical advances introduced during the 1964–65 playoffs. Although a process called "hot processing" was developed for instant replay in the mid-1950s, it wasn't until 1965 that Ty Lemberg, a Retzlaff staffer from CBC Sports, developed a workable technique that enabled replays to become a regular feature. The replay was not very elaborate, as it would only replay a fixed number of seconds preceding the goal. The other innovation was revealed in an intermission when executive producer George Retzlaff gave viewers a demonstration of the new hand-held camera, referred to as the "creepie peepie."

On March 24, 1965, *Hockey Night in Canada* televised a game between Montreal and Toronto at Maple Leaf Gardens in colour for test purposes. It proved successful even without any enhanced lighting. But it wasn't until the 1966–67 season that televised games in colour became the standard. The first colour telecast was the Leafs' home opener on October 22, 1966, and new, powerful lighting of the ice surface was installed, prompting Toronto defenceman Kent Douglas to rub burnt cork under his eyes to block the glare. Terry Sawchuk, who was backup to Johnny Bower that night, actually watched the game from the end of the bench wearing sunglasses!

That same season, slow-motion replays were tested, but the technology had not been mastered, and the picture quality was very poor. A much-improved "slo-mo" was introduced a few years later.

To watch games from this era is to watch an entirely different game from the one we know today, not just in the action on the ice, but in the way the game is presented. Yet, it's essential that we recall how revolutionary and exciting each of these changes was at the time they were introduced.

4

1959–60: Adding Red to the Blue and White

Viewers of *Hockey Night in Canada* were more than a little familiar with the Imperial Oil commercial used during games:

> *"When the tires are humming and the motor purrs,*
> *And your car is eager and the thought occurs*
> *That it's good to be alive in this land of ours*
> *Good to drive in this land of ours*
> *What a great, great feeling,*
> *What a wonderful sense of sheer enjoyment and of confidence*
> *For there's something you're aware of*
> *Your cars been taken care of*
> *At the Esso sign of confidence*
> *At the 'Happy Motoring' sign!"*

There was a new confidence in more than gasoline brewing in Toronto.

An unknown soothsayer named Punch Imlach arrived on the scene, instilled a new work ethic in the team and, miraculously, came close to delivering the Leafs to the Promised Land; this all in his first season after finishing last the year before. Mahovlich and Brewer blossomed, and Bower emerged as the goalkeeper they had hoped he would be. The future looked very bright indeed.

The Montreal Canadiens kept their squad relatively intact, but having won four successive Stanley Cup championships, why would they alter the lineup? Two notable additions to the roster in 1959–60 were Jean-Claude Tremblay on the blue line and Bill Hicke at forward.

Boston's goaltending tandem of Harry Lumley and Don Simmons had worked well and had contributed to their second-place finish in 1958–59. They drafted Aut Erickson from Chicago and introduced Dallas Smith to the team. At forward, the Bruins added Charlie Burns, the only helmeted player in the NHL.

The Chicago Black Hawks, who had made the playoffs the previous spring after a woeful five-year drought, picked up Murray Balfour and Bill Hay from Montreal. An aggressive rookie from the St. Catharines junior squad, Stan Mikita, made his debut that season.

The New York Rangers made few significant changes, claiming Brian Cullen and Noel Price from the Maple Leafs and Irv Spencer from Montreal.

Detroit, after finishing last the previous season, obtained Gary Aldcorn and Barry Cullen from Toronto. Rookies Val Fonteyne, Gerry Melnyk and Murray Oliver were all promoted and joined the club full time.

The Toronto Maple Leafs again held training camp in Peterborough. Tim Daly, the veteran trainer who had served the team since their days at the Mutual Street Arena, hovered around, entertaining both the players and sportswriters with his sense of humour. Johnny Bower and Bert Olmstead, both tied up with responsibilities back home in western Canada, were permitted to arrive late.

Punch Imlach was very confident in the team he had helped assemble. In particular, he was pleased with his defence corps, especially the development of Carl Brewer, who was runner-up to Montreal's Ralph Backstrom for the NHL's rookie of the year in 1958–59. "I have to rate Brewer as the find of the NHL season," proclaimed the coach. Other defence hopefuls joining Brewer in camp were Bob Baun, Tim Horton, Steve Kraftcheck, Al MacNeil, Marc Reaume, Allan Stanley and Howie Young.

Several new faces arrived at camp that fall, including NHL ironman Johnny Wilson, picked up in a trade with Detroit for Barry Cullen. Garry Edmundson, known to his teammates as "Duke," was traded to Toronto from Springfield of the AHL. Ted Hampson was claimed in the draft from the Rangers, and Hank Ciesla arrived from New York in a trade for defenceman Noel Price.

"By the time 1959–60 showed up, we had a confident team," stated Dick Duff. "We had been guys looking for a little direction, a little confidence. Imlach gave that to us when he first came to Toronto. He might have rubbed the other teams and the other coaches the wrong way, but he made us a confident team. We knew what it meant to wear the Maple Leaf sweater."

Leafs Win Home Opener over Chicago
Saturday, October 10, 1959
The Maple Leafs won their first home opener in four years when they defeated the Chicago Black Hawks 6–3 on October 10, 1959. *Hockey Night in Canada* used videotape for the first time to show viewers the game's opening ceremonies, which included the awarding of the J. P. Bickell Memorial Cup to co-winners George Armstrong and Bob Pulford.

Plante, Wearing New Mask, Shuts Out Leafs
Thursday, November 12, 1959
The Leafs were shut out 3–0 by Jacques Plante and the Montreal Canadiens. Plante was wearing a crude mask after suffering facial injuries incurred while blocking an Andy Bathgate shot against the New York Rangers on November 1. The mask, worn against the recommendations of coach Toe Blake and general manager Frank Selke, hadn't hampered Plante's play, but in fact had frightened some fans. Since his injury in that 3–1 win over New York, Plante had defeated the Rangers again, 8–2, on November 5, and two days later tied

Chicago 2–2. During December, Selke, not convinced that Plante should be wearing a mask, insisted that his goaltender undergo vision tests with and without the mask. Although the results were never announced, Plante only ever played one more game without facial protection. In that contest, he lost to the Red Wings 3-0, and never took the mask off again.

Bench-Clearing Brawl Highlight of Debacle against Canadiens
Thursday, December 17, 1959
During an 8–2 trouncing at the hands of the Canadiens, a brawl broke out during the second period. It began when the Leafs' Billy Harris jostled Plante. Both benches emptied, and everyone except Johnny Bower paired off and exchanged punches. Twenty-four penalties were handed out, including four majors and a misconduct.

Regan Gets Curious Christmas Gift from James
Saturday, December 19, 1959
In the last *Hockey Night in Canada* broadcast before Christmas, Larry Regan suffered a broken nose when he was hit by a shot from teammate Gerry James during a 4–2 win over Detroit.

The rambunctious fourth line that the Maple Leafs employed during the 1959–60 season had various nicknames — the Yannigans, the Clothes Line, the Puke Line and, most often, The Rocks. When Leafs' coach Punch Imlach wanted to stir things up, he'd send centre Duke Edmundson and wingers Johnny Wilson and Gerry James over the boards to use their hard-hitting style to make something happen. Most of the hardest hits were provided by a fearless right winger whose aggressive nature came naturally to him. While playing with the Leafs, Gerry James was also crashing through defensive lines in the Canadian Football League. James was a fullback with the Winnipeg Blue Bombers beginning in 1952, and he helped the Blue Bombers win the Grey Cup in 1958, 1959, 1961 and 1962. James was so accomplished as a football player that he was inducted into the Canadian Football Hall of Fame in 1981.

Gerry James was one of the last professional two-sport athletes. In 1954–55, he not only suited up for his first NHL game but also helped his junior club, the Toronto Marlboros, win the Memorial Cup. He earned a regular spot with the Maple Leafs in 1955–56 and 1956–57, then split 1957–58 between Toronto and the AHL Rochester Americans. After breaking his leg in a football game in 1958, James was placed in a cast for three months, eliminating his ability to play with the Maple Leafs that season, but he returned to the Leafs in 1959–60.

Asked in 1958 whether James was a better hockey player or football player, Conn Smythe hedged, saying, "Oh, I don't know. He's a pretty useful hockey player. He won a Memorial Cup as a hockey player and a Grey Cup as a football player." Bob Nevin, a teammate with James both as a Marlboro and as a Leaf, added, "Gerry James was a hero of mine because of the fact he was such a great football player. His hockey never really blossomed. He was a very tough individual and he played hockey more like football."

His scoring record with the Leafs wasn't nearly as impressive as his CFL stats, having scored a mere fourteen goals in 149 regular season games with the Leafs between 1955 and 1960. Gerry became a fan favourite in Maple Leaf Gardens, wreaking havoc against the opposition, something he did very well using his aggressive football instincts.

King Clancy reflected on James' hockey ability. "He played his heart out for the Toronto Maple Leafs and he was a good, solid hockey player. They don't make them like James any more."

Another Masked Netminder Foils Leafs
Sunday, January 10, 1960
Following the lead of the inimitable Jacques Plante, on this date, Don Simmons of the Boston Bruins wore a mask in a contest for the first time, and promptly shut out Toronto in a 4–0 win.

Leafs See Red
Friday, February 5, 1960
After four Stanley Cup championships, eight All-Star selections, a Norris Trophy (the first ever) as best defenceman, and three Lady Byng awards while playing with the Detroit Red Wings, Red Kelly was devastated to learn he had been traded to the New York Rangers on February 5, 1960.

Billy McNeill was dealt along with Kelly, while Bill Gadsby and Eddie Shack were ticketed for Detroit. But there was a hitch — both Kelly and McNeill refused to report to New York. "Twelve-and-a-half years in Detroit and then they trade you. I thought I was out of hockey. I retired," admitted Kelly. "I thought my hockey days were over. When I started playing in the league, I thought, 'If you have a ten-year career, that's a long career.' I played twelve-and-a-half years, and thought, 'That's it. Now I gotta earn a living.' I started to work the next day with a tool company. But hockey was my whole life. I loved hockey ever since I was knee-high to a grasshopper."

That trade was voided, but Maple Leafs' general manager Punch Imlach asked for permission to talk Kelly into renouncing his retirement. Kelly arrived surreptitiously at Malton Airport at 5:40 that afternoon to discuss his hockey future with the Toronto Maple Leafs. He was met there by King Clancy, who drove him to the Westbury Hotel, located behind Maple Leaf Gardens, and Kelly checked in under the name Fay Bainter (who was, in actuality, an American film actress).

Imlach joined Clancy and Kelly for dinner at the Embers, a nearby restaurant. But when they entered, they were horrified to discover that several members of the Canadiens were there having dinner. Maurice Richard said hello, but made no fuss about seeing the trio. Imlach, Clancy and Kelly later retired to Maple Leaf Gardens where, as the Moscow State Symphony Orchestra performed, Kelly was signed to a contract with the Toronto Maple Leafs.

"When I had the contract talk with Imlach, we talked most of the day and then it went until midnight before we agreed," recalled Kelly. "Nothing was ever said about where I was going to play (position-wise) until after I agreed to come to Toronto."

Punch phoned Jack Adams in Detroit and told him he'd send defence-man Marc Reaume to him in return for Kelly. "Fine," he said. "Send Reaume." He then hung up. "Didn't even speak to Red to wish him luck," remembered Clancy. Reaume, from across the Detroit River in Lasalle, Ontario, had been a regular defenceman for Toronto in 1956–57 and 1957–58, partnering on the blue line with Bobby Baun. It was the recently acquired Johnny Wilson, a former Red Wing, who had alerted the Leafs' brass that Adams liked Reaume as a hockey player.

Kelly was delighted to be going to Toronto. He was joining an organization that dearly wanted him and that had a legitimate shot at the Stanley Cup. But Toronto was also his childhood favourite and was located close to his family in Simcoe. "When I went to Toronto, after I agreed to everything with the contract, I was going out the room and Clancy said, 'Red, how would you like to wear number four?' I said, 'That'd be great!' Well, he had asked my wife — I didn't know this — when Clancy was trying to reach me, he talked to her [Andra] and he asked her if there was anything he could do for her. She said, 'Yes. You could give my husband number four!' I was tickled pink of course. I had the number four for nineteen years." That number hadn't been worn since Steve Kraftcheck wore it for eight games in 1958–59.

"After I signed, I told Punch, 'I've been off skates for ten days or so. I'd hate to make a mistake out there and cause a goal,' and Punch said, 'Red, how would you feel about playing centre?' I said, 'Great! No problem.' I didn't care where I played as long as I was playing hockey. He said, 'If we're going to win the Stanley Cup, we're going to have to go through Montreal. I need somebody to check Beliveau.' He said, 'How would you feel if I started you against Beliveau?' I just said, 'Fine. Great. Love it!'"

Leaf Fans Greet New Acquisition
Wednesday, February 10, 1960
The Leafs were scheduled to play Montreal on February 10, but Red did not have his equipment. Leafs' trainer Bob Haggert contacted Lefty Wilson, the Red Wings' trainer, and arranged for Kelly's skates to be flown to Toronto, where they arrived later that afternoon, just before game time. That evening, Maple Leaf Gardens greeted Red Kelly with a huge ovation. "They really applauded and cheered when I came onto the ice," smiled Red. "It made the hair on the back of my head stand up because it was such a great feeling to think that they really welcomed me in Toronto." Unfortunately, the Leafs were doubled 4–2 by the Canadiens that evening.

Imlach placed Kelly at centre with Gerry Ehman and Frank Mahovlich on the wings. Carl Brewer spoke about the line. "All great players make the players around them better. Red Kelly had that effect," he stated. "Mahovlich matured." The Big M spoke glowingly of the effect Kelly had on his game. "Of all the centremen that I've played with, and I've played with Delvecchio and Beliveau and all kinds, Red Kelly, to me, was the greatest centreman that I ever played with," stated Mahovlich. "He had a knack for studying the opposition and making the right move at the right time with them. Very seldom were there times when I didn't know what Red was going to do."

Shack Takes Out Frustrations on Kelly
Sunday, February 28, 1960
The Leafs met the Rangers, and New York's Eddie Shack ran at Red Kelly all night. When the stillborn trade between Detroit and New York was announced, Shack was vocal about his dislike of the Rangers' management. But when Kelly refused to report to New York, the trade was dissolved and Shack was forced to remain with the Rangers — the team he had badmouthed — and blamed Kelly for his misfortune. Toronto dumped 5–3 that night. Shack and Kelly later became great friends while playing in Toronto, and even today, the friendship is among the strongest of the Maple Leafs' players of that decade.

Toronto Trounced by Montreal
Wednesday, March 9, 1960
During practice on March 9, Johnny Bower stumbled and sprained the thumb on his stick hand. Although he played the game against Montreal that evening, Ed Babiuk, a junior from Melville, Saskatchewan, was summoned to stand by for the game. The Canadiens walloped the Leafs 9–4, but Bower didn't blame the score on his injury. "I just had a bad night," he said, shrugging.

Toronto Earns Second-Place Finish

Sunday, March 20, 1960

The seventy-game campaign concluded with, to no one's surprise, Montreal finishing in first place with a dominant ninety-two-point total. In spite of regular derision over sporting a mask, Jacques Plante won the Vezina Trophy for having the best goals-against average. It was the fifth straight year Plante had collected the award.

Following a 3–2 win over Detroit in the final regular season game, Toronto earned a strong second-place finish. Chicago completed the season in third while Detroit was the fourth and final playoff contender. Boston and New York were relegated to observer status.

Bobby Hull of the Black Hawks was the NHL's scoring champion, picking up eighty-one points — one more than Bronco Horvath of Boston. Bob Pulford was Toronto's top scorer, with fifty-two points. Carl Brewer led the NHL in penalty minutes with 150. "Sure, the kid gets penalties," explained King Clancy. "He's bound to. He plays all out."

Gordie Howe was recipient of the Hart Trophy and Doug Harvey of the Canadiens was named winner of the Norris Trophy, his fifth in six seasons. Chicago's Bill Hay was the winner of the Calder Trophy as NHL rookie of the year and Don McKenney of Boston earned the Lady Byng for his gentlemanly play. Allan Stanley of the Leafs was named to the Second All-Star Team.

1959–60 Regular Season Standings						
FINISH	TEAM	GAMES	WINS	LOSSES	TIES	POINTS
1	Montreal Canadiens	70	40	18	12	92
2	Toronto Maple Leafs	70	35	26	9	79
3	Chicago Black Hawks	70	28	29	13	69
4	Detroit Red Wings	70	26	29	15	67
5	Boston Bruins	70	28	34	8	64
6	New York Rangers	70	17	38	15	49

1959–60 Regular Season Scoring

RK	NUMBER	PLAYER	POS	AGE	GP	G	A	PTS	PIM
1	20	Bob Pulford	LW	23	70	24	28	52	81
2	10	George Armstrong	RW	29	70	23	28	51	60
3	9	Dick Duff	LW	23	67	19	22	41	51
4	27	Frank Mahovlich	LW	22	70	18	21	39	61
5	15	Billy Harris	C	24	70	13	25	38	29
6	16	Bert Olmstead	LW	33	53	15	21	36	63
7	12	Ron Stewart	RW	27	67	14	20	34	28
8	26	Allan Stanley	D	33	64	10	23	33	22
9	7	Tim Horton	D	30	70	3	29	32	69
10	19	Johnny Wilson	LW	30	70	15	16	31	8
11	17	Gerry Ehman	RW	27	69	12	16	28	26
12	18	Carl Brewer	D	21	67	4	19	23	150
13	8	Larry Regan	RW	29	47	4	16	20	6
14	21	Bob Baun	D	23	61	8	9	17	59
15	11	Gerry James	RW	25	34	4	9	13	56
16	4	Red Kelly	D/C	32	18	6	5	11	8
17	25	Garry Edmundson	LW	27	39	4	6	10	47
18	14	Ted Hampson	C	23	41	2	8	10	17
19	22	Dave Creighton	C	29	14	1	5	6	4
20	23	Joe Crozier	D	30	5	0	3	3	2
21	4	Marc Reaume	D	25	36	0	1	1	6
22	1	Johnny Bower	G	35	66	0	0	0	4
23	1	Ed Chadwick	G	26	4	0	0	0	0
24	27	Ken Girard	RW	23	1	0	0	0	0
25	23	Pat Hannigan	LW	23	1	0	0	0	0
26	24	Al MacNeil	D	24	4	0	0	0	2
27	14	Rudy Migay	C	31	1	0	0	0	0
		TEAM TOTALS			70	199	330	529	859

RK		PLAYER	POS	AGE	GP	MIN	W	L	T	GA	GAA	SO
1	1	Johnny Bower	G	35	66	3960	34	24	8	177	2.68	5
2	1	Ed Chadwick	G	26	4	240	1	2	1	15	3.75	0
		TEAM TOTALS			70	4200	35	26	9	192	2.74	5

The semi-finals pitted Toronto against the Detroit Red Wings, while Montreal faced Chicago. CBC Television planned to air all of the Leafs' upcoming playoff games, although some would be broadcast on the full network and others on the "minor network" — Toronto and Southern Ontario.

"We're thankful to be in the playoffs," offered Jack Adams, Detroit's GM. "We dumbfounded the experts by getting this far. Most of them picked us to finish a poor last. Now they're picking the Leafs [to win the series]. They could be wrong again!" The Wings featured four players from Detroit's last Stanley Cup win. Alex Delvecchio, Gordie Howe, Marcel Pronovost and Terry Sawchuk were all integral parts of that 1955 championship.

Punch Imlach felt that stifling Gordie Howe's production was key to winning the series, and he planned to have Bert Olmstead shadow the Red Wings' star. Sid Abel simply laughed. "If Olmstead is going to keep track of Howe, he'll have to play an awful lot of positions. I'll use Gordie at both wings, centre and both defence posts to shake him loose."

To avoid distractions, Imlach had his team staying in Peterborough and bussing into Toronto for home games. When not on the ice, the coach had a full complement of motivational films and records he played for his team.

Wings Surprise Leafs with Opening Victory
Game One, Semi-Final – Wednesday, March 23, 1960
The smallest Maple Leaf Gardens' crowd of the season was in attendance for the opening game of the series on March 23. The Red Wings shocked the Leafs with a 2–1 win in game one. The first goal of the game came at 2:38 of the first period, scored by Gordie Howe. Nursing a cold, Bert Olmstead simply shook his head at his assignment of shadowing Howe. "That guy never gets tired. He's stronger when he should be weary than I am when I'm fresh!"

Little-used Len Haley, a twenty-nine-year-old rookie who had scored but once during the regular season, scored Detroit's winning goal at 14:24 of the first.

Carl Brewer scored a sensational goal on a solo effort at 16:04 of the third, but it was too little, too late. The *Toronto Star* wrote, "The Leafs started out as if they were all equipped with two left feet, and before they got straightened away in the second period, it was too late." Cheekily, the paper added, "The Leaf line of Duke Edmundson, Johnny Wilson and Gerry James was the only one that would have beaten a fat man over a knoll." *The Globe and Mail* reported that during the regular season, Edmundson and James were offered an incentive of $25 each if they scored five goals. Both finished the season with four, but King Clancy paid them the bonus money anyway.

Frustrated, Billy Harris said, "It's about time we quit thinking about the Canadiens and concentrated on beating *this* team."

Imlach now believed he could neutralize Howe by utilizing both Olmstead and Mahovlich against the Wings' star. "They are the only two big left wingers I have, and you have to be strong to handle Howe. I tried both Johnny Wilson and Dick Duff against him, but they lack the size to keep up with the big fellow."

The Three Stars of the evening's match were Gordie Howe, Norm Ullman and Carl Brewer.

Leafs Double Detroit for a Tie in Semi-Final Series
Game Two, Semi-Final – Friday, March 25, 1960
Toronto rebounded with a 4–2 win at home. In the last minute of the game, with Toronto up 3–2 and the Wings playing with an empty net so they could skate with an extra attacker, Bob Pulford took a calculated risk and fired the puck from his side of the red line, depositing the puck in the empty cage.

Curiously, after his energy line of Wilson, James and Edmundson had played so well in the opening contest, Imlach relegated them to the bench in game two, with James and Edmundson getting but two short shifts and Wilson just one. "This is no time to gamble," Imlach explained. "I'm going with the guys who put me into the Stanley Cup."

Frank Mahovlich, Johnny Bower and Warren Godfrey were selected as the game's first, second and third stars.

Dressing Room Incentive Pushes Leafs to OT Win

Game Three, Semi-Final – Sunday, March 27, 1960

The teams travelled to the Detroit Olympia for game three. At the conclusion of the first period, Maple Leaf warriors marched into their dressing room, only to discover a huge mound of money. The message on the bulletin board read: "Take a good look at the centre of the floor. This is the difference between losing and winning — $1,250." Imlach did not even make an appearance in the room — his message said all he needed to say.

With Red Kelly leading the Leafs' charge with two goals, playing as though he wanted to prove that the Wings had erred in thinking he was finished just a few months earlier, the teams were tied 4–4 at the end of regulation time. The Red Wings employed oxygen tanks on their bench to keep their players energized. In overtime, Bower was sensational, but neither team was able to score the winner. George Armstrong, speaking to no one in particular, said, "The reason Detroit made the playoffs is that nobody could make them quit. They haven't changed."

Going into a third overtime, Frank Mahovlich declared to his teammates, "We're going to get it. We're going to win." At 3:00 of that period, The Big M did just that, redirecting a shot from Kelly to give Toronto a hard-earned 5–4 victory. "When the light went on, the Leafs on the bench went over the boards as if their pants caught fire," reported *The Globe and Mail*.

"Howe, who was so exhausted he could barely skate to the bench at times, didn't figure in the scoring but only because Bower behaved like a magician," stated *The Globe*. "Kelly played a big game for them but that Bower was a wizard," acknowledged Jack Adams. The Leafs' captain agreed, stating, "There were a lot of good men out there, but the best by a country mile was Bower!"

CBC Television received complaints from 950 viewers about carrying the broadcast to its conclusion, necessitating the cancellation of several programs. A CBC spokesperson replied, "We'd get twice as many complaints if we didn't televise the game, or if we cut it before the final score."

Johnny Bower was chosen as the first star, Red Kelly the second and The Big M, the game-winning goal scorer, was named third star.

Extra Time Provides Wings with Game Four Win

Game Four, Semi-Final – Tuesday, March 29, 1960

Neither team practised the previous day, as players were exhausted and needed a break. Two nights later, still in Detroit, the teams again needed overtime to decide the winner. Gary Aldcorn opened the scoring in the first period with a goal for Detroit, to which Carl Brewer responded with a matching marker in the second. Red Wing rookie Gerry Melnyk scored the game-winning goal on a power play at 1:54 into overtime to tie the semi-final at two wins apiece. "I saw the save and saw Bower go down and the rebound came out," the rookie explained. "There it was! I moved in and threw it up. I knew I had to get it high, and that was it."

Carl Brewer was booed every time he touched the puck. He had had a terrific series, but his petulance had angered the Detroit faithful. In game one, he had elbowed netminder Sawchuk, drawing the ire of opponents and their fans alike. At one point, Warren Godfrey lost his helmet but continued play without it. Brewer flipped the protective gear into the crowd. "I wasn't trying to be a smart guy," he confessed, tongue seemingly planted firmly in cheek. "The thing was lying in our zone. Suppose our fellows trip over it. I just didn't want anybody to trip over it." Later on, Brewer got into a tussle with the penalty-box attendant. "Frank Mahovlich was in there already, serving a misconduct. I got a minor and the first thing I see is Frank throwing a towel on the ice. That's just asking for another ten minutes, so I tossed it right back, hoping the referee wouldn't notice. Then this old gentleman starts to lecture me, shaking his finger under my nose. I argued a bit. He pushed me. Then the referee arrived and he gave me a talking-to. I noticed he later gave the usher a dressing-down, too." In fact, referee Vern Buffey explained to the penalty-box attendant that his duties did not include disciplining players.

The *Toronto Star* indicated that Brewer just might have a dual personality. "He plays hockey in a kind of frenzy, which is completely opposite to his polite, solicitous, civilian conduct. At leisure, he's well-behaved and charming. On the job, he's nasty, irritable but oh so valuable." *The Globe* agreed, and wrote, "Brewer is almost as talented at disturbing the peace as he is at playing hockey, and that is plenty."

Detroit netminder Terry Sawchuk was the game's first star, with Johnny Bower and Gerry Melnyk selected second and third stars respectively.

Stanley Unlikely Hero in 5–4 Toronto Win
Game Five, Semi-Final – Saturday, April 2, 1960
Maple Leaf Gardens hosted the rivals again on April 2. Allan Stanley starred, scoring twice for Toronto in a 5–4 win. Gerry Melnyk shone for Detroit, posting his third goal of the series. Melnyk was chosen as the third star of the game. First star was Red Kelly and Frank Mahovlich was the second star.

Leafs Push Past Detroit; Set Sights on Montreal
Game Six, Semi-Final – Sunday, April 3, 1960
With Toronto leading the series three games to two, the Leafs and Wings played game six back in Detroit on April 3. Murray Oliver and Bob Pulford traded goals in the first period, but Norm Ullman helped Detroit pull away with a 2–1 lead in the second. Toronto responded in kind, adding goals by Pulford, Duff and Mahovlich to collect a 4–2 victory and a berth in the Stanley Cup final against the Montreal Canadiens, who had swept Chicago in four straight games.

Bob Pulford was the first star of the game, Johnny Bower was the second star and Gordie Howe was selected as the third star.

When a tough series ends, suddenly the fierce animosity between the warriors is gone. Immediately after the final buzzer, Terry Sawchuk made his way through the crowd into the Leafs' dressing room to congratulate his opponents, spending a great deal of time chatting first with Johnny Bower and then with former teammate Red Kelly.

Kelly led the series in scoring with nine points on three goals and six assists and, although too gentlemanly to ever admit it, had to have felt some satisfaction in beating his old club. Detroit general manager Jack

Adams went on record as stating, "Kelly wasn't going full for us and we're not sorry we traded him. [Marc] Reaume [who sat out with an injury during the series] will be around for a long time after Kelly is through."

The Stanley Cup final pitted the NHL's two Canadian squads against one another for the second straight spring. The Canadiens had easily dismissed Chicago, winning the series in four games. Jacques Plante had been superb, shutting out the Hawks in two of the four contests, the last two on Chicago ice.

Canadiens Double Leafs to Take First Game of Final
Game One, Stanley Cup Final – Thursday, April 7, 1960
The Stanley Cup final opened in Montreal on April 7 with Danny Gallivan handling play-by-play duties for the national *Hockey Night in Canada* broadcast. Al Cauley, unmistakable with his eye patch, took care of intermission interviews.

As the lineups were scrolled on *Hockey Night in Canada*, fans scratched their heads that two number 1s were listed for the Maple Leafs. Johnny Bower was the recognizable name, and starting goaltender, but the second number 1 was listed as Ed Babiuk. The youngster was a Second All-Star for the junior Melville Millionaires and had played one game, a win, for the AHL Rochester Americans. Babiuk would remain a career minor-league netminder, never playing with Toronto or any other NHL team.

The Canadiens took game one by a 4–2 count. "The defence handled the puck indecisively," wrote *The Globe.* "Playing that way against Montreal is like putting out fire with gasoline." Dickie Moore, Doug Harvey and Jean Beliveau tallied for the Canadiens in the first period, but Bobby Baun and Bert Olmstead closed the gap in the second for Toronto. Henri Richard, later named the game's first star, potted an insurance marker for Montreal. Bernard Geoffrion was the second star of the game while Johnny Bower was named the third star.

Montreal Mounts Lead against Leafs with 2–1 Win

Game Two, Stanley Cup Final – Saturday, April 9, 1960

Game two, played at the Forum two nights later, saw the Canadiens leap to a 2–0 lead within the first five minutes on goals by Moore and Beliveau. Larry Regan beat Plante later in the period, but that was it for scoring.

In spite of the 2–1 win, Toe Blake was incensed at the Leafs' clutch-and-grab tactics, isolating Carl Brewer as a principal culprit. Punch Imlach was pleased with the effort of his team. "If we play that well in Toronto, we'll win," he stated. On the television broadcast, Frank Selke Jr. mentioned, "The Leafs must be wondering just how well you have to play in order to win a hockey game. They certainly played an extremely fine hockey game here tonight." The Three Stars, chosen by Terry Sawchuk, were Jacques Plante, Johnny Bower and Bert Olmstead.

Rocket Collects Final NHL Goal as Habs Take Insurmountable Lead

Game Three, Stanley Cup Final – Tuesday, April 12, 1960

The opponents travelled to Toronto for game three on April 12. Donny Marshall of the Canadiens opened the scoring at 13:54 of the first period.

Conn Smythe announced the death of *Hockey Night in Canada* interviewer Tom Foley during an awkward intermission segment. Foley had provided frequent intermission interviews for the show, mostly from the Montreal Forum, and was auditioning for the job as permanent intermission host. He died when the taxi he was in was involved in a traffic accident shortly after arriving in Toronto on March 17, 1960. Scott Young wrote in *The Globe and Mail*, "Tom Foley was a very good and accurate sports play-by-play announcer and a good-natured and pleasant interviewer."

With a ferocious travel schedule, Foley was the manager of CFRA radio in Ottawa and worked in television, mostly out of Montreal. When the sporting seasons overlapped, he might call a football game in Hamilton on a Saturday afternoon and then conduct intermission interviews at a hockey game that night. A widower, the thirty-eight-year-old Foley left behind four daughters, the oldest being thirteen. "I'm doing too much right now, I know," he had said while covering the Olympic hockey tournament in Squaw Valley. "It's the kind of stuff you have to take while the taking is good, because you never know how long it's going to last." Which, in this case, was tragically true.

Conn Smythe followed up that sad announcement by giving his coach a resounding endorsement. "Punch is a positive thinker and he's brought us, in fourteen months, from last place to twice in the Stanley Cup [final]." The endorsement was moot that evening, as Montreal could do no wrong. Phil Goyette scored twice and the Richard brothers each added a goal for the Canadiens while Johnny Wilson and Bert Olmstead scored for the Leafs in a 5–2 Montreal victory.

Playing with an injured foot and far from his usual form, The Rocket scored his first goal in six games, which turned out to be the final goal of his extraordinary NHL career. Richard was observed picking up the puck after scoring the goal, giving an indication that he was considering retirement.

The first star of the game was Don Marshall, the second was Phil Goyette and Larry Regan was the game's third star.

Despite Valiant Effort by Leafs, Montreal Wins Fifth Consecutive Cup
Game Four, Stanley Cup Final – Thursday, April 14, 1960
Up three games to none, the Montreal Canadiens were hoping to end the season with a victory on April 14 in Toronto and, in doing so, collecting their unprecedented fifth Stanley Cup championship. Jean Beliveau scored at 8:16 with Doug Harvey adding the Habs' second goal of the period just twenty-nine seconds later.

Montreal was leading 3–0 after the second period, with Henri Richard's goal in that period coming on a deflection of his brother's shot at 16:40. Cornell took viewers on a tour of the area from where *Hockey Night in Canada* broadcast at Maple Leaf Gardens. Starting with the actual inter-view studio, the intermission host then showed an area where quiz games were played. Passing the Stanley Cup, which was placed on a nearby table, he then introduced the Imperial Oil set from where Murray Westgate did his live commercials, and then the Leafs' dressing room, where Punch

Imlach's wife and children were introduced. Dodo Imlach, Punch's wife, stated that she was even more anxious than her husband after a game. Son Brent announced that his favourite player was Jean Beliveau, while daughter Marlene, clutching a stuffed animal named Clancy, told Cornell that she liked Gordie Howe.

In the third period, Jean Beliveau scored Montreal's fourth goal, giving the Canadiens' the 4–0 count that would go into the record books as the final score. At the siren ending the game, the Canadiens mobbed goalie Jacques Plante. "Plante played a sensational game, but every one of his teammates was a star," said Foster Hewitt, working the game as the colour analyst on the television/radio simulcast. "The Leafs fought it out right to the end but they were overmatched in this game and in this series. They gave it their best shot, but it wasn't good enough."

Johnny Bower and Red Kelly were the first of the Maple Leafs to venture over to congratulate the victors, shaking hands with their opponents near Plante's crease.

First through the doors of the losing dressing room was Bert Olmstead. He tossed his stick at the rack near the door, went to his place on the bench and fumed, saying nothing. Others followed shortly afterwards — Stewart, Regan and Pulford. No one said a word. Former Leafs' captain Ted Kennedy stopped into the room and stated, "It's no disgrace, boys," but he was virtually ignored. Conn Smythe came in and shook each player's hand and exchanged a few words with every one of them.

"Only a game, but they lost it," wrote Scott Young in *The Globe and Mail.* "And they took it as if it was their lives, instead of their living."

The Canadiens had won eight straight games through the postseason, the only team besides the 1952 Detroit Red Wings, up until that time, to have accomplished the feat of winning the Stanley Cup in the fewest number of games possible.

As the players mingled, congratulating each other, the Stanley Cup was brought out to centre ice and placed on a table. National Hockey League president Clarence Campbell held the microphone and, amidst the booing of the crowd, announced, "Ladies and gentlemen, it is now my privilege and responsibility to present to the winning team, the Montreal Canadiens, the Stanley Cup, emblematic of the world championship. This is the twelfth time in which the Canadiens have won this trophy, the fifth time in succession, and I call upon their captain, Maurice Richard, to accept the trophy."

1958–59 Playoff Scoring

RK	NUMBER	PLAYER	POS	AGE	GP	G	A	PTS	PIM
1	4	Red Kelly	D/C	32	10	3	8	11	2
2	16	Bert Olmstead	LW	33	10	3	4	7	0
3	8	Larry Regan	RW	29	10	3	3	6	0
4	9	Dick Duff	LW	23	10	2	4	6	6
5	20	Bob Pulford	LW	23	10	4	1	5	10
6	18	Carl Brewer	D	21	10	2	3	5	16
7	26	Allan Stanley	D	33	10	2	3	5	2
8	10	George Armstrong	RW	29	10	1	4	5	4
9	27	Frank Mahovlich	LW	22	10	3	1	4	27
10	19	Johnny Wilson	LW	30	10	1	2	3	2
11	15	Billy Harris	C	24	9	0	3	3	4
12	12	Ron Stewart	RW	27	10	0	2	2	2
13	21	Bob Baun	D	23	10	1	0	1	17
14	25	Garry Edmundson	LW	27	9	0	1	1	4
15	7	Tim Horton	D	30	10	0	1	1	6
16	1	Johnny Bower	G	35	10	0	0	0	0
17	17	Gerry Ehman	RW	27	9	0	0	0	0
18	11	Gerry James	RW	25	10	0	0	0	0
				TEAM TOTALS	10	25	40	65	102

Playoff Netminding

RK	NUMBER	PLAYER	POS	AGE	GP	MIN	W	L	GA	GAA	SO
1	1	Johnny Bower	G	35	10	645	4	6	31	2.88	0
				TEAM TOTAL	10	645	4	6	31	2.88	0

Richard grasped the microphone and, with Plante to his left, and, hovering nearby, a man dressed in a clown costume mugging for the TV cameras while holding a sign that read: "Compliments of Tom St. Jean, Sudbury, Ontario," accepted the Stanley Cup from the NHL president for what would be his final time. The Rocket addressed the crowd, saying, "Thank you very much, Mr. Campbell. Ladies and gentlemen, it is always nice to win the Stanley Cup outside of Montreal. The best place to win it is right here in Toronto because the people are really nice and they give us a nice hand any time we score, and they really gave us a nice hand through the series. Thank you very much."

Richard never raised the Cup, but he and Plante leaned down beside it for photographs. When they left, a member of the Gardens' ice crew pushed the table off the ice.

In the *Hockey Night in Canada* studio, Ward Cornell and Rene Lecavalier, from the French-language broadcast, ping-ponged back and forth with interviews, Cornell conducting his in English and Lecavalier in French.

Punch Imlach expressed his disappointment. "I have to give a lot of praise to the Canadiens. I thought they played remarkably well in this series and they certainly proved to be one of the great teams in hockey." Stafford Smythe, introduced mistakenly as Frank Selke Jr. by Cornell, added, "The team probably did better than any of us had hoped for. We'll be back, trying harder than ever next year."

King Clancy summed up the series by stating, "We were beaten by a great hockey team. We have no regrets."

The Toronto Maple Leafs had made substantial progress, reaching the finals for a second straight spring, but still were no match for the powerful Canadiens. Imlach knew he had to beat Montreal to capture the Stanley Cup. Johnny Bower was at the zenith of his career, Frank Mahovlich had the potential to be a superstar and Imlach now had Red Kelly's experience and talent. Their defence was as solid as any in the league. The final piece of this puzzle — Dave Keon — was about to arrive. So were the glory years!

SLAPSHOTS AND SNAPSHOTS
FEELING A DRAFT

During the 1950s, it was apparent that the Chicago Black Hawks were in need of some assistance from the rest of the league. From 1946–47 until 1958–59, the Hawks had missed the playoffs in all but one season (a fourth place finish in 1952–53). A "Help the Hawks" campaign sent Chicago an influx of players, including future thirty-goal scorer Ed Litzenberger from Montreal and veteran Harry Watson from Toronto.

Another method to help distribute talent was an Intra-League Draft. All six NHL teams were allowed to protect a certain number of players, making others available to companion teams for a fee. The Toronto Maple Leafs, bottom feeders in the 1957–58 season, were eager to acquire veteran players to work with the young talent they had coming from their junior teams, the St. Michael's Majors and the Toronto Marlboros.

The Leafs were on the lookout for a rugged veteran who could inspire teammates and find a role as a team leader. Fortunately for Toronto, Bert Olmstead was deemed expendable by the Montreal Canadiens and was not protected. Billy Reay and Stafford Smythe, who were running the draft for the Leafs, happily selected him with their pick. Olmstead proved to be exactly what was needed by the Maple Leafs — a veteran presence who had tasted hockey victory and wasn't afraid of the rough going — and proved invaluable to the Leafs, who made the playoffs that season, and within four years would win the first of four Stanley Cup championships of the decade.

General manager Punch Imlach gambled in 1959, and astonishing to most, did not protect veterans Johnny Bower and Allan Stanley, firmly believing that they would not be claimed due to their age. It was a risk, because had it backfired, it would have been disastrous to the Leafs' visions of a Stanley Cup. As predicted, neither Bower nor Stanley was drafted. Toronto did lose once-promising centre Brian Cullen to the Rangers and winger Gary Aldcorn to Detroit, but neither fit into the Leafs' plans by that point.

During the 1959–60 season, the Leafs traded Marc Reaume, their fifth defenceman, to Detroit for Red Kelly, who was promptly converted to centre. As a result, Toronto was in need of a spare defenceman, and they were fortunate to be able to pluck Larry Hillman from the Boston Bruins in the 1960 draft. Hillman, who was to become a good team man who fought many battles for the Leafs, had just won the Eddie Shore Award as the outstanding defenceman in the American Hockey League. By this time, the Maple Leafs were certainly not a "have-not" team, but were still able to use the draft to fill in holes.

In the Intra-League Draft of 1961, Imlach, seeking depth on defence, claimed bespectacled defenceman Al Arbour, who filled in as a spare defenceman and gave the Leafs' farm team in Rochester a steady, veteran presence.

In that same draft, Johnny Bower was protected, but Toronto lost netminder Cesare Maniago to Montreal. When Bower was injured late in the 1960–61 season, Maniago and Gerry McNamara had both more than capably filled the goaltending role. Imlach and assistant general manager King Clancy should have heeded the advice of Leafs' president Stafford Smythe in protecting Maniago, who went on to have a successful NHL career.

The Maple Leafs, having won the Stanley Cup in 1962, did not pick up any players in the Intra-League Draft of 1962. They did, however, lose young Alex Faulkner to the Red Wings, and more importantly, Bert Olmstead to the Rangers. Olmstead was angry and devastated at not being protected after the sizable role he had played in the creation of the Leafs' dynasty. But the still-competitive Olmstead would be thirty-six years old when the next season started and instead, the Leafs protected former junior star Larry Keenan, who Imlach proclaimed was "the best young player around." Olmstead never did report to the lowly Rangers and bitterly retired.

Again in 1963, the Leafs, having repeated as Stanley Cup champions, made no moves at the draft that June, and with their existing roster, repeated as Stanley Cup champions.

In 1964, the Detroit Red Wings protected young goaltenders Roger Crozier and George Gardner, leaving legendary Terry Sawchuk exposed in the draft. Salivating like Pavlov's dog, the Maple Leafs snapped up Sawchuk, giving them a dynamic one-two punch in goal. Both were nearing the ends of their careers, and Imlach believed that should either falter, he had a top goaltending prospect in Rochester by the name of Gerry Cheevers. In yet another surprising move at the draft, Imlach took a chance and selected former two-time scoring champion Dickie Moore off Montreal's unprotected list. Moore had retired with bad knees after the 1962–63 season and was shocked to be picked up after a year out of hockey. He did report but was largely ineffective for the Leafs. In another comeback attempt three years later, Moore was much more effective with the expansion St. Louis Blues.

Although the Leafs failed to repeat as Stanley Cup winners in 1964–65, the tandem of Bower and Sawchuk did win the Vezina Trophy for having allowed the fewest goals during the regular season. Now, Imlach had a dilemma on his hands. Wanting to retain both, it was certain that Cheevers, an AHL All-Star that year, would be claimed if unprotected. In a desperate move, the Leafs tried to protect Cheevers as a forward. Although Cheevers had played a handful of games at forward in junior, NHL president Clarence Campbell refused to allow the ploy. As a result, forty-year-old Bower and thirty-five-year-old Sawchuk were kept, and would go on to play a vital role in the 1967 Stanley Cup championship, while Cheevers was selected by the last-place Boston Bruins and became a Hall of Fame goaltender.

That same year, Chicago drafted newly acquired defenceman Pat Stapleton from the Leafs. With a firmly entrenched blue-line quartet of Bob Baun, Carl Brewer, Tim Horton and Allan Stanley, little thought was given to losing Stapleton. That is until Brewer unexpectedly quit at that fall's training camp, leaving the Leafs without a defenceman who could consistently move the puck up the ice. The fact that Stapleton became a star player for many years also left Leaf fans wondering "What if?"

In the final Intra-League Draft before the NHL Expansion Draft of 1967, the Leafs had a decision to make: either protect aggressive, young centre Pete Stemkowski or fan favourite Orland Kurtenbach. Imlach reluctantly went with youth this time, protecting Stemkowski. The Rangers immediately drafted Kurtenbach, in turn, dropping speedy John Brenneman from their protected list. The Leafs then took Brenneman for the draft cost of $30,000. Toronto also lost spare centre Wally Boyer to Montreal, who in turn, lost him to Chicago. But the Leafs were pleased to pick up Don Blackburn from the Montreal organization, and were intrigued by his toughness. After Blackburn was compared to Montreal enforcer John Ferguson, Toronto fans were excited to learn of this acquisition. However, Blackburn was not quite the feared player that Ferguson was. In fact, he never suited up for the Leafs and was taken by the Philadelphia Flyers in the 1967 Expansion Draft.

You win some, you lose some.

The Leafs' record in the Intra-League Drafts from 1959 to 1966 was successful in bringing in key elements for the great teams of the 1960s. They did, however, lose a few promising players, but the Leafs in the 1960s were all about winning at that moment, which of course they did.

5

1960–61: VEXED AND PERPLEXED

Having astonished the hockey world by rebounding from a last-place finish in 1957–58 to two consecutive appearances in the Stanley Cup final, the Toronto Maple Leafs appeared poised to regain glories not enjoyed in ten years. But the Montreal Canadiens were not about to relinquish the Stanley Cup, having owned it for five straight years without a battle. And the Chicago Black Hawks, who had also endured a horrific decade, now boasted some of the finest young talent in the game. It would prove to be a very interesting season.

The Stanley Cup champion Montreal Canadiens went into the 1960–61 season without Maurice Richard for the first time since the 1942–43 season. On September 15, 1960, during training camp, The Rocket decided he was no longer capable of playing at the level that had seen him set numerous records — most career goals (544), most goals in a season (50) and most career hat tricks (26) among them — and in an emotional announcement made live via radio, he ended his NHL playing career. Doug Harvey assumed the captaincy from the eight-time Stanley Cup champion. Reg Fleming and Ab McDonald were traded from the

Stanley Cup champs to the Chicago Black Hawks, but youngsters Bobby Rousseau and Gilles Tremblay made their NHL debuts. As more teams added backup goaltenders, the Canadiens followed suit, making Charlie Hodge a full-time understudy to Jacques Plante in the Montreal goal. "Judging by their skill, poise and all-around ice deportment, the Canadiens should maintain their National Hockey League championship monopoly," predicted *The Globe and Mail.*

The Chicago Black Hawks made a relatively large deal with Montreal, receiving Bob Courcy, Reggie Fleming, Cec Hoekstra and Ab McDonald in exchange for Bob Bailey, Lorne Ferguson, Terry Gray, Danny Lewicki and Glen Skov. McDonald was inserted onto a line with Stan Mikita and Kenny Wharram that would be dubbed the "Scooter Line" and would cause opponents no end of headaches. After sixteen seasons, Ted Lindsay retired, although he would return four seasons later playing with the Red Wings.

Detroit made wholesale changes to their lineup for 1960–61. Hank Bassen was added from Vancouver of the WHL to back netminder Terry Sawchuk. Howie Glover was obtained in a trade with Chicago for Jim Morrison, and Pete Conacher arrived in a trade with New York for Barry Cullen. Parker MacDonald came from the Rangers in the Intra-League Draft. Bruce MacGregor was promoted from Edmonton, of the WHL, to shore up the Wings at forward, and Gerry Odrowski made his debut on defence.

After finishing last the season prior, the New York Rangers stockpiled as much potential as they could, adding Ted Hampson from Toronto; Don Johns from Winnipeg, of the WHL; and Jim Morrison from Chicago. Dave Balon and Orland Kurtenbach also made an impact during the season.

Boston's Bruins received Ted Green from the Canadiens and Jim Bartlett from New York. Harry Lumley was replaced in goal by Bruce Gamble.

Toronto was poised for another strong year. Although Gerry James was released and Dave Creighton sent to the minors, neither had made a huge impact on the team. The Leafs claimed Larry Hillman from the Bruins as a fifth defenceman while Bob Nevin was promoted from the

Rochester Americans and David Keon from the St. Michael's Majors.

Johnny Wilson was demoted, destined for Rochester, but refused to report to the Americans because he had had an ongoing disagreement with Steve Kraftcheck, who had started the 1958–59 season with the Leafs but was the playing coach with Toronto's AHL team in Rochester. "Wilson always played well for me," said Imlach. "That's why I'd like to see him go to Rochester because I might want to recall him. This business is getting pretty ridiculous when a player doesn't want to report to a team just because he doesn't like the coach." In retrospect, this was quite an ironic statement coming from Punch Imlach.

The Toronto Maple Leafs' training camp opened in Peterborough once again, and while there were several players holding out with salary disputes, there was one person conspicuous by his absence. Trainer Tim Daly, after more than three decades working with Toronto, retired and was replaced by Bob Haggert, who had earlier served as trainer of the junior Toronto Marlboros. *The Globe's* Scott Young, who, like most journalists, loved to banter with Daly, wrote, "Everybody within earshot roared that he might try continuing to do what he had been doing before he retired: nothing!"

As was tradition, Johnny Bower and Bert Olmstead were excused and allowed to report late to training camp. Joining them in reporting late that fall was Larry Regan, who surprised the Leafs' brass by failing to show up to the season opener.

Dick Duff refused to report to the team over a salary cut. After three seasons with better than a twenty-goal output, Duff had slipped to nineteen in 1959–60, and Imlach was making him pay. The two sides finally came to an agreement with an offer that would match the salary Dick had made the previous season by adding bonus incentives for his goal output.

Tim Horton was also in the midst of a salary dispute and refused to travel to Los Angeles for an exhibition game the Leafs had scheduled. The impasse was finally resolved, and the veteran defenceman joined the team for the commencement of the regular season.

Another star defenceman, Carl Brewer, was nowhere to be seen in Peterborough. "I have no idea where Brewer is," blurted Imlach. "He never told me he wouldn't be here for training camp. I thought a player of Brewer's intelligence would at least show up for training camp."

In fact, Brewer was at McMaster University in Hamilton holding out over $100 owed him through an ankle injury. King Clancy was sent to corral the young blue liner. When asked why he hadn't shown up at the Leafs' training camp, Brewer explained the matter of the $100. Clancy unfolded $200 from his wallet, handed the money to Brewer and implored him to return to the Leafs. But Carl resisted, insisting instead on waiting until a contract had been signed. "It's the principle of the thing," he explained. "If I let them kick me around this early in my hockey career, it will be that way all through my career."

Stan Fischler's *Hockey's 100* described Carl's reputation within the league. "In a sport that treats iconoclasts like lepers, Carl Brewer was regarded by some hockey conservatives as an unimaginable kook who would have been better suited for the ministry or lighthouse work. His clashes with Toronto Maple Leafs' general manager/coach, Punch Imlach, became legend and set the tone for Brewer's later challenges to the hockey establishment. It was Carl as much as any other player who was responsible for the ascendency of the NHL's first union leader, Allan Eagleson."

Defence partner Bobby Baun described Brewer as "an interesting fellow." He explained, "He was Dr. Jekyll and Mr. Hyde. He was brilliant. I think Carl was probably one of the most brilliant guys on the ice. I don't think he ever reached his capability. He could have put Bobby Orr in his hip pocket. Certainly as good a skater and far stronger."

In *The Power of Two*, Sue Foster, Brewer's long-time partner, explained why Carl was considered an enigma within the team. "He was the outsider, the guy who just didn't seem to fit in. Carl was deeply religious, incredibly sensitive, studious, an intellectual and unrelentingly intense. He didn't drink in those days, which made it difficult for him to socialize with his teammates. They seemed uncomfortable with him and certainly were at a loss to understand the complexity or intensity of his personality.

They nicknamed him 'Skitz' — short for schizophrenic."

To the surprise of most, the swift-skating, twenty-year-old Dave Keon was added to the team out of training camp. Most team members served their apprenticeship with one of the Maple Leafs' minor-league affiliates before leaping to the big club, but the youngster impressed everyone with his speed, his dexterity and his skills. Brewer declared Keon "the most complete hockey player I ever saw in the game."

"I had met the veterans [before] because I had practised with the Leafs when they called me up," Keon said. "I practised with them and had gotten to meet them. When you went to training camp, there were eighty or eighty-five guys in camp, so there were four hockey teams there. Everyone was broken up into different teams and different lines. You could be playing with someone from the American League on one wing and someone from the National League on the other. They didn't treat anyone any differently," mentioned Keon. "I didn't think that [I was going to stick with the Leafs]. I was hoping that it would happen, but you can never tell. When I played in the exhibition games, I was fortunate enough that I scored some goals and got some points. It seemed to keep me with the big team, and I was with them when the season started."

Habs Blank Leafs in Season Opener
Thursday, October 6, 1960
The Toronto Maple Leafs opened the season on the road, visiting the Canadiens at the Montreal Forum. Although The Rocket's retirement left a sizable hole in the heart of fans in Quebec, the Richard name stayed prominent on the ice, as Henri scored two goals in this first game of the season, leading Montreal to a 5–0 win over Toronto. The Canadiens scored twice during George Armstrong's high-sticking major, and Toronto seemed to run out of enthusiasm at that point. Leafs' goaltender Johnny Bower played a magnificent game in defeat, in spite of surrendering five goals.

Leafs Suffer Loss to Rangers in Home Opener

Saturday, October 8, 1960

Toronto's home opener took place two days later, with The Right Honourable John Keiller McKay, lieutenant governor of Ontario, performing the ceremonial puck drop between the Leafs and the Rangers. He also presented Johnny Bower with the J. P. Bickell Memorial Trophy for his outstanding contributions to the Leafs in 1959–60.

Duff and Horton both agreed to contracts and played in this contest, which saw Toronto drop their second straight game, losing 5–2 to New York. The Leafs were a disappointment to the Maple Leaf Gardens' opening night crowd that was "liberally sprinkled with mink and social grandeur," according to the *Toronto Star*. *The Globe* remarked, "More colourful on the ice were the 48th Highlanders brass and pipe bands [who appeared at every opening night in Toronto since Maple Leaf Gardens opened]."

With the Rangers surprisingly ahead of the Leafs 3–2 at the end of the second period, viewers learned of Imperial Oil's "Hockey Special" — a toy hockey game available for $5.00 — and watched Carl Brewer and his fourteen-year-old brother Jack playing the game. The *Hockey Night in Canada* intermission then featured J. Frank Willis interviewing Foster Hewitt about his experiences broadcasting Maple Leafs' games, first on radio and later on television. Hewitt mentioned that he rarely missed doing play-by-play on Toronto Maple Leaf games, and other than on one occasion when he had laryngitis, the only other time was during the Olympics, when he was overseas. "I actually missed a few NHL games, but I call them 'substitutions' because I was doing World Hockey at the same time," Foster said. Willis talked about the first Imperial Oil broadcast in 1936 (General Motors had been the only previous sponsor). Imperial Oil had introduced 3-Star gasoline in 1931, which gave its name to the practice of selecting the three best players in games broadcast by *Hockey Night in Canada*. The segment concluded with Willis showing a clip of Foster interviewing Charlie Conacher in the Leafs' dressing room in the 1930s.

Willis then introduced Ward Cornell to the audience as the regular intermission host. "Here is your regular intermission commentator for this season, Ward Cornell, with Syl Apps and Sweeney Schriner."

Rookie Keon Scores First NHL Goal in Tie with Detroit
Sunday, October 9, 1960

The Leafs tied the Red Wings in Detroit by a 3–3 score, but most notable was Dave Keon's first NHL goal, tallied at 14:03 of the first period against Terry Sawchuk in the Detroit net.

"I didn't play much the first two games," Keon remembered. "Then, in the third, I played and scored a goal and I played regularly after that. Bert Olmstead helped me a great deal and he was a big booster of mine. He may have had some influence with Punch, but by and large, Punch liked to make his own decisions. Anyway, I ended up staying the rest of the season."

Olmstead was an immediate fan of the young centre. "Imlach was going to send him to the minor leagues the first year and I said, 'Don't you dare send him down to the minor leagues. It'll kill him! By the end of the first year, he's going to be your best centreman.' I was so damn right."

Larry Regan returned to the team but did not dress for this contest. "Tim Horton, who shattered a section of Herculite glass behind the Detroit goal with one of his explosive shots, gave [Wings' netminder Terry] Sawchuk shinny shell shock with his brutal shooting," reported *The Globe*.

Imlach Creates Successful Line out of Kelly, Mahovlich and Nevin
Saturday, October 29, 1960

Mired in last place with a record of three wins, two ties and four losses going into the televised Saturday night game, rookie Bob Nevin was asked if it was as much fun to play in the NHL as it was elsewhere. "It will be a lot more fun when we start winning," he responded. But Toronto was quickly getting untracked, and erupted for an 8–4 pasting of the Rangers.

Imlach placed Red Kelly at centre, with Bob Nevin and Frank Mahovlich on the wings, and The Big M responded with three goals (and a misconduct). Bert Olmstead scored two for the winners.

Mahovlich Erupts and Shack Arrives
Saturday, November 5, 1960

The Big M was on a tear, and scored four goals against the New York Rangers' rookie goalkeeper Jack McCartan, a former standout with the gold-medal-winning U.S. Olympic hockey team, in a lopsided 7–3 victory. "When Mahovlich wants to go, nobody stops him," shrugged Terry Sawchuk. "Mahovlich took over like big Chas [Charlie Conacher] used to in his heyday," remarked King Clancy. "He turned those Ranger defencemen inside out with his shifts, change of pace and stickhandling."

The humiliated Rangers, who were getting spanked on a regular basis, knew that changes to their roster had to be implemented. Muzz Patrick, New York's general manager, said of Eddie Shack, "He's just a river skater," and sent the rambunctious forward to Toronto in exchange for Pat Hannigan and Johnny Wilson, two players tagged by Imlach for Rochester of the AHL.

A highly touted junior, Shack had collected just sixteen goals in 141 regular season games with the New York Rangers, and was called "an NHL flop" by the *Toronto Telegram*. "I was just happy to get out of New York," sighed Shack, who was declared "one of the most vigorous Leafs" in his first game with Toronto, a 2–0 loss to Chicago on November 9. Shack was an underrated piece of the dynasty's puzzle as he provided colour to the team, added an intimidation factor and had a scoring touch, as he showed in 1965–66 when he collected twenty-six goals.

From Worst to First
Saturday, November 19, 1960

Within a month, the Maple Leafs went from last place to a tie for first with the Montreal Canadiens and the Detroit Red Wings. Much of the credit for this surprising turnabout was heaped on Frank Mahovlich and Johnny

Bower. Detroit's GM, Jack Adams, commented, "The big guy keeps putting them in and the old guy [Bower] keeps kicking them out." That night, viewers of *Hockey Night in Canada* watched Toronto double Montreal 6–3.

A Toronto/Montreal match-up on *Hockey Night in Canada* was a rare treat for hockey viewers. Montreal and Toronto both traditionally played at home on Saturday nights, and the Canadiens only visited the Leafs once per season on a Saturday night during the 1960s. The mid-week games were not yet televised, so this was the only opportunity to see the rivals play before a national audience during the 1960–61 regular season.

Richard Riles Leafs in Montreal Win
Thursday, December 1, 1960

As Toronto's race for first place against the Canadiens continued, so did the rivalry between the two teams. A penalty-filled third period erupted into a free-for-all at 16:22. That final period featured several bouts, including Tom Johnson versus Bob Baun, Dickie Moore versus Bob Pulford, Marcel Bonin versus Carl Brewer and the title bout, Frank Mahovlich versus Henri Richard. The diminutive Richard high-sticked The Big M and the two started swinging. The "Pocket Rocket" gave up a substantial size differential, and the tiff earned Richard two misconducts in the process. When he stuck to hockey, Henri was the best player on the ice, as he scored two goals in a 6–3 Montreal win.

The unlikely feud between these two stars carried on, and in a later contest, Mahovlich was accused of shooting the puck at Richard's face.

Imlach was fined $200 for publicly criticizing the officials after the game. The Leafs' coach suggested that referee Frank Udvari and linesmen Loring Doolittle and George Hayes should have been selected as the Three Stars of the game for helping the Canadiens win.

Leaf Injuries Mount as Stanley Suffers Broken Jaw
Wednesday, December 7, 1960

Although the Leafs were humiliated 6–2 by Montreal, the bigger story was the rash of injuries experienced by Toronto. Larry Regan was out with a sliced tendon, Ron Stewart first had a thigh abscess removed and then broke his ankle, Tim Horton sat out with two injuries and Carl Brewer suffered torn knee ligaments.

During this contest against the Canadiens, Allan Stanley suffered a broken jaw when he fell on Bill Hicke's skate and had the blade go right through his cheek. "Stanley was down on the table in the hospital," explained trainer Bob Haggert. "[Dr.] Jim [Murray] was feeling around and putting his hand inside his mouth to feel where the cut was. His finger came through [Stanley's] cheek! I jumped about three feet. Of course, Stanley couldn't see it because he was lying there. I remember Jim saying, 'Oh my God, I've got to sew him up on the outside and the inside,' and then deal with a broken jaw." Dr. Murray, shaking his head, said, "He knocked a piece out of the upper jaw."

TV Viewers Enjoy Two Rarities
Saturday, January 7, 1961

During Toronto's 4–1 win over the Bruins, Ward Cornell conducted two interviews that can today be considered rarities. Cornell first spoke with Johnny MacMillan of the Leafs. When MacMillan signed with Toronto in October 1960, he was a graduate of Denver University, one of the first players to join the NHL from U.S. college hockey. The Milk River, Alberta, native spent parts of four seasons in Toronto before he was picked up by the Detroit Red Wings on waivers during the 1963–64 season.

That interview was followed by one with Boston's Willie O'Ree, who broke the colour barrier in the NHL when he played for the Bruins against Montreal on January 18, 1958. The Fredericton native played just two games in 1957–58, but became a regular in 1960–61, playing forty-three games. He scored four goals and had ten assists in his NHL career, all during that season.

O'Ree remembered how his path to breaking the NHL's colour barrier took place. "[A coach] said I could be the 'Jackie Robinson of hockey.' He taught me a lot of things, and he says you have to take a lot, being the first coloured player in any pro league or in the National League, so I went along and played as hard as I could." After playing a year of junior in Kitchener in 1955–56 (a season in which he lost the sight in one eye), Willie joined the Quebec Aces of the Quebec Hockey League. "That year I ended up with twenty-two goals and I was out four weeks with a foot injury." The fleet-footed winger made his debut with Boston in 1957–58, and when asked if he had encountered any troubles being the first black hockey player in the NHL, he told Cornell, "None that you could say that were troubles. I heard a few jeers, but all hockey players hear that." Years later, while working with the NHL's Diversity Task Force, O'Ree commented on his pioneering role in hockey. "They called me the 'Jackie Robinson of hockey,' but I didn't have the problems he had. I was never refused service at a hotel or restaurant, and I was accepted by my teammates." He admitted that the taunts he heard, mostly in the U.S. cities, didn't bother him. "I just wanted to be a hockey player, and if they couldn't accept that, that was their problem, not mine."

Tussles, A Tie and Tim
Wednesday, January 18, 1961

One of the strengths of Leafs teams in the late 1950s and early '60s was their team spirit. Players could rely on teammates standing up for each other on the ice. There was no intimidation on these Leafs teams. And no player epitomized a team player more than Tim Horton. His teammates always knew that they had their backs covered when Horton was on the ice — or even off the ice.

On January 18, 1961, the Leafs and the Rangers were involved in a bench-clearing brawl that resulted in a whopping $575 in fines to players leaving their respective benches. It began when "Dirty Bertie" Olmstead clashed near the Ranger blue line with "Leapin' Lou" Fontinato, and the two started swinging. The two combatants had had a running feud since Olmstead patrolled left wing with the Montreal Canadiens. Olmstead later admitted his role in starting this fight. "I may have high-sticked him. At least he thought I did."

Olmstead had indeed brought his stick up against the Rangers' enforcer (a term not coined until well after the era), and in the ensuing fight, a

Fontinato punch connected square against Olmstead's face. Fights in that era were heated and bitter, and it seems particularly odd that combatants, after being separated on the ice, were then asked to sit beside each other in a single penalty box. If a referee sensed further trouble, a police officer was asked to sit between them. On this evening, a husky constable took his place in the middle of the penalty bench to forestall a further outbreak.

As was the rule, with matching majors, the home team's player was let out of the penalty box before the visitor. When their five-minute penalties expired, and with the Rangers killing a penalty, Olmstead blocked Fontinato's path to the ice. This, of course, infuriated the Rangers' defenceman, who jumped Olmstead and proceeded to start hammering away on him. "They had the play in our end and he wouldn't let me out of the box, so I went after him," Fontinato later said. And how did Olmstead see it? "Well, the play was in their end and we had a man advantage and I wasn't in any hurry. I guess that made him mad." The competitor in Olmstead caused him to do anything to give his team an edge.

Both linesmen intervened at this point, but an enraged Tim Horton jumped off the Leafs' bench and roared over to the melee. Fontinato had separated from the linesman when Horton, using his brute strength, attacked him and bear hugged him to the ice. Although it is popularly believed that Horton never threw punches in a fight, he certainly did on this night. Horton rained punches on the prone Fontinato, and was then joined by Olmstead. As Horton uncharacteristically shoved a linesman, Rangers' goalie Gump Worsley skated to the bench, exhorting his teammates to join the fray, with the Leafs following in response.

Once the combatants were finally pried apart, Fontinato gestured obscenely to the crowd and then skated wildly around the mass of players, before being calmed down by his teammates. Horton, still angry, tried to attack Fontinato once again as the numerous photographers on the ice beat a hasty retreat. Fontinato was finally escorted off the ice, bleeding badly from a skate cut to his leg.

A stretcher was brought out with the intention of wheeling Fontinato to the infirmary in order to tend to his lacerated leg, but the Rangers' defenceman kicked away the stretcher. He claimed that he was kicked, but no one was certain when or how. His nose was bashed but not broken, which was a minor victory of sorts for Leapin' Lou, since in his previous fight he had his nose plastered all over his face by Gordie Howe.

Olmstead, meanwhile, was sporting a black eye and a cut above his left eye that refused to stop bleeding. The injury was caused by the final punch Fontinato landed in their first fight. "He got in a real good punch," remarked Olmstead.

Elsewhere, Leafs' captain George Armstrong suspected that he had broken his thumb when John Hanna's skull got in the way of a punch. Two photographers also suffered injuries —- one was kicked in the shins and the other cut his finger.

Horton never again lost control of himself like he did on that night, but his leadership was further established and his teammates knew beyond a shadow of a doubt that Horton would back them up whenever necessary.

Obscured by the fighting was the fact that Toronto pulled a point out of the fire against the Rangers. Down 4–3 with under a minute to go, Imlach pulled the goalie for an added attacker, and the strategy worked. Red Kelly scored the tying goal at 19:35.

The Big M Breaks Big Franchise Record
Wednesday, January 25, 1961
Frank Mahovlich, the NHL's leading scorer at that point, had been on fire all season, and scored two goals in a 5–3 win over Montreal. The pair of goals gave him thirty-nine for the season, establishing a Toronto franchise record for most goals in a season. The record had been previously held by Babe Dye of the Toronto St. Pats, with thirty-eight, since the 1924–25 season. Mahovlich also set a new Maple Leafs' record, breaking Gaye Stewart's record of thirty-seven in 1945–46, matched by Tod Sloan 1955–56. Mahovlich, who showed about as much excitement as an accountant arriving at a correct total after he beat goalie Charlie Hodge for the second time in the game, said he felt no special elation.

Trainer Bob Haggert reflected back on Mahovlich's career. "I always say he was a far greater player than a whole lot of people ever realized. He had the ability to make difficult things look extremely easy. A lot of people thought he was loafing out there. He had incredible ability and was one of the very few players in that era who could make the people come right out of their seats."

Red Kelly Breaks Leaf Assist Record
Saturday, February 11, 1961
In a 6–3 victory over the Bruins, Red Kelly set a Toronto Maple Leafs' record for most assists in a season, edging Ted Kennedy's mark of forty-three from 1950–51. "The best line I played on was with Nevin and Red Kelly, when we played together in nineteen sixty-one," stated Mahovlich.

Bower Hurt as Toronto's Fiery Streak Continues
Sunday, February 12, 1961
The Leafs enjoyed their fourteenth consecutive game without a loss in a 4–2 win over the Red Wings, but they suffered a loss of a different kind. At 7:17 of the third period, Johnny Bower wandered from his crease to clear a puck and was smeared by Howie Young. "The puck was shot down and the defence got caught," recalled Bower. "I could see an opportunity to beat Howie Young to the puck. He was a very fine skater with good speed, but I had the jump on him. I remember Punch saying, 'When you are going to do something, don't hesitate. Just go and do it, no matter what happens.' I went away out of the net to get it and as soon as I got to the puck, I shot it and Howie Young came at me about the same time. He ploughed into me and that's when I pulled a hamstring muscle." Young was assessed a charging major on the play. "The leg pinched me every time I moved," Johnny said. "I had trouble gaining my feet. My teeth were a little bent, too. He got me with his elbow."

Although shaken up with an injury to his left knee, Bower finished the game. "How I ever finished, I don't know. The pain was there and I was very lucky the players knew I was hurt, too. They tried a lot harder, particularly in my defence." After the game, Bower was hospitalized, but admitted that he didn't want to come out of the net because it might jeopardize his shot at earning the Vezina Trophy. "I was in the race for the Vezina Trophy at the time. There were a couple of times I remember where we were down a goal [nearing the end of a game] and Punch would be yelling at me to come off but I wouldn't even look at the bench. I didn't want them to score a goal into an open net. But I'll tell you, I sure heard about it when the game was over!"

Don Simmons, who had been acquired from the Bruins on January 31 in a swap of goaltenders that sent Ed Chadwick to Boston, had yet to report, so Gerry McNamara of the EPHL's Sudbury Wolves was called up to replace Bower. McNamara, long-time chattel in the Leafs system, had bounced around the minors since tending goal at St. Michael's College. His tour of duty had taken him from Pittsburgh to Buffalo, Cleveland, Winnipeg, Hershey, Rochester and Sudbury before finally making his NHL debut with Toronto.

Clancy Coaches in Clutch

Thursday, February 23, 1961

After a 4–2 loss to New York on February 19, Imlach left the team for a brief Florida vacation, but owing to a U.S. airline strike, did not arrive at the February 23 game until the second period. With King Clancy behind the bench, the Leafs doubled Montreal 4–2.

At 18:19 of the second, Dick Duff was whistled for hooking Ralph Backstrom. As he argued the call, he was assessed a misconduct, and as he sat in the penalty box, threw his stick out onto the ice and was ejected from the game. The Leafs were already shorthanded through injury, with Bower, Olmstead and Pulford missing, joined by Armstrong who tore knee ligaments during the game. And to make matters worse, they lost a second goaltender. McNamara was injured and Cesare Maniago of the Spokane Comets in the Western Hockey League was summoned to replace him.

Bob Nevin scored a disputed goal at 17:35 of the third to give Leafs a 3–2 lead, but the goal judge did not put on the red light, stating that the puck hit the crossbar. When referee Eddie Powers signalled a goal, the Forum fans went wild. "I saw Nevin with the puck and saw him shoot," explained Powers. "I saw the puck beat Plante and saw a bulge in the back of the net. I knew it was a goal." Defenceman Jean-Guy Talbot, one of a multitude of Habs surrounding Powers at centre ice, was so incensed that it appeared as though he knocked Powers to the ice, although the referee himself confessed that he had tripped over a discarded stick. Nevertheless, when Talbot was sent to the dressing room, fans observed him giving the finger across the throat sign. It took several minutes for play to finally resume as fans continued to toss debris onto the ice surface in disgust. Police escorted Powers to the dressing room after the game. The league fined Talbot $75 for his petulant gestures.

Mahovlich's Scoring Championship Jeopardized
Sunday, February 26, 1961

Cesare Maniago saw his first NHL action that weekend, subbing for Johnny Bower in both home-and-home games against the Red Wings. Viewed by his family in Trail, British Columbia, Cesare and the Leafs defeated the Red Wings 3–1 on *Hockey Night in Canada*. "In 1961, I was called up to play with the Leafs when Bower was hurt. I would wear his actual jersey because there were no names on the back and the team only had one jersey for the goalie position," noted Maniago.

With Toronto facing Detroit that weekend for the first time since Young charged Bower, the Leafs tied Detroit 2–2. But of bigger consequence was the sense of deja vu. When Maniago left his crease to corral a loose puck, Young piled into him. Tim Horton immediately came in and drove Young to the ground. Both were given major penalties.

With forty-five goals to his credit and on pace for a fifty-goal season, Frank Mahovlich was taking physiotherapy for a bruised elbow when he suffered a thigh infection that forced him to briefly check into the hospital. The stay was short, and The Big M was back in the lineup for the next game. Toronto edged Montreal 3–1 on March 1, with Mahovlich scoring once to give him forty-six on the season. To further hinder The Big M's run at a fifty-goal season, his centre was injured in a game on March 4. Red Kelly left the game against the Rangers with a pulled groin muscle. His loss was felt clearly by the Leafs, as they lost their number one centre, but in addition, Mahovlich cooled off without his pivot.

Leafs Edge Rangers in Spectacular Comeback
Saturday, March 4, 1961

Toronto's Maple Leafs made an astounding comeback against the Rangers, scoring four goals in the third period alone to squeak past New York with a 5–4 win. Frank Mahovlich scored his league-leading forty-seventh goal with an outstanding effort in the contest, reviving hope of a fifty-goal season.

Meantime, in a game on March 9, Bernie Geoffrion recorded a hat trick against the Rangers in a 6–1 Canadiens' victory. The three goals gave Boom Boom forty-six, just one behind Mahovlich.

Penalty Record Established in Tie With Hawks
Saturday, March 11, 1961

A penalty record was established in a tie game against the Black Hawks. The chippy contest erupted in the third period when Pierre Pilote slashed Eddie Shack and both benches cleared. Afraid that a metaphoric match might be tossed onto the powder keg, police arrived on the ice surface to quell the melee and, to the amusement of fans, were slipping and sliding like Keystone Kops as they attempted to restore order. Eight of the combatants earned misconducts and the twenty-one players that leapt the boards to join the brouhaha were fined $25 apiece. The 2–2 tie was overshadowed by the forty-one penalties called by referee Frank Udvari.

Maniago Subs for Bower; Surrenders Geoffrion's Milestone Marker
Thursday, March 16, 1961

Bower, having just returned from a previous injury, appeared to be on the verge of winning the Vezina Trophy when he strained a leg muscle and withdrew from the game. Replaced by Cesare Maniago, the unfortunate backup surrendered a goal to Bernie Geoffrion; his fiftieth of the season. Fans littered the Forum ice with debris. The milestone marker gave Boom Boom the acclaim of being the second player in NHL history to score fifty goals in a season. "I'm glad it's over, that I have tied Rocket's record," said Geoffrion. "The pressure was terrible. It got so I couldn't eat or sleep."

Montreal defeated the Maple Leafs 5–2.

Leafs Conclude Terrific Season with Second-Place Finish

Sunday, March 19, 1961

Toronto chased after first place through the latter half of the season, competing with Montreal for top spot. With five games remaining, both teams had been tied for first with eighty-four points. While they beat Boston 6–2 on March 18 and tied the Rangers 2–2 in the final game of the schedule on the 19th, they could only have grabbed top spot if Montreal lost, which they did not do, blanking Detroit 2–0. The Leafs, who had been burdened with injuries all season, played that final contest without Armstrong (knee), Bower (leg), Kelly (groin) and Shack (thirty-stitch gash behind left knee), then lost blue liner Bobby Baun.

During the second period, Bobby Baun suffered a cut to his neck during a pileup in the Leafs' crease. He skated to the team bench under his own steam, grabbed a towel to hold to the cut and then walked to the Madison Square Garden infirmary. After a couple of stitches, Baun returned and readied himself for the third period, but after one shift, the cut began to bleed again and started to swell. Done for the night, on the team bus after the game, Bob began gasping for breath. "Bob was unable to talk when I left him at the hospital," said Harold Ballard. "He wrote (in his book) that he thought he was going to die while waiting for the players to get on the bus after the game." Tim Horton and King Clancy rushed him to St. Clare's hospital, where doctors performed two operations on him. "They called it a hematoma," Ballard told reporters. "That's a collection of blood in the tissue. This caused [Baun's] mouth to swell under the tongue, forcing the tongue down his throat, which prevented him from talking or breathing." After a moment to reflect, Ballard added, "Bob just has too much guts for his own good."

The final contest of the regular season saw Marcel Paille in goal for the Rangers and Gerry McNamara for the Leafs. The 2–2 tie allowed Johnny Bower to win the Vezina Trophy by two goals over Glenn Hall of Chicago, wrestling the crown for lowest goals-against average away from five-time winner Jacques Plante, who finished third. The NHL's oldest player at thirty-six, Bower earned a $1,000 bonus for the win. He gave both Cesare Maniago and Gerry McNamara $100 each as thanks. "Those two rookies did a great job while I watched from the sidelines," he said.

Frank Mahovlich's quest to reach fifty goals in a season was halted with his forty-eighth goal of the season, scored at home on March 18. Coach Imlach had Mahovlich on the ice almost constantly in the third period, trying to help Frank get the milestone goals. "I had thirty goals halfway through the season and then everybody was excited and no one had ever dreamt that this could have been done because Maurice Richard, ten years previously had done it," recalled Mahovlich. "Here, all of a sudden, I had thirty goals in thirty games or some ridiculous thing like that. I didn't get fifty. I just reached forty-eight goals, which isn't bad. It didn't quite work out in Toronto but I was able to score over forty goals with two other clubs after that." Mahovlich again chased the fifty-goal plateau in 1968–69, finishing with forty-nine as a member of the Detroit Red Wings.

Red Kelly, who centred Frank during the 1960–61 season, had a sensational season, his first at forward, scoring twenty goals and an astonishing fifty assists. Only Jean Beliveau, with fifty-eight, contributed more helpers through the 1960–61 season. Kelly reflected back on the talented Mahovlich. "He should have scored, but Frank needed somebody to holler at him sometimes. Not badly, just to say, 'Frank, you should be doing this or that.' Sometimes, he seemed to be thinking of something else. That's just the way he was sometimes. His concentration had gone away from the game a little bit." But Kelly also admired the skill of The Big M. "There was nobody more graceful than Frank skating down the ice. Those long strides — he was a beautiful skater. Once he got started, you couldn't stop him. And he had a tremendous reach. He was strong and big, and I knew that if I could get the puck to Frank, it would be in the net. I was always a good passer. I could pass the puck on my forehand or backhand."

Both linemates were rewarded for their fine seasons. Kelly was recipient of the Lady Byng as the league's most gentlemanly player, and Mahovlich was voted onto the NHL's First All-Star Team, as was Johnny Bower, who, in spite of injury woes at the end of the season, took home the Vezina Trophy. Allan Stanley, meanwhile, was selected as a Second Team All-Star.

1960–61 Regular Season Standings

FINISH	TEAM	GAMES	WINS	LOSSES	TIES	POINTS
1	Montreal Canadiens	70	41	19	10	92
2	Toronto Maple Leafs	70	39	19	12	90
3	Chicago Black Hawks	70	29	24	17	75
4	Detroit Red Wings	70	25	29	16	66
5	New York Rangers	70	22	38	10	54
6	Boston Bruins	70	15	42	13	43

1960–61 Regular Season Scoring

RK	NUMBER	PLAYER	POS	AGE	GP	G	A	PTS	PIM
1	27	Frank Mahovlich	LW	23	70	48	36	84	131
2	4	Red Kelly	D/C	33	64	20	50	70	12
3	11	Bob Nevin	RW	22	68	21	37	58	13
4	16	Bert Olmstead	LW	34	67	18	34	52	84
5	14	Dave Keon	C	20	70	20	25	45	6
6	15	Billy Harris	C	25	66	12	27	39	30
7	26	Allan Stanley	D	34	68	9	25	34	42
8	9	Dick Duff	LW	24	67	16	17	33	54
9	10	George Armstrong	RW	30	47	14	19	33	21
10	20	Bob Pulford	LW	24	40	11	18	29	41
11	23	Eddie Shack	LW	23	55	14	14	28	90
12	12	Ron Stewart	RW	28	51	13	12	25	8
13	7	Tim Horton	D	31	57	6	15	21	75
14	21	Bob Baun	D	24	70	1	14	15	70
15	18	Carl Brewer	D	22	51	1	14	15	92
16	22	Larry Hillman	D	23	62	3	10	13	59
17	24	Johnny MacMillan	RW	25	31	3	5	8	8
18	8	Larry Regan	RW	30	37	3	5	8	2
19	17	Gerry Ehman	RW	28	14	1	1	2	2
20	19	Johnny Wilson	LW	31	3	0	1	1	0
21	1	Johnny Bower	G	36	58	0	0	0	0
22	25	Garry Edmundson	LW	28	3	0	0	0	0
23	24	Gary Jarrett	LW	18	1	0	0	0	0
24	1	Cesare Maniago	G	22	7	0	0	0	2
25	24	Jack Martin	C	20	1	0	0	0	0
26	1	Gerry McNamara	G	26	5	0	0	0	2
		TEAM TOTALS			70	234	379	613	844

Regular Season Netminding													
RK		PLAYER	POS	AGE	GP	MIN	W	L	T	GA	GAA	SO
1	1	Johnny Bower	G	36	58	3480	33	15	10	145	2.50	2
2	1	Cesare Maniago	G	22	7	420	4	2	1	17	2.43	0
3	1	Gerry McNamara	G	26	5	300	2	2	1	12	2.40	0
			TEAM TOTALS		70	4200	39	19	12	174	2.49	2

The rookie of the year trophy, the Calder, went to Toronto's Dave Keon, who edged out teammate Bob Nevin for the award. "Bobby Nevin and I both had good years, and maybe I was a bit surprised," admitted Keon, who used a stick straighter than a Baptist preacher. "We were the two individuals who were going to decide who won it. It ended up being me."

Other NHL individual awards went to Montreal's Doug Harvey, who captured the Norris Trophy for the seventh time in eight seasons, and Boom Boom Geoffrion, whose sensational scoring spurt in the final weeks of the season earned him ninety-five points (including fifty goals) and the Art Ross Trophy as the NHL's scoring leader. He was also Hart Trophy winner as the league's most valuable performer.

After flirting with a first-place finish throughout the season, chasing and being chased by the Montreal Canadiens in some sort of shinny dogfight, talk was that 1961 was the year that the Maple Leafs would win the Stanley Cup, stopping cold the Canadiens' attempt to win six championships in succession. The pieces were in place — reliable goaltending, a solid defence corps, scoring forwards, youth, experience, skill and grit. And all led by a coach who willed the team into the Stanley Cup final in his first two years on the job.

The semi-finals lined up with first-place Montreal facing third-place Chicago, while the second-place Maple Leafs would meet the fourth-place Red Wings. Toronto finished twenty-four points ahead of Detroit during the regular season, giving every amateur prognosticator the indication that the Leafs would take the series in a cakewalk. But, as we've come to appreciate, in hockey anything can happen.

The Captain Crushes Wings in Overtime
Game One, Semi-Final – Wednesday, March 22, 1961

With Johnny Bower still struggling with his leg injury, Imlach started Cesare Maniago, who surrendered a goal to Alex Delvecchio at the fourteen-second mark of the first period. Bob Nevin tied it up at 2:20 of the second. The seesaw battle continued as Howie Young scored his first NHL goal early in the third, putting Detroit ahead 2–1, but Ron Stewart bounced a puck past Sawchuk at 14:26 of that period, tying the game and forcing overtime. Regulation time saw the Leafs and Wings deadlocked at two goals apiece.

During the first overtime, there was a hush over the crowd when Bert Olmstead, who had earned assists on both Leafs' goals, was nailed into the boards by Gordie Howe. Olmstead struggled off the ice and was taken to the hospital, replaced in the Leafs' lineup by Johnny MacMillan. Olmstead was diagnosed with strained knee ligaments, but it was unclear whether he would return to play in that series.

At 4:51 of the second overtime, George Armstrong scored the sudden-death winner on a pass from Dickie Duff to win the game, 3–2. After missing twenty-three regular season games to injury, the Leafs' captain commented through heavy breaths, "I'll tell you one thing…that is a good way to get in shape in one easy lesson." He was selected as the first star of the game, with Bob Nevin and Terry Sawchuk second and third stars.

"This isn't the Detroit team we were beating all season," commented Conn Smythe. "Half the time or more we were playing against Hank Bassen in goal, not Sawchuk. We weren't playing against Howie Young either. The way he's playing now, he helps them a lot."

Punch Imlach stated that Johnny Bower would be ready to take over from his jittery understudy for game two.

Detroit Bounces Back to Even Series
Game Two, Semi-Final – Saturday, March 25, 1961
Detroit evened the series, winning 4–2 at Maple Leaf Gardens.

Billy Harris was credited with the opening goal when Detroit's Howie Young banged Marcel Pronovost's clearing attempt into his own net past a stunned Sawchuk.

In spite of Imlach's statement, Cesare Maniago played goal for Toronto, and fanned on two second-period long shots, one by Marcel Pronovost and the other a short-handed marker by Leo Labine. "These bouncing shots had me confused and then they started flipping them at me all the time," said Maniago.

In the third, Vic Stasiuk and Gerry Melnyk responded with a goal each, countering Frank Mahovlich's late-period tally. Maniago had not looked sharp in this game, won by the Wings 4–2.

"The beating might do us a world of good," suggested Dave Keon. "We could have been getting a bit complacent."

Wings Win with Shutout to Take Series Lead
Game Three, Semi-Final – Sunday, March 26, 1961
The series moved to the Olympia for game three, with both teams having earned a win. Johnny Bower replaced Maniago, who had proven to be shaky in the Leafs' goal.

The game was scoreless through two periods of play until Gordie Howe beat Bower with a backhander at 4:51 of the third. "He owned the puck when he was on the ice, controlled the game like a puppeteer pulling the strings in a Punch and Judy show," stated the *Toronto Daily Star*. Just 1:24 later, Val Fonteyne scored to put the game away for Detroit.

The Three Stars in this 2–0 Detroit victory were Gordie Howe, Allan Stanley and Terry Sawchuk.

Leafs on Brink of Elimination following Showdown in Motown
Game Four, Semi-Final – Tuesday, March 28, 1961
Imlach inserted Bert Olmstead back into his lineup for game four, and

Bert responded with a power play goal in the first period. Dave Keon scored a breakaway goal at 17:48 of the period, but the tally was wiped out by referee Frank Udvari when Ron Stewart was called for interfering with Marcel Pronovost on the play. Instead of being up 2–0, Toronto had Stewart in the penalty box beside Olmstead, who had been given a misconduct for throwing his stick in disgust. Leo Labine then scored to tie the game.

In the second, Carl Brewer's weak clearing pass was picked off by Vic Stasiuk, who fed Howe. Gordie fired a rocket past Bower into the top corner to put Detroit up 2–1. Marcel Pronovost later got in behind the defence for a breakaway. Bower's poke check only got a piece of the puck, and it slithered past the netminder for a goal.

With the Leafs down 3–1 and the net empty for an additional attacker, Val Fonteyne put the game away with an empty net goal at 19:55.

"We had to win in Detroit," recalled Imlach several years later. "We were winning 1–0. Keon is going in on a breakaway and scores the goal. I see [referee Frank] Udvari put his hand up and he blows the goddamned whistle and gives us a penalty. [Ron] Stewart took the guy from behind. If Udvari had been up with the bloody play, he wouldn't have seen Stewart hook him to start with. He should have called the play and not let the goal go in, because as soon as Keon touched the puck, it is supposed to be a penalty against us and out it goes. But, when he let it go, it is crisis against Detroit. We got the penalty and they tried to score and went on and won. That is part of the game. Those are the damn things you remember, you know. You remember the good ones and you also remember the things that really cost you, and that was one of the things that really cost us."

"You can talk about penalties and everything else but you have to give credit to the guy in goal," said Bert Olmstead. "He's playing like the Sawchuk of old."

"We had enough chances to win six games," fumed Imlach. "We didn't finish them off and when we did, Sawchuk beat us."

The Red Wings, counted out before they had even stepped onto the ice for the opening faceoff in game one, were now on the verge of eliminating the Maple Leafs.

Detroit Underdogs Bury Leaf Chances at Stanley Cup

Game Five, Semi-Final – Saturday, April 1, 1961

The first day of April was no joke for Toronto. Heavily favoured to win the Stanley Cup, they were outplayed, outskated and outscored by the hungry Red Wings, who dumped Toronto 3–2.

Gordie Howe scored a shorthanded goal at 4:36 of the opening period. Len Lunde then golfed a Howe pass past Bower for a power play goal at 14:11.

Early in the second period, Al Johnson made it 3–0 for Detroit. Red Kelly, hobbling through a leg injury, banged a shot past Sawchuk with Pete Goegan in the penalty box to make it 3–1.

In the third, Terry Sawchuk raced out to beat fleet-footed Dave Keon to a loose puck, but instead, cleared it onto the Leafs' stick. Keon then stepped past Sawchuk and fired the puck into an empty net to make it 3–2.

With a minute to play, the Leafs pulled Bower for an extra skater and looked dangerous, but Sawchuk stole two sure goals, then Mahovlich fired the puck wide with an open net with eight seconds to play. The Toronto fans, who had booed The Big M frequently through the game, increased the derision as the Maple Leafs skated off in defeat. Mahovlich was one of several Leafs who did not remain on the ice after the buzzer to congratulate the Red Wings. Bert Olmstead and Tim Horton were the others.

Detroit goaltender Terry Sawchuk took a beating during the game, getting a crosscheck from Eddie Shack in the second period, and took four stitches to the eye in a goal crease pile-up in the third, but was hailed as the difference in the series. Sawchuk, Howe and Larry Hillman were chosen as the game's Three Stars.

"You could sum it up this way," explained Detroit GM Jack Adams. "Our club suddenly gelled, and we got hot just at the right time. On top of that, we got great goaltending from Terry Sawchuk. That was the whole story."

So angered by the result were Conn Smythe, Bert Olmstead and Larry Regan that none of them showed up for the team photograph.

"We could have won in nineteen sixty-one," Punch Imlach maintained years later. "If we had gotten by Detroit, we would certainly have knocked Chicago out. What happened to us was injuries. Bower got hurt. I remember Howie Young charged Bower in the crease and put him out and Olmstead and Kelly were hurt."

There was much discussion over whether the 1961 Stanley Cup final was going to be carried by CBC Television. At that time, the CBC only had rights to games played by the Montreal Canadiens and the Toronto Maple Leafs; home games during the season and all games in the playoffs. However, with both teams eliminated in their respective semi-finals, the CBC's worst nightmare became reality.

Canada's national broadcaster had to work out a solution that would allow them to carry the Stanley Cup final between Chicago's Black Hawks and the Detroit Red Wings, or face the wrath of angry viewers.

CBC Television convinced the Red Wings that their Canadian viewers in Windsor had a vested interest in the final. As a result, after signing a special contract with the Red Wings that offered the broadcast as a public service to the Windsor market, the CBC was able to carry the series, then linked the signal to Toronto and relayed the coverage nationwide. As a result, Canadian hockey fans were able to watch the Stanley Cup final between Detroit and Chicago, which was won by the Black Hawks, four games to two.

Chicago's captain, Ed Litzenberger, accepted the Stanley Cup from NHL president Clarence Campbell. It was the franchise's first championship since 1937–38. Chicago had gone through decades of futility, missing the playoffs fourteen times between Cup celebrations. And to this day, the Chicago Blackhawks have yet to win again since April 16, 1961, the longest period without a Stanley Cup championship of any current NHL team.

Through the entire Original Six Era, the Toronto Maple Leafs won the Stanley Cup nine times, the Montreal Canadiens collected the Cup ten times and the Detroit Red Wings were presented with the Stanley Cup on five occasions. In an era of "haves" and "have nots," neither the Boston Bruins nor the New York Rangers claimed the Stanley Cup at all during that twenty-five-year period. The Chicago Black Hawks won the Stanley Cup but once during that time — in 1961.

It was a bitter pill to swallow for the Maple Leafs, whose lofty expectations were dashed by Detroit. The Leafs had all manner of individual triumphs through the season: leading the NHL in goals scored, Mahovlich's forty-eight-goal season, a Vezina for Johnny Bower, First All-Star Team selections for both Mahovlich and Bower, the Calder for Dave Keon and the Lady Byng for Red Kelly. But Toronto seemed to run out of steam chasing Montreal for first place (and Montreal, also eliminated in the semi-final, seemed to be drained for the same reason). Injuries also had played a role. Bower's injuries had kept him out of the lineup for twelve games during the regular season, and George Armstrong, Bobby Baun, Red Kelly, Bert Olmstead and Eddie Shack, all key components of that Leafs team, were injured during the playoffs. Imlach believed that the injuries had cost Toronto first place as well as left the team tired for the playoffs. But the truth was that the Toronto Maple Leafs had a roster that was second to none in the NHL. They had but one thing to do — they had to learn how to win.

SLAPSHOTS AND SNAPSHOTS
LARRY THE LEECH

Karl Elieff was the Maple Leafs' physiotherapist from 1955 to 1974, and was recognized as one of Canada's foremost experts in the field. He was with Team Canada during the 1972 Summit Series and also treated such world-class athletes as Mario Andretti, Jack Nicklaus and the skating Jelineks.

Always open to new approaches, Elieff and trainer Bob Haggert once joined trainers from hockey, football and baseball at a conference of the National Trainers' Association. "We met this fellow from Gainesville, Florida, who told us that whenever any of their players got hurt and ended up with a hematoma [a collection of blood, usually clotted, in a tissue or organ], they used to use leeches," explained Elieff.

During the playoffs that year, Bert Olmstead was determined to continue playing in spite of sporting an eye which was swollen shut. Elieff and Haggert looked at each other, and the physiotherapist said, "Why don't we do what the hell they do in Florida? Let's get one of those leeches!"

The Leafs' physiotherapist hailed a cab and headed to Starkmans Chemists, and returned to the Gardens with a leech. He and Haggert then told Olmstead of the plan. "Bert said he didn't care what the hell we did, as long as we got him on the ice," Elieff recalled.

"We didn't want anybody to see this so we plunked him down in the trainer's room, which was off the main dressing room, and put the leech [fondly nicknamed 'Larry the Leech'] over Bert's eyelid, which was completely shut." Assistant trainer Tommy Nayler walked in, took one horrified look, shook his head and left. Imlach took a quick glance and he, too, was gone.

Larry latched on to Olmstead's eyelid, did his job and drew the blood, allowing the assistant captain to see out of his eye once again. But Elieff and Haggert were stymied in knowing how to remove the satiated leech. After discussing various methods of removing it, the two simply shrugged.

"The thing was pulled off and [Olmstead] had a little bit of bleeding but Bobby Haggert stopped it and out went Bert. We found out later that if you applied a lit cigarette to it, the leech would come right off."

Elieff said, "When it came to the playoffs, we did just about anything to get them back on the ice, and it had to take a person like Bert Olmstead to do this, too."

6

1961–62: The Curse of Barilko Lifted

Denied the opportunity to claim the Stanley Cup in 1961, the Maple Leafs were more determined than ever to win the championship. All the pieces seemed to be in place: great goaltending, an outstanding defence corps, goal scoring, checking and a work ethic instilled by Punch Imlach that was going to bring victory, if it didn't kill the team first.

The reigning Stanley Cup champions had a terrific core — Glenn Hall in goal, Pierre Pilote and Elmer Vasko anchoring the blue line, Bobby Hull, Stan Mikita, Bill Hay, Kenny Wharram and a group of young Turks now starring at forward. Nonetheless, they tinkered with their lineup, strengthening it with Bob Turner on defence in a trade with Montreal and forwards Bronco Horvath from Boston and Gerry Melnyk from the Red Wings. Rookie Chico Maki graduated to the NHL.

Montreal expressed bitter disappointment at their poor play-off showing by shaking up their roster. After fourteen All-Star seasons, Doug Harvey was moved to the Rangers to become player-coach, with Montreal receiving Lou Fontinato in exchange. The Habs also added Cesare Maniago as depth in goal, receiving the netminder from Spokane of the Western Hockey League in the Intra-League Draft.

After a last-place finish, Boston made wholesale changes, moving Phil Watson in as coach. The Bruins added Orland Kurtenbach from New York and Cliff Pennington and Terry Gray in a trade with Montreal. Youngsters Ted Green, Pat Stapleton, Ed Westfall and Tom Williams all got their shot at a regular NHL spot.

The Rangers were also upset at missing the post season, and shook up their roster. They picked up perennial All-Star Doug Harvey from Montreal and secured Al Langlois from the Canadiens for John Hanna. Vic Hadfield was selected from Chicago in the Intra-League Draft, while Jean Ratelle found a spot in the lineup after a sterling junior career.

The Detroit Red Wings picked up Chicago's captain, Ed Litzenberger, in a trade, and bolstered their blue line by trading Les Hunt to the Rangers for Bill Gadsby, and sent Pete Conacher, John McIntyre and Marc Reaume to Hershey of the AHL for Howie Young. Sid Abel planned to give junior Larry Jeffrey every opportunity to make the team.

Punch Imlach tinkered with his lineup the least of all the GMs. Don Simmons was added from Boston as a backup to Johnny Bower, replacing Cesare Maniago, in whom the coach had lost faith. Al Arbour was a valuable Intra-League Draft addition from the Stanley Cup champion Black Hawks. Dave Creighton was shipped to Buffalo of the AHL with Toronto receiving Dick Gamble. Larry Regan was released and became playing coach of the Pittsburgh Hornets of the AHL.

Leafs Start Strong with Season-Opening Win
Thursday, October 12, 1961

While training camp and an exhibition scheduled readied NHL teams for the 1961–62 season, some manoeuvring was taking place to get the players all signed. Allan Stanley finally signed, leaving Bob Pulford and Billy Harris unsigned and ineligible for the opening faceoff of the season. "I'm very happy with the raise I got," said Stanley, a Second Team All-Star in 1960–61. Imlach warned that if his two Leaf regulars didn't sign, he was quite prepared to summon Bill Dineen and Bruce Draper to join the NHL squad. As it turned out, both Harris and Pulford signed on the eve of the season opener.

The season was also starting with the lineup hit by injuries. Carl Brewer was suffering from an elbow infection, so Imlach had Arnie Brown standing by should Brewer not be able to play in the season opener. Larry Hillman had injured his shoulder in an exhibition game against Chicago, but Al Arbour was newly available to fill that fifth defenceman spot. Bert Olmstead would also miss the season opener due to injury.

The Maple Leafs started the season on a positive note, beating the Detroit Red Wings 4–2 in that city's opener.

Toronto's Home Opener Provides Second Win of Season
Saturday, October 14, 1961

As had become the annual tradition in Toronto, the 48th Highlanders Pipe and Drum Corps performed on the ice surface before the opening faceoff. Rt. Honourable Louis St. Laurent, the former prime minister of Canada, opened the Leafs' NHL season at home by dropping the ceremonial puck between George Armstrong and Don McKenney of the Boston Bruins. St. Laurent also presented the J. P. Bickell Award to Red Kelly as Toronto's MVP of the 1960–61 season.

The Maple Leafs edged Boston 3–2. Although they had won two straight out of the gate, Punch Imlach was concerned about the lack of firepower when the team had the man advantage. Injured Bert Olmstead was entrusted by Imlach to create a power play, the glaring weakness in the Leafs' game. "Olmstead's absence from left wing is the main problem with Leafs' powerless powerplay," noted *The Star*.

New Ownership Takes over Toronto Maple Leafs

Thursday, November 23, 1961

With a 5–2 victory over Chicago, the Leafs briefly enjoyed sitting in first place. Red Kelly had a hat trick in the victory, which was only the second win by Toronto at Chicago Stadium in two years.

But beyond the momentous game, it was a historic date in Toronto Maple Leafs' history. On November 23, 1961, Conn Smythe, after thirty-four years, vacated the president's chair at Maple Leaf Gardens.

"Stafford [his son] and I talked for three days over various aspects of the deal and finally reached an agreement," wrote Conn. "At the time, I thought I was selling only to him, and gave me the assurance that the honesty and class I had tried to bring to the place would continue. A few days later, when he told me he was selling part of my shares to Ballard and Bassett, I exploded. 'That's a lousy deal! That's the worst business mistake you could ever make! You have the whole pot and now you're going to get a third instead, so that every time this place makes a million dollars, you're going to give two-thirds away!'"

But, on that date, the deal was begrudgingly consummated by the elder Smythe, who tendered his resignation as president and managing director in favour of his son. Conn was rewarded with a retiring salary of $15,000 per year for life, an office, secretary, car, driver and seats to home games. Conn succeeded W. A. H. MacBrien as chairman of the board of directors, a position from which he resigned in March 1966.

Stafford Smythe and his partners, Harold Ballard and John Bassett, purchased Conn's 45,000 shares in Maple Leaf Gardens for a price estimated at $2,000,000, gaining 65 percent of Gardens' stock as a result. Stafford assumed the presidency from his father. "It's a great satisfaction to me that my son, who not so long ago as stick boy, congratulated me on winning the Stanley Cup, now has a chance to do the same thing as president," commented Conn.

The forty-year-old Stafford listed a number of areas he would to like addressed at the venerable old arena. "We'll get together with our engineers to see what can be done about our seating capacity," he said. The Leafs had a waiting list of six thousand anxious to subscribe to season tickets.

By installing seats at the north end, it was hoped they could accommodate at least two thousand of those hopefuls.

In addition, the trio of owners planned to put more non-hockey events into Maple Leaf Gardens. "Now that Toronto has a centre for the performing arts, we'll concentrate on that area of business where we have the field to ourselves."

Despite Injury Woes, Leafs Hot Streak Continues
Wednesday, November 29, 1961
The Maple Leafs were faced with a lineup at the Gardens' infirmary in late November. During the 2–2 tie with Montreal, Dave Keon and Ron Stewart suffered groin pulls, and Johnny Bower had a badly swollen ankle after stopping a blast. Yet, even with such adversity, the Leafs hadn't lost a game in the four played since the new ownership had assumed command or in eleven games played at home.

Gerry Cheevers Makes his NHL Debut
Saturday, December 2, 1961
The Leafs dumped Chicago 6–4, with goaltender Gerry Cheevers making his debut in the NHL. It had been a topsy-turvy season already for the young St. Catharines native. He turned pro that season with the Pittsburgh Hornets of the American Hockey League, moved over to the AHL's Rochester Americans for nineteen contests and then spent most of the season with the Sault Thunderbirds of the Eastern Provincial Hockey League. It was during his tenure with the Sault that Gerry saw his first NHL action. "Johnny Bower was hurt and so was Donny Simmons, who was playing down in Rochester," Cheevers recalled. "I got a call on Friday night and took the train down from the Sault. We played Chicago and it was a great thrill — no mask, Bobby Hull, scared to death. Billy Harris got three goals. Then we got on the train and played the next night in Detroit. We got beat 3–1. I'll never forget that night. Gordie Howe came down, shot what I thought was a routine wrist shot and knocked the stick right out of my hands! I thought, 'Ooh. They're a little bit bigger and stronger up here!'"

Cheevers was returned to the Thunderbirds as soon as Johnny Bower was able to step back into the crease. "They were the only two games I played in the NHL until I went to Boston," stated Gerry. "The Leafs won the Stanley Cup that year. During the playoffs, Johnny Bower got hurt and Donny Simmons played goal, so I was the standby goalie in the stands. My thought was that if Donny Simmons got hurt, they'd never find me, and if they did find me, it wouldn't be worth it anyway!"

Billy Harris picked up his second career hat trick, replacing Keon on a line with George Armstrong and Dick Duff. Harris was regarded as hockey's best pinch-hitter. In spite of abundant skills, he was a centre on a team, with Dave Keon, Red Kelly and Bob Pulford playing the same position. "Even though I realize Punch thinks of those three before he gets to me, when he's considering centres, I still feel there are times when I could spell off Keon, Kelly or Pulford, especially if they have been killing a penalty," Billy stated. Imlach admitted that he felt Harris was a defensive liability and not rugged enough to play regularly.

Leafs Add Veteran Leadership to Roster
Sunday, December 31, 1961
During the era, there was never a break of any appreciable length for NHL teams. Most players were accustomed to having Santa Claus arrive several days early for their children, as games were routinely scheduled for Christmas Day. In 1961, Toronto played in Chicago on December 25, and tied the Black Hawks 3–3. The two teams faced off in Toronto on December 27 and again tied, this time a goaltenders' duel resulting in shutouts for both Toronto's Johnny Bower and Chicago's Glenn Hall.

On December 29, Imlach picked up Eddie Litzenberger off waivers from Detroit for $20,000. "This guy can mean first place for us," claimed the coach, who slotted the big centre between Mahovlich and Nevin, replacing Red Kelly, who hurt his right knee after sliding into a goalpost.

Litzenberger had been to hell and back in the previous two years. While returning home from a 3–1 victory over the Rangers on January 19, 1960, the Black Hawks' captain and his wife Doreen, who was driving, skidded and crashed into an abutment on the Edens highway. Mrs. Litzenberger suffered extensive injuries and died the next day, while the Chicago forward, who had enjoyed three consecutive seasons with thirty or more goals, suffered kidney and liver injuries and was briefly in critical condition. The couple's son, two-and-a-half-year-old Dean, was cared for by Glenn Hall's wife, Pauline, during Ed's convalescence. Litzenberger returned to the Black Hawks on March 5, scoring twice in a 5–0 win over New York. He was horribly affected by the death of his wife, and after captaining Chicago to a Stanley Cup championship in 1961 he bounced from Detroit to Toronto, where he would finish his NHL career.

Litzenberger seemed to be rejuvenated by his fresh start in Toronto. On December 30 he played his first game against his former teammates and did not look out of place. That night, Johnny Bower was back in goal for Toronto, replacing Don Simmons, who had played several games with a broken bone in his hand. The Leafs defeated Detroit 6–4. On January 10, Toronto continued a six-game winning streak by toppling Boston 7–5, and Litzenberger was the game's first Star. "The thunder was back in his shot and he was moving the puck well," wrote *The Daily Star*.

Toronto Loses Game…and Duff
Thursday, January 11, 1962
Two big losses took place on this night for Toronto. Their unbeaten string of eight games was snapped by the Canadiens with a 4–2 decision. In that game, Dick Duff broke his foot, and it was thought that his season had come to an end, although he did return later in the campaign.

Shack Returns, and then Exits Again
Saturday, February 17, 1962
Injuries continued to plague the Leafs through the heart of the season, and yet they seemed to be able to stay the course and continue winning hockey games. Eddie Shack had freshly returned from tearing the ligaments in his left knee on Christmas Night, when he re-injured the knee in a 4–2 win over the Rangers. "Shack travels like a one-man cavalry charge, his

elbows riding wide and high as his legs pump and his head bobs around with his big nose cutting the air like a prow in front," described Scott Young in *The Globe*.

Imlach juggled the roster, occasionally inserting spare defenceman Al Arbour at centre. To replace Shack, Larry Keenan was called up from Rochester. During the course of the 1960–61 season, Punch announced that Bruce Draper and Larry Keenan were the two best junior players he had seen that season. "I didn't see anyone better," he declared. "They should be good enough to give the big boys a run for their money [when they were invited to training camp with the Leafs in the fall of 1961], and if they can put some of them out of a job, it's there for them. I hope they do." Keenan, so highly touted, played his only two games in a Leafs' uniform on February 18 and 21.

Simmons Sensational as Sub
Saturday, March 10, 1962
The Leafs' injury woes continued. While handling an Eddie Shack shot in the pre-game warm-up, Johnny Bower injured his left thumb and was pulled from the lineup. In his place skated Don Simmons, his fractured left cheekbone protected by his mask and playing with injured knees on which trainer Bob Haggert kept icepacks between periods. Nevertheless, Simmons shut out the Red Wings 2–0.

Toronto Removes Detroit from Playoff Contention
Saturday, March 24, 1962
The Leafs ended any hopes the Red Wings may have had in making the playoffs by skating to a 2-all draw on the Saturday night in Toronto. Al Arbour, who had been chained to the bench through most of the latter half of the season, scored the Leafs' first goal.

Toronto concluded the regular season in Boston on Sunday, March 25. Dave Keon was rested and did not dress for the game. He observed, "Sometimes you can learn more from the bench. Every player should sit out one or two games to observe." Imlach, resting his starters, had

Kelly and Armstrong both play just four shifts to ready themselves for the playoffs.

The game concluded with a 5–4 loss to the Bruins, and cost Bower his shot at the Vezina. Bower faced fifty-five shots, the most he'd faced all season. "He was a leaping, diving acrobat," reported *The Globe*.

That same night, Bobby Hull scored his fiftieth goal of the season, an NHL milestone reached only by Maurice Richard and Boom Boom Geoffrion to that point. Through the 1961–62 season, Hull scored but six goals against the Leafs — four on Bower and two on Simmons. By comparison, "The Golden Jet" scored ten times against Vezina winner Jacques Plante.

Although they had led the league for part of the season, the Toronto Maple Leafs finished second, with eighty-five points. Montreal led the NHL in 1961–62, compiling ninety-eight points. Third place went to Chicago, while the New York Rangers took the fourth and final playoff berth. The Red Wings and Boston were left out of playoff contention.

Bobby Hull was the NHL's Art Ross Trophy winner, collecting thirty-four assists to go with his fifty-goal season for eighty-four scoring points. While Andy Bathgate of the Rangers also finished with eighty-four points, the scoring championship went to the Black Hawks' star on the basis of having scored more goals. Frank Mahovlich was Toronto's top scorer, finishing fifth in the league with seventy-one points on thirty-three goals and thirty-eight assists.

1961–62 Regular Season Standings						
FINISH	TEAM	GAMES	WINS	LOSSES	TIES	POINTS
1	Montreal Canadiens	70	42	14	14	98
2	Toronto Maple Leafs	70	37	22	11	85
3	Chicago Black Hawks	70	31	26	13	75
4	New York Rangers	70	26	32	12	64
5	Detroit Red Wings	70	23	33	14	60
6	Boston Bruins	70	15	47	8	38

1961–62 Regular Season Scoring

RK	NUMBER	PLAYER	POS	AGE	GP	G	A	PTS	PIM
1	27	Frank Mahovlich	LW	24	70	33	38	71	87
2	14	Dave Keon	C	21	64	26	35	61	2
3	10	George Armstrong	RW	31	70	21	32	53	27
4	4	Red Kelly	D/C	34	58	22	27	49	6
5	11	Bob Nevin	RW	23	69	15	30	45	10
6	20	Bob Pulford	LW	25	70	18	21	39	98
7	7	Tim Horton	D	32	70	10	28	38	88
8	9	Dick Duff	LW	25	51	17	20	37	37
9	16	Bert Olmstead	LW	35	56	13	23	36	10
10	26	Allan Stanley	D	35	60	9	26	35	24
11	15	Billy Harris	C	26	67	15	10	25	14
12	2	Carl Brewer	D	23	67	1	22	23	89
13	23	Eddie Shack	LW	24	44	7	14	21	62
14	25	Ed Litzenberger	C/RW	29	37	10	10	20	14
15	12	Ron Stewart	RW	29	60	8	9	17	14
16	21	Bob Baun	D	25	65	4	11	15	94
17	3	Al Arbour	D	29	52	1	5	6	68
18	8	Les Kozak	LW	21	12	1	0	1	2
19	24	Johnny MacMillan	RW	26	31	1	0	1	8
20	1	Johnny Bower	G	37	59	0	1	1	4
21	22	Arnie Brown	D	20	2	0	0	0	0
22	1	Gerry Cheevers	G	21	2	0	0	0	0
23	17	Brian Conacher	LW	20	1	0	0	0	0
24	8	Alex Faulkner	C	25	1	0	0	0	0
25	22	Larry Hillman	D	24	5	0	0	0	4
26	8	Larry Keenan	LW	21	2	0	0	0	0
27	1	Don Simmons	G	30	9	0	0	0	0
		TEAM TOTALS			70	232	362	594	762

Regular Season Netminding

RK		PLAYER	POS	AGE	GP	MIN	W	L	T	GA	GAA	SO
1	1	Johnny Bower	G	37	59	3540	31	18	10	151	2.56	2
2	1	Don Simmons	G	30	9	540	5	3	1	21	2.33	1
3	1	Gerry Cheevers	G	21	2	120	1	1	0	6	3.00	0
		TEAM TOTALS			70	4200	37	22	11	178	2.54	3

In preparation for the playoffs, one hundred seats behind each goal were added to Maple Leaf Gardens. In addition, the Leafs would be sporting new sweaters, and for the first time, had numbers added to the sleeves.

The Stanley Cup semi-final pitted the Maple Leafs against the New York Rangers.

Toronto Doubles New York to Open Stanley Cup Playoffs
Game One, Semi-Final – Tuesday, March 27, 1962

It had been twenty years since the Leafs and the Rangers had met in post-season action, and four years since New York had participated in the playoffs at all. Player-coach Doug Harvey was applauded for his efforts to re-introduce his Rangers to Stanley Cup competition.

Game one was a listless affair, won 4–2 by the Maple Leafs on their home rink.

Dave Keon opened the scoring when he picked the puck off former Leaf Johnny Wilson and fired the puck into the far side of the Rangers' goal past Gump Worsley.

On a second-period power play, Red Kelly cradled the puck behind the net, but as he passed it out front, it hit Doug Harvey and caromed into the Rangers' goal at the twenty-four-second mark. Midway through the period, Ken Schinkel batted a Dave Balon rebound past Bower to narrow the score. Bower put up a mild protest but let it die just as quickly. But less than two minutes later, Horton and Pulford broke in on a two-on-one, with only Al Langlois back. Horton took Pulford's pass, swept past the defender and backhanded the puck past Worsley. Then, with thirty-five seconds left in the period, New York captain Andy Bathgate dished a pass from the wing in front to Earl Ingarfield, who made no mistake on the backhand.

With the Rangers' net empty late in the period, George Armstrong took a pass from Tim Horton and fired the puck into the empty goal with forty-one seconds remaining.

The Three Stars of the game were Bob Pulford, Dave Keon and Andy Bathgate, chosen by Detroit defenceman Bill Gadsby. Punch Imlach countered with, "I'll tell you this, Tim Horton was the best player on the ice by a country mile." *The Globe* concurred: "He still lugs a puck out of his own end with an unparalleled verve and effectiveness, slaps in shots from the point that make the crowd go oooh and ahhh and plays all-star defence behind his own blue line. If one man won the game for the Leafs, it was Tim Horton."

Leafs Take Two-Game Lead with Win Over Rangers
Game Two, Semi-Final – Thursday, March 29, 1962
Both coaches — Punch Imlach for the Leafs and Doug Harvey for the Rangers — vowed that their teams could improve on their efforts from game one. The second contest, again played in the heat of Maple Leaf Gardens, saw the Rangers seem to wilt from the Toronto effort. Andy Bathgate had another frustrating time trying to elude Ed Litzenberger, who had been assigned the role of keeping the Rangers' captain off the scoresheet. Doug Harvey, looked upon to lead the Rangers out of the wilderness, was all but invisible. In fact, *The Globe* wrote, "Sometimes he moved like a tired old man." Gump Worsley, on the other hand, was at his acrobatic best for the Rangers, but was unable to steal the win singlehandedly for New York. Gump stoned Keon on a breakaway in the third in what may have been his finest save.

There was no scoring in the first period. George Armstrong gave the Leafs the lead midway through the second when he fired a hard shot that Worsley got most of, but not enough to prevent from entering the net. Earl Ingarfield, who was a doubtful starter due to stomach flu, made the most of a scramble in front of Bower to poke the puck over the goal line. Late in the period, Bob Pulford roared in from the left wing and drove a Bob Nevin rebound past Worsley to restore the Leaf lead at 18:08.

There was no scoring in the third period, giving Toronto a 2–1 win and a two-game lead in the series.

Former Leaf Scores Twice as Rangers Rebound
Game Three, Semi-Final – Sunday, April 1, 1962

The Rangers altered the lineup for game three, played at Madison Square Garden. Ken Schinkel was out with a broken toe and Camille Henry was benched, giving rookie Rod Gilbert a spot in the Rangers' lineup.

Viewers of *Hockey Night in Canada* were excited to finally see a game televised from Madison Square Garden in New York, but had to endure watching the game from unique camera angles as the two main cameras were placed at the blue lines.

Tim Horton opened the scoring with a low blast from the blue line that eluded Worsley in the Rangers' net at 5:59 of the first period.

Jean-Guy Gendron then slipped between Stanley and Horton on the Toronto defence and backhanded a shot past Bower to tie the score early in the second. George Armstrong put the Leafs ahead by cashing in his own rebound at 6:46, but nineteen seconds later, Johnny Wilson fired a shot from well out that caught Bower by surprise and tied the game at 2–2.

With ten seconds to play in the period, Al Arbour, subbing for the injured Carl Brewer, blew a tire and fell while retreating with the puck in his zone. "I don't know whether I stepped on something or not," he said. But the puck slid away, and Johnny Wilson was only too pleased to pick it up and fire it low to Bower's left for his second goal of the night, to give the Rangers a 3–2 lead. Arbour took one horrified look at the puck sitting behind Bower in the Leafs' net and flung his stick against the boards. After the game, Punch Imlach explained what Arbour had done wrong. "One, he never should have gone back in the first place. Two, he never should have turned his back to the play unless he's got eyes in his rear end. And three, he never should have lost the puck. He knows that. I don't have to tell him." A sullen Arbour commented, "I felt like jumping out the window."

Red Kelly replaced Arbour on defence in the third period, and with Rod Gilbert serving an interference penalty, scored at 4:47 to tie the game. George Armstrong took a penalty ten seconds later, and as fast as you can say slap-chop, Earl Ingarfield won the draw to Dean Prentice, who passed it in front of the goal, where Andy Hebenton scored for New York at 5:00. The Rangers scored again when Gilbert fired a shot that the Leafs' net-minder blocked, but gave up a ten-foot rebound. With no Toronto defence-men close by, Bower skated out to clear the puck but was beaten there by Johnny Wilson, who fired at the seemingly open net. Somehow, Bower got his right pad up to make the save. Dave Balon then picked up the puck and fired it high over Bower into the Leafs' goal for what became the game-winner at 8:17 of the third. Bob Pulford later scored for Toronto, but it was too little, too late.

The Rangers won 5–4. Punch Imlach was less than pleased with the play of Johnny Bower. "I'd have to say our guy had an off day."

The win at home for New York got them back into the series, which then stood with Toronto up two games to one.

Rangers Tie Series with 4–2 Win
Game Four, Semi-Final – Tuesday, April 3, 1962

In the first minute of the game, Rod Gilbert intercepted a pass Allan Stanley intended for Dick Duff, and beat Bower cleanly for his first NHL goal. Johnny Wilson then snagged a pass made by Bob Baun from behind his net and got it over to Gilbert, who showed great patience in waiting for Bower to make his move, then tucked the puck into the Leafs' cage. "I've never been so thrilled in my life," beamed Gilbert, who had been summoned from Kitchener-Waterloo of the EPHL.

At 11:59 of the third, Bob Pulford scored a power-play marker. The Rangers negated that goal when Doug Harvey fed Gilbert, who made a move on Bob Baun that left Dave Balon in the clear. Balon shot and scored at 14:03. But not long afterwards, Bob Nevin picked up a shot that Tim Horton fired wide and beat Worsley to narrow the gap. With fifty-two seconds left, the Leafs pressed for a late goal, but Horton was checked near the Rangers' blue line, and Andy Hebenton picked up the loose puck and fed it to Jean-Guy Gendron, who sent the puck the length of the ice for an insurance goal. Rangers 4, Toronto 2.

Kelly Scores Overtime Winner to Push Rangers to Brink of Elimination
Game Five, Semi-Final – Thursday, April 5, 1962

Carl Brewer, who suffered a charley horse that required surgery, returned to the Toronto lineup in game five. Bert Olmstead, with a bum shoulder, was also expected to return to the active roster for Toronto. "Imlach told me to practise at ten and two today," reported Olmstead. "I told him if he wanted me to play, I wasn't going to practise twice, so he told me to work with the rest of the team at two." Olmstead had another comment for Imlach. "I want to know if I'm going to get compensation if I re-injure my shoulder and can't take care of my farm this summer." As it turned out, Olmstead was not ready to play and did not dress in the semi-final for Toronto.

Ron Stewart, who had earlier been benched by Imlach, replaced Eddie Shack in game five and scored the game's first goal when he converted a pass from Red Kelly at 7:46 of the first.

The Leafs' second goal was scored by Frank Mahovlich on a deflection midway through the second period. Earl Ingarfield and Jean-Guy Gendron replied with goals for New York that tied the score at the end of regulation time.

With nothing decided in the first overtime period, play moved into a second extra frame. Early on, Mahovlich fired a long shot that Gump Worsley easily turned away. Andy Bathgate took the puck behind Worsley in the New York net, but his attempted pass to Camille Henry seemed to hit Kelly's skate and landed at Mahovlich's feet in front of the Rangers' net. The Big M tried again, but Worsley blocked his shot. Gump sprawled to smother the puck but it slithered out and Kelly poked it home at 4:23 to end the contest. "It was a big win for us," stated Kelly. "As soon as I passed the puck to Frank, I went as fast as I could for the net. [Worsley] lost the puck when he fell down. He thought he was lying on it but I was on him so fast that I spotted it lying beside his shoulder and tapped it in." Playing-coach Doug Harvey argued that the whistle should have been blown, but referee Eddie Powers claimed he saw the puck. "Ten thousand angels could swear I was right but it wouldn't change the decision," huffed Harvey.

Both netminders were sensational, but the Rangers' Gump Worsley kicked out fifty-three shots, many in spectacular fashion, to earn an ovation from the Maple Leafs' faithful. Punch Imlach paid tribute to Worsley after the game. "He played a fantastic game. I've seen a lot of good ones, but I've never seen anything like that!"

Leafs Reach Stanley Cup Final with Decisive Win over Rangers
Game Six, Semi-Final – Saturday, April 7, 1962

In one of the oddest scenarios in hockey playoff history, one repeated several times through the years, Madison Square Garden was booked for a circus every spring. As a result, the Rangers should have hosted game six, but because of the tenant, the contest was instead played at Maple Leaf Gardens.

Toronto held a 3–1 lead after one period. George Armstrong tucked a backhand into an open net at 9:36 after Worsley ventured out of his crease to corral a loose puck and was unable to scramble back in time. On the second goal Ed Litzenberger cleanly won the faceoff, getting the puck to Bob Pulford, who wired it past Worsley. Keon scored his first of two at 17:52 before Andy Bathgate earned his first goal of the series twenty-eight seconds later to conclude the period's scoring.

Andy Bathgate scored his only goal of the series early in the second period, but that marker was matched when Duff scored a disputed goal at 3:27 of the second. While the Rangers argued that it was gloved into the net, Duff claimed it bounced in off the back of his glove. Mahovlich scored a highlight reel goal, breaking from centre ice, eluding Larry Cahan at the Rangers' blue line and, while watching Worsley go down to block the shot, slipped it into the Rangers' goal at 5:01. At 17:34, Armstrong placed a perfect pass onto the tape of Duff's stick, waiting at the lip of the crease, and Duff scored his second of the night to put Toronto up 6–1.

A shot by Red Kelly was stopped by Worsley, but Keon got two chances to bury the rebound and did so at 9:53 of the third to give Toronto a 7–1 lead, which stood as the final score.

With three assists and a strong game, Tim Horton earned *Hockey Night in Canada*'s first Star, chosen by Milt Schmidt of the Bruins. Dave Keon and Dick Duff, both with a pair of goals, collected the second and third Star honours.

The Rangers had not won a game on Toronto ice in sixteen games going into the contest, and the Maple Leafs made certain the streak extended to seventeen games.

Meanwhile, the Chicago Black Hawks and Montreal Canadiens battled in the other semi-final series, resulting in Chicago earning the right to compete for the Stanley Cup again by defeating the Canadiens four games to two.

There was almost no Stanley Cup for the teams to compete for. During the third period of game three in the Hawks/Habs semi-final, police arrested Ken Kilander, a twenty-five-year-old Montreal native, who attempted to walk out of Chicago Stadium with the Stanley Cup. The Cup had been on display near the Madison Street side of the rink. Kilander picked the lock of the trophy case holding the Cup, grabbed Lord Stanley's legacy and walked towards the exit. A sixteen-year-old usher, Roy Perrell, could see nothing but the legs of a man with the rest of his body hidden behind the Cup. Kilander asked Perrell if he'd be kind enough to hold the door open for him. Perrell refused and called for police help. Sergeant Jerry Cortapassi subdued Kilander, and the Cup was locked away in its travel case. Police reported that they believed Kilander had been drinking.

The thief offered two stories as to why he was trying to steal the Cup. In one, he claimed he was returning the trophy to Montreal, where it rightfully belonged. But in another, the Montreal native admitted he had been offered $400 by some Montreal hockey writers to deliver the Stanley Cup to their Chicago hotel. Both Perrell and Sgt. Cortapassi admitted that Kilander had offered them $250 if they would allow him to take the Cup to the Lasalle hotel where the Montreal writers were staying. Kilander was known to the team; he followed them around the NHL circuit, earning his way by playing piano in local nightclubs in each city.

Montreal coach Toe Blake simply shook his head. "We want the Cup, sure! But we want to win it, not steal it."

Ken Kilander was fined $10 and placed on unofficial probation by Judge Hyman Feldman of Chicago. The Stanley Cup was fine, and would be at the centre of sports attention for the next two weeks.

Hockey fans were ecstatic. "CBC plans complete radio and television coverage in English and French of the Stanley Cup hockey final between Toronto Maple Leafs and Chicago Black Hawks," stated a media release issued earlier that day by the Canadian Broadcasting Corporation. "All games in the best-of-seven series will be broadcast right through from the opening faceoff."

During the 1961–62 regular season (and including the semi-finals), televised games began at 9:00 p.m., one hour after the game's opening faceoff. Fans anxiously waited to discover the score of the game in progress from announcer Bill Hewitt. To be able to watch each of the Stanley Cup final contests in their entirety was a real treat.

The Toronto Maple Leafs had dismissed the New York Rangers four games to two in the opening round of the 1962 playoffs, while the defending Stanley Cup champion Chicago Black Hawks eliminated the Montreal Canadiens in a gruelling six-game semi-final. The opening game of the Stanley Cup final pitted the Leafs, second-place finishers during the regular season, against Chicago, who completed the seventy-game schedule in third. The two teams had met in a Stanley Cup final only once before — in 1938. That year, Chicago won the best-of-five series three games to one to claim the Stanley Cup.

Toe Blake, coach of the vanquished Canadiens, believed that Toronto could handle the Black Hawks and would claim the Stanley Cup. "Chicago can't win in Toronto, and that's all the edge Toronto will need. Otherwise, the teams are pretty closely matched," he noted. "They [Toronto] never made a mistake, and not one of their guys had a bad series. Leafs will have a better balance than we did in this series and they'll force a few of the Hawks to play badly, something we couldn't do."

Hap Day, architect of the previous Leafs' dynasty (six championships in ten seasons between 1945 and 1951), predicted a Stanley Cup victory for Toronto. "This is the Leafs' year," he stated. "They have the horses to go all the way."

Rudy Pilous, coach of the Black Hawks, dismissed the soothsayers. "[The win over Montreal] is just the first stage in our program to prove this is the best hockey club in the business," he stated. "Stage two is coming up. We're already Stanley Cup champions, but that doesn't seem to impress anybody. We have the scoring champion in Bobby Hull, the All-Star centre in Stan Mikita and a magician in goal. We've just beaten a great team in four straight [Montreal was up two games to none over Chicago, but the Hawks rebounded]. I think we'll get around to the rest of the proof in the next week or two."

Leafs Draw First Blood in Stanley Cup Final Opener
Game One, Stanley Cup Final – Tuesday, April 10, 1962

At the Maple Leafs' practice the day before the final was to begin, teammates were horrified to see Johnny Bower pull on a pair of striped underwear. "Where are the lucky red ones?" demanded captain George Armstrong. "I wore them for three weeks, but don't worry, I'll have them on again Tuesday night," came Bower's reply. Armstrong laughed, "I'd like to see you wear them, but I hope you'll have them washed!"

At 8:00 on Tuesday, April 10, televisions across the country were tuned for the first game of the Stanley Cup final, a series tagged by sportswriters as "The Punch and Rudy Show" after the opposing coaches. As the second hand swept the top of the hour, the announcer began: "Garry Moore, sponsored by Coca Cola Limited and the makers of Cheer and Spic and Span; Red Skelton, sponsored by the Ford Motor Company of Canada Limited; and Front Page Challenge, sponsored by DuMaurier Cigarettes, will not be seen tonight. Tonight, from Maple Leaf Gardens in Toronto, the first game of the Stanley Cup finals between the Chicago Black Hawks and the Toronto Maple Leafs."

Following the Esso jingle, the announcer continued, "The Stanley Cup playoffs, brought to you by Imperial Oil Limited, brought to you on behalf of Imperial Esso dealers and Imperial Esso Agents from coast to coast."

Play-by-play announcer Bill Hewitt then joined the broadcast with his usual introduction: "Hello Canada and hockey fans in the United States, Bill Hewitt from Maple Leaf Gardens in Toronto, and the teams are skating around prior to the start of the first period." Following the playing of "God Save the Queen" by the orchestra in Maple Leaf Gardens, Hewitt added, "All set now to start the first period."

Chicago's principal marksman, Bobby Hull, had scored fifty goals during the regular season, and his eighty-four points earned him the Art Ross Trophy as the NHL's scoring champion, so it surprised no one that he opened the scoring early in the contest. Toronto's Tim Horton had wrestled Bronco Horvath to the ice at 3:20 of the first, and while he was serving a holding minor, Chicago defenceman Pierre Pilote delivered a pass along the blue line to Stan Mikita, who faked a shot and passed to Hull. Although he initially misplayed the puck, Hull recovered and fired a wrist shot past Bower. It was the fourth time in the post-season that spring that The Golden Jet had scored the first goal of the game.

It didn't take long for all hell to break loose. Midway through the first, Murray Balfour of the Hawks slammed into Bob Baun after goaltender Bower froze the puck. Baun gave Balfour a glove to the face, which precipitated a minor melee. Bobby Hull moved in and grabbed Baun, and the two traded punches. Linesman George Hayes grabbed Hull, so Baun took the opportunity to get in a couple of extra licks. "Nobody was holding Baun, but it doesn't matter. Fights are a waste of time and energy anyhow," said Hull after the game.

Meantime, while Bob Pulford and Balfour wrestled behind the net, Carl Brewer of the Leafs and Jack Evans of Chicago traded blows. "Suddenly, from the throng emerged the large and handsome Jack Evans, dangling Carl Brewer at the end of one arm while attempting to extract something from Brewer's eye, possibly the bridge of Brewer's nose," reported *The Globe and Mail*. "One could see nothing but flying fists for nearly a minute between these two, before finally they gripped one another closely, waltzed a few steps and finally came to a halt." When the dust settled, referee Eddie Powers eschewed fighting majors in favour of roughing minors to Baun, Brewer, Hull and Evans. "If those weren't fights, I never saw a fight," blurted Conn Smythe, shaking his head.

Although Chicago was first on the scoreboard and stronger in the first period, it was the Leafs that dominated play for the final forty minutes. Only the sterling work of Chicago goaltender Glenn Hall kept the game close. Dick Duff ignited the spark under the Leafs. Late in the first period, he laid a huge bodycheck on Pierre Pilote behind the Hawks' goal, earning a penalty in the process. But on his return, he never let up, nailing Pilote three additional times.

During the first intermission, Ward Cornell of *Hockey Night in Canada* spoke with Montreal goaltender Jacques Plante. "I think that Chicago had the puck in Toronto's end of the rink more than the other way around," noted Plante. Viewers also saw Babe Pratt, a member of the 1945 Stanley Cup champion Maple Leafs, predict that Toronto would defeat Chicago in six games. He also commented that the Toronto/Chicago final would be a "slam bang, keep the ambulances ready" kind of series.

Detroit Red Wings' star Gordie Howe added, "I see one thing brewing out there and it's an awful feud between a few individuals. I see the series is going to be long and rugged."

Early in the second, Duff threaded a pass through Jack Evans that arrived on the stick of Dave Keon in front of Hall. Keon made no mistake tipping the puck behind Hall to tie the game. Later in the second, with Eric Nesterenko in the penalty box serving a minor for roughing up Brewer after the whistle, Frank Mahovlich drove the puck past the screened Black Hawks' netminder to put Toronto ahead 2–1.

Montreal coach Toe Blake visited the *Hockey Night in Canada* studio during the second intermission, as did injured Maple Leaf Bert Olmstead, who had at one time been a member of the Canadiens under Blake. "I didn't know I wasn't going to dress until six-thirty this evening," Olmstead admitted. "This is a real first-class hockey game. It's tough, but we should see some outstanding goaltending."

Bobby Hull made a spectacular rink-long dash that resulted in a breakaway early in the third, but was thwarted by Johnny Bower. Just past the six-minute mark, Dickie Duff stole the puck from "Moose" Vasko in the Chicago zone and caught a glimpse of George Armstrong standing to the left of Glenn Hall. The Leafs' captain took the feed and scored Toronto's third goal. Tim Horton added an insurance marker late in the game when his sixty-foot slapshot glanced off Hawks' defenceman Dollard St. Laurent, changed direction and eluded Glenn Hall to conclude the scoring. The Maple Leafs, 4–1 winners, outskated, outshot and outplayed the Hawks and "played with a reckless vigour," according to *The Globe.*

Gordie Howe selected the Three Stars of the contest: Dick Duff, Dave Keon and Bobby Hull. Foster Hewitt commented, "That was a very convincing win by the Toronto Maple Leafs in the first game of the series, which may be called the "black and blue series" before it's over."

"We were tired and let down after a tough series with Montreal," explained Rudy Pilous. "I'm not happy over the loss, of course, but I'm glad it was four to one. They've had their noses rubbed into the dirt. Maybe they'll get mad now!"

Jack Evans was more direct. "There is only one way of overcoming what they're doing to us and that is to do the same thing to them, only more so."

Toronto Wins Battles as Well as War in Game Two
Game Two, Stanley Cup Final – Thursday, April 12, 1962
With a day in Toronto between games one and two, several Black Hawks toured Casa Loma on April 11, while coach Rudy Pilous spent the day in Fort Erie watching the ponies. The Maple Leafs, meantime, were awarded a rare day off from skating, with the exception of the "Black Aces" — the boys either out of the lineup or playing minimally. Eddie Shack played just the final thirty-six seconds of game two, and earned a cut to the chin

in the process. He was joined in the skate by Al Arbour, Billy Harris, Larry Hillman and Bert Olmstead, as well as a surprise guest. There, enjoying a brisk skate, was forty-two-year-old Max Bentley, a member of the Stanley Cup-winning Leafs teams of 1948, 1949 and 1951. In fact, Max assisted on George Armstrong's first NHL goal in 1951–52.

Billy Harris scored a power play goal on his first shift of game two, played at Maple Leaf Gardens in Toronto. The tally, the sole goal of the first period, resulted when Chicago's Reggie Fleming passed the puck from behind his own net but had it blocked by Ron Stewart, who got the puck over to Tim Horton at the right point. Horton's slapshot was deflected away by Glenn Hall, but Harris picked up the rebound and, twirling to his backhand, deposited the puck into the Chicago net.

Murray Balfour watched the end of the game from East Toronto General after being checked into the boards by Carl Brewer late in first period. Balfour slid down the boards to the ice, where he remained, dazed. He was helped to the bench, stayed there for a few shifts, and then retired to the dressing room. There, team doctors felt he'd be better diagnosed at the hospital. After closing a two-stitch cut, Balfour nursed a lemon-sized goose egg. The diagnosis: a mild concussion. "It was the cleanest check I ever made," shrugged Brewer. "He just put his head down at the wrong time. I was trying to take him out of the play and was watching the puck. I hit him with my shoulder and he banged into the boards." Balfour vowed payback against Brewer and was to exact his revenge two years later.

"I don't know why there was no major penalty on the play," huffed Pilous. "There was intent to injure and blood. [Referee Frank] Udvari apparently thought it was tomato juice!"

Between periods, Ward Cornell chatted with Max Bentley, who had played for both Toronto and Chicago during his Hall of Fame career. "I guess I'll cheer for the Leafs in Toronto and the Hawks in Chicago," he told the viewing audience. "Actually, I guess I'm for Toronto. I'm always feuding with my brother Doug. He sticks with the Hawks and I stay with the Leafs."

Referee Frank Udvari waved off a Stan Mikita goal in the second period, and Coach Pilous was incensed. "I think Udvari blew his whistle too quickly," he bellowed. The second period of game two went scoreless.

As if to make up for earlier indiscretions, Referee Udvari waved off a third-period goal by Eddie Litzenberger of the Leafs, claiming his stick was too high. Later, Ron Stewart nabbed a clearing pass from Dollard St. Laurent, deked both him and defence partner Jack Evans, then slid the puck to Frank Mahovlich, who made no mistake and put the Leafs up by two.

Chicago roared back. Ken Wharram of the Hawks passed from behind the net to Ab McDonald in the slot. McDonald's shot dinged off the crossbar, but Mikita, who had circled from behind the net, pounced on the puck and shoved it into the Toronto net.

The *Toronto Daily Star* claimed that "George Armstrong played his finest game as a Leaf. He controlled the puck as if it were attached to his stick by a string." Midway through the third, Armstrong backhanded the puck high over Glenn Hall to give the Leafs their third goal. Mikita responded with his second goal at 18:27 of the third, slapping a rebound past Bower. Incidentally, both Mikita markers were scored with Davey Keon on the bench, and Leafs' coach Punch Imlach vowed that from that period on, he'd match the two star centres in order to stop Mikita's production.

As if Frank Udvari didn't have enough scorn to shoulder, in the third period, Frank Mahovlich was in the clear and reaching for the puck when Elmer Vasko pulled him down. Punch Imlach was livid, waving his fedora as if he was fanning a bonfire. Toronto players demanded a penalty shot, but Udvari resisted, standing firm in assessing a simple minor to Moose.

"I wasn't very happy about the officiating, but it would be a mistake to say it won or lost the game," stated Pierre Pilote.

"That was an extremely important win for the Toronto Maple Leafs tonight," said Foster Hewitt in his analysis of the game. "It wasn't just the fact that they won the game, but it was the way that they did it."

Max Bentley selected the game's Three Stars. George Armstrong was the first Star, Frank Mahovlich the second and Glenn Hall was the third Star. "Glenn Hall was sensational," wrote the *Star*. "His work was mainly responsible for keeping the score to a 3–2 count for the Leafs."

"We were skating well but the puck didn't roll for us," commented Rudy Pilous. "I thought we came back well from the other loss but we haven't quite reached that necessary point. I'm sure we'll get back in stride on our home ice."

Hall the Hero as Hawks Blank Leafs

Game Three, Stanley Cup Final – Sunday, April 15, 1962

After losing two in Toronto, Chicago vowed they would return home and "knock the Leafs loose from their skate rivets and outscore them at the same time," according to the *Daily Star*. Rudy Pilous said, "There are a lot of guys on the Leafs playing way above their ability."

Both lineups for game three, played in Chicago, were altered. Murray Balfour was medically cleared to play after suffering a concussion, although Gerry Melnyk dressed in case Balfour's headaches lingered. Balfour sported a leather helmet in game three. Bert Olmstead, who had been out for five weeks nursing a broken shoulder suffered in Chicago on March 11, dressed and was back in the Toronto lineup, adding veteran savvy to the contest.

Bruising bodychecks by the Hawks dictated the tempo of the game. Bobby Hull and Bob Baun continued their feud, hitting each other at every opportunity. "Bobby Hull and I used to run at each other like two bull moose in rut," mentioned Baun, recalling that the two had battled on-ice since they were twelve or thirteen years old. "He was always playing left wing and I was on right defence."

Dollard St. Laurent rocked Dave Keon with his head down, spinning him to the ice with a solid bodycheck. After that, the *Daily Star* claimed, "Leafs attackers moved into the Hawk zone as if skating through a minefield."

Both Toronto and Chicago shadowed their opponent's top gun. Toronto used Eddie Shack and Bob Nevin to blanket Bobby Hull, while Eric Nesterenko was employed to cover Toronto's Frank Mahovlich. At one point, the rowdy Chicago fans attempted to hang Maple Leafs' star Frank Mahovlich in effigy from the stadium's top balcony. The dummy was laughingly removed by chief usher Les Modesti.

Between the first and second periods, Punch Imlach was interviewed by Ward Cornell, and mentioned, "I thought that our team weren't skating as well as what they had in the first two games. Once we start to skate, we'll be a little harder to handle."

Cornell also spoke with retired Hawks' star Doug Bentley ("I'm pulling for Chicago all the way") and Jack Adams, the Wings' GM, who was thoroughly enjoying the contest. "This is a great hockey game, but it's real playoff hockey and that period proved it's the greatest game in the world!"

Stan Mikita opened the scoring at 4:35 of the second period, picking the puck up off Allan Stanley's glove and rifling it past Bower. Four minutes later, with Brewer sitting in the penalty box, Pierre Pilote roared down the wing, flipped the puck past Stanley and onto the stick of Ab McDonald. He avoided a poke check from Bower and tucked the puck into a yawning net.

Down 2–0, Toronto coach Punch Imlach shuffled his lines in the third to get his team going, dropping Red Kelly back to defence and adding Ron Stewart to a line with Keon and Mahovlich. "Our regular lines weren't doing anything and I thought a shuffle might help," he admitted after the game.

Late in the third, with the Leafs' goal empty for the added attacker, Bronco Horvath took a pass from Eric Nesterenko, fired wide but picked up the loose puck and deposited it into the net to cement the victory. Dick Duff argued vehemently that Nesterenko had carried the puck in his hand past a Leaf defender, but it was to no avail. In fact, referee Powers assigned a misconduct to Duff. "[Nesterenko] skated right by me with the puck in his hand, from behind his blue line almost to the red line," explained Duff, still fuming after the game. "Powers said he didn't see it. What the hell was he looking at?"

Following the shutout, George Armstrong admitted, "We didn't play well. You have to skate to beat the Hawks and we weren't moving." Punch Imlach waxed philosophical after the loss. "It's not like motors where you push a button and the lights come on. But hell, you get beat, you give the guy who beat you a little credit. At no time did we control this game. You only succeed in hockey through hard work. We didn't work at the job and the Hawks beat us to the puck all evening."

Meanwhile, the Hawks were much more pleased with this effort than they had been with their play in Toronto. "My defence played a wonderful game. They gave everything that little extra effort," stated Glenn Hall. "Jack Evans broke up two dangerous plays while lying flat on the ice after being knocked down."

"I notice that Shack didn't get on the ice until Toronto was behind 2–0," snarled Coach Pilous. "And he didn't even play in the first two games of the series. So why does he become so valuable when Leafs are behind? I'll tell you why! Imlach sent him out there to try to rough up some of our players. He knew the game was lost so he told the 'Wild Bull of the Pampas' [Shack] to take a run at our guys." Shack picked up three minors, but failed to ignite his team.

The Three Stars of the game, as chosen by Gump Worsley, were Glenn Hall, Johnny Bower and Dollard St. Laurent. Foster Hewitt's comments included, "The Chicago Black Hawks went on that ice with all the determination Rudy Pilous said they would on Chicago ice." He added, "I thought that Johnny Bower played a tremendous game in goal to keep that score in reasonable proportion."

Pilous cautioned, "We can still play better. It's going to be a tough haul but I won't mind as long as we win that last game. We still have to prove that we can win on Toronto ice."

Clarence Campbell, the NHL's president, was angered by Chicago's public-address announcer, Bob Foster, who he believed was "acting like a cheerleader." Foster introduced Glenn Hall simply as "Mr. Goalie" and Eric Nesterenko as "Swoop." Later, following Mikita's goal, Foster detailed that it was the centre's seventeenth point of the playoffs, just three shy of an NHL playoff record. "The public-address system is a part of the game," Campbell stated in his reprimand of Foster. "The announcer is, in effect, a game official. He must act impartially at all times. To act like a cheerleader is completely wrong. The public-address system can be an obvious public menace if it isn't handled correctly." The Hawks' GM Tommy Ivan said the team would comply with the president's ruling.

Gump Worsley suggested that the NHL should clamp down on the organist instead of the public-address announcer. "He stirs the crowd up more than the announcer when he plays music to every Hawk bodycheck," said Gump. The crowd never got tired of the organist playing 'Three Blind Mice' every time the referee and two linesmen take to the ice prior to a game.

With the victory, the Black Hawks got back into the series. "Chicago too good to lose four straight," declared the *Toronto Daily Star*.

Bower Injured in Leafs' Loss

Game Four, Stanley Cup Final – Tuesday, April 17, 1962

The Black Hawks evened the series by defeating Toronto 4–1 that evening in Chicago, but the Leafs lost more than the game. They also lost their star goaltender.

During the first period, Bill Hewitt's play-by-play suggested that Johnny Bower "did the splits" when he grasped for a Bobby Hull drive that was ticketed for the open corner of the Toronto net. "It's one of the fastest shots I've seen since I've been up here in this league," Bower explained to the *Hockey Night in Canada* viewers. "I really had to move fast for it; I didn't really know I could move that fast," he said with a chuckle. In his autobiography, *The China Wall*, Johnny explained further. "I stretched to get my foot behind my glove, to give the glove some backing. If I'd missed it, it would have gone in." The Leafs' netminder trapped the puck and saved the goal, but in doing so, felt a snap in his left leg. "I thought all the muscles were going right up to my stomach, the way it felt."

Bower continued playing for several minutes, including allowing a Chicago goal that saw Bobby Hull pick a Mikita pass out of the air and fire it into the Leafs' goal to open the scoring. But with just over five minutes remaining in the first period, George Armstrong skated over to the crease and spoke to his goaltender. Bower recalled, "He came up to me and said, 'Punch says you're not doing too well with your lateral movement and you're not moving around too fast.' I said, 'I'm okay, really I am.'" But when Imlach threatened Bower with a $500 fine (it was actually $25), the response was different. "I think I broke the world's record going to the bench!"

In actuality, Bower skated gingerly to the Leafs' bench and indicated to Imlach that he was unable to continue. *Hockey Night in Canada* viewers heard the public-address announcer summon the Leafs' spare goaltender: "Mr. Don Simmons. Don Simmons. Please report to the Leafs' dressing room." Simmons was dressed in civilian clothes and had been watching the activity from the stands.

According to *The Globe and Mail*, Don Simmons was "considered a fringe NHL goaltender by most." The *Chicago Tribune* concurred, adding, "Simmons has a glaring weakness known to every player in the league." The newspaper claimed that Simmons struggled with shots to his stick side. "That is why he failed to make the grade with the Boston Bruins and why he is a minor league goalie." The *Toronto Daily Star* also weighed in. "The rap against Simmons is that he is a good mechanical netminder but not a fiery competitor. Simmons wears a mask, following the example of Montreal's Jacques Plante. He had fractured a cheekbone while playing for Rochester in the AHL."

In June 1961, Punch Imlach had been criticized when he protected Simmons and left Cesare Maniago expendable in the NHL's Intra-League Draft. Maniago was quickly picked up by the Montreal Canadiens. "I see no reason why Simmons can't handle the goaltending assignment if Bower is out," said Imlach at that time.

The *Toronto Daily Star* later decreed that spare goalies should be dressed with the rest of the team, eliminating the need to stop the game while the netminder, sitting in the stands in civilian clothes, heads to the dressing room to pull on his equipment. The statement came as a result of the delay while Simmons changed into his gear. In this contest, the teams retired to their dressing rooms to conclude the first period and 5:20 was added to the start of the second period. The last time a netminder had been called out of the stands to replace an injured teammate in a Stanley Cup final was in 1953, when on April 11, Boston's "Sugar Jim" Henry was injured and replaced by Gordon "Red" Henry.

Commenting on the loss of Bower, Red Burnett of the *Toronto Daily Star* wrote, "This could be the end of the ancient's great career."

During the intermission, Tom Johnson of the Montreal Canadiens compared the defence corps of the two teams. "Tonight, Baun and Brewer have been a little more effective. They were bodychecking well, blocking shots and clearing the puck well."

Don Simmons, wearing Bower's number 1, led the Maple Leafs onto the ice to start the second period. Just prior to Bower's injury, Bobby Hull had picked a Mikita pass out of the air and fired it into the Leafs' goal to draw first blood. Bobby Hull quickly scored his second goal of the game on a power play at the forty-six-second mark, blasting a rocket past Simmons in the Leafs' net. Stafford Smythe, president of the Toronto Maple Leafs, had stood behind the bench with Imlach until Hull's second goal, then retreated to a seat. The second period ended with the Hawks leading 2–1, Toronto's goal a power-play marker into the top left corner by Red Kelly.

Ward Cornell conducted a fascinating interview with Roy Edwards between the second and third period. Paralleling Simmons in the Toronto goal, Edwards, also a southpaw, was the spare netminder for the Black Hawks during the Stanley Cup final, a role he had filled the previous year as well, getting his name engraved on the Stanley Cup as a result. Edwards divulged a secret during the *Hockey Night in Canada* broadcast. "Reggie Fleming has been practising a shot along the ice on my stick side, which is the same side as Donny Simmons. I hold the stick in my left hand and catch with my right and so does Simmons." Fleming would score in that exact manner later in that game.

Frank Selke Jr. spoke with Al Arbour, the fifth Leafs' defenceman who was being used sparingly in the final. Arbour and Ed Litzenberger had both been members of the Chicago Black Hawks when they won the Stanley Cup in 1961. Litzenberger, who had been the Hawks' captain, was traded to Detroit in June 1961, then was claimed on waivers by Toronto from Detroit on December 29, 1961. Arbour was claimed by Toronto from Chicago in the Intra-League Draft in June 1961.

With Allan Stanley scrambling to get back into the play after sitting out a minor, Reggie Fleming scored at 7:31 of the third. The red light did not go on, but the goal judge ruled that Fleming pushed Simmons' hand and the puck into the goal. Toronto protested wildly. The goal judge stated it was clearly a goal, but the official timer had stopped the clock too early in anticipation of a whistle, and in doing so, automatically cut off power to the goal light. At centre ice for the faceoff, Bob Pulford made a disparaging remark and was sent to the penalty box with a misconduct. Reg Fleming scored a fourth goal for Chicago, who finished with a decisive 4–1 victory, and the series tied at two.

For his efforts, Fleming was named the first Star of the game, with Bob Nevin and Stan Mikita falling in as Stars two and three.

"Hawks' three additional goals could not be blamed on Simmons," wrote *The Globe*. "He played with his usual dexterity, but this was one game the Hawks were determined to win regardless of who happened to be in the Leafs' goal." Simmons wasn't happy with his game. "I didn't play as well as I wanted to," he told the *Toronto Daily Star*. "You can't sit out for a month and expect to be ready because no practice is ever like a game. It's just a matter of getting the feel, that's all."

Johnny Bower was resting overnight in Chicago's Swedish Covenant Hospital with a pulled hamstring.

Rudy Pilous was concerned that the Leafs might rally behind Bower's injury. "I don't know if Bower will play in Toronto on Thursday, but if he doesn't, the Leafs may be more inspired and just that much tougher. They will play better defensively as a team to help him [Simmons]." Imlach appeared to have no qualms about his substitute netminder. "Simmons is a good goalie and has a good playoff record."

Bobby Hull tagged the conversations, showing confidence in the Hawks' momentum. "If we can retain our strength, and I'm sure we will, we'll win in Toronto." Tim Horton responded, "We'll take over again in Toronto. We've come too far to fold."

Simmons Stars as Leafs Dump Chicago

Game Five, Stanley Cup Final – Thursday, April 19, 1962

The series moved to Toronto for game five, and while pundits decried the possibility of Simmons returning to the goal for Toronto, suggesting that freezing Bower's injured leg was a better choice than a second-rate netminder, Punch Imlach made the choice to take to the ice with Simmons. In addition, Toronto benched Ed Litzenberger in favour of dressing defenceman Al Arbour. Toronto enjoyed an offensive bonanza in game five, doubling Chicago 8–4.

Hockey Night in Canada viewers were informed that Toronto coach Punch Imlach had such a severe case of the flu that after game four in Chicago, he stretched out in the aisle of the plane as it returned to Toronto. Nevertheless, he was behind the bench for the Maple Leafs for the fifth game of the final.

Bob Pulford opened the scoring at the seventeen-second mark, dribbling a backhand through Hall's feet. Seventeen minutes later, Pulford scored a second, putting the puck over Hall's glove on a long shot.

The Hawks roared back, scoring two more unanswered goals, both by Ab McDonald, to start the second. Stan Mikita assisted on both of McDonald's game five tallies. That second point set two NHL records — most assists in a playoff year (fifteen, one more than Boston's Fleming Mackell in 1958) and points in a playoff year (twenty-one, one better than Gordie Howe in 1955 for the Detroit Red Wings).

Both teams seemed to have found the Achilles heel of their opponent's netminder — Glenn Hall in the Chicago goal was having difficulty with rising shots to his glove side. Don Simmons was struggling with shots low to his stick side.

Billy Harris tied the score, deflecting a shot from the point by Tim Horton. Dave Keon made a spectacular rush on the power play, dishing off to Horton inside the Chicago blue line. Horton's shot went wide, but Mahovlich snatched the puck and tried to jam it in. In the scuffle, Keon darted in and poked the puck past Hall from the lip of the crease. Mahovlich scored just before the second period concluded, from the lip of the crease. Toronto went up 5–3 when Red Kelly stripped Bobby Hull of the puck, getting the puck to Mahovlich, who scored on a good second effort just before the second period concluded.

George Armstrong deflected a shot from Carl Brewer past Hall to open the scoring in the third period. Mahovlich fired a scorcher delivered with such velocity that he fell to the ice as he scored his second goal of the night, putting the Leafs up 7–3. Bob Turner, on a penalty kill, broke through centre and used Horton as a screen, firing the puck past Simmons. Pulford then scored the final goal of the game, his third, with Pierre Pilote serving an elbowing penalty.

Doug Harvey picked the Three Stars, and selected Bob Pulford, Ab McDonald and Dave Keon. Kudos also went to Bert Olmstead, who was digging the puck out of the corners in his usual style, and seemed to inspire his teammates, especially Bob Pulford. "The first game Olmstead came back, I scored three goals in that game," Pulford reminisced. "He went into the corners and he just knew he was going to come out with the puck. That was probably one of the best games I ever saw him play."

"They say a team that won't be beaten, can't be beaten, and that was the story of the Toronto Maple Leafs tonight," offered Foster Hewitt in his post-game remarks. "That was the most impressive win and performance of the Maple Leaf team, not only this year, but in many years in a playoff."

"It was a tense evening of hockey with players of both teams ready to forget the principles of the game and resort to the back-alley tactics that disgraced the fourth game in Chicago on Tuesday night," wrote *The Globe and Mail.* Boisterous Leafs' fans, mimicking the Chicago faithful, pelted the ice with eggs on several occasions during the lopsided win.

The game turned even uglier. Angry fans attacked Chicago equipment manager Walter "Gunzo" Humeniuk after he hit a Toronto supporter who was baiting Stan Mikita and Ab McDonald. "It was my fault," admitted Gunzo. "He was riding Mikita and some of the players and I asked him to quit. He kept it up so I hit him. I think we talked him out of pressing charges."

Leafs Break Curse of Barilko; Win First Cup Since 1951

Game Six, Stanley Cup Final – Sunday, April 22, 1962

It wouldn't be a playoff series without the obligatory cliches, but with the Toronto Maple Leafs up three games to two, the backs of the Chicago Black Hawks were clearly up against the wall. The series returned to rowdy Chicago Stadium for game six of the 1962 Stanley Cup final. The Maple Leafs, able to collect the Stanley Cup with a win that evening, hoped to have lightning strike twice — they had won the Stanley Cup on April 22, 1945, beginning what was to be the franchise's first dynasty.

While injured Johnny Bower insisted on watching the game on television, too nervous to watch from the stands, Don Simmons returned to the crease for Toronto again in game six, and kicked out all but one shot for the Leafs. The ten-foot shot from Bobby Hull on a Murray Balfour pass from behind the Toronto net eluded Simmons on his stick side, breaking a scoreless tie at the 8:56 mark of the game. With 11:05 remaining in the third period. 16,666 Black Hawks' fans erupted and rained a shower of debris onto the ice surface. While organist Al Melgard provided a soundtrack to the mayhem, the maintenance crew collected the various programs, hats and boots. "Joy reigned unrestrained," wrote The *Chicago Tribune*.

But the break in the action disrupted the Black Hawks' momentum, a fact later confirmed by several members of the team.

The Maple Leafs stormed back. Less than two minutes later, Bobby Baun took a shot from the point. Frank Mahovlich picked up the rebound and passed it to Bob Nevin, who drove an eight-foot shot easily into the back of the Hawks' net, knotting the score at one apiece. "That was probably the most gratifying goal of my career," he later recalled. "I was just lucky enough to be in the right spot and get the tying goal." In his book, *The Big M,* Frank Mahovlich remembers the play well. "I thought I made a real good play in that game. I could see Bobby Nevin out of the corner of my eye at centre and I gave him the pass. He fired it into the net and scored the tying goal."

Three minutes later, Nevin broke into the clear but was hooked by Chicago's Eric Nesterenko. While the Leafs argued for a penalty shot,

Nesterenko was sent to the penalty box by referee Frank Udvari, who called a minor penalty. On the ensuing power play, Tim Horton sent a shot at the Hawks' net. Hall made the save, but the rebound caromed out to Dick Duff, who over skated the puck, swung at it and missed, but on a second try connected on his backhand, and at 14:14 of the third, tucked the puck behind Hall. Dick Duff, who had been at fault on Hull's goal, called the go-ahead marker, which turned out to be the Stanley Cup-clinching goal, "the biggest goal I ever scored."

Tim Horton took a penalty with ninety seconds left in the game. With a minute remaining in regulation, Rudy Pilous motioned for goaltender Hall to come off the ice in favour of an extra attacker, but Toronto's defence blanketed the Hawks, and they were unable to tie the score. "We went into our defensive mode for the last five minutes, and I don't think they had a single scoring chance the rest of the way," recalled Bob Baun in *Lowering the Boom*. "Ronnie Stewart and Bob Pulford were the penalty killers, but Punch tapped us," remembered Keon, referring to himself and Nevin. "We went out with Baun and Brewer. We were second-year guys, but after we killed that penalty, we felt we were part of it, that this was his [Punch Imlach's] way of telling us we had finally arrived as Leafs." Both Keon and Nevin regard those final ninety seconds as their personal highlight from the era.

The seconds dragged like decades to the Leafs, but as the final buzzer sounded, Don Simmons sprinted from his crease into the arms of his teammates, who had poured over the boards to mob him. The Toronto Maple Leafs had won the Stanley Cup! The first since 1951! They had defeated the reigning Stanley Cup champion Chicago Black Hawks!

At the conclusion of the game, George Armstrong noticed the puck lying in the corner and grabbed it, vowing to display it in a hotel he owned in Hamilton. Armstrong also made certain coach Punch Imlach was included in the on-ice celebration.

One by one, the Leafs retreated down the stairs to their dressing room — Olmstead, Simmons, Litzenberger (who was not dressed for the game), Keon, Baun, Mahovlich. The team was quickly summoned back to the ice for the formal Stanley Cup presentation. Billy Harris hurried to get his camera and missed the team photograph with the Cup. As Johnny Bower emerged, with most of his pads removed, organist Al Melgard began playing "Old Soldiers Never Die," and Bower's teammates chided him.

Clarence Campbell, the NHL president, was booed as he stepped out onto the ice, but after George Armstrong accepted the Stanley Cup, the fans gave the new Stanley Cup champions a very warm round of applause. Bobby Hull orchestrated a haphazard line of Hawks congratulating the victors. The organist played "That Old Gang of Mine" and "Auld Lang Syne," as the Leafs celebrated on-ice with the Stanley Cup.

Following a brief on-ice celebration, which included the captain handing the Stanley Cup to his teammates, Armstrong carried the Cup down the stairs to the visitors' dressing room, then sat the trophy in the corner, where he and Dickie Duff laughed in celebration.

Television viewers were not able to witness much of the celebration. The Stanley Cup had barely left the ice when Ward Cornell conducted brief interviews with Dave Keon and Punch Imlach, and with that, *Hockey Night in Canada* concluded for another season.

"[The] Leafs proved that they're the kind of battlers who swim upstream," declared the *Toronto Daily Star*. "The ancient basin probably has been won by greater teams, but never has gone to a gamer one!"

In an article written for the *Toronto Daily Star*, George Armstrong commented, "I've been playing organized hockey since I was 10 or 11. That's 20 or 21 years in the sport. In all that time, it's been my one and only aim to play for a Stanley Cup team. Every player feels the same. Outside of four fellows — Red Kelly, Bert Olmstead, Al Arbour and Eddie Litzenberger — none of us had made it before. As a matter of fact, we hadn't even come close. We're very happy and consider ourselves very fortunate."

Using Armstrong's nickname, Conn Smythe stated, "The Chief is the best captain, as a captain, that the Leafs ever have had."

1961–62 Playoff Scoring

RK	NUMBER	PLAYER	POS	AGE	GP	G	A	PTS	PIM
1	7	Tim Horton	D	32	12	3	13	16	16
2	9	Dick Duff	LW	25	12	3	10	13	20
3	10	George Armstrong	RW	31	12	7	5	12	2
4	27	Frank Mahovlich	LW	24	12	6	6	12	29
5	4	Red Kelly	D/C	34	12	4	6	10	0
6	20	Bob Pulford	LW	25	12	7	1	8	24
7	14	Dave Keon	C	21	12	5	3	8	0
8	12	Ron Stewart	RW	29	11	1	6	7	4
9	11	Bob Nevin	RW	23	12	2	4	6	6
10	15	Billy Harris	C	26	12	2	1	3	2
11	21	Bob Baun	D	25	12	0	3	3	19
12	26	Allan Stanley	D	35	12	0	3	3	6
13	2	Carl Brewer	D	23	8	0	2	2	22
14	25	Ed Litzenberger	C/RW	29	10	0	2	2	4
15	16	Bert Olmstead	LW	35	4	0	1	1	0
16	3	Al Arbour	D	29	8	0	0	0	6
17	1	Johnny Bower	G	37	10	0	0	0	0
18	24	Johnny MacMillan	RW	26	3	0	0	0	0
19	23	Eddie Shack	LW	24	9	0	0	0	18
20	1	Don Simmons	G	30	3	0	0	0	0
				TEAM TOTALS	12	40	66	106	178

Playoff Netminding

RK	NUMBER	PLAYER	POS	AGE	GP	MIN	W	L	GA	GAA	SO
1	1	Johnny Bower	G	37	10	579	6	3	20	2.07	0
2	1	Don Simmons	G	30	3	165	2	1	8	2.91	0
				TEAM TOTALS	12	744	8	4	28	2.26	0

Bob Baun looked around the dressing room, a huge smile cemented to his face. "Bert Olmstead, the 'windmill,' sat quietly in his chair," Baun recalled in his autobiography. "Of course, he'd been here before; this was his fifth Stanley Cup victory. He was shaking his head, as if he thought we could have done better. That image left an impression on me, and I believe all of us, for the rest of our lives." Baun recalled that Olmstead was almost dismissive of the win, reminding the Leafs, "You guys haven't won anything yet!" Coming from a player who was enjoying his fifth Cup championship (three of which had come as part of the Montreal Canadiens' dynasty of five consecutive championships between 1956 and 1960), the words caught the team off guard, but for many, resounded deep within them.

Bert Olmstead's role as de facto assistant coach for the Maple Leafs can't be understated. During the playoffs, he often reprimanded players who were less than serious. "Cut out the fooling around; we're in a Stanley Cup series," he told Eddie Shack at one point. And his temper wasn't reserved solely for teammates. "Harold Ballard came down and I can remember Bert Olmstead being upset at it," said Baun. "You never saw Ballard and all of a sudden, you see him right when we're about to win the Stanley Cup. He was coming into the dressing room, patting guys on the back before the game and Olmstead told him off."

"Wow, what a great feeling! That was a dream come true, a childhood dream to have my name engraved on the Stanley Cup," recalled Billy Harris in *The Glory Years*.' "I remember looking at Bert Olmstead and Dave Keon. Bert, at age thirty-five, was subdued, tired, hurting and relieved that it was over. Dave had just turned twenty-two and was elated, energetic, and his boyish smile revealed that a dream had come true for him. Bert never again put on his hockey equipment. Dave played for another twenty seasons."

Harris reflected on Olmstead's role. "The day before we won our first Stanley Cup, we flew to Chicago and checked into the LaSalle Hotel around eight-thirty p.m. About nine of us walked two blocks to the Morrison Hotel, entered the bar and ordered a round of beer. After one beer, we got up to leave when Bert ordered us to sit down, saying, 'Let's have one more. We'll sleep better.' Twenty-four hours later, we won our first Stanley Cup; Bert, his fifth and last. I can still see Bert after our championship game sitting in the dressing room at the Chicago Stadium in his wet underwear, wearing an expression on his face of absolute satisfaction that we had accomplished what we had set out to accomplish, and puffing on his cigarette."

Olmstead had been a fixture on Montreal's Stanley Cup-winning teams, and when Montreal left the thirty-two-year-old Olmstead unprotected in the Intra-League Draft, Toronto was ecstatic to receive the wily veteran. It was deemed that Olmstead could assist the Leafs' young centremen, could act as the team's enforcer as well as be employed to shadow Gordie Howe, and time proved that Olmstead did all three.

Olmstead was a vociferous leader in the dressing room and was used to winning with Montreal, and he became increasingly frustrated with the Leafs. It was reported that Olmstead was going to leave the team early in his first year with Toronto. At one point, there was a dressing room tiff when Olmstead told Frank Mahovlich that he didn't care for his lackadaisical effort, and the two almost came to blows.

Later, when Eddie Shack played on Olmstead's line, Shack crashed into Olmstead on the ice. Bert grabbed Shack's sweater and asked what colour it was then asked what colour his own sweater was. Olmstead's confrontational methods did do the things that he was brought to Toronto for — he helped the Leafs' centremen, primarily Pulford; he did the policing and fought battles for the Leafs and he did cover Gordie Howe and others.

When Punch Imlach fired Billy Reay and took over as coach, he went to Olmstead to ask if he would still play for him, in spite of his closeness to the former coach. When assured he would, Punch made Olmstead an assistant coach and had him run the occasional practice. Olmstead, however, quit the position, as he felt he wasn't consulted enough.

Olmstead's leadership was credited with helping bring a winning atmosphere to the Leafs. Toronto made the playoffs on the last game of the season in 1959 and went on to win the Stanley Cup in 1962. When the Leafs won the Cup in 1962, Olmstead let his victorious teammates know that they really hadn't won anything yet. The ultimate goal was a dynasty!

Olmstead was left unprotected in the draft that summer, and much to the veteran's chagrin, the Rangers picked him up. The bitter Olmstead had felt that he would be the successor to Imlach as Leafs' coach at some point. But the fighting spirit that Olmstead exhibited from his first moments as a Leaf rubbed off on his teammates, and eventually, the Leafs did become the dynasty that Olmstead knew they were capable of becoming.

Rudy Pilous, Chicago's coach, was angry that his Hawks were unable to pull out the victory. "We should have stayed in front once we got there," he told *The Tribune*. "We should have protected the lead." Although disappointed with the result, Pilous was still pleased with the effort of his team and acknowledged his opponents. "We played six very tough games against Montreal and six more against Toronto. They played well when they had to and certainly deserve to win."

Pilous found his way through the crowd and waded into the Leafs' room, shaking hands with the victors one by one. "Hey, Big M," he said, shaking Mahovlich's hand. Frank replied, "How are you, Rudy?"

"Not so good tonight," came the reply.

Mahovlich remembered not really knowing what to do after winning the Cup. "The game is over and everything is done," he recalled in his biography. "I went down to the [dressing] room and they brought the Stanley Cup there. I had never lifted it up. It was so light that I decided to pick it up over my head. While I had it over my head, a guy clicked a photo and it made the front page of the paper. It's a great memory."

Asked to what he attributed the Leafs' victory, Punch pointed to his three centres. "Dave Keon, Bob Pulford and Red Kelly — those three are better than any three of the Hawks, and I'm including Stan Mikita in there."

This Stanley Cup final established an NHL record with eighty-seven penalties assessed over the six games. It had been a tough series between two tough competitors. Ron Stewart had barely been able to play, with ribs bruised so badly that they had to be frozen. Bob Pulford played five games with a shoulder frozen to erase the pain. "We didn't want to say anything when the series was going on," said Coach Imlach.

Pulford recalled the intense pain he faced daily. "I tore all the muscles out of my shoulder and they froze it two and three times a game," he remembered. "I wouldn't get frozen until after the warm-up, and then they'd freeze me and I'd have to go, sometimes midway through the second period, and get frozen again. The first time they did it, I remember going home that night and crying, it was so painful after the freezing came out. In those days, it was all about winning. It was the type of team we had. I went to see the doctor and as long as I wasn't going to do any permanent damage to myself, there was no reason not to do it, so I had it frozen all the time."

"This club had the ability, guts and desire that go to make up a championship team," boasted Imlach. "I called them to win the Stanley Cup back in September and they didn't let me down. I knew when they skated out for the game that they'd come back winners. You could sense it. We just outplayed them, and we couldn't be denied."

"Imlach may not be the best coach in the world, but at least you know where you stand with him," Tim Horton told the *Daily Star*. "Imlach will chew you out for an error, but you're back the next shift. You have to play in this league to know what this does for your confidence."

Not everyone was quite so complimentary of the coach. One of the Leafs' directors tried to convince Imlach to allow the team to stay over in Chicago to enjoy the celebration, but Punch refused, threatening Eddie Shack that he'd be abandoned if he wasn't ready for the trip to the airport. Shack recalled the threat in his book, *Clear the Track*. "When we won the first Cup, we were in Chicago Stadium wahooin' and having a beer in the downstairs dressing room, and Imlach comes in all cranky and pissed off, like we just lost. Then he says, 'If you aren't on the goddamned bus in fifteen minutes, you won't be on this team next year!' No congratulations, no 'Nice goin'' or anything. What a crabby bastard. He couldn't even loosen up and have a beer with us!"

The Leafs' plane touched down at Malton International Airport (today known as Pearson) at 3:30 in the morning, and was greeted by two thousand fans, including a kilted bagpiper and two trumpeters, who forced their way into the customs area as the team was going through the immigration ritual. A chant of "Go Leafs Go," smothered the area. "We were overwhelmed by the tremendous reception we were given at the airport," commented George Armstrong. "At that hour of night, the whole place was jammed with people. It meant a great deal to us and we appreciated it very much indeed!"

Punch Imlach emerged carrying the Stanley Cup through the crowded airport. Extra police had been assigned to crowd control, although there were no reported problems. The Stanley Cup was carried high over the crowd as the fans surged to touch it. The Cup was placed in a police cruiser for safekeeping, and the fans returned to the arrivals area to greet their heroes.

As the players emerged, they were hoisted onto the shoulders of fans. Dick Duff, one of the first to be lifted from his feet, waved the Stanley Cup winning goal stick he clutched as a memento. While several players, including George Armstrong, Billy Harris and Bob Nevin were hoisted, several players, including Frank Mahovlich, Bert Olmstead, Bob Pulford and Ron Stewart, didn't emerge from the main door and were able to slide away undetected. Allan Stanley and Johnny Bower stopped for some time to sign autographs.

George Armstrong presented the puck used by Dick Duff to score the Stanley Cup winning goal to Dodo Imlach, the coach's wife, who was there with a number of other players' wives to greet the team at the airport. "Mrs. Imlach asked for it two weeks ago," he mentioned. "She said she wanted the puck that won the Stanley Cup, and I said I'd see that she got it. I know that goal meant as much to Punch as it did us…maybe more." Armstrong also had the final puck used in the game, which he intended to display in a hotel he owned in Hamilton.

That night, Imlach took the Stanley Cup home to Scarborough. The intent was for it to later be placed on display in the lobby of Maple Leaf Gardens. "That's providing they can get it away from me," laughed the coach. "I don't feel like letting it go."

The players got some sleep, and then attended a victory celebration on Monday, April 23, at the Etobicoke home of Stafford and Dorothea

Smythe. Stafford and partners Harold Ballard and John Bassett, the new owners of the Toronto Maple Leafs Hockey Club, had struck gold in their first season of ownership, and were ready to celebrate along with the team and valued employees. Several players were missing —- Don Simmons and Allan Stanley were unable to attend and Bert Olmstead had returned to his farm in Saskatchewan.

"Bert had his station wagon half packed before the last game, and the next morning he pointed his car west and headed back to Saskatchewan, because he had a lot of work to do at his wheat farm in Sceptre," recalled Billy Harris. But that posed a problem for the Maple Leafs, as they were scheduled to have the team photo taken with the Stanley Cup that next day. "What the Leafs did for that particular team picture was get the office boy, that year it happened to be Bill Collins, who played briefly in the NHL, and had him come down and dress up in a Leaf uniform, sit in the front row and have his picture taken. But in the official team picture, they transposed Bert Olmstead's head onto Bill Collins's body, so that in the team picture, you're looking at Bert Olmstead's head but not his body. It's a bit of an embarrassment to an organization to have a team picture and not have a prominent member of the team in the picture. Because of Bert, the official team picture was always taken very early in the playoffs, usually during the first playoff series, just to avoid any absentees."

Although a Stanley Cup party was no place to decide on the team's future, Stafford Smythe was already thinking strategically about the years ahead. "I'm not in favour of tampering with success," he stated. "My only concern is Imlach's health. If he tells me he's working too hard, a coach will come in immediately. Right now, Punch doesn't feel that way. He wants to do both jobs." In the back of his mind, Smythe was already sizing up John Crawford for the coaching position, should the decision need to be made. The long-time Bruin defenceman was coaching the Leafs' AHL affiliate, the Rochester Americans.

Just prior to the party, the National Hockey League announced the bonuses that would be awarded to each of the Maple Leafs. The players earned $750 for finishing second during the regular season, $1,500 for eliminating the New York Rangers in the semi-final, and $1,800 for winning the Stanley Cup. The bonus money would make an appreciable difference to each of the players, but George Armstrong wrote in the *Toronto Daily Star* about a more significant difference. "There's a difference between being an NHL player and being a Stanley Cup champion. I think a lot of fellows grew up, became men, when we won that Cup in Chicago. I know I did!"

Under cloudy skies on a warm Wednesday afternoon, the City of Toronto staged a celebration parade for the Stanley Cup champion Toronto Maple Leafs. The headline of the *Toronto Daily Star* on April 25, 1962 read: "50,000 Cheer Leafs in City Hall Salute."

Led by the Queen's Own Rifles, the ticker tape parade saw each of the Leafs' players seated in a convertible driven up Bay Street from Wellington to City Hall at Queen Street. But the city's police department was caught short-staffed, not anticipating such an enormous crowd and ensuing pandemonium. Only the first four of fifteen convertibles carrying the Stanley Cup champions to City Hall were able to get through the crowd. "It was craziness," recalled Lori Horton in her book, *In Loving Memory — A Tribute to Tim Horton*. "The players had to get out of their cars and walk through Simpson's department store to get to City Hall. The cars just couldn't make it through the crowd anymore."

Standing in his convertible, Eddie Shack danced the Twist, the current sensation spawned by Chubby Checker's hit song. Exuberant fans mobbed the players, pulling their hair and ties and stealing their handkerchiefs. Several of those lining the parade route fainted in the seventy-four-degree heat.

The players and their families were finally able to congregate on the steps of what is now Old City Hall. "We were all up front for the ceremony, but the crowd was so big, the police had to hold them back to protect us," recalled Lori Horton, whose husband Tim likely enjoyed his best period as a hockey player during the 1962 Stanley Cup playoff. On the steps of City Hall, Mayor Nathan Phillips declared Toronto "the hockey capital of the world." At the top of the flagpole fluttered a giant Canadian flag, although this time it was blue and white to honour the hometown heroes. Each player was introduced, but the noise level was so high that the introductions were lost. So many fans were on hand to welcome the conquering heroes that the reception had to be moved from the front steps of city hall to the second-floor council chamber. "I don't think that in the history of Toronto we've had such a large crowd around City Hall," crowed Mayor Nathan Phillips. "This is the greatest reception ever tendered in this city." Metro Chairman William Allen re-marked, "Even the Queen never had a crowd like this." The crowd, esti-mated at more than fifty thousand, was the largest crowd ever to con-gregate at Toronto's city hall.

Mayor Phillips awarded each member of the team and management beautiful gold-plated City of Toronto cufflinks. Each player was then asked to sign the official civic guest book. Eddie Shack, who earlier had danced the twist in his parade car, sat in the mayor's chair during the re-ception. "You've got to learn to relax in this business," he laughed.

Allan Stanley was deeply moved by the reception given to the Leafs that day by the city of Toronto. "You couldn't believe it! Every hockey player knows [that winning the Stanley Cup is the greatest thrill in hock-ey] because he's seen those Stanley Cup parades, like the first one they had in Toronto. You couldn't imagine the experience, just hundreds of thou-sands of people and on to the city hall and that's in your honour. You are a part of the team — that's really something."

Following the enormously successful civic reception, the players, management and staff, along with their families, were treated to a buffet luncheon and photographs with the Stanley Cup back at Maple Leaf Gardens. While there, Stafford Smythe granted each of the Gardens' employees an added week's vacation with pay to thank them for their contributions through the season.

Reflecting back on this first Stanley Cup championship, Bob Baun said, "No matter what we Leaf players did from that day on, our lives would be changed forever. Torontonians are mad about hockey, and that made us ultimate heroes."

Johnny Bower recalled his first championship. "Wow, what a great feeling! That was a dream come true, a childhood dream to have my name engraved on the Stanley Cup."

Tim Horton may very well have been at his playing zenith that season. He led the Leafs in post-season scoring with sixteen points (three goals and thirteen assists), setting an NHL record for most playoff points by a defenceman. After playing for twelve NHL seasons, winning the Stanley Cup was a great reward — and relief — not just for Tim, but for his wife Lori, too. "The actual winning of the Stanley Cup was a very emotional thing for me," she said. "I would have my whole section in tears. I would start to cry and they'd start!"

Like Bower and Horton, Allan Stanley was a veteran who was enjoying his first Stanley Cup victory. After earning catcalls from the Broadway boo-birds while playing in New York, he had bounced back significantly, and was overwhelmed by being part of his first Stanley Cup championship. "The first Cup win is the most exciting thing that happened in my whole career," he claimed. "No matter what money you make out there, you're working for one thing, and that's supremacy in hockey in the NHL. That's represented by the Stanley Cup, and it's something you can't buy, you've got to earn and some people, even with twenty years in the league, have never been on it. There's no excitement like it!"

While it was the first Stanley Cup victory for many members of the team, it was win number five for Red Kelly, who had won the Stanley Cup with the Detroit Red Wings on four earlier occasions.

On June 6, 1962, CBC Television viewers watched with rapt attention as Earl Cameron read the lead story that evening. "The remains of former Toronto Maple Leaf hockey player Bill Barilko have been found in the northern Ontario wilderness. The provincial minister of mines and forests, Mr. (Wilf) Spooner, said tonight that members of his staff had identified the remains of both Mr. Barilko and Dr. Henry Hudson in the wreckage of a seaplane in dense bush forty-five miles north of Cochrane. The two men disappeared on a flight on a fishing trip eleven years ago."

At 8:15 that evening, the plane was positively identified as having belonged to Dr. Hudson. By methodically piecing together parts of the fuselage discovered at the site, they were able to read the letters CF-FXT, the registration assigned to Hudson's Fairchild 24 plane. "The engine was buried in muskeg but most of the fuselage was lying on the surface," reported Joe Shalla, the acting forest protection supervisor, who was one of several at the site following the discovery.

After a horrific decade, starting with the disappearance of Barilko during the summer following his Stanley Cup winning goal, the Toronto Maple Leafs finally began to pull themselves out of their tailspin in 1958–59.

From April 21, 1951, to April 22, 1962, the Toronto Maple Leafs had gone without winning the Stanley Cup. On June 6, 1962, a mere forty-three days after the first Stanley Cup victory since his disappearance, the skeletal remains of Bill Barilko had been found in the impenetrable northern Ontario forest. It was as though a curse had been lifted.

Once the Leafs' winning touch had, at last, been recovered, so too was Bill Barilko.

SLAPSHOTS AND SNAPSHOTS
FROM DREAMS TO DONUTS

Until the National Hockey League Players' Association was established in 1967, making players' wages respectable, most NHL players were forced to take summer employment. Tim Horton had spent summers working in the Smythe gravel pits, but in looking for a job that would follow hockey after his retirement, fell into a career that has become his legacy.

Horton had experimented with several businesses before hitting pay dirt with coffee and donuts. A used-car dealership preceded Horton's venture into fast food. Horton tried his hand at hamburger and chicken restaurants, opening five short-lived outlets.

A Tim Horton Do-Nut shop opened in Toronto in 1963. While the burger and chicken enterprises were failing, the donut market began to fly in southern Ontario. In April 1964, without benefit of fuss or fanfare, a Tim Horton Donut Drive-In opened in a former gas station on Ottawa Street in Hamilton.

Immediately successful, the store capitalized on the donut craze sweeping the province. Coffee was all but an afterthought, contributing only 20 percent to revenues. At that time, coffee and donuts were the only products offered, although there were as many as forty varieties of donuts, including two original creations — the Dutchie and the apple fritter.

A former Hamilton policeman, Ron Joyce, bought the franchise in 1965 and added another later that year. Joyce had learned the fast-food business as a Dairy Queen franchisee. While Tim could only afford to spend one day a week during the hockey season on his outside businesses, he quickly realized that he needed a partner. In stepped Ron Joyce.

"I was working there [in the donut shops] all the time," said Joyce. "Once Tim accepted the fact that I wasn't going to stay there just as an operator, that it had to be more than that, we became partners." Horton and Joyce consummated their business partnership in October 1966. The paperwork was completed, and on December 1, 1966, Ron Joyce joined Tim Horton as partners in Tim Donut Ltd.

In a between-period interview on *Hockey Night in Canada*, Horton was asked by Ward Cornell about plans for retirement. The thirty-eight-year-old Horton answered, "Things are quite hectic these days, trying to combine business with hockey."

Cornell replied, "You're talking about your new donut chain."

"Yes, Tim Hortons Donuts," responded the veteran defenceman. "It's nice of you to let me get a word in about it. If I may..."

"No," Cornell interrupted with a grin.

"Well heck, I'm going to anyway," said Horton, soldiering on. "I'd like to say thanks to all you nice people in Hamilton and Burlington..."

Cornell groaned, and after Horton had thanked each store by city, the host jokingly handed Horton a bill for the publicity. "And we'd like to thank you for paying to be on *Hockey Night in Canada*," he said with a laugh.

By 1970, the first Toronto Tim Hortons opened at Kennedy and Eglinton, in the city's east end.

On February 21, 1974, Tim Horton died in a horrific single-car accident on the highway in St. Catharines. Just forty-four years of age, Horton was still playing hockey, and was returning to Buffalo after his Sabres had been beaten 4–2 by the Maple Leafs in a game in which he was injured but was still selected as one of the game's Stars. "He was hurting too bad to play a regular shift in the third period," recalled Punch Imlach, the Sabres' coach at the time. "We faded without him and lost the game to the Leafs. After the game, he and I took a little walk up Church Street and had what was our last talk. He was down in the dumps because he didn't like to miss a shift and he felt he had cost us the game. I got on the bus with the team. Tim drove the cursed car back to Buffalo. He didn't make it." On his way back to Buffalo at 4:30 the morning of February 21, 1974, Horton lost control of his speeding sports car on the highway near St. Catharines, rolling it several times. He was killed instantly.

At the time of his death, there were forty Tim Hortons Donuts in existence.

"No finer person, teammate or hockey player ever lived," said emotional Leafs' captain, George Armstrong.

Maple Leafs' president Conn Smythe sits in front of his 1957 executive team. Standing left to right are coach Billy Reay, Silver Seven chairman Stafford Smythe and short-termed general manager Howie Meeker. (Imperial Oil–Turofsky/Hockey Hall of Fame)

Howie Meeker, strumming a guitar, is surrounded by his "Crew Cuts" — from left to right: Al MacNeil, Bob Pulford, Pat Hannigan, Bob Baun and Gary Collins.

(Imperial Oil–Turofsky/Hockey Hall of Fame)

Punch Imlach looks on as defenceman Carl Brewer signs his contract before the 1958 season. Contract negotiations and conflicting personalities would later drive a wedge between the two. (Imperial Oil–Turofsky/Hockey Hall of Fame)

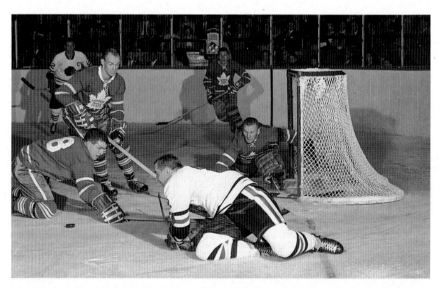

On October 11, 1958, Johnny Bower played his first game as a Maple Leaf, defeating Chicago 3–1. Aided by Carl Brewer (left), a Bower poke check thwarts Danny Lewicki of the Black Hawks. (Imperial Oil–Turofsky/Hockey Hall of Fame)

Frank Mahovlich (centre) scores the overtime winner against Harry Lumley in game four of the 1959 semi-final against the Bruins, giving the miracle Maple Leafs momentum and confidence. Boston's Leo Boivin (20) and Toronto's Bert Olmstead (16) and Gerry Ehman (17), who scored the o/t winner in game three, look on. (Imperial Oil–Turofsky/Hockey Hall of Fame)

Maple Leafs' coach Punch Imlach and veteran Bert Olmstead, briefly a playing assistant coach, take to the blackboard to detail strategy to the team.

(Imperial Oil–Turofsky/Hockey Hall of Fame)

Dave Keon (second from right) learned his craft on the outdoor rinks of Rouyn-Noranda. It is ironic that this Hall of Famer from Quebec was known as a "Hab killer" for his tenacity and prowess against the Montreal Canadiens.

(Courtesy of the Keon family)

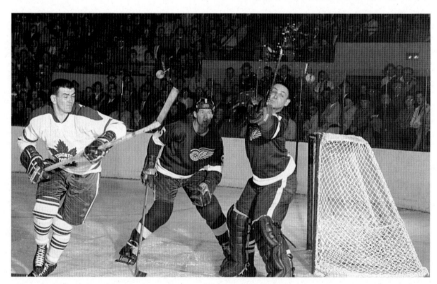

Detroit netminder Terry Sawchuk reaches to knock down a puck as Dave Keon of the Leafs (left) and Warren Godfrey (centre) look on in this semi-final game in March 1961. Godfrey was one of just two players regularly wearing a helmet at that time (Charlie Burns was the other). (Imperial Oil–Turofsky/Hockey Hall of Fame)

Red Kelly, playing his first shift as a Maple Leaf (February 10, 1960), tumbles over Jacques Plante behind the Canadiens' net. Montreal went on to double Toronto 4–2. Minutes earlier, Kelly had been greeted with a thunderous ovation from the fans at Maple Leaf Gardens. (Imperial Oil–Turofsky/Hockey Hall of Fame)

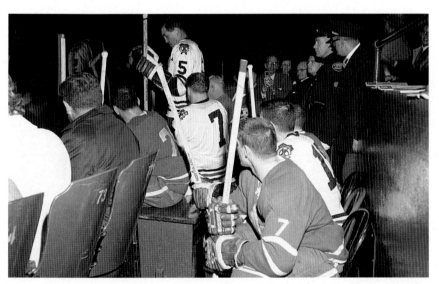

Astonishing to today's fan is the sight of both teams seated in the same penalty box. In game one of the 1962 final, the congested sin bin required additional seating for the overflow crowd, which featured Bobby Hull (7) and Jack Evans (5, standing) of the Black Hawks, and Tim Horton (7) of the Maple Leafs.

(Imperial Oil-Turofsky/Hockey Hall of Fame)

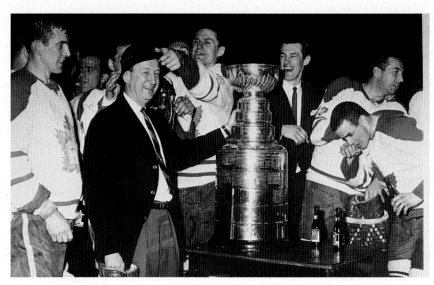

The Maple Leafs celebrate their 1962 Stanley Cup victory, the franchise's first since 1951. Punch Imlach is having his fedora pulled down by Allan Stanley while surrounded (left to right) by Don Simmons, Al Arbour, Ed Litzenberger (in suit), Ron Stewart and Dave Keon. (Imperial Oil–Turofsky/Hockey Hall of Fame)

Flanked by owners Harold Ballard and Stafford Smythe, Leafs' captain George Armstrong waves to the crowd while clutching hockey's greatest prize during the 1962 Stanley Cup parade. (Graphic Artists/Hockey Hall of Fame)

Scrawled on hotel stationery, this note confirmed the sale of The Big M to Chicago by Toronto: "I will pay $1,000,000 for Frank Mahalovich [sic]. Jim Norris." Harold Ballard signed the note, adding, "Excepted [sic] by Maple Leaf Hockey Club." The note was witnessed by Leafs' board member Jack Amell.

(Hockey Hall of Fame)

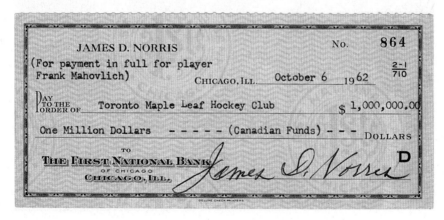

The million-dollar cheque backed up the sale of Mahovlich to the Black Hawks.

(Hockey Hall of Fame)

Trainer Bob Haggert throws his arms into the air and the team rejoices as Toronto wins their second consecutive Stanley Cup in 1963. The Leafs were at the apex of the dynasty, finishing first and winning both playoff series in five games.

(Graphic Artists/Hockey Hall of Fame)

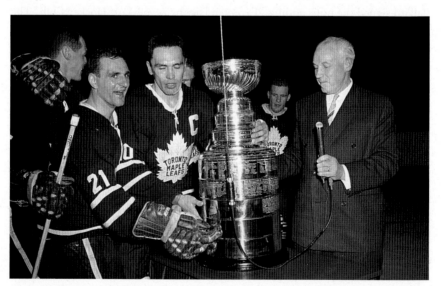

Jubilant Leafs Eddie Litzenberger, Bob Baun, George Armstrong and Kent Douglas (left to right) celebrate as NHL president Clarence Campbell awards the Stanley Cup to the 1963 Maple Leafs. (Imperial Oil-Turofsky/Hockey Hall of Fame)

Off-season fishing buddies but on-ice rivals, Gordie Howe and Johnny Bower embrace on the ice, waiting to be interviewed by *Hockey Night in Canada's* Frank Selke Jr. (Imperial Oil-Turofsky/Hockey Hall of Fame)

With the crowd chanting his name, Eddie Shack gets the privilege of carrying Lord Stanley's Cup to the dressing room after scoring 1963's Stanley Cup-winning goal.

(Graphic Artists/Hockey Hall of Fame)

Andy Bathgate scored the Stanley Cup-winning goal against Terry Sawchuk on April 25, 1964, earning the Maple Leafs a third straight championship. Punch Imlach believed that Bathgate was the final piece of the puzzle required to win it all again in 1964. (Graphic Artists/Hockey Hall of Fame)

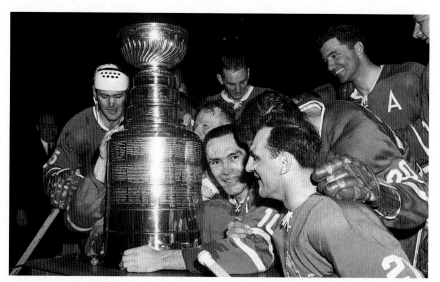

The 1964-vintage Toronto Maple Leafs circle the table that holds the Stanley Cup, theirs for a third spring in a row. Toronto emerged as the victor after rebounding in the dramatic series that included Bob Baun's historic game-winner scored on a broken leg. (Graphic Artists/Hockey Hall of Fame)

George Armstrong carries the Stanley Cup from the parade procession to the steps of Old City Hall. The Leafs' longest-serving captain was hosted by a different Toronto mayor in each of the four Leafs' Cup wins. (Graphic Artists/Hockey Hall of Fame)

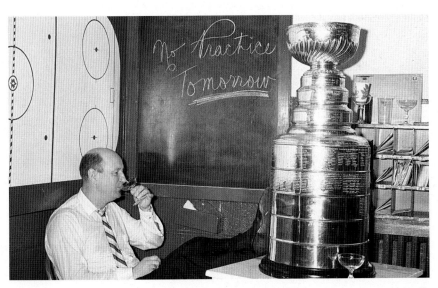

After a long, challenging season, Punch Imlach's blackboard message says it all!
(Graphic Artists/Hockey Hall of Fame)

With Punch Imlach hospitalized during the 1966–67 season, King Clancy took over as interim coach, changing the mood of the team and helping propel them to their fourth Stanley Cup championship of that decade.

(Graphic Artists/Hockey Hall of Fame)

The 1967 Toronto Maple Leafs surround kneeling captain George Armstrong, cradling the Stanley Cup for a fourth and final time. Note the bespectacled intruder to the left of Larry Jeffrey, in a suit, holding crutches.

(Graphic Artists/Hockey Hall of Fame)

George Armstrong (right), here with his cousin, was a fan of the Toronto Maple Leafs from the time he was a youngster. He'd one day captain the Leafs, and played with no other team during his 21-year NHL career. (Courtesy of the Armstrong family)

One of the greatest captains ever to pull on a blue-and-white sweater, George Armstrong faces a phalanx of photographers after his team's 1967 victory.

(Frank Prazak/Hockey Hall of Fame)

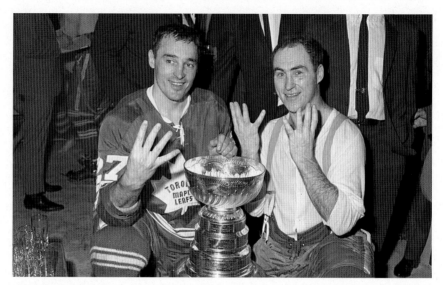

With the 1967 win, linemates Frank Mahovlich and Red Kelly indicate the number of Stanley Cup championships they each have won. (Graphic Artists/Hockey Hall of Fame)

Punch Imlach and his "Over the Hill Gang" enjoy a final hurrah following the 1967 win. Standing left to right are Imlach, Marcel Pronovost, George Armstrong, Red Kelly and Allan Stanley. Kneeling are Johnny Bower and Terry Sawchuk.

(Graphic Artists/Hockey Hall of Fame)

Bob Baun kept his ties to Tim Horton long after his hockey career had ended, successfully operating two Tim Horton franchises in the Greater Toronto Area.

(Roly Harris)

In 2007, at a fortieth anniversary fundraising tribute to the Maple Leafs, Bob Baun shared a special moment with Tim Horton's daughter, Jeri-Lynn.

(Courtesy of Hersh Borenstein)

Terry Sawchuk, his wife and son pose in the hallway of Maple Leaf Gardens with a table full of team and individual trophies, including the Stanley Cup and the mysterious Air Canada Trophy (aka Trans-Canada Airlines Trophy), presented to Sawchuk as the Leafs' 1967 playoff MVP. (Graphic Artists/Hockey Hall of Fame)

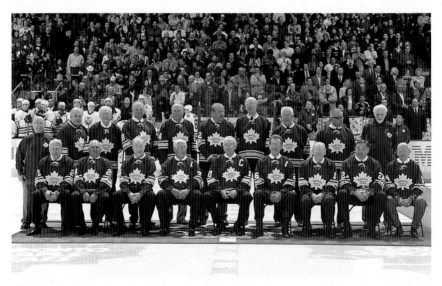

In 2007, the 1967 Toronto Maple Leafs were gathered together for an on-ice reunion at the Air Canada Centre, forty years after they had celebrated the franchise's last Stanley Cup championship. Dave Keon's rare appearance at the ACC was a tribute to the bond between members of the dynasty. (Graig Abel)

7

1962–63: EVEN BETTER THE SECOND TIME AROUND

The reigning Stanley Cup champions had every reason to feel confident. The talent-laden lineup was a nice mix of youthful exuberance and veteran experience. Having tasted victory once, the Maple Leafs wanted to taste it again. But there were five other teams who were determined to make every attempt to thwart the Toronto club.

The Montreal Canadiens made few changes to their lineup for the 1962–63 season, in spite of the fact they were eliminated in the semi-finals after finishing first overall in 1961–62. Defenceman Al MacNeil was dispatched to Chicago, making room for newcomers Terry Harper and Jacques Laperriere, who joined the squad later in the season when Lou Fontinato and Tom Johnson were injured. Red Berenson found a spot in the lineup. The Canadiens sold defenceman Gary Bergman and forward Bill Sutherland to Quebec of the WHL.

Chicago believed they were going to compete for the Stanley Cup again, and stood pat, for the most part, with their lineup. Al MacNeil joined the team from Montreal in a trade for Wayne

Hicks and Johnny McKenzie. Dollard St. Laurent was sold to Quebec of the AHL.

The Rangers added Jim Neilson to their defence corps, and Rod Gilbert became a regular at forward. Jean-Guy Gendron was chosen from the Canadiens and Bronco Horvath from Chicago in the Intra-League Draft. Doug Harvey, who had served as player-coach, relinquished the coaching reins to play defence full time.

GM Muzz Patrick took over behind the bench.

The Detroit Red Wings picked up Doug Barkley from Chicago in a trade for Len Lunde and Johnny McKenzie. The Intra-League Draft provided Alex Faulkner from Toronto, Barclay Plager from the QHL's Quebec Aces and Floyd Smith from the New York Rangers. Rookie Ed Joyal also cracked the lineup.

Boston, who had been mired in a prolonged slump, won but fifteen games in 1961–62. The Bruins decided to make wholesale changes to their roster. Goaltenders Bruce Gamble and Don Head were dropped in favour of Ed Johnston (Spokane of the WHL) and Bob Perreault (received from Hershey of the AHL for Ed Chadwick and Barry Ashbee). Veteran Warren Godfrey was drafted from Detroit, Wayne Hicks from Montreal and Irv Spencer from the Rangers.

The Stanley Cup Champion Toronto Maple Leafs chose to remain virtually constant with their roster. Coming off the franchise's first Stanley Cup win in eleven years, Coach Imlach was anxious to get back to defend the crown. Training-camp invitations went out to all team members and prospects, notifying all that no jobs were safe. "We have a good crop of rookies and they will get every opportunity to make the club," wrote Imlach, also insisting that everyone report in shape. "I expect you to report in good condition and not more than seven pounds over your playing weight, with a minimum of being able to do twenty push-ups, twenty sit-ups and thirty knee bends." He added, "Let's get ready for the competition and not sorry."

Rookie Jim Mikol cracked the Leafs' lineup out of training camp. "He showed us enough to rate a good look," said Imlach. Mikol would play but four games with Toronto, all in October 1962, before he was sent to the minors.

One player who did stick was Kent Douglas, who had been acquired from the Springfield Indians of the AHL in June 1962. To get Douglas, Toronto surrendered five prospects who were unlikely to crack the NHL roster — Roger Cote, Dick Mattiussi, Bill White and Jim Wilcox — plus the loan of Wally Boyer. A former "wild man" in junior, senior and minor pro hockey, the defenceman with the big shot had recently impressed everyone with his level-headed play. "Douglas is a sure-fire bet to be rookie of the year," said Imlach, the Leafs' soothsayer. "I've liked everything he's done so far."

After his fifth and most recent Stanley Cup championship, Bert Olmstead was not protected in the NHL Intra-League Draft. On June 4, 1962, the Rangers claimed Olmstead, and he furiously refused to report to New York. The Canadiens offered to buy him from the Rangers, but the deal never transpired and he retired instead. "I knew I played goddamned well enough to be protected," Olmstead said. "I also knew that the people who were coming in to take my place, whoever they were, weren't near the hockey player I was." Punch Imlach, looking to the future, said, "We have to give those kids from Rochester a chance. That's [Bruce] Draper, [Larry] Keenan and [Jim] Pappin. They've got a year [of pro hockey] under their belts. Whoever plays the best will make the team. But when a team wins the Stanley Cup, somebody has got to be pretty good to break in." Several players have suggested that Imlach saw Olmstead as a threat to his position with the team.

There had been other changes on the team, although not ones directly involving the product on the ice. For some time during the previous season, Frank Mahovlich and his girlfriend, Marie, had quietly made plans to be married, but were concerned about how Punch Imlach would frown on the distraction to The Big M's play. They announced their engagement only after the season had ended. Having kept the secret for several months, the couple was married on June 13, 1962, at Toronto's Holy Rosary Church, followed by a reception at the Royal York Hotel.

On June 18, 1962, Red Kelly made the unusual move of running for public office, and won the Liberal seat in Toronto's York West riding. "When I was traded to Toronto, I stayed at the Westbury [hotel], and Keith Davey worked at the radio station [CKFH] right across the road," he explained. "He was a hang of a hockey fan and used to come into the restaurant there." Davey was sales manager of Foster Hewitt's radio station from 1949 to 1960, and then entered politics and was appointed national campaign director of the Liberal Party of Canada. "He used to come in and eat breakfast in there. So, he's the one who talked me into going into politics. I was interested in Canada and guessed I was near the end of my playing career. He took me over and introduced me to [Prime Minister Lester] Pearson over at the Park Plaza. He thought Pearson was going to talk me into running. I said that I didn't think I could play hockey and be a member at the same time. Pearson agreed and said it would be very tough to do. Davey thought he would talk to me and persuade me, but Pearson used other tactics. Pearson was a great negotiator. He was pretty smart; I thought the world of him. The reason that I ran is that I thought he would be good for our country. Anything that I could do to get him in would be good for the country."

Red won the election by a healthy margin over the incumbent, Progressive Conservative candidate John Hamilton, who had held the seat since 1954, and for three years Kelly embarked on the dual career — hockey player and member of Parliament.

"I came home [to Toronto] to practise in the morning, then I'd catch a plane and go to Ottawa for the afternoon and evening sessions and then come home on the last flight, the midnight flight, and get home at one or one-thirty in the morning. Then, I'd go down and practise in the morning and then all over again, do the same thing. Most of the nights, we played on Saturdays, Sundays and Wednesday nights. The House didn't sit on Wednesday night and it didn't sit on Saturday or Sunday. The only time I had a real problem is when we played in Montreal on a Thursday night. We were in a minority position, so could be defeated. One night, we had votes on a whole pile and I couldn't get away."

Red combined hockey and politics into one highly successful, and for a short time, frantic career. "We had another election in sixty-three because we were a minority government and we defeated Diefenbaker on a vote of confidence." In that election on April 8, 1963, Kelly buried his opponent — lawyer Alan Eagleson, who ran as the Progressive Conservative candidate in York West. "We came back as the government in a minority position in sixty-three and we won the Cup again in sixty-three." Kelly decided not to run in the next election, which took place on November 8, 1965. "It felt like taking two two-hundred-pound bags of grain off each shoulder," he admitted. "It was sort of like a new world."

Maple Leaf Gardens went through its own metamorphosis during the off-season.

Under Conn Smythe's fiefdom, the Gardens was a relatively busy venue, with hockey, wrestling and occasional forays into basketball (the Huskies), political and religious conventions, as well as the occasional musical program. But while Stafford Smythe engrossed himself in the hockey operation, Harold Ballard did a remarkable job of increasing revenue for Maple Leaf Gardens. He negotiated a television contract that garnered an additional $700,000 for the Gardens. He also reduced the number of dark nights at the venue by adding closed-circuit boxing matches, rodeos and religious revivals and concerts from big-name touring acts. "He started what has become the biggest operation in Canada for bringing in rock groups," said Dick Beddoes. "I don't think Old Man Smythe knew what a rock group was, unless it was a collection of hard-hitting defencemen! And it was Ballard who made sure that when the Baptists or Shriners come to town for a convention, they wound up at the Gardens. That's Ballard. That has been his major accomplishment on the business side — just keeping the joint open."

Maple Leaf Gardens was also reconfigured in 1962. By reducing the size of existing seats and finding new areas in which to expand, 981 new seats were added. But some of those came at the expense of the organ loft and removal of the Queen's portrait. "If people want to see pictures of the Queen, they can go to an art gallery," blustered Ballard, adding, "Besides, what the hell position can a Queen play?" When the dust had settled, the capacity of Maple Leaf Gardens was increased to 13,718.

CCM and Ford paid about $15,000 a year to have signs at either end of the rink, Schick razor blades were advertised on the escalator risers and the Zamboni sported advertising for Dominion. "He sold everything," said George Mara, one of the Silver Seven management team. "Everything he did was a money-maker."

Ballard and Smythe decided to add a private members' club within Maple Leaf Gardens. The Marlboro Athletic Club leased space from Maple Leaf Gardens for $250,000, and after the stores along Church Street were removed, the Hot Stove Lounge was born. Initiation fees were sold for $100, along with an annual membership of $50, and once a customer bought one, he was first in line for Maple Leafs' season tickets when they became available. "Mr. Ballard said good sporting types, without regard for race or religion, will be eligible for membership," reported *The Globe and Mail*. The Hot Stove Club was a not-for-profit venture, with the newspaper reporting, "Profits, which Mr. Ballard expects to be substantial, will go entirely to amateur hockey."

Thanks to Harold Ballard's creative foresight, along with an outstanding era of hockey, the profits of Maple Leaf Gardens grew from $300,000 in 1961 to $900,000 three years later. And shares grew in price from $26.50 in 1961 to $114,750 in 1965 before the stock split five for one. "We're not in the business to lose money," Ballard remarked.

A Cool Million for a Big M
Saturday, October 6, 1962

One of the most gigantic stories in the hockey world in 1962–63 didn't take place on the ice. In fact, it didn't even take place in an arena.

On October 6, 1962, the NHL All-Star Game took place at Maple Leaf Gardens. In what was recognized as a dull affair, the defending Stanley Cup champions, the Maple Leafs, beat the All-Stars, 4–1. Other than a tussle between Carl Brewer and Don McKenney, the game was largely forgettable. But the activity that happened afterwards was anything but forgettable.

Following the annual All-Star dinner at Toronto's Royal York Hotel, some of the executives decided to relax over cocktails. "A game of highball roulette burst beyond the bounds of party privacy late Friday night," *The Globe* reported.

The story began when Maple Leafs' executives bemoaned the fact that they had been unable to sign Frank Mahovlich to a deal for the upcoming season. James Norris, chairman of the board of the Chicago Black Hawks, stated that he would pay any amount to get Mahovlich. When Leafs' vice-president Harold Ballard asked Norris to quantify the amount, Norris replied, "A million dollars," to which Ballard blurted, "Sold!"

Norris and Ballard shook hands on the deal, and Norris gave Ballard $1,000 in $100 bills to show his good faith. Finding a piece of paper, Ballard then wrote, "We except [*sic*] on behalf of Maple Leaf Gardens." Jack Amell, a member of the Silver Seven, also signed the sheet. Punch Imlach was present but refused to shake hands on the deal and left for home.

With Ballard's agreement, Norris then contacted Johnny Gottselig, the team's publicity director, and told him to make the announcement of the transaction. At 12:53 Saturday morning, the announcement arrived in the newsrooms of United Press International and Associated Press and was sent out to media outlets across North America.

Shortly afterwards, Stafford Smythe arrived in the suite and was informed of the transaction by King Clancy. "Everything's on hold," he told Norris, later saying, "I will not consider such a deal. If he [Norris] would like to meet me in my office at noon and make the same offer, I am interested."

"A report that Frank Mahovlich had been sold to the Chicago Black Hawks for $1,000,000 early Saturday morning was denied by Maple Leafs' president Stafford Smythe, who admitted the fantastic offer had been made by Jim Norris, chairman of the Chicago Black Hawks' board," reported *The Globe and Mail*. Norris stated, "I have offered the Maple Leafs one million dollars for Mahovlich." General manager Tommy Ivan confirmed the offer had been made. "I believe this is the greatest sum ever offered for an athlete," commented Ivan. "Mr. Norris has always wanted Mahovlich and laid the money on the line for him."

While the negotiations were unfolding, Frank Mahovlich was told by his father that he had been traded. "I hadn't signed a contract, but I didn't figure I was going to be traded," he said. The Big M drove to Maple Leaf Gardens, but when hounded by reporters, offered his scepticism. "I think it's a lot of guff," he said. "Some people were happy and just got carried away. Personally, I want to stay in Toronto and play my hockey here."

At noon, Stafford Smythe, Harold Ballard and a roomful of reporters greeted Tommy Ivan, general manager of the Hawks, who delivered the cheque, as promised, on behalf of Jim Norris. But Ivan was rebuffed by Smythe, claiming he had no authority to make such a deal without conferring with the board of directors. Ivan left with his boss's personal cheque. Norris was livid and insisted that the transaction was legal, as he had a slip of paper confirming the sale signed by two executives from Maple Leaf Gardens. Norris forced the issue with NHL president Clarence Campbell, who ruled that the sale was null and void on the grounds that "no responsible member of the Maple Leaf organization had accepted the bid."

The hands of fate work in mysterious ways. The opening game of 1962–63 pitted these two rivals against one another on October 10, 1962, in Chicago. "There's no doubt about it, they welched on the deal," said Norris on the eve of the season opener. "I still regard Mahovlich as my property. We shook hands on it. That's been my way of doing business."

Stafford Smythe decided not to accompany the team to Chicago for that season-opening contest.

The order to cancel the deal had come from on high. Conn Smythe, even though he no longer owned the team, ordered Stafford to renege on the deal. "Connie Smythe told me that he cancelled the deal, and that was that," head scout Bob Davidson stated in *The Big M*. "Harold Ballard didn't know a hell of a lot about hockey. He just thought it was a great thing to be offered a million dollars."

"After that, Ballard didn't like me because he was embarrassed by the whole situation," admitted Mahovlich in his biography. From that moment, the relationship between Mahovlich and the Maple Leafs changed for the worse. The incident created resentment towards The Big M. "Instead of going to Chicago, I ended up playing for a team that didn't even want me — and yet, wouldn't trade me. I would have felt better in Chicago, where they would have let me play."

Leafs Open Season on Right Foot

Wednesday, October 10, 1962

Chicago Stadium was extremely warm for the opening game of the campaign. The mercury rose above ninety degrees in the rink, and the ice was slow and watery. The rink attendants didn't even bother to flood for the third period.

The Maple Leafs beat Chicago 3–1 in that opening game. George Armstrong scored twice, once on a power play then during a penalty kill. Bob Baun scored the other Toronto goal, while Ken Wharram collected Chicago's lone goal.

Toronto Ties Bruins in Home Opener

Saturday, October 13, 1962

Toronto's opening-night tradition continued, with the 48th Highlanders taking to the ice prior to the contest between the Maple Leafs and the visiting Boston Bruins. The rhythm of the drums and skirl of the pipes had taken place at every Leafs' home opener since Maple Leaf Gardens opened in 1931, and as was de rigueur, the Highlanders performed "The Maple Leaf Forever." Conn Smythe, past-president of Maple Leaf Gardens, strutted to centre ice to present the J. P. Bickell Award to Dave Keon prior to the opening faceoff.

The Leafs tied Boston 2–2, with Bruins' goaltender Bob Perreault named the game's first Star. He was accidentally high-sticked by teammate Ted Green and had to excuse himself for several minutes to seek medical attention. "Physicians decided there was no fracture when Perreault refused to stop talking during tests," the *Star* reported. Although a rookie, Boston was already Perreault's third NHL team. "Last year, our goalie [Don Head] couldn't stop anything and it wrecked the confidence of the team," said Bruins' coach Phil Watson.

Between periods, Punch Imlach liked to be alone, plotting the immediate future of his team. He would head out into the corridor outside the Maple Leafs' dressing room, pour himself a coffee and pace. His between-period talks tended to be brief. "I don't want to spend much time in there," he said, referring to the dressing room. "They've got a lot on their minds. I'd be talking too much. They wouldn't be listening anyway."

Beginning early in the 1962–63 season, there was one mission at the core of Imlach's existence. "Finishing first and winning the Stanley Cup is one thing we haven't done," stated Punch. "I'd like that." Toronto hadn't accomplished that feat since 1947–48 with Hap Day behind the bench.

Bower Falters; Imlach Goes to Plan B
Saturday, November 3, 1962

The Red Wings bombed Toronto 7–3 for Detroit's second win over the Maple Leafs within a week. Following the game on *Hockey Night in Canada*, Imlach announced that Don Simmons would replace Johnny Bower in goal for Toronto. The Leafs won the next five games, although Johnny Bower was back in net after Simmons became ill.

Fleming Taunts Leafs in Shutout Loss
Thursday, November 22, 1962

While the final score showed the Hawks 1, Toronto 0 (Pierre Pilote scored on a second-period power play for Chicago), the game was like a powder keg, ready to explode. The two teams hadn't liked each other for a long time, but the Mahovlich incident prior to the start of the season just exacerbated the hatred.

In the second period, Kent Douglas fenced with Stan Mikita, which immediately drew a crowd. Eddie Shack, making his first appearance of the game at 19:07 of the third, traded punches with Murray Balfour, and that set off a flurry of fights. Allan Stanley duked it out with Elmer Vasko, while Reggie Fleming, who had already served three minor penalties in the third period alone, raced to grab Shack but was intercepted by Tim

Horton, who tackled him like a wrangler at the Calgary Stampede. Later, Fleming stood in front of the Leafs' bench and taunted them. Dick Duff tried to scramble over the boards to get at Fleming, but was grabbed by his jersey as teammates restrained him.

Bower Breaks Boom Boom's Bone
Wednesday, December 5, 1962
Toronto hosted Montreal, and the netminders, Bower and Plante, staged a virtual clinic in goal through the game. Toronto ended up winning 2–1. "It was a great hockey game," asserted Imlach. "Plante and Johnny Bower came up with tremendous goaltending to hold the score down. We played it a little too tough for them and deserved to win." Bower, Plante and Bob Nevin were the Three Stars.

At 7:22 of the third, with Duff in the penalty box, Boom Boom Geoffrion fired a shot at Bower that the netminder dove to stop. Bower's chin hit Geoffrion's wrist. Toronto's goalie was dazed but returned to his crease. Geoffrion retired to the clinic at Maple Leaf Gardens, where X-rays showed a fractured bone in his wrist.

Who's on First?
Saturday, December 15, 1962
Red Armstrong was called up from Sudbury of the EPHL to dress for the Leafs, after Baun and Nevin both suffered knee injuries in a 4–3 loss to Detroit on December 9. The addition of Armstrong caused some confusion on the Leafs' bench during the 8–2 victory over Boston. Imlach barked out the next line: "Red, take right wing with Harris and Pulford." Red Kelly glanced up, confused, and got ready to take the next shift. "Not you, Red, I mean Armstrong." The captain stood up, ready to clamber over the boards. "No, no. Not you, Chief." Billy Harris finally jumped in. "His name's Norm. Call him Norm." Imlach said, with a chuckle, "Norm, Harris and Pulford — get ready!"

Armstrong scored on his first shift with the Maple Leafs, with five minutes remaining in a Leafs' blowout. He ended up being a career minor leaguer, playing just seven games with the Leafs that season but spending eleven seasons in the American Hockey League before dying in an industrial accident in July 1974.

Keon Picks Up Two Goals and Two Minutes in Penalties
Saturday, January 12, 1963
Dave Keon was awarded the Lady Byng Trophy that night for being the NHL's most gentlemanly player of 1961–62. That night, Keon scored two goals and (gasp) earned a minor penalty as Toronto edged Detroit 2–1.

Keon's penalty, his first of the season and only his fifth in three seasons, resulted when Wings' defenceman Howie Young rode Keon into the boards and held him up there. "I was trying to break loose, and when I did I hit him on the head," admitted the gentlemanly Keon. "It was sort of a chain reaction. I might have been a little browned off."

Boom Boom Tossed and Montreal Lost as Kelly Pots Three
Thursday, January 31, 1963
Red Kelly potted a hat trick, leading Toronto to a 6–3 spanking of the Montreal Canadiens at the Forum. Going into the final period, the score was deadlocked at two apiece. During that period, Kelly was in all alone on Jacques Plante when Jean-Guy Talbot jumped him from behind. Referee Eddie Powers pointed to centre ice, indicating a penalty shot. The puck was placed at the centre faceoff dot amidst a massive chorus of boos. Kelly slowly skated in towards the Montreal goal and fired a low shot past Plante's glove side.

The feisty Habs earned more than their share of penalties during that game. Toe Blake's tirade from the bench earned his team a bench minor in the second. Billy Hicke was whistled for a misconduct after arguing a call in the third. Bernie Geoffrion scrapped with Toronto's Carl Brewer in the third. Both were assessed a minor and a misconduct. When Geoffrion refused to conclude his antics, continuing to challenge Brewer in the box, Boom Boom was tossed from the game.

After the contest, sportswriters were entertained by Blake. "[Powers] is too inconsistent. Some of his calls were bad and he missed so many that you have to say his work is putrid," Blake claimed. "The whole league is getting bush all around." He told a French newspaper that Powers handled the game as though he bet on it.

Kelly Adds Helmet to Equipment
Sunday, February 17, 1963
It was a curious sight to see Red Kelly wearing a helmet after suffering a concussion on February 13 when he was crashed into the boards by Detroit's Howie Young. At the time, only Charlie Burns of the Bruins was regularly sporting a helmet. That night, the Rangers defeated Toronto 4–1. Kelly would make the helmet a permanent part of his equipment until the 1966–67 season, when he discarded the headgear.

Leafs Begin Ten-Game Unbeaten Streak
Thursday, February 27, 1963
After battling with Detroit and Chicago for first place through the season, Toronto went on a tear and began a ten-game unbeaten streak that thrust them into second place, one point behind Chicago. They doubled Chicago 6–3 to begin the string, which included seven wins and three ties.

The animosity continued, too. A title bout featured Kent Douglas against Reg Fleming. After taking matching slashing penalties, the two exited to the penalty box, but it was there that the fight began. The match spilled out of the box and into the nearby aisle in front of the box seats. Jack Evans, already serving a minor, was confronted by the Leafs' Frank Mahovlich, who leapt in and grabbed Evans to pull him from the tussle. Later, Evans said, "I had no thought of interfering. I said to Mahovlich, 'You take your man and I'll pull Fleming away.'"

Linesmen Matt Pavelich and Ron Wicks restored order until the combatants returned to the ice. Referee John Ashley assessed both battlers minors for slashing, majors for fighting and game misconducts for renewing the fight. Douglas was also assessed a holding penalty. Conn Smythe, in Toronto from his retreat in Florida, enjoyed the spectacle, repeating his mantra, "If you can't lick 'em in the alley, you can't beat 'em on the ice."

Overshadowed by the scrap was Frank Mahovlich's four-point effort — a goal and three assists. Leafs' coach Punch Imlach was especially pleased to see his star left winger go to the aid of Kent Douglas.

Leafs Capture First Place
Wednesday, March 20, 1963

The Maple Leafs went into the game against Montreal needing only a tie to clinch first place. That was a challenge at the best of times, but Mahovlich sat out while suffering from the flu, and Bobby Baun injured his knee on the first shift of the game.

With a minute to go in the game, Montreal was up 3–2. Imlach pulled Simmons for the extra attacker. The Canadiens controlled the puck, but an attempt at an insurance goal went wide. With twenty seconds remaining, Bob Nevin was able to dump the puck into the corner to the left of Jacques Plante. Duff stripped Terry Harper of the puck behind the Montreal goal and tapped it to Bob Nevin. Keon cut in front of Plante, picked up the pass from Nevin and flipped a backhand past Plante for his second goal of the game at 19:52. "I just shot on my backhand and it went between Plante's feet," explained Keon. The game ended eight seconds later with Toronto tying Montreal 3–3, but more importantly, they had secured first place.

"We didn't really deserve a tie the way we played in the third period," Keon commented amidst players in a jubilant dressing room. "We stopped skating and the Canadiens, as usual, never stopped skating. We slowed down and let them get a goal ahead."

"I was a little worried before the game," admitted Imlach. "Our guys were really nervous. They had all been in the Stanley Cup playoffs before, but this is the first time they have had a chance to finish first. As a result, they were afraid to make mistakes."

The *Toronto Star* wrote, "Leafs' manager-coach George Imlach, whose persistence in playing Simmons in goal in recent games has been questioned by hockey swami, was again vindicated. Simmons made several superlative saves when Leafs' defences relaxed."

"Even when Punch said a few weeks ago that Johnny [Bower] was going to play all games for the rest of the season, I was still ready," said Simmons. "Punch gets these hunches about who should play goal. Don't ask me how or where he gets them, but he hasn't been wrong too often."

For Red Kelly, this was his ninth first-place finish — eight occurring with the Red Wings' dynasty. Kent Douglas had been on five first-place finishers, all prior to his NHL debut. One was with Winnipeg and three with Springfield.

"We were a very happy group of little boys masquerading as men," wrote Billy Harris in *The Glory Years*.

That ecstasy quickly turned to agony. The next day, Keon's eighteen-month-old son, Richard, died of pneumonia at the Hospital for Sick Children. The tragedy occurred one day before Keon's twenty-third birthday. At the time, David and his wife had two other children — David Jr. (two and one-half years) and Anne-Marie (five months).

Keon missed the last two games of the regular season mourning the death of his son. In a 2–1 Red Wings win on Saturday, March 23, Gordie Howe and Alex Faulkner scored for Detroit and Red Kelly for Toronto. On Sunday, March 24, Parker MacDonald, Eddie Joyal and Gordie Howe contributed to the Wings' 3–2 win. Ed Litzenberger and Tim Horton scored goals fifteen seconds apart in the second period for Toronto.

In spite of the back-to-back losses, the final standings showed Toronto finishing in first place, one point ahead of the Black Hawks. Montreal in third place and Detroit in fourth were also playoff-bound. The Rangers and Bruins missed the post-season.

\multicolumn{6}{l}{**1962–63 Regular Season Standings**}					
FINISH	TEAM	GAMES	WINS	LOSSES	TIES	POINTS
1	Toronto Maple Leafs	70	35	13	12	82
2	Chicago Black Hawks	70	32	21	17	81
3	Montreal Canadiens	70	28	19	23	79
4	Detroit Red Wings	70	32	25	13	77
5	New York Rangers	70	22	36	12	56
6	Boston Bruins	70	14	39	17	45

1962–63 Regular Season Scoring

RK	NUMBER	PLAYER	POS	AGE	GP	G	A	PTS	PIM
1	27	Frank Mahovlich	LW	25	67	36	37	73	56
2	4	Red Kelly	D/C	35	66	20	40	60	8
3	14	Dave Keon	C	22	68	28	28	56	2
4	20	Bob Pulford	LW	26	70	19	25	44	49
5	10	George Armstrong	RW	32	70	19	24	43	27
6	9	Dick Duff	LW	26	69	16	19	35	56
7	11	Bob Nevin	RW	24	58	12	21	33	4
8	12	Ron Stewart	RW	30	63	16	16	32	26
9	15	Billy Harris	C	27	65	8	24	32	22
10	23	Eddie Shack	LW	25	63	16	9	25	97
11	7	Tim Horton	D	33	70	6	19	25	69
12	2	Carl Brewer	D	24	70	2	23	25	168
13	19	Kent Douglas	D	26	70	7	15	22	105
14	26	Allan Stanley	D	36	61	4	15	19	22
15	25	Ed Litzenberger	C/RW	30	58	5	13	18	10
16	21	Bob Baun	D	26	48	4	8	12	65
17	17	Bronco Horvath	C	32	10	0	4	4	12
18	18	Norm Armstrong	RW/D	24	7	1	1	2	2
19	8	Johnny MacMillan	RW	27	6	1	1	2	6
20	3	Al Arbour	D	30	4	1	0	1	4
21	16	Jim Mikol	LW/D	24	4	0	1	1	2
22	17	Rod Seiling	D	18	1	0	1	1	0
23	1	Johnny Bower	G	38	42	0	0	0	2
24	18	Andre Champagne	LW	19	2	0	0	0	0
25	17	Bruce Draper	C	22	1	0	0	0	0
26	22	Larry Hillman	D	25	5	0	0	0	2
27	24	Don Simmons	G	31	28	0	0	0	0
		TEAM TOTALS			70	221	344	565	816

Regular Season Netminding

RK		PLAYER	POS	AGE	GP	MIN	W	L	T	GA	GAA	SO
1	1	Johnny Bower	G	38	42	2520	20	15	7	109	2.60	1
2	24	Don Simmons	G	31	28	1680	15	8	5	69	2.46	1
		TEAM TOTALS			70	4200	37	22	11	178	2.54	3

After going undefeated through ten consecutive games (seven wins and three ties), there was clearly a letdown by the Maple Leafs. Coach Imlach remained positive. "They'll bounce back for the opening game of our Stanley Cup semi-final against Montreal Canadiens at home."

Gordie Howe finished the season as the NHL scoring champ with eighty-six points, five more than Andy Bathgate of the Rangers. "I think I got a bigger kick out of winning this scoring title than I did my first one," admitted Howe. "There was more satisfaction because a lot of experts thought that at thirty-five and in my seventeenth season, I'd slow down a mite." Howe was also awarded the Hart Trophy as the NHL's most valuable player.

Chicago picked up two individual's awards. Goalie Glenn Hall won the Vezina for the the fewest goals allowed by a team, while Pierre Pilote was awarded the Norris Trophy as the best defenceman.

It was a season of predictions coming true for Punch Imlach. Not only did the team finish first, but Kent Douglas was named the Calder Trophy winner as the NHL's rookie of the year. In addition, Dave Keon was awarded the Lady Byng Trophy as the league's most gentlemanly player. It was the second straight season winning the award for Keon, who had totalled just four minutes in penalties in those two NHL seasons.

The first-place Toronto Maple Leafs faced the third-place Montreal Canadiens in the Stanley Cup semi-final, but the rankings were deceiving, as the Canadiens collected just three fewer points than Toronto.

Bower the Hero as Toronto Takes Series Lead
Game One, Semi-Final – Tuesday, March 26, 1963
Toronto orchestrated a tight, defensive game that earned a 3–1 victory over the Canadiens in game one, played at Maple Leaf Gardens in front of the smallest crowd of the season. Bob Pulford opened the scoring at 3:10 of the first period on a shot that deflected off J. C. Tremblay's stick past Jacques Plante. Johnny Bower assisted on the goal.

Pulford, Dick Duff and George Armstrong scored unanswered goals before Jean Beliveau spoiled Bower's shutout bid in the third period. The first two periods were energetic and entertaining, but the pace slowed considerably in the third.

The Globe believed that "the humidity, oppressive at times, caught up to both teams."

Leafs Win Game Two on Lucky Goal
Game Two, Semi-Final – Thursday, March 28, 1963
A perennial concern, netminder Jacques Plante regularly found that his asthma acted up when he was in Toronto. As a precaution, the Canadiens summoned Charlie Hodge from Quebec in the AHL, replacing Ernie Wakely, who had been the stand-by goaltender.

A few eyebrows were raised when scribes noted that Maurice Richard was practising with the Canadiens in Maple Leaf Gardens. "I just came out for my own benefit," suggested The Rocket.

After losing game one, Montreal came out strong, and Jean Beliveau answered the bell, scoring the game's first goal. Stealing the puck from Bobby Baun, the Habs' captain fired a shot from well out that zipped past Bower in the Toronto goal. Just forty-seven seconds later, Toronto evened the score when their captain, George Armstrong, bounced a puck off Plante into the Montreal net.

Allan Stanley scored in the second to put his team up by a goal. "Plante didn't have much of a chance on that one," the defenceman stated. "It hit one of the Canadiens and deflected over his shoulder." The play went back and forth, and Terry Harper knotted the score on a pass by Henri Richard. Later in the second period, Dave Keon, in trying to deke Jacques Plante, lost control of the puck, yet watched as it rolled under the Montreal goaltender's stick for the winning goal.

Allan Stanley, with a goal and an assist, was the first Star of the 3–2 Leaf win. Second honours went to Dave Keon and Terry Harper was the third Star of game two.

Bower Blanks Canadiens, Puts Habs Backs against the Wall
Game Three, Semi-Final – Saturday, March 30, 1963

After two games in Toronto, the series shifted to Montreal for games three and four. Toronto coach Punch Imlach, who regularly imposed fines for various team infractions, was forced to swallow a spoonful of his own medicine when traffic tie-ups on the 401 forced him, assistant GM King Clancy, Red Kelly and Tim Horton to miss their flight. Harold Ballard insisted that no one was immune and fined Imlach and Clancy $100 each. "Not enough," laughed Dick Duff. "This is the playoffs. Should be $1,000 each."

The fact that the series shifted locales made little difference, as Johnny Bower earned his first-ever playoff shutout, blanking Montreal 2–0 in his thirty-eighth career playoff contest. Eddie Shack's second-period goal opened the scoring and proved to be the winner. The entertaining forward had earlier almost cost his team a goal after earning a five-minute major for carving Ralph Backstrom with his stick. While Shack was serving his time, Carl Brewer earned a penalty. Angered by the call, Conn Smythe protested by waving his coat, and it took the gendarmes to calm him down. The Maple Leafs limited the Canadiens' chances and easily killed off the penalties.

Bob Pulford scored in the third to polish off the Canadiens and put Toronto clearly in the driver's seat with a commanding three-game-to-none advantage in the semi-final.

Detroit general manager Jack Adams selected the game's Three Stars for *Hockey Night in Canada* and chose Bob Pulford, Johnny Bower and Jean Beliveau.

Leafs Surrender Win but Maintain Series Lead
Game Four, Semi-Final – Tuesday, April 2, 1963

After winning in Montreal on Saturday night, the team flew home and then practised at Maple Leaf Gardens on Sunday before returning to Montreal for game four of the semi-final.

The Leafs, anxious to close out the series, maintained the close checking that had identified their post-season success to that point, and the Canadiens, shaking off the shackles, were able to rebound.

Ron Stewart began the scoring, picking up the Leafs' only goal at 6:12 of the first period. From that point on, Jacques Plante was afforded outstanding protection, with special mention of the role played by rookie Terry Harper. Coach Blake mentioned that the turning point was when his netminder stoned Dave Keon on a third-period breakaway. "When I saw Keon skating in alone, I thought, 'There goes the ballgame.'"

Henri Richard tied the score early in the second. In the third, Gilles Tremblay added the first of his two power-play goals. As Harper and Frank Mahovlich continued their feud, The Big M cross-checked his opponent and earned a penalty. While he looked on from the penalty, Tremblay scored the Canadiens' third goal, and the game ended in a 3–1 Montreal win, averting elimination.

Frank Mahovlich was enduring the toughest post-season of his storied career. Already hit by the flu bug, The Big M took eight stitches in the lip during an altercation with Boom Boom Geoffrion in game one. Finding it difficult to eat, Mahovlich lost weight and found his energy zapped through the entire playoff.

Henri Richard earned first Star honours, Johnny Bower was the second Star and Terry Harper was the game's third Star.

Imlach admitted, "You have to give them the credit. They played a better brand of hockey and they had the breaks."

Bower and Keon Star as Toronto Eliminates Montreal
Game Five – Semi-Final – Thursday, April 4, 1963
Game five, back in the friendly confines of Maple Leaf Gardens, was a blowout for Toronto.

Dave Keon scored at 4:56 of the first to put the first goal on the board, and before the period was through, Dick Duff and Ron Stewart had added to the score. Keon scored his second goal of the contest in the second period, and the Leafs' fifth and final goal of the game came off the stick of

Kent Douglas during the third period. Johnny Bower earned his second shutout of the post-season, stopping thirty-five shots, as his teammates smothered the Canadiens, eliminating them from further playoff action. After losing in game four, Imlach assigned Bob Pulford to shadow Jean Beliveau and Keon to blanket Henri Richard, and the strategy completely threw Montreal off their game. Particularly grating to the Canadiens' management was the truculent Leafs' winger Eddie Shack running at the smaller Montreal players, getting them off their game.

"Those six guys — Tim Horton, Carl Brewer, Allan Stanley, Bob Baun, Kent Douglas and Bower — were the difference," suggested Imlach.

Dave Keon was named first Star of the game and was introduced by Frank Selke Jr. from the Montreal broadcast crew of *Hockey Night in Canada* as a "Hab killer." Johnny Bower skated out as the second Star and Dick Duff took third Star kudos.

"This is the same Toronto team we beat in four games in 1960," said Frank Selke Sr., the Canadiens' GM. "They've matured."

Toe Blake ventured into the exuberance in the Leafs' dressing room and shook the hands of each player, as well as Punch Imlach. Imlach grinned in the aftermath of the Leafs' victory. "This was the first time in three tries my team has been able to beat the Canadiens. Why shouldn't I be happy?"

There was a changing of the guard in Montreal following this series. Game five of the semi-final was Jacques Plante's last game as a Hab. He was traded to the Rangers with Phil Goyette and Don Marshall that summer. And the Canadiens vowed that they wouldn't be pushed around any longer. In due time, Montreal would toughen up with the addition of John Ferguson and Ted Harris.

While Toronto had finished off Montreal, the Detroit Red Wings defeated the Chicago Black Hawks in six games to earn a berth in the Stanley Cup final. Through the regular season, the Wings had finished fourth, and the last time a fourth-place club had won the Stanley Cup was in 1948–49, when the Leafs took the championship. But Detroit was not to be taken lightly. They were the only team to hold an edge over the Leafs through the regular season, winning seven, losing six and tying one in their fourteen games.

"I wouldn't sell this Detroit team short," cautioned Chicago coach Rudy Pilous, whose Chicago Black Hawks were erased from the playoffs by Detroit. "If the Wings keep hustling the way they did against us, they'll put up a tremendous argument [against the Leafs]. They're a good-skating club and they never give up. They keep flying at you, keeping you off balance. An upset wouldn't surprise me a bit."

Baldy Cotton, Bruins' head scout, commented, "The Leafs will win because they have the better third line. I think the Wings can match any two lines Imlach can toss out, but they haven't a third line to compare to his."

To no one's surprise, Punch Imlach was confident. "I don't think Detroit has three centres to match Keon, Kelly and Pulford," he stated. "And show me where they have five defencemen as good as the five I can put on the ice. And either one of our two guys [Bower and Simmons] can come up with the big game. They won't suffer by comparison to Sawchuk." Imlach planned to assign Eddie Shack to shadow Gordie Howe, and looked to Frank Mahovlich to lead the way in scoring, stating, "I'm expecting him to have a big series." In addition, he called up Gary Jarrett and Jim Pappin from Rochester for insurance.

George Armstrong was cautious and said, "I know we're not taking them lightly. We look for a tough series." Team owner Stafford Smythe added, "I can never forget the semi-final series in 1960–61. We were heavily favoured in that one, and they knocked us off in four straight after we won the first game."

All of the games in the Stanley Cup final were going to be televised from the opening faceoff.

Duff Sets an NHL Record as Leafs Romp to Win in Game One
Game One, Stanley Cup Final – Tuesday, April 9, 1963
The afternoon of the game, Imlach received a newspaper clipping from a Detroit source that claimed that Sid Abel predicted that "They'll take

Toronto and they'll do it easier than the Chicago series." Punch used this as his pep talk before the game. It seemed to fire up the team, as Toronto came out of the first game with a 4–2 win.

Dick Duff set an NHL record for the fastest two goals from the start of a playoff game. He scored his first at the forty-nine-second mark and followed it with his second at 1:08, just nineteen seconds later, to give Toronto a quick 2–0 lead. "Those goals came off perfect shots," said Sawchuk. "On the first one, Duff whipped the puck with one of the fastest wrist shots I've seen. He had me on the move because I had to worry about Armstrong cutting in from the right side and he put the puck between me and the post."

"We were two goals down before our boys realized the game had started," sighed Detroit coach Sid Abel.

Later that period, Bob Nevin scored another for Toronto. Tim Horton was sitting out "a siege of repentance in the sneezer," according to the *Star's* colourful writer Milt Dunnell, when Nevin scored Toronto's third goal. But after taking a 3–0 lead, the Leafs let the Wings up off the canvas in the second, with Jeffrey scoring twice for Detroit. "Letting down is a habit of theirs," shrugged Imlach. "They didn't do anything when we had a two-man advantage for the first fifty seconds of the second period, and from then on, they stopped skating."

Bob Nevin scored an insurance goal, his second of the game, to secure the Toronto win in game one.

"Personally, I don't think either team played well," said Sid Abel. "We were bad in the first period, Leafs were bad in the second and I thought we both came back in the third and played the way we should."

Frank Mahovlich suffered a knee injury after being checked by Bill Gadsby in the first period. He was treated in what Bill Hewitt announced as "the Gardens hospital," and then returned for a brief skate during a stoppage in play. Feeling okay, The Big M played one shift, making a solo rush, but knew something was wrong and was taken to the hospital for overnight observation.

Gadsby admitted that Mahovlich was a tough player to stop. "He takes that wide sweep and then pulls in behind you. This time, he was just beginning to pick up speed. That's the reason I was able to nail him. It was a good clean hit," said Gadsby. "Those knee-to-knee jobs usually hurt." Referencing Gadsby, the *Toronto Daily Star* wrote, "He gives and he receives. There are more stitches in Gadsby's face than there are in a custom-made topcoat." Gadsby simply shrugged. "You've got to play hard. Otherwise, you won't last." The veteran Detroit defenceman claimed to still feel pain from damage inflicted by a Bill Barilko bodycheck years before.

Johnny MacMillan, recuperating from an infected elbow, was expected to take the Big M's place in the lineup but he, too, was unable to play. Ed Litzenberger was assigned the task instead.

Larry Jeffrey starred for Detroit with two goals in a losing cause. Norm Ullman played a strong two-way game for Detroit, and added assists on both of Jeffrey's goals to establish the playoff point-scoring lead. "Man for man, there isn't a better checker in the National Hockey League than Norm Ullman," offered Bob Pulford.

Dick Duff scored two goals for Toronto, and had a good feeling about the game. "I knew in the warm-up I was in for a good night," admitted Duff. "I took two little shots and 'zing' — they whipped in." The Leafs' feisty winger was chosen by Bernie Geoffrion as *Hockey Night in Canada's* first Star. Jeffrey, who scored twice, was second Star while Bob Nevin, who scored twice, took the third Star.

"Brewer played a vigilant, tough game," stated *The Globe*. "He invariably zigged and zagged out of the Leafs' zone with the puck when the Wings threatened."

After the game, Brewer wasn't talking about the win. In fact, he was espousing the benefits of a new vitamin pill that halts male pattern baldness. "Eddie Litzenberger says me and Baun have got to watch it. If we don't, the club will have a new line: Brewer, Baun and Imlach!"

Déjà vu: Leafs Win by Score of 4–2
Game Two, Stanley Cup Final – Thursday, April 11, 1963
The fear of losing Mahovlich for most, or all, of the final with his knee injury, turned out to be overstated. Doctors diagnosed that the injury was a deep bruise, nothing more, so while The Big M missed game two, he was

scheduled to return for game three, when the series shifted to Detroit.

Imlach had to make a major decision during the season. He only had room on the roster for one extra player, with both Bronco Horvath and Ed Litzenberger to choose from. Imlach decided to send Horvath to Rochester of the AHL and to keep Litzenberger. "Litz stayed for one reason. He worked harder," said Imlach. Litzenberger, inserted into Mahovlich's spot in the lineup, came up big with a three-point game. Said Imlach, "He vindicated the decision to keep him on the team all season. He produced in the clutch. It pays a coach to be lucky and to have solid, versatile players on the bench for emergencies. Litz made me look good."

Litzenberger appeared to be on his way to NHL stardom while playing with the Black Hawks. Using his size and shot, he enjoyed three consecutive thirty-plus goal seasons, starting in 1956–57. But his career seemed to suffer after the car accident in which he lost his wife. He was Detroit property briefly, but when made available, the Leafs grabbed him for the $20,000 waiver price during 1961–62. "I wanted him but I couldn't play him much," explained Imlach. "I had to use him as a spare. One thing he does good is faceoffs. If I've got an important faceoff where I want the puck, Litz is my guy."

Litzenberger opened the scoring at 5:31 of the first, banging in his own rebound. Later that period, he earned an assist when Ron Stewart broke into the clear, deked Sawchuk and tucked a backhander into the back of the net at 18:43 for Toronto's second goal.

At the forty-nine-second mark of the second, Bob Nevin scored on a rebound from an Allan Stanley shot to put Toronto up 3–0. Gordie Howe, fighting off the effects of intestinal flu, was Detroit's most determined player and scored the first of his two goals less than a minute after Nevin. Ron Stewart scored his second goal on a power play, assisted by Litzenberger, to give Toronto a 4–1 lead going into the third period.

Howe scored his second goal in the third period, but it was too little too late. Toronto earned their second straight 4–2 victory.

The Leafs weren't challenged in either of the first two games, and were capable of playing better. So were the Wings, or they would never have dismissed Chicago in the semi-final. Sid Abel admitted his troops looked tired, and he spelled off Gadsby and Barkley with Howie Young on defence. Young had been banished to occasional power-play shifts only, having taken too many foolish penalties during the Chicago series. "The Leafs played a big game Thursday," admitted Abel. "They had the puck most of the night and when they didn't have possession, they were pressing us into mistakes."

Bobby Hull appeared on *Hockey Night in Canada*, choosing the game's Three Stars, and selected former teammate Ed Litzenberger, followed by Ron Stewart and Gordie Howe.

While the Red Wings appeared tired, the *Star* noted that the Leafs "weren't puffing hard enough to extinguish a match." Dick Beddoes in *The Globe* called the Red Wings "an embarrassment of poverty," and suggested that a Leaf sweep in four games "would be the humane thing" to put the Wings out of their misery.

Leaf Discard Scores Two to Topple Toronto
Game Three, Stanley Cup Final – Sunday, April 14, 1963

With the Maple Leafs leading the series two games to one, game three was scheduled for Detroit's Olympia. Sid Abel sequestered his team in Toledo, where they bussed into Detroit for the two games played at home. After three games in five days for the Red Wings, the coach initiated a number of team-building exercises, like bowling, away from the distractions of the players' homes. "Home ice should pick us up," said Abel.

The Wings were heartened by the fact they had been down two games to none against Chicago in the semi-final, and proceeded to come back and win the next four. "We came back from that and we can come back from this," said Abel, who briefly considered replacing Sawchuk in goal with Hank Bassen for the third game but decided against it.

Meanwhile, the Leafs flew to Detroit for game three, except for Carl Brewer, who hated flying and took the train instead. The team stayed in nearby Dearborn.

Sid Abel had created a cabinet of veteran Wings to assist him with team decisions. This group was comprised of Alex Delvecchio, Bill Gadsby, Gordie Howe and Marcel Pronovost. Abel ended up benching defenceman Howie Young, a move dictated by his cabinet after he compromised the team by taking terrible penalties at inopportune times and giving the puck away too frequently through the playoffs. Young was replaced by Lou Marcon from the Pittsburgh Hornets, who never saw a shift.

Mahovlich returned for game three, used sparingly at first, but then, after testing his sore knee, took his regular shift as the game progressed.

Vic Stasiuk scored Detroit's first goal on a screened backhand at the thirty-three-second mark of the game. The Wings had successfully waived Stasiuk through the league in December, sending the veteran to Pittsburgh. Stasiuk balked at going to the minors and retired, but reconsidered and reported to the Hornets in January. He was recalled by the Red Wings and was an important component of the playoff run. Stasiuk was one of only five current Red Wings to have played on Detroit's last Stanley Cup championship squad in 1955. The others were Delvecchio, Howe, Pronovost and Sawchuk. Both Larry Hillman and Red Kelly, playing with Toronto, were also on that team.

Dave Keon evened the score at 14:56. Although he lost control of the puck as he cut through the crease, the puck crossed the goal line to tie the score.

At 8:13 of the second period, Alex Faulkner fired a thirty-foot rocket that went in off the post past Bower. It was the first of two goals the former Leaf scored that night.

Tim Horton scored Toronto's second goal at 13:06. A rebound from a Red Kelly chance bounced out front of Sawchuk, struck Horton's skate and went in.

Faulkner tipped a Marcel Pronovost shot from the point to give Detroit the lead at 13:39 of the second in the seesaw battle. With no scoring in the third, Faulkner's goal proved to be the game-winner, his third winning goal of the playoffs. Each of the game-winning goals was scored on successive Sundays. "There were fireworks and dancing in the streets [of Newfoundland] when, on two occasions, he shot the winning goal in Detroit's semi-final upset over the Chicago Black Hawks," wrote the *Star*.

Alex Faulkner had been plucked from the waiver wire by Detroit from Toronto for the $20,000 waiver price in June 1962. "If Detroit hadn't drafted him, I was going to deal him off to Springfield," admitted Imlach. The plan had been for Toronto to acquire Kent Douglas and Floyd Smith from the AHL Indians, but Detroit stifled that deal by drafting both Faulkner and Smith.

Faulkner was the first Newfoundlander to play in the NHL. Discovered by King Clancy during a goodwill mission to Newfoundland, Alex was invited to go to Rochester for a tryout with the Americans in December 1960. Allowed to play five professional games before he'd lose his amateur status, he scored two goals in two games for Rochester and was immediately signed to a pro contract by the Maple Leafs. He played his only game as a Maple Leaf on December 7, 1961, spending both seasons with Rochester. "Let's face it, I can never thank King Clancy enough for getting me a break in pro hockey," Faulkner said. "I could make ten thousand a year as an athletic director down there [in Newfoundland]. That's not bad for a guy with a grade ten education, but as long as I can hang on in the NHL, I'll stay here."

"It's Newfy's night," said Howe. "Did you see the way he kept bouncing back when they knocked him down? And he's never out of position around the net." Howie Meeker, the former Leafs' coach who was living in St. John's at that time and making his debut as a *Hockey Night in Canada* analyst, boasted, "Alex is to Newfoundland hockey fans what Babe Ruth was to baseball." Alex was chosen as the game's first Star. Marcel Pronovost and Tim Horton were Stars two and three.

The 3–2 win was Detroit's best effort to date in the final. "Detroit could have won this game by a more commanding margin but for the alert goaltending of Johnny Bower," reported *The Globe*.

"I told you fellows not to write us off, that a three-day rest and home ice would be worth two goals to us," declared Sid Abel. "We were the aggressors. We skated, we checked, we forced the play and we finally started to hit." Bill Gadsby added, "We were dead tired in Toronto. That three-day rest did us a world of good."

Conversely, Punch Imlach was furious. "King [Clancy] and I thought this was our poorest game as a team in a month-and-a-half. We weren't skating, gave the puck away too much, our wings weren't coming back and we didn't knock enough of them down." The coach tried to shake the team up by replacing Baun with Douglas. "I was trying to get something going. It's no good standing pat when nothing is working. Several of our guys had off nights." King Clancy, ever the optimist, pointed out the Leafs' best player. "I thought Tim Horton was tremendous. He nailed big Gordie [Howe] a couple of beauts and really lugged that puck."

Toronto Again Wins 4–2; Takes Commanding Series Lead
Game Four, Stanley Cup Final – Tuesday, April 16, 1963
Both teams practised in Detroit, although remaining away from distractions at their respective hotels. Trainer Bob Haggert put the Leafs through a brief practice, while scout Johnny Mitchell did the same for Detroit. Ed Litzenberger said the Leafs' Dearborn hotel was so quiet, "You startle the guests if you're not careful turning the pages of your newspaper."

Detroit goalie Terry Sawchuk had experienced a mediocre series, to that point, re-injuring his elbow, and again there was talk of Hank Bassen starting in goal for Detroit in game four.

Howie Young had "finally exhausted the inexhaustible patience of manager-coach Sid Abel," according to *The Globe*. The twenty-six-year-old bad boy was dropped from the Red Wings' lineup for game three, and did not accompany the team to their hotel for game four. Detroit newspapers suggested Young was through as a Red Wing.

Toronto took the fourth game, played in Detroit, 4–2 over the Red Wings, putting them up three games to one. The Wings played their most efficient game of the final, led by the fine play of Gordie Howe and Bill Gadsby, and in spite of the Leafs committing several errors, Johnny Bower came up big in the Leafs' net.

"We don't think the Detroit Red Wings can play a better hockey game than they turned in while losing to the Leafs 4–2," claimed the *Star*.

Howe opened scoring for Detroit, firing a shot from the faceoff circle that hit Bower's glove and fell behind the goal line into the net at 2:54. "The puck flipped on end, hopping like a Mexican jumping bean jazzed up on morphine," wrote *The Globe*. The goal was considered soft by Imlach, who contemplated pulling Bower in favour of Don Simmons at that point. "It hit my glove and rolled right over. You saw the guy who fired the shot. Howe's been beating guys for seventeen years. Give him credit instead of looking for my mistake," responded Bower.

George Armstrong scored at 1:17 of the second to knot the score, but Ed Joyal fooled Bower, coming out from behind the net and tucking the puck into the empty goal while Bower looked the other way. At 17:41 of the second period and with the Wings shorthanded, Kelly executed "a masterpiece of sleight of hand." He faked a drop pass to Mahovlich, used Gadsby as a screen and then fired a missile past Sawchuk, as Litzenberger skated by, serving as yet another screen.

Dave Keon scored the winning goal at 9:42 of third, the result of tenacious effort. The nimble centre deked Floyd Smith and Pete Goegan and then passed to Armstrong in front of the net. The captain went in too quickly, and Keon scooted in to claim the puck. He tried to pull the puck across in front of Sawchuk, but lost control. The puck hit the sliding Sawchuk in the pads, rebounded out and hit Norm Ullman's skate, finding the back of the net.

Red Kelly scored his second goal of the game at 17:43 to ice the victory. "By whacking in a pair of goals, Mr. Kelly put himself in a precarious position," wrote the *Star*. "He doesn't drink a drop — and they're not going to fill that Stanley Cup with ginger ale."

Dick Duff was at his feisty best throughout game four. At one point, he flipped Howe's stick into the crowd. When he was challenged, he skated over to the Red Wings' bench and offered to spar with veteran Vic Stasiuk.

Hockey Night in Canada asked guest commentator Gump Worsley to choose the Three Stars, and he selected Keon, Bill Gadsby and George Armstrong.

Detroit got strong games from defensive veterans Gadsby and Marcel Pronovost, while Terry Sawchuk played his best game of the series. "It was a question of breaks, and the Leafs cashed in better than we did," said Abel.

The Wings were unanimous in their praise of Johnny Bower, whom they acknowledged as the difference-maker in the contest. "He may not have been best in the league during the season, but no one has been close to him on the playoffs," stated Gordie Howe, who sarcastically acknowledged Toronto's close-checking. "The Leafs have a whole team of checkers. With the Hawks, you worried about one guy [Nesterenko]. With the Leafs, you have the whole team grabbing and clutching. They're pretty good at it."

After both Red Wings' goals, the game was held up for more than five minutes as workers cleared debris from the ice, ranging from eggs to a splattered bottle of ink. Just before the end of the game, players and fans alike ducked when two loud firecrackers were discharged. Sid Abel blamed the debris-tossing on fans from across the river in Windsor.

As the Leafs made their way to the dressing room at the conclusion of the game, they were pelted with garbage, boos and profanity. Fans shouted derisive comments at coach Imlach, who countered with, "Go home, you've seen your last game of the season!" Carl Brewer took a water balloon square in the face. Police were summoned but there was no further activity.

The *Toronto Star* stated: "This Stanley Cup final between the Maple Leafs and the Detroit Red Wings boils down to one word: 'desire.'"

Toronto Wins Second Straight Stanley Cup!
Game Five, Stanley Cup Final – Thursday, April 18, 1963
The location switched back to Maple Leaf Gardens, and because the final could be decided that night, the Stanley Cup was on hand. The Toronto Maple Leafs had the upper hand on Detroit, with a three-games-to-one lead, and playing in front of Leafs' faithful gave Toronto a further, albeit psychological, advantage.

Dave Keon opened the scoring on a breakaway at 17:44 of the first period, while teammate Allan Stanley was sitting out an elbowing penalty. Delvecchio contributed a goal for Detroit at the forty-second mark of the second period, driving the puck in off the goalpost, past Bower. "We quit skating in the second period," explained Imlach. "We played like dogs."

Leafs scored twice in the final seven minutes of the third period. The score was 1–1 until midway through the third period when Eddie Shack, "who had aroused the crowd with his convulsive rushes," deflected a Kent Douglas shot past Sawchuk at 13:28. "I was cruising near the goal and the puck hit the stick on the handle and went in," he offered. "I never even saw it. All I wanted to do was get the hell out of the way."

At the previous morning's workout, Johnny Bower decided to forgo his goal pads and skated as a forward, while Don Simmons blocked shots. For fun, Bower bodychecked Kent Douglas, but the play almost turned disastrous as Douglas's oft-injured right shoulder popped out of its socket. After some deliberation, Douglas insisted on playing, saying, "This is the fourth straight season I've had the bubbly and I don't want to miss it!" Douglas was part of three Calder Cup championships with the Springfield Indians, and in his rookie season with the Maple Leafs, would then add the Stanley Cup. It was his shot that Shack deflected for what would become the Stanley Cup winning goal. "I fielded the puck with my skate and was able to put tremendous force into my shot," Douglas told reporters. "Fortunately, it hit Shack's stick and went past Sawchuk."

The action in the final moments was furious. With the Leafs up 2–1, Bob Pulford was called for holding at 18:07. Coach Sid Abel summoned Sawchuk to the bench for a sixth skater, and what ensued was a frantic attack. Bower used his skate to make a superlative save on Detroit rookie Eddie Joyal, "who seems destined for greatness in the National Hockey League." Bruce MacGregor then hit the post. Norm Ullman unleashed a shot that struck Gordie Howe as he tangled with Bower in the crease. An ensuing whistle allowed Bower to head to the bench to have his catching glove repaired after it was sliced by Howe's skate. "Tension stayed thicker than sour cream," noted *The Globe*.

The subsequent faceoff took place in the Leafs' end. During a scramble, Keon was pulled down. He quickly gained his legs and relieved the pressure being asserted by the Red Wings by golfing a backhand that wobbled crazily and eventually slid into the empty Detroit goal with five seconds remaining in regulation. The victory was secured. Keon's reaction? He flung his stick and arms into the air and bolted into the embrace of George Armstrong. "Sure I was shooting at the net on that last shot, but if I missed, I wasn't going to be sad," he said after the game, seated in his underwear, his face showing fatigue.

The Globe reported, "An explosion of sound rocked the Gardens and Toronto fans, normally the most decorous in the league, even threw programs and a few hats on the ice." The crowd of 14,403 gave their Maple Leafs a thunderous ovation. The Toronto Maple Leafs had won their second Stanley Cup championship in as many years!

The Maple Leafs gathered around Bower, congratulating him on his fine effort, patting each other and celebrating enthusiastically. The Red Wings could only look on. "There wasn't a player on either team who didn't contribute his last ounce of energy," reported the *Star*. The teams lined up to shake hands, a wonderful longstanding tradition in hockey. Ed Joyal was the only Red Wing who refused to shake hands with the victorious Maple Leafs. "I just didn't feel like it," he said, shrugging.

There were a number of standout performances in game five. Terry Sawchuk, who had been erratic through the final, was superb in this contest for Detroit. Red Kelly was outstanding for Toronto, and seemed to have a monopoly on the puck throughout the final two periods. Imlach singled out Bower and Keon as his most valuable players. Keon, of course, was outstanding through the entire series, and especially in the deciding game, underscored by his two-goal effort. Johnny Bower's play belied his age. "That Bower has to be the youngest forty-year-old that ever skated on this planet," chuckled Rangers' coach Red Sullivan. He was selected by Dickie Moore on *Hockey Night in Canada* as the first Star of the game. Moore chose Keon and Shack as the second and third Stars.

"We gave it our best shot," said Bill Gadsby, who played in his first Stanley Cup final in seventeen NHL seasons. "It wasn't good enough, but we scared the hell out of a lot of people before that final whistle. I've been around this league a long time and never played with a club that had so much spirit." Gordie Howe added, "For a team that wasn't even supposed to be in the playoffs, we showed up rather well."

Clarence Campbell presented the Stanley Cup to Toronto's captain, George Armstrong, who gathered his teammates for a photograph around the table where the Cup sat. "Everybody in here," he shouted. "It belongs to all of them."

One player was conspicuous by his absence. Carl Brewer had had a challenging night. With five minutes left in the third period, he broke the radius bone in his arm while attempting to check Andre Pronovost in front of the Leafs' bench. Brewer missed the speedy winger and used his left hand to cushion his blow as he tumbled into the boards. He immediately got up, shook off his glove, skated to the dressing room and was on his way to the hospital as the celebration was taking place. It was his second incident with Pronovost. In the first period, Pronovost's stick had clipped Brewer's upper lip for three stitches.

While a few of the Leafs remained on the ice, most of the team retreated to the dressing room, led by Eddie Shack who, by scoring the Cup winning goal, earned the right to carry the Stanley Cup into the crowded victors' dressing room. Jammed with family, well-wishers, newspaper reporters and photographers, through the din, the players could still hear the Maple Leaf Gardens' faithful chanting, "We want Shack! We want Shack!" It wasn't to be. "Nattily attired in his skin, with a glass in one hand, [Shack] was holding court for newsmen," joked *The Globe*.

Ward Cornell and Frank Selke Jr. ventured down to ice level to speak with some of the competitors for *Hockey Night in Canada*. While fans shouted, "We want Keon!," the Leafs' star was nowhere to be found. The broadcasters instead spoke with Johnny Bower, Allan Stanley and Gordie Howe. While Stanley was being interviewed, he was all but drowned out by the insistent crowd's rhythmic, "We want Keon! We want Keon!" Just as *Hockey Night in Canada* was signing off the air, Keon emerged from the dressing room celebration to wave to the crowd, and the building shook with cheering. The program wisely stopped rolling its credits so viewers could hear the centre's reaction to the victory. "I'm glad we won tonight and didn't have to go back to Detroit," he said. Ward Cornell then had a word with Punch Imlach, who announced that in his opinion, Keon was "the best hockey player in the business!"

1962–63 Playoff Scoring

RK	NUMBER	PLAYER	POS	AGE	GP	G	A	PTS	PIM
1	14	Dave Keon	C	22	10	7	5	12	0
2	10	George Armstrong	RW	32	10	3	6	9	4
3	4	Red Kelly	D/C	35	10	2	6	8	6
4	20	Bob Pulford	LW	26	10	2	5	7	14
5	26	Allan Stanley	D	36	10	1	6	7	8
6	9	Dick Duff	LW	26	10	4	1	5	2
7	12	Ron Stewart	RW	30	10	4	0	4	2
8	7	Tim Horton	D	33	10	1	3	4	10
9	11	Bob Nevin	RW	24	10	3	0	3	2
10	23	Eddie Shack	LW	25	10	2	1	3	11
11	25	Ed Litzenberger	C/RW	30	9	1	2	3	6
12	21	Bob Baun	D	26	10	0	3	3	6
13	19	Kent Douglas	D	26	10	1	1	2	2
14	27	Frank Mahovlich	LW	25	9	0	2	2	8
15	1	Johnny Bower	G	38	10	0	1	1	0
16	2	Carl Brewer	D	24	10	0	1	1	12
17	15	Billy Harris	C	27	10	0	1	1	0
18	8	Johnny MacMillan	RW	27	1	0	0	0	0
		TEAM TOTALS			10	31	44	75	93

Playoff Netminding

RK	NUMBER	PLAYER	POS	AGE	GP	MIN	W	L	GA	GAA	SO
1	1	Johnny Bower	G	38	10	600	8	2	16	1.60	2
		TEAM TOTALS			10	600	8	2	16	1.6	2

Mayor Donald Summerville and hundreds of others crammed into the humid dressing room to celebrate with the champions, and Dave Keon violated one of his personal rules. A non-smoker, he puffed on a cigarette while downing swallows of champagne. "It only happens once a year," he said, laughing.

Gordie Howe visited the Maple Leafs' dressing room to congratulate his opponents. Johnny Bower handed Howe a bottle of champagne. "I wouldn't have agreed to bait his hook when we go fishing this summer if he hadn't given me the champagne," said Howe, laughing. Bower, who allowed just sixteen goals in twelve playoff games, then took his champagne and clicked glasses with John Jr., who was seated beside his Dad in the dressing room. John Jr. was drinking Canada Dry, ironically, the "champagne of ginger ales."

Ed Litzenberger reminded anyone within range that this was his third Stanley Cup championship in a row. He won with Chicago in 1961 and with the Leafs in 1962 and 1963.

Kent Douglas, nursing his shoulder, laughed, telling reporters that when he was the star of the Noranda midget hockey team, the stick boy was none other than his Toronto teammate, Dave Keon.

Leafs' captain George Armstrong had a plaster on his face to cover a cyst. Asked if it bothered him, he said, "Hell, in the Stanley Cup final, a guy should be able to play on a broken leg!" Ironically, Bob Baun would do exactly that one year later!

During the dressing-room celebration, Duff, Keon and Mahovlich, as well as their former coach, Father Ted Flanagan, began to sing the St. Michael's College school song, which brought good-natured derision from the Marlie alumni in the room. While Keon had drawn the loudest cheers on the ice after the game, the fans weren't so hospitable to Mahovlich, who was booed. The Big M had gone scoreless through both the semi-final and the final series.

Led by the mischievous Keon, team executives Stafford Smythe, Harold Ballard and Punch Imlach were tossed into the shower, suits and all. Funny enough, none of them seemed to mind.

As the dressing room crowd began to thin, Imlach, still damp from his impromptu shower, sat down with reporters and delivered a soliloquy worthy of Shakespeare. "Humility is something I usually don't believe in, being a positive thinker. But at the moment, I'm full of humility because of the one-hundred-and-ten-per-cent cooperation I have received from my players — the world champion Maple Leafs — and the fans. The experts said my old players — Johnny Bower, Red Kelly and Allan Stanley — were over the hill. I knew they were wrong. They're a special breed of athlete. This is a sound hockey club, real champions with just the right blending of age and youth. I have tried to teach my men that you don't wait for things to happen; you have to go out and make them happen. That is what they did this season and that is why they are league champions and Stanley Cup champions."

Imlach's soothsaying, along with the influence of Norman Vincent Peale's book (*The Power of Positive Thinking*), had worked, with both a first-place finish and the Stanley Cup, as Punch had predicted. "Punch could put a setting of sparrow's eggs under a Plymouth Rock and come up with a brood of meadowlarks," suggested the *Star*. Imlach then confirmed that he would continue in the role of both coach and general manager for the Maple Leafs. "As long as they play for me, I won't hire a coach," he said.

That night, the team was treated by the owners to a celebration party at a downtown Toronto restaurant. Hundreds of fans waited excitedly outside the premises to greet their heroes upon their departure.

The City of Toronto hosted a parade for the new Stanley Cup champions the next day — Friday, April 19. The weather prognosticators had threatened showers, but the rain never did transpire. Fans began to gather at 9:00 a.m., and by the time the parade began at noon, more than forty thousand people had jammed Bay Street to salute their victors, a sizable number but down from the fifty thousand who had gathered the year before. In order to get a better look, fans climbed onto the roofs of cars. One radio station's cruiser left that afternoon with its roof caved in. Police Chief James Mackey noted that six hundred officers lined the parade route to ensure that mayhem didn't spoil the celebration.

As the clock in city hall struck twelve, the red-coated civic honour guard marched up Bay Street, leading the tickertape parade. The band struck up "Hail, Hail, the Gang's All Here," as the procession of convertibles made its way up Bay Street from Wellington to city hall.

Captain George Armstrong sat with the Stanley Cup in the lead car of the parade as a raw wind whipped up the street. As the tickertape floated down onto the parade from the windows of buildings lining Bay Street, fans chanted, "We want Keon!"

The fans surged as the players arrived at city hall, and police were needed to hold back the anxious throng. While climbing the stairs of the venerable old building to where the civic reception was to take place, the captain nearly dropped the Stanley Cup!

Ed Fitkin served as the master of ceremonies from the top of the stairs at city hall, standing beside W. A. Hewitt, father of Foster and grandfather of Bill, the Leafs' broadcasters. Fitkin introduced Mayor Donald Summerville, who was wearing the trappings of his office as he shouted, "You are OUR world champions!" His worship then addressed the fans, saying, "This is a tremendous crowd! This is young Canada. I bet everyone out there has a pair of skates!"

Each player was introduced, with Keon, Shack and Bower receiving the loudest cheers from the crowd. Every one of the players was handed a gold tie clasp that bore the insignia of the City of Toronto. The gift gave players a matching set, as in 1962, they had received cufflinks from the city.

Then the players accompanied Mayor Summerville into his office, where they signed the visitors' guest book. In the previous year, Eddie Shack had caused some mayhem by sitting in the mayor's' chair, but this year's celebration was much more subdued.

Highlights of the Maple Leafs' game five win, along with the dressing room celebration and the Stanley Cup parade, were shown on CFTO-TV that night at 8:00 p.m., and repeated the next day.

Once the civic reception concluded, the Maple Leafs headed over to Maple Leaf Gardens with their families, as well as the staff and their families, for a quiet party where each employee had his or her picture taken with the Stanley Cup. That night, Stafford Smythe held a party at his Edgehill Road home in Etobicoke.

The Toronto Maple Leafs had accomplished everything they targeted at the start the season. The team finished first for the first time in fifteen years, and was virtually unbeatable in the playoffs. Having won their second consecutive Stanley Cup championship, the word "dynasty" was being whispered (shouted, by some).

Each returning player was asked to return his Stanley Cup ring from 1962. Leafs' management then replaced the existing stone with a larger diamond to commemorate the sensational season.

The Maple Leafs knew they had something very special. The youngsters had developed into terrific hockey players and the older veterans were as reliable as they had ever been. And Imlach's "spare parts" were valuable in providing depth. The team had meshed into a most remarkable machine, and the only thing holding them back from dominating through the entire decade, if you listened to the critics, was that Father Time would soon catch up to the core of the team.

SLAPSHOTS AND SNAPSHOTS
THE MAPLE LEAFS: PAY TV AND MOVIES

During the early 1960s, Sunday night in Toronto was "Hockey Night in Etobicoke." The northwest Toronto suburb of Etobicoke had many homes hooked up to the Pay TV network, a co-operative venture between the International Telemeter Company of New York and Famous Players Canadian Corp. Besides the various events and movies that were available, customers could drop $1.25 in change into the coin box attached to their black-and-white television set and watch Maple Leafs' road games. The first experimental out-of-town broadcast took place on February 28, 1960, with the Leafs visiting the New York Rangers. The test was so successful that the original number of eight away games was increased to all thirty-five road games for the 1962–63 and 1963–64 seasons.

Along with the privilege of watching the game from the comfort of your living room, there was an annual fee of $15 fee for the slot-machine Telemeter box to watch "feevee." The additional $1.25 was then was paid for each game a viewer decided to watch.

Etobicoke was selected as the experimental site because surveys had indicated that 60 per cent of the local population had not been to a theatre in a year, leading to the belief that these people would prefer their entertainment at home. Of the fifty thousand homes in Etobicoke at the time, only about fourteen thousand were wired for pay television. One resident whose home was located outside the Pay TV area gladly paid the $1,100 fee to extend the wiring to his home. In addition, it should come as no surprise that Harold Ballard and Stafford Smythe, co-owners of the Toronto Maple Leafs, both resided in Etobicoke.

In an era when *Hockey Night in Canada* viewers were accustomed to seeing only half of the broadcast (the games were joined in progress at that time), the Toronto road games were shown in their entirety, a welcome feature for those with access to "Telemeter Hockey." Film clips of previous Toronto Maple Leafs' games were shown during the intermissions.

For the 1962–63 season, the average number of subscribers for each of these hockey games was only one thousand, although games originating from the Montreal Forum had a greater number of viewers.

Although visiting clubs did not share in any monies from free television and radio broadcasts of NHL games, and they didn't receive any percentage of the live gate, with Pay TV the visiting clubs did receive a share of the television rights.

Even NHL president Clarence Campbell endorsed the concept of Pay TV. Campbell, who in 1949 expressed concern that televising games would be detrimental to the game and keep people away from the rinks, recognized the benefits of television. "Pay TV is the only available additional box office we have left. It won't stand up to the live article, but it helps develop more hockey fans. The greater exposure the better. Pay television is a perfect outlet."

The offering of "live" sports events to customers in Etobicoke and the adjacent town of Mimico remained popular through the 1963–64 season. However, because of the high installation and production costs, including rights fees for first-run movies and hockey games, there just were not enough subscribers to offset the thousands of dollars in losses to International Telemeter and Famous Players Canadian Corp. Although there was demand for the service in other parts of Toronto, those areas were never wired up, and the Pay TV experiment could not be continued. Eventually, some out-of-town games were shown on free television, but the experience could not match the excitement of the "feevee" experiment in Etobicoke in the 1960s.

LEAFS AT THE MOVIES

When "Leafs TV," the club's digital television station, announced that a number of the Toronto Maple Leafs' broadcasts would be available for fans to watch at movie theatres, it was thought that it was an original, groundbreaking idea.

In fact, there was a precedent.

For the 1962–63 season, the Maple Leafs, together with Trans-Canada Telemeter, announced that non-televised games would be available for viewing in selected theatres around Toronto. Homes in the Toronto suburb of Etobicoke were already able to access the Leafs' away games via their Telemeter boxes. Until the completion of the Telemeter installations for the rest of Toronto could take place, fans could attend the theatres to watch their Maple Leafs play in the four American cities.

The newspaper ads proclaimed, "For the first time, a new type of Sports Entertainment! Through the magic of Eidophor, YOU CAN SEE MAJOR LEAGUE HOCKEY on a Big Theatre Screen — every minute of every Maple Leaf Away Game — Beamed Live — play by play to the College Theatre." The ad noted "All Seats Reserved: $1.25, $2.00, $2.50."

The "magic of Eidophor" seemed like some new space-age technology, but it was essentially a thirty-foot giant screen projection or closed circuit. But what was enticing was that the entire game would be shown, a novel idea at the time.

In the initial closed-circuit telecast, on October 10, 1962, the Maple Leafs treated their fans to a 3–1 victory over the Black Hawks at raucous Chicago Stadium. According to *The Globe and Mail*, there was an "overflow of fans, and the wide-screen performance drew as many cheers, howls and groans as can be heard at Maple Leaf Gardens." The College Theatre was filled to capacity with 1,500 fans joined by 50 standees lining the rail in the lobby. For the season, 92 per cent of the seats were sold, and plans were made to expand.

Outside of a few technical flaws, the fans were generally pleased with the picture quality. The enthusiasm generated by the crowd was partly because the action seemed much faster on the giant screen than watching at home on a small television set. Bill Hewitt handled the play-by-play, but there was no intermission content.

Every effort was made to recreate the experience at Maple Leaf Gardens and represent an "electronic arena." Official programs and souvenirs were sold at the theatres. As a gesture to the Leafs' players, their wives were provided with season tickets for all the games as guests of Trans Canada Telemeter.

Mr. Winik, executive vice-president of the parent company, International Telemeter, considered the evening a success except for some technical flaws in the picture that would later be rectified. The next Sunday night game from New York had already sold more than half of capacity. With all seats sold for every game played at Maple Leaf Gardens, and the Leafs having just won the Stanley Cup, the success of this venture was not surprising. According to Toronto Maple Leafs' president Stafford Smythe, the Leafs would get a minimum guarantee or 25 per cent of capacity, whichever was greater, for the broadcast rights. Under the NHL's television revenue split, the Leafs paid 25 per cent of the Pay TV revenue into the league pool.

The success of playing to 85-per-cent capacity in 1962–63 prompted ads for the 1963–64 season stating, "A New Era of Entertainment — Share the crowd excitement of the close-up action that almost puts you in the game — On The Giant Screens of 9 Theatres!" Season tickets were available guaranteeing the same seat for each game. Theatres in Oshawa, Hamilton and St. Catharines were among those added to carry the broadcasts.

Viewing hockey games at the theatres did have its critics. Some fans preferred the quiet atmosphere at home over the hubbub of the crowd in the theatres. Long-time Leafs' fan John Arnott, a fan of Billy Harris, complained that he missed his favourite player scoring his hundredth NHL goal when there was a glitch in the picture.

During the 1963–64 season, four home games were added to the theatre schedule, viewed by what was deemed an "average-sized audience," and by the 1964–65 season, discounted seats were being offered: "Hockey Fans Who Purchase a Regular Ticket May Bring Ladies, Students, Children To See This Game at ½ Price! Also, To The First 50 Kids in Each Theatre, an Authentic Maple Leaf Hockey Player Calendar."

The logistics of presenting out-of-town broadcasts to movie theatres and to the experimental home Pay TV subscribers in Etobicoke was costly to Trans-Canada Telemeter, and the venture ran its course after the 1964–65 season. The concept, as we now realize, was well ahead of its time.

8

1963–64: Overcoming Injuries and the Odds, to Win Again

The five "also-rans" from the previous season made a number of roster changes prior to the 1963–64 season, but the two-time defending champions from Toronto, not surprisingly, did little tinkering to their lineup. Their only change of consequence was the addition of rookie Jim Pappin, although they added depth for their AHL lineup by securing Don Cherry, from Spokane of the WHL (when that team was purchased by the Leafs), and Les Duff from Hershey of the AHL, in return for Bruce Draper and Gene Ubriaco.

Concerned with their third-place finish and premature elimination in the playoffs of 1962–63, the Montreal Canadiens underwent significant changes, aimed at strengthening their lineup. A shocking trade with New York saw netminder Jacques Plante and forwards Phil Goyette and Don Marshall move to the Rangers in exchange for Gump Worsley, Dave Balon, Leon Rochefort and Len Ronson. To insure that their smaller forwards would no longer be pushed around, the Habs bought John Ferguson from the AHL's Cleveland Barons and traded Gary Bergman, Wayne Bobby, Fred Hilts, Lorne O'Donnell, John Rodger and Brian Smith to Springfield of the AHL in order to receive Ted Harris, John Chasczewski, Bruce Cline, Terry Gray and Wayne Larkin. Injuries brought Dickie Moore's career to a premature (but not permanent) conclusion.

Ferguson and Bryan Watson, both tough guys, were introduced to the NHL. Along with fellow tough guy Ted Harris, who joined the Habs in 1964–65, there would be no more intimidation of the Montreal players. The balance of power was beginning to shift. The Montreal Canadiens certainly had sufficient talent, but with the acquisition of Ted Harris and even more so, John Ferguson, Montreal was now the team to beat.

Boston, following yet another last-place finish, received Tom Johnson from Montreal on waivers. Andy Hebenton was drafted from the Rangers and Wayne Rivers from Detroit. In order to receive defenceman Bob McCord from Springfield of the AHL, the Bruins sent Bruce Gamble, Terry Gray, Randy Miller and Dale Rolfe to the Indians. Also out was Bob Perreault, who was sold to San Francisco of the WHL. Shuffled into the lineup were Gary Dornhoefer and Orland Kurtenbach.

The Black Hawks dropped Rudy Pilous from behind the bench and hired former Leafs' coach, Billy Reay. Phil Esposito made his debut, and Howie Young was picked up from the Red Wings. For goaltending insurance, the Hawks received Jack McCartan from the Rangers in the Intra-League Draft.

Along with Plante, Goyette and Marshall, New York added Val Fonteyne from the Red Wings. Former captain Red Sullivan returned as coach, having taken over behind the Rangers' bench halfway through the previous season.

Meanwhile, Detroit already presented a formidable lineup. Through the draft, they added Irv Spencer from Boston and Ted Hampson from the Rangers. A deal that would pay sizable dividends saw the Wings deal Howie Young to Chicago for Ron Ingram and goalkeeper Roger Crozier. Rookies Paul Henderson and Pit Martin looked good in the Detroit lineup.

As had become tradition, the Maple Leafs conducted their training camp in Peterborough. Prior to the season opener, Toronto had a series of exhibition games slated in western Canada. Punch Imlach had also orchestrated an exhibition game in Quebec City, which took place before the western swing.

On September 22, after a few drinks, Tim Horton and Bob Pulford challenged each other to a contest to see who could knock over the most garbage cans along Quebec City's Grand Allée. It wasn't long before three police cars pulled up beside the duo, and although Horton offered to buy the officers a beer, the Leafs' veterans were arrested for disturbing the peace. Horton called Imlach and explained the situation. In court, he and Pulford were found guilty and ordered to pay a fine of $50. "It was probably a stupid thing to do," admitted Pulford. "Imlach didn't think it was too funny."

Horton, the longest-serving Leaf, had surprised his teammates by mentioning that he was considering taking flying lessons with Bob Baun. It was well known in the dressing room just how bad Horton's eyesight was. "Without his glasses, Tim can't tell a comma from a cockroach," joked Bob Haggert.

At that junction, it was inconceivable that Horton would have the time to fly. He and his wife, Lori, had four daughters. Tim also owned four hamburger places, three donut shops, and was a partner in an industrial contracting firm. "Nothing serious, these things," he shrugged. "We pay the rent."

Leafs Bury Bruins in Season Opener
Saturday, October 12, 1963

This season was the first for *Hockey Night in Canada* to begin televising games from 8:30 p.m., which meant viewers, for the first time, were treated to two intermissions.

Following the 48th Highlanders, Prime Minister Lester B. Pearson dropped the puck for the ceremonial faceoff between George Armstrong, the Leafs' captain, and Leo Boivin, sporting the "C" for the Bruins.

During the first intermission, the prime minister strode to centre ice to present Dave Keon with the J. P. Bickell Award as the Leafs' most valuable performer during the previous season. It was the second straight season Keon was recipient of the honour.

It seemed only fitting that Red Kelly, Liberal member for York West, would score in the presence of the Liberal prime minister. Frank Mahovlich with two, Bob Nevin and Armstrong scored for Toronto in a 5–1 Leafs' victory. The game's Three Stars were Frank Mahovlich, Orland Kurtenbach of the Bruins and Johnny Bower.

Nasty Fight Prompts Leafs to Divide Penalty Boxes
Thursday, October 30, 1963

The Leafs doubled Montreal 6–3 in a chippy contest. Early in the second, Pulford tangled with John Ferguson, then later took offence to a hit from Terry Harper. Their bout started behind the Leafs' net. "I went in with my stick up because that's where his was," commented Harper. Pulford stated, "He hit me with his stick. I don't know if it was intentional, but you know how it is, you lose your temper." Harper skated away with Pulford down on the ice, but the Leafs' forward caught up to Harper near the Leafs' bench and the two duelled, first with sticks and then with fists. The two continued their battle in the penalty box, mere feet away from NHL President Clarence Campbell. Pulford said, "He said something that would have made any man fight." Harper recounted, "He hit me in the penalty box while I was sitting down. I was surprised, but that's where I got in my best licks. He challenged me in the box and I told him he didn't have the guts."

The entire penalty box incident was viewed by millions on the midweek CTV telecast, undoubtedly embarrassing NHL executives.

In spite of serving nineteen minutes in penalties, Pulford still scored a shorthanded goal and assisted on two others. Ed Litzenberger, J. C. Tremblay and Tim Horton were the Three Stars of the game.

After the altercation, Leafs' owner Stafford Smythe began lobbying the league to have divided penalty boxes. "It's ridiculous to ask two guys who've been trying to knock each other's heads off to sit quietly side by side," he remarked. "We've tried policemen, but that didn't work out too well. Linesmen are supposed to go in to break it up but they didn't do it here." One of the concerns was that wiring and controls for the score clock were located in that same area. Smythe vowed that Maple Leaf Gardens could separate the penalty boxes at some point that season. In fact, the Montreal Forum beat Smythe to the punch, initiating the divided penalty box in a game on November 9 against the Chicago Black Hawks.

Brewer Returns to Club as Bad Blood with Hawks Continues
Saturday, November 9, 1963
Carl Brewer had been sitting out, regaining strength from the arm injury suffered in the previous season's Stanley Cup final, and was also awaiting a new contract, which was agreed upon and signed in time to return to the Leafs' lineup for the 3–3 tie against Chicago. He was chosen as one of the Three Stars, picked up three minors and was, in Imlach's words, "the best defenceman on the ice, either team."

Kent Douglas was demoted to Rochester, in part because of Brewer's arrival and also for curfew violations that angered Imlach. Gerry Ehman was also sent to Rochester.

Don Simmons was in goal, replacing Bower, who was out with an injured toe. Denis DeJordy replaced Glenn Hall in the Black Hawks' goal after the first period when Hall became ill.

"[Stan] Mikita, who spent most of the night looking for trouble, got plenty," announced the *Star*. He was high-sticked by Bob Pulford in the second period. Then, with four minutes remaining in the game, tussled with Shack. Howie Young came to his defence, but Shack won both bouts, jumping Young from behind. Mikita then engaged Baun in a scrap. Mikita ended up with eight stitches and four penalties.

Toronto Loses a Friend

Tuesday, November 19, 1963

Toronto City Council was challenged by the City Radio and Press Club in a charity hockey game at George Bell Arena, with proceeds going to flood victims in Italy. Billy Harris and Bob Pulford were honourary coaches, and Frank Mahovlich and Eddie Shack were the referees.

Toronto Mayor Donald Summerville, who had been a goaltender for the Timmins Gold Diggers of the Northern Ontario Hockey Association in 1936–37 and had also been a practice goaltender for the Leafs during the 1930s, was in net against the team of local media members. The mayor had only been in the crease for a few minutes when he made his way towards the dressing room. 1050 CHUM morning man Al Boliska playfully wrestled with the mayor just before he left the ice surface. On his way to the dressing room, Summerville chatted with local reporters and was asked by the arena manager to sign the guest book. Summerville arrived in the dressing room and commented that he felt tired. He reached for his medication, but before he was able to take anything, he slumped to the floor, unconscious. The arena manager started artificial respiration while the team trainer, Max Hurley, ran to find his wife, a doctor who was in the crowd watching the game. An attendant from St. John Ambulance and the fire department were also summoned. Hurley's wife, Dr. Geraldine Arthur, was unable to find a pulse.

While the men massaged the mayor's chest, the ambulance arrived, and, escorted by police and Controller Phil Givens, took Mayor Summerville to the hospital, where he was pronounced dead. The coroner pronounced the cause as an acute coronary occlusion. It was not well known that Summerville had a heart condition, although he had had a mild heart attack in 1961. He kept nitroglycerine around in case he needed it. The game continued for its full twenty minutes, the players oblivious to the tragedy.

Phil Givens was the first to be informed of the mayor's death. As president of Toronto City Council, Givens assumed the mayoral duties until council was able to select a successor to finish Summerville's term. Council, in fact, chose Givens to replace Donald Summerville as mayor.

Mayor Summerville had presided over the Toronto Maple Leafs' Stanley Cup parade and civic reception in 1963. On the day of the mayor's funeral, the world was rocked by the announcement that U.S. President John F. Kennedy had been assassinated in Dallas.

Leafs and Wings Play in Spite of Pre-Game Bull
Saturday, November 30, 1963
The Canadian Championship Rodeo was held at Maple Leaf Gardens from November 24 to 29. And although detractors had advised the owners of the Maple Leafs against hosting the rodeo because of the ramifications to the ice, Stafford Smythe dismissed the naysayers with a wave of his hand, and as a result, foam chips, sawdust and soil needed for the event were dumped directly onto the Gardens' ice. Smythe had been assured that cleaning up after the rodeo would not pose a problem to ice conditions; however, over the five days, the unprotected ice surface warmed and bonded with the soil and sawdust, as well as the waste from the animals.

When the Gardens' crew tried to remove the layer of dirt and sawdust, they encountered a near-impossible task. "The earth and sawdust melted into the ice and then it froze again to a cement-like consistency," explained Harold Ballard. "When we started to lift the surface, it refused to move. We had to bring in two hundred extra workers [including members of the junior St. Michael's Majors and Toronto Marlboros] to aid our regular staff of seventy-five, and it was a miracle that we got any kind of surface ready by 8:30 [for the game to be broadcast on *Hockey Night in Canada*]. We had two bulldozers, four front-loaders, a grader, two sweepers, fifteen trucks and two hundred and seventy-five men trying to get the ice in shape. We had to truck twenty tons of snow from Richmond Hill to fill the holes caused by the bulldozers and men using fifty flat picks to dig the earth, sawdust and other things out of the ice." All the work left the ice terribly pockmarked and the puck bounced uncontrollably.

Had it not been for radio and television commitments, the game, almost certainly, would have been cancelled. The coaches met and discussed the situation, arguing over whether the game should be played. Detroit coach Sid Abel said, "It wasn't fit for a hockey game." He lodged a formal complaint with NHL President Clarence Campbell. As it was, the game was an hour and fifteen minutes late in starting, the first time a game had ever been delayed.

Roger Crozier, replacing injured Terry Sawchuk in the Detroit crease, was struck on the cheek by a Frank Mahovlich slapshot that sent him to the dressing room, although he returned after ten minutes. Larry Jeffrey recalled that the shot took off because it was slapped from a patch of cement where the ice was negligible. After visiting the hospital following the game, it was discovered that the plucky young netminder had suffered a double fracture of the cheekbone.

Before the second period, George Armstrong, on behalf of the Toronto Maple Leafs Hockey Club, presented Gordie Howe with an award to commemorate his 545th goal, which surpassed Maurice Richard as the NHL's all-time goal scorer.

The Three Stars of the 1–1 tie were Bob Pulford, Parker MacDonald and Roger Crozier.

Hideous Fight Mars Game, Scars Leaf
Saturday, December 7, 1963

During the 1960s, one of the fiercest rivalries was between the Chicago Black Hawks and the Toronto Maple Leafs. These two star-studded teams had enormous physical encounters during their fourteen regular season games. Through the seventy-game schedule during this six-team era, each team played the other five teams seven times at home and seven times away. Many of those games were back-to-back weekend encounters.

The Hawks and Leafs both had skilled players — Bobby Hull, Stan Mikita and Kenny Wharram for Chicago; Frank Mahovlich and Dave Keon for the Maple Leafs — but both also had physical players. Bob Baun, Kent Douglas and the rambunctious Eddie Shack of Toronto were equally matched by the slugging Reggie Fleming, the tough Murray Balfour and the incorrigible Howie Young, representing Chicago.

At the best of times, Chicago and Toronto hated each other. Hate is such a strong word, but it was appropriate in the case of these two teams. Both teams had the talent to battle for league supremacy, and both utilized hard-checking styles of play. The fact that they played each other so many times also contributed to the possibility of fireworks.

The donnybrook of December 7 had been simmering since March 1961. Chicago defenceman Pierre Pilote was on one of his headlong rushes when he appeared to be speared by Eddie Shack of the Leafs. Pilote responded with a vicious swing of his stick, grazing the now-dazed Leaf. Seeing this, Shack's linemate Bert Olmstead challenged Pilote, and a succession of fights was started. The main combatants were Pilote and Olmstead, joined by the Hawks' resident tough guy, Reg Fleming, who was grappling with Leafs' defenceman Larry Hillman. With all this mayhem going on around him, Shack, feeling that he likely instigated the affair, pulled away from trainer Bob Haggert, who was attending to him, and squared off with Hawks' centre Stan Mikita. The angry Hawks, noting the size differential, threw their sticks at the flailing Shack, but to no avail. The Hawks, having seen enough pain inflicted on their star, leapt off the bench, led by Bill Hay, with the Leafs following immediately.

Fans in attendance, as well as those watching the nationally televised contest, remember watching the amusing attempts by Toronto police officers slipping and sliding out on the ice trying to break up the now lengthy and bitter brawl. It was believed to be the first time, and possibly the last, that police intervened in the breaking up of an on-ice fight.

The major participants of the brawls were appropriately fined for their indiscretions and were undoubtedly warned about proper behaviour in future matches.

Looking back at the December 7, 1963, contest, the Leafs were inspired by spectacular goaltending from Don Simmons, who collected his second consecutive shutout (he had blanked Montreal 3–0 on December 4). They scored a goal in each of the three periods, one apiece from George Armstrong, Frank Mahovlich and Eddie Shack. Late in the third period, it looked as though Toronto was going to earn its first win in six meetings that season against Chicago. Simmons briefly left the game in the third period after making an awkward save on Howie Young, but returned to stone the Hawks.

Reggie Fleming and Eddie Shack had continued a personal feud, and they seemed to be especially belligerent this particular night. In a radio interview prior to the game, Shack alleged that "Fleming was only dangerous when he was behind a player. Face-to-face, he was a little cat who would run away." That set the stage for what was to come.

Midway through the third, Shack earned a penalty for high-sticking for rudely planting his stick around Fleming's neck and hauling him down. Fleming waited until the next time both were on the ice together and, with just three minutes and three seconds to go before the end of the game, Fleming exacted his revenge, viciously spearing Shack in the solar plexus. With Shack kneeling on the ice, gasping for air, Fleming was tagged with a five-minute major.

Bob Baun apparently didn't believe a five-minute major was enough punishment, and rushed to the penalty box, where he grabbed Fleming. Referee Frank Udvari, who refereed that previous fight-filled contest two years earlier, noted that the Leafs were bent on revenge and he thought that the best way to prevent another incident would be to send Fleming directly to the dressing room. But to get there, Fleming had to cross to the other side of the ice and pass sixteen Leafs. Thirty minutes, sixteen penalties and $850 later, "Rugged Reggie" finally did make it to his dressing room.

What transpired in the meantime was a bitter, bench-clearing brawl, as vicious as there ever was. Besides Fleming being challenged by, in turn, Baun, Hillman and Dick Duff of the Leafs, various other fights broke out. Even Shack, who had appeared near death, made a miraculous recovery and dashed into combat.

Carl Brewer, still nursing an injured arm, was tangled up with Ab McDonald when Murray Balfour hit him on the back of the head. Balfour then engaged Brewer in an open-ice battle. As they waltzed around the length of the ice and along the boards, Balfour pulled the sweater over Brewer's head. Balfour then pushed Brewer towards the boards by the players' benches. During this era, with teams facing each other fourteen times through the regular season, players had long memories to fuel vendettas, and Balfour, no doubt, remembered the concussion Brewer gave him a few years earlier. "Murray Balfour put his head down and was running me into the boards," Brewer later told Leafs TV. "I didn't realize the bench was open, and as it turned out, I fell back through the bench — under the bench — and that was the end of the fight."

Stan Mikita recalled, "Murray Balfour chased Carl Brewer around the ice like a greyhound after a rabbit. He finally caught up to him near the Leaf bench, stuffed him through the gate and proceeded to punch the snot out of him."

Balfour boasted, "I drove him into the bench and I was on top of him, beating the hell out of him. He started yelling, 'Bobby! Bobby!' Then Haggert and Imlach landed on me. I don't know who hit me, but it wasn't one of them." Balfour suffered a nasty gash on his forehead, but it wasn't clear how the cut was inflicted.

The Hawks, including coach Billy Reay, were livid, accusing the Leafs' trainer of hitting the unsuspecting Hawks' player. But Haggert pleaded innocence. He claimed that when Balfour was hammering Brewer, he grabbed the Hawk, but then Bill Hay grabbed him. At that point, a spectator joined in to even the sides.

TV cameras captured the image of fans coming to Brewer's aid, and when the combatants were finally separated, Balfour had the nasty gash above his eye. Brewer revisited the event, stating, "Fortunately, a friend of mine came down from the stands, Dick Shatto, who proceeded to punch out Balfour." Shatto was a star running back with the Canadian Football League's Toronto Argonauts. When he saw Brewer was in trouble, he bolted from his seat in the stands and joined the scrap before being restrained by a police officer and Leafs' co-owner John Bassett.

Howie Young, astonishingly, had not involved himself in the melee to any great degree up to that point. He skated to the Leafs' bench, peered into the stands and asked a spectator in a seat directly behind the bench if he'd been involved. "Yes, I was down there," said the fan. "You're not so tough," challenged Young. "Come on down here." Up stood Shatto, who was poised to leap down again, when quick intervention by a police constable stopped him.

The mystery has always been, who cut Balfour? Brewer simply shrugged and said, "It wasn't me." That was apparent to anyone watching the fight. Balfour stated, "Brewer didn't hit me. It was either Haggert or Imlach." Others had seen Haggert swinging, but Haggert, who was behind the bench and witness to the punch-up, said a spectator had caused the damage, and although he recognized the individual, he had no intention of naming him. Television cameras captured Toronto Argonauts' star Dick Shatto leaping from the stands to join the fray, but he professed innocence. While there is some question as to whether Shatto ever connected with a punch on Balfour, there is no doubt that Balfour was cut by a phantom punch.

There may be an answer to this mystery. The Maple Leafs had been filming their home games as far back as 1945; the footage was used to improve the play of their team. Don "Shanty" McKenzie had played football for the Argonauts in the early 1940s before serving with Conn Smythe's 30th Sportsman Battery during the Second World War. After returning home, Shanty was hired by Smythe to work at Maple Leaf Gardens, which he did for forty years before retiring as the building superintendent. In his early years at Maple Leaf Gardens, McKenzie also played with the Toronto Argonauts, from 1950 to 1953 (Dick Shatto joined the team a year after McKenzie retired from football).

As part of his duties at Maple Leaf Gardens, Shanty was given the task of filming the Maple Leafs' home games using a sixteen-millimetre camera situated in the green seating section. Some years after the Brewer/ Balfour incident, Leafs' centre Billy Harris, who was wrestling with Pierre Pilote during the fracas, asked Shanty if he had managed to zero in on the fight at the bench with his camera. According to Harris, Shanty admitted that the footage clearly showed the guilty party as Jack Hoult, the box office manager of the Maple Leaf Gardens, who was related to the Smythe family by marriage. This, of course, would have to be kept secret. Hoult may very well be whom Haggert was protecting. Shanty went on to say that the film of the game was "not available." It doesn't show up in the collection of Leafs' films, so chances are that the evidence is lost. But perhaps the mystery has finally been solved.

In the end, eleven Leafs and an equal number of Hawks were fined for leaving their bench to fight. Baun received a major, a misconduct and a game misconduct. Ron Stewart and Larry Hillman each received a major and a misconduct. Fleming received his original five minutes for spearing as well as five for fighting, a misconduct and a game misconduct. Balfour received a major and a game misconduct, Mikita earned a major and a misconduct, and Chico Maki was tagged with a misconduct. "I missed Brewer," admitted referee Frank Udvari. "He should have got something."

The newspapers called the game a renewal of their "sizzling vendetta." Even the coaches, Reay and Imlach (who had fired Billy Reay as coach of the Leafs several years earlier) exchanged profanities publicly after the game.

Because of the severity of the incident — including the possibility that a spectator had inflicted injury upon a player — this fracas between the rival teams resulted in additional notoriety and bad press. This game was just another event in the longstanding enmity between the two teams.

The fight left an indelible imprint on Brewer, who never truly recovered from the embarrassment. "I was never the same player after that. Psychologically, it destroyed me." In Susan Foster's book, *The Power of Two,* she quoted from notes left by Brewer prior to his death. "Murray Balfour — he ruined my life because our fight shamed me. I forgive myself for being afraid. I was afraid because Murray caused it. Yet I was brave. I played the games, but lived with the destructiveness of fear. I could have confronted my fear; I did not. My fear was unnecessary."

Ferguson's Presence Leads Montreal to Victory over Leafs
Wednesday, December 18, 1963
In an attempt to curb having their smallish, skilled forwards pushed around, as they had been during the post-season in 1962–63, the Montreal Canadiens purchased bruising John Ferguson from the AHL's Cleveland Barons in June 1963. Ferguson had registered 126, 146 and 179

minutes in penalties during his three-season AHL tenure, but had also proven that he could score, registering seasons of thirteen, twenty and thirty-eight goals in 1960–61, 1961–62 and 1962–63.

During his rookie season with Montreal, Ferguson made a name for himself as a fighter who routinely bowled over opposing goalies (or anyone else in his wake). On one occasion, in payback for a previous hit, Johnny Bower tripped Ferguson as he crossed through the goal crease. The hard-charging Montreal winger smashed into the boards rather violently. Much to the dismay of the Leafs' coach, Bower skated over to see whether Ferguson was injured. But Ferguson warned Bower that he better keep his head up. From then on, Bower admitted, "I was afraid to leave the net to get the puck when Ferguson was on the ice." The Leafs' defencemen wanted Bower to corral the puck on shoot-ins. "I wouldn't do it because I was a little scared because I saw Fergie," said Bower. "When he wasn't on the ice, I was okay, but he bothered me a little bit."

Ferguson's presence changed the complexion of games. On this night, Montreal dumped Toronto 7–3.

Imlach Gives His Team a Holiday Gift
Wednesday, December 25, 1963
Punch Imlach was told that Bobby Rousseau of the Montreal Canadiens had scored five goals in one game after reading Norman Vincent Peale's *The Power of Positive Thinking,* and decided that the book would make an ideal Christmas gift for his team. On the Christmas Day train trip to Boston for that evening's contest against the Bruins, Punch distributed a copy of Peale's bestseller to every member of his team. The book had the desired effect, as Toronto dumped Boston 5–1 that night.

"There's No Place Like Home," says Johnny Bower
Saturday, January 4, 1964
Regular viewers to *Hockey Night in Canada* could barely wait for this January 4 contest, as it was the first return of the Hawks to Maple Leaf Gardens since the notorious Brewer/Balfour brouhaha.

The fireworks didn't transpire as anticipated, but there was drama nonetheless. Frank Mahovlich scored twice, and Johnny Bower back-stopped Toronto to a 3–0 shutout win over the Hawks that evening. It was Bower's third consecutive shutout at Maple Leaf Gardens. He blanked Detroit on December 21 and Boston on the December 28.

The game wasn't without its nastiness. Leafs' owner Stafford Smythe contacted NHL president Clarence Campbell, complaining that Howie Young spat in his direction and used profanity while serving a penalty. Young was suspended for five games and wrote a letter of apology to Smythe.

Simmons Shell-Shocked as He Surrenders Eleven Goals
Saturday, January 18, 1964
Dick Beddoes reported in *The Globe and Mail,* "January 18, 1964, will be distinguished as the date when the lamb backed the butcher into a corner in Maple Leaf Gardens and carved his initials on him with a meat cleaver."

The Boston Bruins skated to a sinful 11–0 win over Toronto. Belea-guered Don Simmons, once a Bruin and now filling in for the injured Bower, took a pounding against his former team. After the first period, Boston was already up 6–0. Rookie Gary Dornhoefer, with his parents looking on, opened the onslaught at the fifty-three-second mark of the first, and it was all downhill from there for Toronto.

Television viewers were anxious, as always, for *Hockey Night in Canada* to begin, anticipating what the score might be. They were greeted by, "Hello Canada and hockey fans in the United States. Bill Hewitt here at Maple Leaf Gardens in Toronto — the score, Boston Bruins six, the Toronto Maple Leafs nothing. Six-nothing for the Boston Bruins. They've just scored. Their sixth goal — Kurtenbach scoring on a long shot and it comes with just six seconds left."

With the boos of the crowd in the background, sportswriter Hal Walker, serving as commentator between periods that evening on *Hockey Night in Canada,* spluttered, "It's hard to believe. I've been covering games here for years and I've never seen a Toronto team so humiliated as they were in the first twenty minutes."

It was a game never to be forgotten by members of both squads, but for Peter Stemkowski and Arnie Brown, it was their first-ever NHL game. "I remember sitting on the bench thinking, 'I'll sure never forget my first NHL game,'" remembered Stemkowski. "I had a few shifts that night but my name only shows up in the penalty stats." (He served the Leafs' too-many-men-on-the-ice penalty late in the second period.) Arnie Brown was Ward Cornell's second-period intermission guest. "It feels good to be here but it's a little rough out there tonight," smirked Brown. Asked whether he was surprised to be playing as much as he was, Arnie stated, "Yes. The way those things started going in there in the first period, I guess Punch thought to maybe change something up, so I got a chance."

After the second period, the score was 10–0. "Punch didn't say much behind the bench that night, but I could tell just by looking at him that he was in a rage," remembered Eddie Shack. "With the score 10–0, he sent me and [Billy] Harris over the boards, so I turned to him and said, 'What do you want us to do, tie it or win it?' I don't think he appreciated my humour!"

Towards the conclusion of the game, fans at Maple Leaf Gardens chanted, "Go Bruins go!" and began yelling, "We want ten!" The loudest cheer of the evening, a mocking gesture by the hometown fans, was when Boston's Ted Green flipped a harmless shot from outside Toronto's blue line that Simmons caught, and the crowd cheered wildly. At the buzzer that mercifully brought the debacle to a conclusion, Bill Hewitt commented, "And the Boston Bruins have swamped the Toronto Maple Leafs at Maple Leaf Gardens, and they are getting a standing ovation from the crowd, a real sportsmanlike gesture by the crowd here tonight."

Dean Prentice collected three goals and three assists, Andy Hebenton also earned a hat trick, and Murray Oliver had two goals and two assists as the Bruins feasted on Simmons and the Leafs.

"Toronto goalie Don Simmons was constantly left bereft of aid, deserted by a defence that came down with an acute case of clumsy pacifism," stated *The Globe*. "Don't blame Simmons for blowing," said Boston coach Milt Schmidt. "His defence was standing around like so many statues." The *Star* wrote, "Simmons played poorly, of course, but on at least four goals, the Boston snipers had time to adjust their sights and gauge wind drift before pulling the trigger."

The Three Stars of the game were Dean Prentice, Andy Hebenton and Gary Dornhoefer. "You certainly couldn't pick a Leaf tonight," added Foster Hewitt.

"We were all wondering what the hell was going on, and I'm sure the Leaf players were as well," stated Dornhoefer in Howard Berger's *Maple Leaf Moments*. "We didn't have a whole lot of offensive firepower on that team. Most nights were an exercise in survival for us."

In that week, the Leafs lost 6–3 to Boston on Sunday, January 12; 5–4 to Rangers on Wednesday the 15th, and, of course, the 11–0 debacle. Don Simmons had been in goal for all three games. The twenty-two goals surrendered by the Leafs all but ensured that Johnny Bower would not be in contention for the Vezina Trophy in 1963–64. This goaltending travesty helped convince Imlach that the team required a sizable makeover, which it got a month later.

Don Simmons took it all in stride. "Some nights were good and others were bad, but you took whatever came and pushed forward," he told Howard Berger. "As a goalie, you couldn't do anything else."

The very next night, the morose Maple Leafs travelled to Chicago to tangle with the first-place Black Hawks. The Leafs, needing a change in goal, looked to Gerry Cheevers in Rochester, but he was injured. His backup, Ed Babiuk, was not deemed NHL calibre. Imlach chose not to promote Gary Smith from the junior Marlboros, so quickly summoned Al Millar, their Western Hockey League goaltender with Denver, but his plane from San Francisco was grounded due to an equipment malfunction and he was unable to make the trip. As a result, it was necessary that Simmons tend goal, and in spite of his horrific output of the previous games, Toronto rebounded, playing solid, sound, defensive hockey, and Simmons responded with a shutout in a 2–0 victory. "This was not a one- or two-man show; it was a team effort with every Leaf doing a job," reported the *Star*. "Leafs backed Simmons' netminding with one of their most robust performances of the season," wrote *The Globe.* "The improvement in Leafs' defensive play over recent outings was almost unbelievable." Don Simmons agreed: "A goalkeeper is only as good as his teammates, and mine were great tonight." Billy Harris and Ron Stewart scored the goals, both in the second period.

Blockbuster Deal Lands Bathgate and McKenney
Saturday, February 22, 1964

The Toronto Maple Leafs and New York Rangers were set to play Saturday night's *Hockey Night in Canada* contest, but earlier in the day, the two teams pulled off a blockbuster trade. Toronto picked up Andy Bathgate, fourth in league scoring at that point, along with Don McKenney, in exchange for Dick Duff, Bob Nevin, Arnie Brown, Rod Seiling and Bill Collins. The trade addressed the needs of both teams. Toronto was in a scoring slump and needed production, and the Rangers, accepting that they were likely to miss the playoffs, needed to build for the future, especially in the area of defence. "Toronto Maple Leafs traded for today's proven ability, plus goals; New York Rangers traded for tomorrow's potential, and defence," said *The Globe.*

"Andy will do two things that'll make a tremendous difference for Leafs," explained Muzz Patrick. "He's an expert on the power play where the Leafs need help, and he has an excellent shot. With those improvements, they'll be awfully tough to beat. Losing him will hurt us, but we had to do something about our defensive record. That's what's holding us back."

"They forced us to give up two National Leaguers, plus the best NHL prospect from Rochester [Arnie Brown], the guy who should win the rookie award in the Western League [Bill Collins] and the best player on the Canadian Olympic Team [Rod Seiling]," said Smythe.

"You know what you got," said New York's assistant general manager, Emile Francis. "You just got the Stanley Cup right back before you lost it."

"We couldn't win with Bathgate despite his admitted prowess," remarked New York Rangers' president William Jennings. "Leafs got a great in Bathgate and a fine one in McKenney. They should help them repeat for the Stanley Cup. I hope they do." He continued, explaining how the Rangers were strengthened by the trade. "We are searching for muscle and hustle. We got good wingers in Dick Duff and Bob Nevin and three fine young players, the kind [coach Red] Sullivan wants. Now I think we are moving in the right direction, building for the future. I feel we'll have the Stanley Cup here in three seasons."

The Rangers had originally arranged to trade Bathgate to Toronto a month earlier, but the trade was scuttled when details leaked out before Muzz Patrick could discuss it with the Rangers' board of directors. The original trade was Duff for McKenney. "They wouldn't even talk about Bathgate if we weren't willing to give up Seiling. Seiling was the clincher," admitted Stafford Smythe.

Punch Imlach had mixed feelings about the trade. "I've grown to like the fellas who played for me," he told *Hockey Night in Canada*. "We've come quite a way from last place to winning two Stanley Cups. It was hard to get rid of Dick Duff. I looked for all the excuses not to do it. I'm lucky I'm going on the road tonight, as my daughter told me not to come home because I'm letting Dick go. I know there are a lot of people who feel the same way. I think Stafford Smythe wanted to make the trade more than I did. I was looking for excuses."

Imlach refused to allow personal feelings get in the way of doing his job. "Sometimes, you have to do things that you don't want to do if you are going to do your job. You can't let sympathy or friendship interfere with what you have to do as a manager and a coach. Of course, it hurts the player just like it would hurt anybody else that you have to sit down or be traded or whatever. But, that is part of the job as a manager and a coach. You just have to do those kinds of things or you are going to get fired yourself."

Bathgate was ecstatic about the trade to Toronto. "You dream of something like this, but it just doesn't happen," said the ten-year veteran of the Rangers. "Although I've been in the New York organization since I was nine, there's a soft spot in my heart for the Leafs. They're a good team and a contender and I think I can help them. I hope I can live up to Punch's expectations. I know they are having problems on the power play." He continued, "In New York, we had a nucleus for a solid team and it seemed that we'd just get it going and it would start falling apart. I was not helping the team very much in New York. In Toronto, they had a winning tradition. They have a championship team here and I hope we'll help them from here on in."

When Bathgate arrived in Toronto, his family became welcome additions to the Eddie Shack household. He and Shack had been teammates with the Rangers for two seasons.

Don McKenney was taken aback by the deal. "I was surprised by the trade," he told Ward Cornell on *Hockey Night in Canada*. "The Leafs already have four good centremen."

Not everyone was pleased about changing clubs. Dick Duff expressed his regret about leaving Toronto and the Maple Leafs. "I came to Toronto when I was fifteen years old and was twenty-eight when I left. I'd been familiar with the areas in the city and the building and the guys that I played with, and Toronto was the focal point of NHL exposure." He was candid in believing that New York got the better of the deal. "It won't look like such a good trade three years from now," he predicted. "These other guys and I will be playing, and the fellows Toronto got will be ready to pack it in. I think I'll get more opportunity to play with the Rangers. They're a young team with a future."

Harold Ballard also weighed in. "This deal was made for the present. As far as the future is concerned, we have so many good men in junior hockey and below that our farm team is getting jammed up." Rod Seiling was one of those young players who had starred at the junior level for the Leafs. He learned of the trade in a radio report, and although angered at first, was told by his father upon returning home that the Leafs had been trying to contact him all day. "It was quite a shock to me when I heard my name mentioned and I thought, 'This is a heck of a way to hear you've been traded!'" He later said, "I'm really happy. I think there'll be a better chance of making the NHL with the Rangers. They haven't got too many good young players coming up."

At the time, Bob Nevin said, shrugging, "You've got to expect these things when you're a professional athlete. They own you, after all." But many years later, he stated in *The Power of Two*, "There was no purpose in the trade, other than for Imlach to show everybody who was running the show."

Duff and Nevin had been part of the Leafs' organization for years, and were extremely popular with their teammates. Bob Pulford admitted, "I thought it was a bad trade. Duff and Nevin were great players and when the playoffs came, you knew that they were going to be there." In notes left by Carl Brewer, he agreed. "Carl felt the trade was absolutely absurd," wrote Susan Foster, Carl's life partner. "We gave up Dick Duff, who was probably one of the greatest playoff performers of all time, and Bob Nevin, who went on to play for the Rangers for seven years as their captain." The idea that it was a bad trade was a sentiment held not so secretly by a number of team members.

Bathgate was a skilled hockey player, no doubt, but never fit into the team in Toronto. When asked on Leafs' TV how he was received by his new teammates, Andy responded, "I think it was a little cool. Most of the fellows, maybe eight of them, had played their junior hockey together and had grown up together, being Toronto boys. Dickie Duff was very popular and got a lot of important goals for the Leafs. I don't know why Punch made the trade, but you have to give up something to get something. It was my first time traded and I had to adjust. You have to do it on the ice."

In his autobiography, Bob Baun wrote, "When McKenney and Bathgate arrived, they were greeted with stony silence. Andy came on quite gregariously, and Timmy Horton took it upon himself to welcome him to the Leafs: 'Well Alice, you can shut up and go sit down in the corner!'" Horton and Duff had been very good friends, both alumni of St. Michael's College and regular church-goers together on the road.

The dressing room was never quite the same again. This was the first trade of regulars made by Imlach since taking over the role as Toronto's general manager, and the Leafs' players now realized that if Duff and Nevin could be dealt, they were all vulnerable from that point on.

Five hours after the trade, the same two teams played each other. On the Saturday *Hockey Night in Canada* broadcast from Maple Leaf Gardens, the Leafs beat Jacques Plante and the Rangers 5–2. With the newly arrived McKenney on his wing, Dave Keon found more room to manoeuvre. "Don skates, moves the puck and is always in position," said Keon. McKenney observed, "I feel five years younger already. This is my kind of hockey!" McKenney, whose wife was expecting a baby and remained at their home in Boston, was one of the Three Stars in his first game as a Leaf. The others were Ron Stewart and Camille Henry.

The next night the teams played again, this time at Madison Square Garden. During the 4–3 Toronto win, with Keon scoring the winning goal at 19:32, New York fans chanted, "Muzz must go! Muzz must go!"

Detroit Leaves Leafs in Stitches
Saturday, March 21, 1964
The Leafs faced Detroit in a home-and-home weekend series that concluded the 1963-64 regular season. The Leafs won the Saturday *Hockey Night in Canada* contest 5–3 in Toronto.

Johnny Bower was cut for fifteen stitches on the cheek in the Saturday game, yet still was named one of the Three Stars. While Bower was diving to clear a loose puck, Wings' rookie Paul Henderson took a poke at it and caught Bower in the cheek. Don Simmons stepped into the crease in relief.

Terry Sawchuk had troubles in the Wings' net. Keon flipped a puck from centre ice that skipped past him for Toronto's third goal. Andy Bathgate picked up two assists in the game to tie Jean Beliveau's NHL record of fifty-eight assists in a season.

Even more rare was the spectacle of mild-mannered Red Kelly involved in a Saturday night fight. After Kelly scored the winning goal, Al Langlois rode him hard into the boards, cutting him for four stitches by his right eye. Kelly, a former boxing champion while in high school, swung viciously at Langlois with his stick before players from both teams jumped in.

Final Contest of 1963–64 Season

Sunday, March 21, 1964

The second game in two nights saw the Leafs and Wings meet again, this time at the Olympia in Detroit. Johnny Bower played the first twenty-six minutes of the game before making way for Don Simmons. Pat Rupp made his NHL debut in the Red Wings' goal so Detroit could rest Terry Sawchuk. Frank Mahovlich scored twice for Toronto. Bob Baun scored the winning goal that evening with a shot that caromed off the back-boards, hit Rupp's skate and went into the net. It would prove to be the only NHL game the young netminder would play. Toronto beat the Wings 4–1 to conclude the regular season.

Going into that final game of the regular season, the race for the Vezina Trophy for the principal goaltender on the team with the best goals-against average was tied between Charlie Hodge of the Canadiens and Glenn Hall of Chicago. Chicago beat Boston 4–3 and Montreal bested the Rangers 3–2, so Hodge took the Vezina by a single goal. The Leafs' goaltenders finished a mere five goals out, undoubtedly hurt by the 11–0 drubbing against Boston.

The Maple Leafs finished well, winning nine, tying two and losing four times following the trade. The newest Leafs were on fire. Don Mc-Kenney scored nine goals and contributed twenty-six points in his fifteen games in blue and white. Andy Bathgate scored three and collected eighteen points in the same number of games. Imlach was more than pleased with Bathgate's efforts. "Andy did exactly what I'd had in mind when I made the deal."

The Leafs finished the regular season in third place. Montreal Canadiens' coach Toe Blake called his team's first-place finish "the most satisfying" of his seven regular season titles. "I certainly don't want to knock those other six years, but those teams were expected to win and we were picked to finish fourth or fifth this season." Chicago finished second, just one point behind the Habs. Detroit took the final playoff berth. New York and Boston were well back, missing the playoffs for the second straight season.

1963–64 Regular Season Standings						
FINISH	TEAM	GAMES	WINS	LOSSES	TIES	POINTS
1	Montreal Canadiens	70	36	21	13	85
2	Chicago Black Hawks	70	36	22	12	84
3	Toronto Maple Leafs	70	33	25	12	78
4	Detroit Red Wings	70	30	29	11	71
5	New York Rangers	70	22	38	10	54
6	Boston Bruins	70	18	40	12	48

Dave Keon was the team's scoring leader, although Andy Bathgate's totals, with both of his teams that season, saw him finish fourth in the league that season with seventy-seven points.

Stan Mikita won the Art Ross Trophy as the league's scoring champion, accumulating eighty-nine points (as well as 146 penalty minutes). Jean Beliveau was awarded the Hart. Ken Wharram of the Hawks took the Lady Byng and Jacques Laperriere won the Calder Trophy. Pierre Pilote was recipient of the Norris with Toronto's Tim Horton the runner-up. Horton was also selected to the NHL's First All-Star Team. "Horton's play [is] characterized by steadiness rather than dash," wrote *Canadian Press* in November 1963. "Missing a flair for the dramatic, his work went largely unrecognized between his sophomore year of 1953–54 and last season." *The Globe and Mail* added, "He was one of those steady defencemen who never set many fires but was always around to put them out."

Habs Blank Leafs in Opening Game of Semi-Final Series
Game One, Semi-Final – Thursday, March 26, 1964
The first-place team played the third-place finisher, while the second- and fourth-place teams also paired off in the first round of the playoffs. This meant that the Toronto Maple Leafs would first have to topple the Montreal

RK	#	PLAYER	POS	AGE	GP	G	A	PTS	PIM	ESG	PPG	SHG	GWG
		1963–64 Regular Season Scoring											
1	14	Dave Keon	C	23	70	23	37	60	6	16	7	0	2
2	27	Frank Mahovlich	LW	26	70	26	29	55	66	20	6	0	4
3	20	Bob Pulford	LW	27	70	18	30	48	73	13	1	4	1
4	4	Red Kelly	D/C	36	70	11	34	45	16	10	1	0	2
5	10	George Armstrong	RW	33	66	20	17	37	14	13	7	0	3
6	7	Tim Horton	D	34	70	9	20	29	71	7	2	0	7
7	26	Allan Stanley	D	37	70	6	21	27	60	5	1	0	1
8	23	Eddie Shack	LW	26	64	11	10	21	128	11	0	0	5
9	12	Ron Stewart	RW	31	65	14	5	19	46	12	0	2	1
10	18	Jim Pappin	RW	24	50	11	8	19	33	11	0	0	0
11	11	Bob Nevin	RW	25	49	7	12	19	26	5	1	1	1
12	15	Billy Harris	C	28	63	6	12	18	17	5	1	0	2
13	21	Bob Baun	D	27	52	4	14	18	113	4	0	0	2
14	9	Andy Bathgate	RW	31	15	3	15	18	8	3	0	0	0
15	9	Dick Duff	LW	27	52	7	10	17	59	5	2	0	0
16	17	Don McKenney	C	29	15	9	6	15	2	6	3	0	1
17	2	Carl Brewer	D	25	57	4	9	13	114	4	0	0	0
18	22	Larry Hillman	D	26	33	0	4	4	31	0	0	0	0
19	25	Ed Litzenberger	C/RW	31	19	2	0	2	0	2	0	0	0
20	8	Gerry Ehman	RW	31	4	1	1	2	0	0	1	0	1
21	3	Al Arbour	D	31	6	0	1	1	0	0	0	0	0
22	19	Kent Douglas	D	27	43	0	1	1	29	0	0	0	0
23	1	Johnny Bower	G	39	51	0	0	0	4	0	0	0	0
24	16	Arnie Brown	D	22	4	0	0	0	6	0	0	0	0
25	8	Ron Ellis	RW	19	1	0	0	0	0	0	0	0	0
26	8	Johnny MacMillan	RW	28	13	0	0	0	4	0	0	0	0
27	24	Don Simmons	G	32	21	0	0	0	0	0	0	0	0
28	17	Peter Stemkowski	C	20	1	0	0	0	2	0	0	0	0
		TEAM TOTALS			70	192	296	488	928	152	33	7	33

Canadiens if they hoped to reach the final and go on to win a third successive Stanley Cup championship. "There are no soft spots in the playoffs," said Dave Keon, to which Bobby Baun responded, "It's going to be a battle."

Regular Season Netminding												
RK		PLAYER	POS	AGE	GP	MIN	W	L	T	GA	GAA	SO
1	1	Johnny Bower	G	39	51	3009	24	16	11	106	2.11	5
2	24	Don Simmons	G	32	21	1191	9	9	1	63	3.17	3
		TEAM TOTALS			70	4200	33	25	12	169	2.41	8

Charlie Hodge and the Canadiens blanked Toronto 2–0 in the opening contest of the 1964 semi-final series between the long-time rivals. Boom Boom Geoffrion and Ralph Backstrom scored for the home team in a game that set an NHL playoff record for most penalties in a game (thirty-one).

Toronto Edges Montreal in Spite of Brewer's Bad Manners
Game Two, Semi-Final – Saturday, March 28, 1964
The Leafs evened the series with a 2–1 win in game two, also played at the Montreal Forum. Red Kelly scored one goal, while Frank Mahovlich, who his coach lauded for "playing his best game in three years," scored the other. Jean Beliveau responded for Montreal. Carl Brewer earned four of Toronto's eight minor penalties.

Montreal Wins Game Three with Seconds to Spare
Game Three, Semi-Final – Tuesday, March 31, 1964
Toe Blake, coach of the Canadiens, admitted that his team stole the game from Toronto, winning 3–2 at Maple Leaf Gardens. The score was 1–1 after the first period, with Claude Provost and Bob Pulford trading goals. Pulford scored again in the second period. While the Leafs outplayed Montreal for fifty-seven minutes, J. C. Tremblay took advantage of Toronto's sloppy defensive play to tie the score at 17:25 of the third. Then, at 19:35, Henri Richard scored what proved to be the winning goal.

Series Evened in Raucous Affair
Game Four, Semi-Final – Thursday, April 2, 1964
After two relatively calm contests, game four erupted once again, with thirty penalties called between the two teams.

Hockey Night in Canada signed on at 8:30, joining the game in progress late in the first period. Ward Cornell greeted viewers during the first intermission with a brief synopsis of the game to that point. "We have a fast-moving game and a very rough period of hockey," fans were told. Ed Fitkin then described the plays with his videotaped highlights, which included Andy Bathgate giving the Leafs an early lead. Fitkin then said, "Right after that, Ron Stewart triggered a brawl in the Leaf zone when he cross-checked Dave Balon." Then, in a rare and surprising treat for viewers, the entire lengthy brawl, which had been initiated at the 3:46 mark, was shown. The tag team match involved Dave Balon versus Ron Stewart and Henri Richard versus Eddie Shack.

Showing entire fights wasn't common in *Hockey Night in Canada* intermissions. In fact, this might have been the first time. In game one, the Montreal video crew had shown a brief Andy Bathgate/J. C. Tremblay tiff, but this scrap was certainly longer and more intense.

Ron Stewart, likely in payback to Balon for slamming Bob Baun into the boards during the previous game, easily handled Balon. The other bout had the fiery Henri Richard exchanging blows with the Leafs' Eddie Shack. The *Globe and Mail* reported, "At one stage of their tussle, Shack and Richard were at a standoff, each with a strong clutch on the other's arms and sweater. Shack suddenly lowered his head and butted the "Pocket Rocket" in the face." It was a head butt that would make local wrestling promoter Jack Tunney proud. The result was a termination of the match, leaving Richard with a nasty cut above his eye. The diminutive centre deserved a great deal of credit, because he never backed down from his much larger opponent.

Glaring from the bench was Montreal's rookie enforcer, John Ferguson. Ron Stewart felt the wrath of Ferguson's fury in a surprise attack at the end of the game. As for Shack, he and Ferguson had a running feud for years.

An already tense rivalry between Toronto and Montreal escalated and became increasingly bitter. Before the next game at the Forum, Henri's brother, The Rocket Richard, shouted to Shack, "'ey Shack! Good t'ing you never 'it my brudder wit your nose, eh? You coulda split 'im in 'alf!"

Meanwhile, all of the talk in the newspapers and amongst fans was about Shack's head butt, labelled a "coco bonk" after one of the weapons in the arsenal of Toronto wrestler Sweet Daddy Siki. Shack, in fact, would call himself "Sweet Daddy Shacky."

Lost amongst all the shenanigans was that Frank Mahovlich had a hand in all the Leafs' goals in a 5–3 victory that evened the series at two games apiece. The Big M scored twice and assisted on goals by Armstrong, Bathgate and Kelly. Four of the Toronto goals took advantage of power-play opportunities. Jean Beliveau, Jacques Laperriere and J. C. Tremblay tallied for the Habs.

Montreal Edges Ahead in Seesaw Series
Game Five, Semi-Final – Saturday, April 4, 1964

The teams returned to the Montreal Forum, and the home squad again took the victory, putting the Canadiens up three games to two with a 4–2 win. Claude Larose, summoned from the Omaha Knights of the CPHL to replace the injured Beliveau, scored for Montreal, joined by Dave Balon, Claude Provost and Bobby Rousseau. Don McKenney scored both of Toronto's goals.

Bower Beats Habs with Shutout
Game Six, Semi-Final – Tuesday, April 7, 1964

Refusing to roll over, Toronto rebounded in their return to Maple Leaf Gardens, stoning Montreal 3–0 and evening the series at three games apiece. Johnny Bower starred for the Blue and White, slamming the door on a potent Canadiens' offence, especially in the first period. In spite of the score, Charlie Hodge was strong for the Canadiens, keeping the outcome respectable. Don McKenney scored in his second straight game, with Bathgate and Baun also collecting goals for Toronto. Baun's goal was particularly memorable as he raced in on a breakaway after escaping the penalty box, shot on Hodge and fanned on the puck, yet the puck still found its way into the goal, fooling Hodge.

Toronto Wins 3–1; Earns Shot at Third Stanley Cup!

Game Seven, Semi-Final – Thursday, April 9, 1964

The Toronto Maple Leafs and Montreal Canadiens had never played a seventh game in a playoff series until April 9, 1964.

After sitting out two games with a knee injury, Jean Beliveau, the captain of the Canadiens, returned for the pivotal game in this semi-final series. Dave Keon scored twice in the first period to jump-start the Leafs, his second goal earned on a shorthanded breakaway. Ralph Backstrom cut Toronto's lead to 2–1 in the third, but Keon put the victory away with a goal scored into an empty net late in the game; his hat trick was secured. Johnny Bower was sensational again for Toronto, especially in the third period when he stopped seventeen shots, and was named the game's first Star. He posed with a "good luck" wreath around his shoulders, sent to Montreal by loyal Toronto fans.

Both semi-final series in the spring of 1964 went the full seven games. Toronto had eliminated Montreal, while the Red Wings polished off the Chicago Black Hawks. Ab McDonald of the Hawks was interviewed on *Hockey Night in Canada,* and credited Norm Ullman and Gordie Howe with leading Detroit past his Black Hawks in the semi-final. Andre Pronovost, who only scored seven goals during the regular season, scored four in the semi-final against Chicago.

"We beat the best team in the National Hockey League and we'll take our chances against Toronto," said Sid Abel, as he prepared his Red Wings for the 1964 Stanley Cup Final. "We're dog-tired and we're hurting, but you can't give the Leafs any edge for those reasons. They had a seven-game series too and it couldn't have been easy. And remember, their mixture of key veterans and younger players is about the same as ours, so I think you'd have to rate us about even."

Although Carl Brewer had suffered a rib injury after taking a hit from Terry Harper, the Toronto Maple Leafs survived their series with Montreal relatively unscathed. The same couldn't be said of Detroit. Larry

Jeffrey suffered a concussion, his third of the season, after colliding with Wayne Hillman of the Hawks. Terry Sawchuk had also suffered a concussion in the semi-final after being knocked cold by a Reggie Fleming hit. During the semi-final, the Red Wings used three goaltenders — Sawchuk, Bob Champoux (who filled in when Sawchuk pinched a nerve in his left arm) and Roger Crozier, who bounced like a lacrosse ball between Pittsburgh and Detroit five times that spring.

The Maple Leafs beat the Red Wings eleven out of fourteen times during the regular season. "The Leafs will win their third successive Cup," predicted *The Globe*, "but it will occasion little surprise if the Wings triumph. They were the best team in the league during the last half of the schedule. There was nothing girlish in their dismissal of Chicago in the semi-final. To write them off as pushovers is presumptuous folly."

Toronto Beats Detroit 3–2 to Take Game One of Series
Game One, Stanley Cup Final – Saturday, April 11, 1964
"From Toronto, the Stanley Cup finals," stated the announcer as fans tuned in en masse to watch *Hockey Night in Canada.*

"A Hollywood script writer would have discarded this finish to the opening game of the best-of-seven Stanley Cup final at the Gardens Saturday night as being too fantastic. You had to see it to believe it," wrote the *Toronto Star*.

Detroit opened the scoring at 4:31 of the first period when Bruce McGregor took a goalmouth pass from Doug Barkley and fired it gloveside past Johnny Bower. Thirteen seconds later, Allan Stanley fired a slapshot from the point that George Armstrong tipped past Terry Sawchuk to tie the score. Midway through the period, with Eddie Shack in the box, George Armstrong earned a ten-minute misconduct. During the power play, Gordie Howe whistled a shot from inside the blue line past a helpless Bower to give Detroit a 2–1 lead at 10:25. Vezina Trophy winner Charlie Hodge analyzed the first period and thought that both teams were playing "a little cozy."

During the first intermission, Jack Dennett gave viewers an overview of playoff overtimes, including Bill Barilko's dramatic Stanley Cup winning goal of 1951. With no television coverage during that era, hockey fans saw little recorded hockey action. Occasionally, newsreels, which ran prior to movies, might show hockey highlights. The lower angle shot of the Barilko goal shown by Dennett was shot by Shanty McKenzie, an employee of Maple Leaf Gardens entrusted by Conn Smythe to film games. Other than a newsreel shown at theatres, filmed images of this historic goal would have been the very first time hockey fans saw Bill Barilko's Stanley Cup winning goal.

There was no scoring during the second frame. During the intermission, *Hockey Night in Canada*'s Ward Cornell introduced a feature on Red Barber, the Maple Leaf Gardens' public-address announcer from the facility's opening night in 1931.

Frank Selke Jr. then spoke with Bob Goldham, a shot-blocking defenceman during an NHL career that included stops in both Toronto and Detroit. "I think I'll be cheering for the Toronto Red Wings," he laughed, "Make it easy that way."

The teams entered the rink to strains of organist Ralph Fraser playing "The Maple Leaf Forever." Toronto came back for the second time in the contest when George Armstrong scored the second of his two goals at 4:02 of the third. With the score 2–2, the game presented a dramatic and unexpected finish.

The Red Wings had the Leafs on the ropes and were overpowering Johnny Bower through the latter half of the third. With Allan Stanley serving a minor penalty late in regulation time, Bob Pulford poke checked the puck away from Norm Ullman, then took off down the wing with Gordie Howe in pursuit. With Sawchuk out to cut down the angle, Pulford lashed a backhand that flew over the goalie's shoulder and gave Toronto a 3–2 lead with two seconds to spare. "The puck came to Ullman, but he never had control of it," explained Pulford. "I poked at it and I think it hit my shoulder and bounced out over the blue line. Then I was gone." Howe said, "He had a stride on me. I might have caught him if he hadn't switched to the backhand. When he did that, I was done."

Debris rained down on the ice following the goal. "That goal could win us our third straight Cup," said Leafs' president Stafford Smythe. "Our fellows played badly and that win has to give them a shot in the arm, while it could kick the stilts from under the Wings. It's hard to bounce back after taking that kind of a kick in the teeth from Lady Luck."

"They must live right," sighed Bill Gadsby. "We played better than they did." Pulford didn't disagree. "It's luck when you pull it out like that. I hardly believe it myself." Detroit coach Sid Abel didn't sound dejected when he added, "It would have been nice to take the first game, but we've come back before.

The Three Stars, chosen by guest analyst Charlie Hodge, were George Armstrong, Bob Pulford and Gordie Howe, who was booed when his name was announced.

While Jim Pappin was playing in this opening game of the Stanley Cup final, his wife, Karen, gave birth to a baby girl at home in Sudbury. "She looks just like her Daddy," said the new mother. The proud father announced, "We named her Merrill Bernadette."

Wings Win Overtime Thriller to Tie Series
Game Two, Stanley Cup Final – Tuesday, April 14, 1964
The two teams had dramatically differing philosophies regarding practices. This became a point of great derision between the Leafs and the Wings. While Toronto worked out hard each day, including game days, the Red Wings did not practise between games.

"No team in hockey works harder or more regularly than the Maple Leafs," reported *The Globe*. "They're on the ice every day, win or lose, weary or fresh. Few clubs take life easier than the Detroit Red Wings. They seldom practise."

Sid Abel leaned heavily on his veterans — Alex Delvecchio, Gordie Howe, Bill Gadsby, Marcel Pronovost and Terry Sawchuk shouldered most of the load for the Red Wings, and it was Abel's belief that they needed as much rest as possible in order to carry the burden for the team. "We're in shape now after playing hockey since September — seven months. I think it's more important at this stage to maintain a fresh outlook," he said.

Through the course of the final, the Red Wings stayed in Toledo when playing their home games, and just outside Toronto for games at Maple Leaf Gardens. In both cases, Abel bussed the team to nearby racetracks — the Toledo and the Fort Erie tracks. "The racetrack just happens to be handy for getting their minds off hockey," commented Abel. "You can get bored by constant practise, and boredom kills effort faster than anything else. Hockey players are human beings and I treat them that way." Bill Gadsby concurred. "That Punch Imlach must be nuts," he said. "His old guys like Kelly, Stanley and Armstrong can't take it. The business of working out every day is killing them. I looked at some of them and they were bushed, but we had something left because we haven't practised for five weeks."

"Hockey is my business and I'm going to make it my players' business until I win the Cup for a third straight time," replied Imlach. "There's only one way to win, and that's by sweat. There's no substitute for hard work."

Hockey Night in Canada asked Emile Francis, assistant GM of the Rangers, his opinion. "From what I've seen, the amount of work Leafs do won't hurt anybody. You should practise regularly." Bob Nevin, the former Leaf who had been traded to New York, said, "It certainly didn't hurt us the last two years. We won two Stanley Cups. It never hurt anyone to get out and work."

Game two was also played at Maple Leaf Gardens. There were modest alterations to the lineups of both teams. For Toronto, Carl Brewer had hoped to be part of the roster, but his tender ribs prohibited him from lacing up his skates. Brewer was replaced by Larry Hillman, with Al Arbour dressed as the fifth defenceman. "Larry Hillman has given it a good shot as his stand-in, but he is neither as mobile nor as talented as Brewer," commented the *Star*. Imlach shuffled his lines, even resurrecting the HEM Line (Harris, Ehman and Mahovlich) that had been so productive for

Toronto in 1959. The Detroit Red Wings made a modest change, inserting Bob Dillabough from Pittsburgh for Alex Faulkner.

Allan Stanley and Norm Ullman traded goals in the first period, but Detroit leapt ahead with goals from Eddie Joyal and Floyd Smith to give them a 3–1 lead going into the second intermission.

With nine minutes left in regulation time, Toronto was trailing 3–1, but the fortunes quickly were reversed. First, Red Kelly scored at 11:37 to make it 3–2. Then, at 19:17, Andy Bathgate shot the puck from the corner, towards the net, and it ended up behind Sawchuk. Both teams thought Bathgate had scored, but the referee ruled that Gerry Ehman had been the last to touch the puck. Al Langlois returned to the ice from serving a tripping minor two seconds earlier but was unable to scramble back into the play.

The first Stanley Cup final game to go into overtime in five years was about to be decided in sudden death.

Just past the 7:00 mark of overtime, Norm Ullman stickhandled beautifully over the Toronto blue line, passing to Howe, who then took the puck behind the net and threw the puck out front, where Larry Jeffrey was alone, and banged the puck past Bower to end the game at 7:52. "I didn't have to move my stick. I just snapped my wrists and it was game ball," said Jeffrey. "It happened so quick. I think Bower was still watching Howe." The Leafs' netminder concurred with Jeffrey's assessment. "I had the short side covered, and it went across and into the far corner. I was watching to see what Howe was going to do and I couldn't see the play after he passed."

Jeffrey, who was getting married on June 6 that year, beamed, and made reporters laugh when he said, "I need the winners' share for winning the Stanley Cup to cover our expenses!"

Pierre Pilote of the Chicago Black Hawks chose the Three Stars, and named Larry Jeffrey, Bob Pulford and Norm Ullman.

The exciting contest was witnessed by a number of dignitaries. Opposition Leader John Diefenbaker and his wife Olive, celebrating her birthday, were in the stands for the game. After delivering a speech in Toronto, Robert Kennedy, the attorney-general of the United States, arrived with his wife in the third period and stayed to watch the Red Wings take game two with a thrilling 4–3 win.

The Wings never quit skating, picked off Leaf passes with relative ease and consistently beat the Leafs to the puck. Sid Abel stated, "We outchecked them, outshot them and the Leafs come up with a tie in regulation time. It would have been a steal if we lost it." *The Globe and Mail* reported, "The absence of Carl Brewer from the Leaf defence was especially notable. Leafs had no one capable of getting the puck quickly out of their territory and were unable to prevent Wings putting sustained pressure on Bower."

Wings Snatch Last-Minute Victory in Game Three
Game Three, Stanley Cup Final – Thursday, April 16, 1964

Prior to game three, NHL president Clarence Campbell introduced the concept of adding a trophy for the most valuable player of the playoffs. "Baseball picks the best player in the World Series and gives him a car. The National Football League awards an automobile to the top man in its final. It would be a good idea for the NHL to do the same thing." Campbell suggested that the NHL should reward each spring's recipient with a cash award, possibly $2,000. The NHL president intended to present the idea of a playoff MVP at the next meeting of the NHL Board of Directors. Rumours immediately swirled that Campbell was going to propose that the trophy be named to honour Conn Smythe. Campbell denied that idea, stating that the concept was in the formative stage at that point. "It will be up to [the league governors] to decide on whom to name it after." Stafford Smythe commented, "I will put Dad's name up, and don't think there will be any difficulty. I'm sure other hockey men recognize what he has done for hockey and will be anxious to honour him in this way." Frank Selke agreed. "I can think of nothing more appropriate than to name a trophy after Conn." Even the senior Smythe added his remarks. "I would be pleased if this one had my name on it," he said. "I've always admired the best in hockey — the best team and the best players. No one stars in the Stanley Cup finals without being a dandy."

Game three, the first game of the series played in Detroit, saw the hometown club completely dominate play. The Red Wings were up 3–0 at the end of the first period. At 2:40, Johnny Bower took Norm Ullman's shot off the chest, and the puck bounced up high. Floyd Smith picked up the stray puck and backhanded it into the Leafs' goal. Just under a minute later, Bower stopped Doug Barkley's shot, but the rebound strayed just beyond the crease. Bower sprawled to corral the puck, but Bruce McGregor got to it first and scored on the prone goaltender. Then at 14:47, just seven seconds into a Bob Baun minor, Alex Delvecchio sent a quick pass to Norm Ullman, who rifled the puck at the net. Floyd Smith deflected it in flight to score Detroit's third goal.

During the first intermission, Frank Selke Jr. spoke with Marty Pavelich, the former Red Wing who, along with Ted Lindsay, did play-by-play on closed-circuit broadcasts exhibited in Detroit-area movie theatres. Almost four thousand spectators had watched games in that manner. Although they weren't the original team — the first play-by-play man was a basketball announcer that didn't know hockey terminology — Pavelich mentioned that, "things just couldn't be any better."

The teams returned to the ice at the Olympia, but the crew had experienced problems with the glass behind the Wings' net and replaced it with screen, which remained there for the rest of that game.

At 4:16, Andy Bathgate, from the right point, fired a slapshot towards Sawchuk, who was screened in the Detroit goal, and caught the short side to make the score 3–1 at the end of the second.

Hockey Night in Canada's Frank Selke spoke with Ted Lindsay about how he still liked to work out once a week through the season with the Red Wings. "Terrible Ted" had retired following the 1959–60 season, but would make a successful one-season comeback in 1964–65. Ward Cornell and Roger Crozier then discussed the goaltender's yo-yo schedule, bouncing back and forth between the Pittsburgh Hornets of the AHL and Detroit of the NHL during that spring's playoffs.

In the third, Dave Keon banged in a shot from behind the net off Norm Ullman's elbow at 7:34. Then, for the third time in the three games of the final, the Leafs scored a late goal to tie the game. This time, Don McKenney played hero at 18:47.

As regulation time evaporated, and with the teams deadlocked at three apiece, it seemed certain that the game was going to go into overtime for the second time in as many games. But Howe and Delvecchio remedied that. With less than a minute to play, Howe was readying to take a shot on Bower when he spotted Delvecchio alone in front of the net. "I shoved it to him and Bower had no chance because he was playing me to shoot," said Howe. "Gordie and Andre [Pronovost] worked it over to me and Bower was on the other side of the cage," explained Delvecchio. With seventeen seconds left in the game, Alex Delvecchio had scored the game winner, and gave Detroit a two-games-to-one lead in the best-of-seven final. "That was a gift," Delvecchio later told *Hockey Night in Canada.* "Gordie did all the work. All I did was tip it in." Delvecchio was relieved to have scored. "I was on the ice when McKenney tied it up, so I just had to get it back."

While the Detroit captain was being mobbed by his teammates, Carl Brewer went back to console his netminder. It was Brewer's first game of the Stanley Cup final. "Ribs don't bother me, and we'll be back," he said. To numb the pain, the Leafs' defenceman had received a shot before the game and midway through the contest.

Toe Blake, coach of the Montreal Canadiens, chose the Three Stars of the contest. First was Delvecchio with the winning goal, second Star was Bill Gadsby and the third Star was Floyd Smith.

The door to the Maple Leafs' dressing room was locked for an extended period of time after the game. Imlach addressed his team, the members of which were annoyed, but seemingly not disheartened. As they exited, Toronto's assistant general manager, King Clancy, punched a Detroit fan who refused to get out of his way. The fan was assisted into the Toronto dressing room, where an icepack was applied to his right eye.

Keon Scores Two to Knot Series at Two Games Apiece
Game Four, Stanley Cup Final – Saturday, April 18, 1964

Game four, like its predecessor, was played at Detroit's Olympia Stadium. Several Maple Leafs' fans, who made the trip down from Toronto, were unable to find tickets for the game, and instead watched the game on closed-circuit theatre TV.

One of the issues discussed by the Leafs, both privately and publicly, was that they simply weren't shooting frequently enough. It was an issue addressed by Imlach with his key forwards, particularly Andy Bathgate. Johnny Bower told reporters, "I wish our guys would shoot as hard, accurate and often at Terry Sawchuk in these games as they do at me in practice!"

Bathgate took the directive to heart, and it resulted in the winning goal of a 4–2 Leafs' victory. Toronto started strong for the first time in the final. They also played a full sixty minutes for the first time in the series.

Dave Keon scored the first two goals of the game, with Bathgate scoring the third and Frank Mahovlich collecting an insurance goal at 18:09.

On the winner, scored at 10:55 of the third, The Big M outreached Marcel Pronovost for the puck and passed to Red Kelly, who then punched the puck to Bathgate near centre ice. Bathgate drove into the Wings' end, with Kelly flanking him on the far wing. Doug Barkley tried to angle Bathgate away, but using Kelly as a decoy, he rifled a shot from the faceoff circle that whistled past Sawchuk into the top corner.

"The blade of my stick is curved," explained Bathgate. "When I slap a puck from long range, it rises and then somehow drops as it reaches the goal. I knew I had to shoot high at Sawchuk because he leans down low and has beaten me a lot that way."

Bathgate admitted that the winning goal was long overdue. "It's about time I delivered for these people," he said. "They've been real patient with me since I came from New York." Bathgate, who had struggled in adapting to the Leafs' style after arriving from the Rangers just a month prior, said, "I've been trying to play a better defensive game. They [the Leafs] play the puck ahead all the time, whereas in New York we used to move the puck around quite a bit, but I'm starting to catch on." Dick Duff, who had been a principal in the Bathgate trade, stated, "It was Bathgate's best moment as a Leaf."

Bathgate was excited, knowing that his goal had put Toronto back into Stanley Cup contention. "You think all your life when you're a kid that it'd be a dream to play in Maple Leaf Gardens and you dream that you might have a chance to be on a Stanley Cup hockey team," he said.

Bobby Hull selected the game's Three Stars. Number One was Bathgate. "He played very well defensively and offensively," Hull told *Hockey Night in Canada* viewers. Star two was Dave Keon, while Gordie Howe was named the third Star.

After the game, the Toronto Maple Leafs took the train from Windsor back to Toronto, and after congratulating each player in turn for an outstanding effort, Punch imposed a 1:15 curfew on the train. When it arrived in Toronto, the players continued sleeping in their berths, as the train was parked in a siding near Union Station. They then reported directly to the Gardens for a 9:30 practice.

Detroit Doubles Leafs, Takes Series Lead
Game Five, Stanley Cup Final – Tuesday, April 21, 1964
Joining Bill Hewitt in the broadcast booth for game five on *Hockey Night in Canada* was Keith Dancy from CBC Montreal. The series shifted back to Maple Leaf Gardens with the teams tied at two wins apiece.

"The Detroit Red Wings, riding their usual determination plus great goaltending and occasionally unbelievable good fortune" took Game Five with a 2–1 win," announced *The Globe and Mail*. "The Lord and the Twelve Apostles couldn't keep the Wings under control tonight," said Conn Smythe.

Midway through the first, Alex Delvecchio's attempt was stopped by Bower, but as Baun and Delvecchio piled up around the crease, the puck was jarred free from the scrum and popped into the net by Gordie Howe.

Eddie Joyal, in spite of suffering through the flu, scored the eventual winner at 7:50 of the third when he fired a rocket that went between Bower's pads as he was screened by Allan Stanley on the play. George Armstrong scored at 14:57 with the Wings two men short, but it was too little, too late.

Terry Sawchuk, dripping in perspiration, told reporters, "That was the toughest game I've had all season. I've never been as tired in my life! Man, was it hot out there, and those last five minutes seemed like a year!"

The Leafs missed a dozen good scoring chances, including several breakaways. Eddie Shore, the Hall of Fame defenceman, commented, "The Leafs should have won by four goals if they had put the puck where they should have — up high. If they'd done that, it would have been a contest. They insisted on shooting the puck at Sawchuk instead of over him. They seemed unable to lift the puck."

Don McKenney suffered ligament damage in his right knee when he collided with Al Langlois in the first period and would miss the remainder of the playoffs.

Sid Abel smiled confidently, saying, "For the first time in the series, I feel really confident we can take them." The series now saw Detroit up three games to two, with the sixth game back at the Olympia in Detroit.

Baun Scores Miraculous OT Winner on Broken Foot
Game Six, Stanley Cup Final – Thursday, April 23, 1964
With a victory at home in game six, the Detroit Red Wings would claim the Stanley Cup for the first time since 1955. Red Wings' coach Sid Abel, bowing to superstition, refused to allow the Stanley Cup to be included in the baggage compartment of the train Detroit took from Toronto. He ordered baggage handlers to "get that thing outta here." Instead, NHL president Clarence Campbell travelled with the championship trophy.

The Wings kept their composure amidst the excitement and anticipation. Veteran Bill Gadsby was quietly hoping to celebrate his first-ever Stanley Cup championship. Ex-Leaf Johnny MacMillan took no added satisfaction out of playing against his former team. "The greatest satisfaction is getting on the ice. I wasn't getting any ice time [in Toronto]."

The Leafs made a minor adjustment in their lineup, inserting Ed

Litzenberger for Don McKenney, who was out for the duration of the playoffs with torn ligaments. "McKenney played exceptionally well in the time he joined the club," Imlach later recalled. "Of course, he never played that well again. Those things happen, that a player will play over his head for a length of time and if you are fortunate enough to get him at the right time, timing means everything, it makes a big difference to your team."

Carl Brewer was still struggling with his rib injury, and endured so many needles to freeze his ribs that he quipped, "I'm almost afraid to drink water. I might spring a few leaks!"

Toronto drew first blood, with Bob Pulford scoring a shorthanded goal at 17:01 of the first period. Allan Stanley had stopped Norm Ullman at the Leafs' blue line, and broke up the wing with Pulford on his flank. Stanley dished the puck to his teammate, who made no mistake in depositing the puck behind Sawchuk.

A flurry of goals marked the second period. Detroit tied the game on a goal by Paul Henderson at 4:20. After taking a long pass from Pit Martin, Henderson broke in behind the Leafs' defence and beat Bower gloveside. Martin made it 2–1 Detroit at 10:56 after Johnny MacMillan's pass from behind the Leafs' net hit his stick in the crease and went in.

Bob Pulford scored his second goal of the game, a shorthanded tally on a cross-crease pass from Ron Stewart at 14:56 to knot the score again. Exactly one minute later, Parker MacDonald tripped Tim Horton at the Maple Leafs' blue line, giving Gordie Howe a clear path to the net. Howe made no mistake, putting the puck behind Bower on a backhand. That made it 3–2 Detroit. But the period wasn't over — the Leafs battled back, and after bang-bang passes from Stewart and Keon, Billy Harris scored at 17:48 to conclude the scoring in the period.

"I wore a uniform and sat on the bench, but I was a spectator," sighed Billy Harris in *The Glory Years*. "I began questioning my ability to play the game, and I started to feel like an outsider." The Leafs were down 3–2 in the second period when Harris got into the game. "Imlach was so desperate, I got the tap on the shoulder. I hadn't played two shifts back-to-back in two months. David [Keon] was tired and had the puck in front of our bench. I gave him a shout as I broke towards the goal and I was able to deflect the pass he directed at the net, past Sawchuk."

Between the second and third periods on *Hockey Night in Canada*, Ward Cornell addressed the rumour of Dickie Moore's return to the NHL with Bernie Geoffrion. Little did either realize, but Moore would join the Toronto Maple Leafs in 1964–65 after spending twelve seasons with the Canadiens, retiring due to injury after 1962–63.

There was no scoring in the third. While the Red Wings fought ferociously to collect the Stanley Cup in front of their own fans, the Maple Leafs defended with equal strength. Prior to overtime, Ted Lindsay predicted a Wings' win, with the goal to come from the stick of Norm Ullman. Harry Howell thought Bob Pulford would score the deciding goal, while Jerry Toppazzini predicted Gordie Howe would score the OT winner.

In fact, it was Bob Baun at 1:43 who scored the winning goal. Carl Brewer dumped the puck into the corner to the left of Sawchuk. Baun explained the goal in detail. "It was Junior Langlois' shot around the boards, blindly, which was a cardinal sin for a defenceman. I just managed to make it to the blue line in time or I would have thrown our guys offside. It came off the boards and it was rolling and I just took a slap at it and the puck was going end over end. Bill Gadsby happened to be stopped in front of the netminder, Terry Sawchuk. It hit the shaft of his stick, changed direction and went by him. I've called it a triple flutter blast, with a followup blooper." Baun's one-timer, from inside the blue line, bounced once on the way and changed direction, eluding Sawchuk and earning the victory for the Leafs. "I think the funniest part of that whole story was that I used to call Bill Gadsby 'Jinxy.'" Although he was an All-Star defenceman, Gadsby never played for a Stanley Cup champion, and opponents needled him about being a jinx to the teams he played for.

"I wasn't trying to get my stick on it," Gadsby said. "The goddamned thing just took a weird bounce. That's the way it goes." Sawchuk added, "I had a good line on that lousy bouncer by Baun, then at the last minute, it hits the shaft of Gadsby's stick and shot to the top corner. I never had a chance."

Baun was an unlikely hero. At 13:15 of the third period, he was carried off the ice on a stretcher. "I blocked a shot [from Alex Delvecchio] in front of the net during killing the penalty," he explained. "It was numb then. I couldn't figure what was wrong. Then when I went into the faceoff with Gordie Howe, I heard a snap and it caved in underneath me." Baun crumpled to the ice and crawled to the front of the net before the puck went into the crowd. "I tried to get up but there was no way I could put any weight on it. My leg just turned to cream cheese. It was the most unusual thing I ever had happen to me." He was carried off the ice on a stretcher and taken to the infirmary in the Olympia. "I couldn't believe I was going off on a stretcher. The guys who looked at it didn't think I could hurt it any more than I already had, so they froze it and taped it up and I went back to play the game. There was no sensation. You couldn't feel a thing from the knee down. You might say, 'How could you skate?' and I still think, well, how could I skate? You could, there was no problem."

The defenceman returned and played one shift in the latter stages of the third period. "They froze my leg then and it's alright now," Bobby told *Hockey Night in Canada*. "Of course, I can't feel it. It could be a pinched nerve. I forgot all about the pain when I saw my blooper shot shoot up into the top of the Wings' goal."

Late in the third, Red Kelly had been checked by Bill Gadsby and left the game with a damaged knee. He was in the dressing room at the start of overtime. While getting ready to return to the bench, he heard a roar. "It wasn't loud enough for a Detroit goal, so I knew the Leafs must have scored!"

In fact, the first Star of that sixth game was playing on a broken bone in his right ankle. The incident has become legendary. Sid Abel was less amused. "It's hard to believe he could get back on the ice so quickly."

Toronto's team physician, Dr. Jim Murray, explained how Baun was able to continue playing on a broken leg. "Bob played with the so-called broken leg, but it was a broken leg that he wasn't going to do himself any permanent damage with, because it was the small bone of the leg. He knew exactly. He saw the X-rays and everything else. You couldn't let anybody with the main bone of the leg between the knee and the ankle go play. Ever."

Baun was determined that, with the seventh game of a Stanley Cup final looming, he was going to be part of the Leafs' roster. "You don't think I'm going to miss the last chapter over something like this, do you?" One medical opinion confirmed that Baun would not risk permanent damage to his ankle by having it taped and injected with a painkiller. "I knew I was hurt quite badly, but the doctors at that time were great friends of mine. I had enough faith in them, that I couldn't hurt myself seriously, and I think that was the key to the whole thing. I kept it in ice for two days right after the game, through to game time and I never came out of an ice bucket. You know, it was more pain than the leg itself."

Maple Leafs Win Third Straight Stanley Cup as Bower Blanks Wings!
Game Seven, Stanley Cup Final – Saturday, April 25, 1964
There are few things more exciting in hockey than a seventh game in a Stanley Cup final. The NHL had expanded the Stanley Cup final to a best-of-seven series in 1939. Since that date, the Cup had been awarded following a seventh and deciding game in 1942 and 1945 (won by the Toronto Maple Leafs); and in 1950, 1954 and 1955, with the Red Wings winning the championship in a seventh game. June 23, 1964, was just the sixth time a seventh game was necessary for a team to clinch the Stanley Cup championship. In fact, 1964 was the first time both semi-final series and the final had gone the full seven-game distance.

During that era, the Supreme Court of Canada ruled that the federal Lord's Day Act promoted the observance of the Christian Holy Day, and prohibited business from opening on Sundays, as well as sporting events from taking place. As a result, all sporting events were required to be completed prior to midnight on Saturday. National Hockey League President Clarence Campbell assured *Hockey Night in Canada* viewers that Toronto's curfew would have no effect on game seven. "This game will be played to a conclusion."

It had been an excruciatingly long season for the Maple Leafs. Riddled with injuries, Toronto was about to play their 101st game of the season, including exhibition games, regular season contests and playoff matches. In fact, some of the best shots of the playoffs took place before the game: Carl Brewer was injected with painkillers to ease the pain of his torn rib cartilage. Red Kelly was shot with painkillers for his strained knee ligaments. Baun had his leg frozen after fracturing his fibula. George Armstrong played with a damaged shoulder. Don McKenney, who had torn knee ligaments in a previous game, was told just hours before the game that his wife had given birth back in Boston.

Hockey Night in Canada signed on, with CBC sportscaster Fred Sgambatti providing colour commentary to Bill Hewitt's play-by-play, on the final game of the 1963–64 season

Bobby Baun took a regular shift, showing no sign of weakness. Andre Pronovost crashed Baun into the boards in the third period, but Baun was none the worse for wear. "I couldn't feel a thing from the knee down. I got hit a couple of good checks and belted a few Wings without an ache. The only time it bothered me was when I tried to skate backwards."

Early in the first period, Al Langlois fanned on a shot from the point, allowing Andy Bathgate to pick up the puck in full stride and beat Sawchuk from twenty-five feet out to put Toronto up 1–0 at 3:04. Bathgate was so wound up after the goal that he skated away from any teammates trying to congratulate him

Bathgate was one of a handful of NHL players using a curved stick at the time, and during the first intermission, Bobby Hull explained to Montreal netminder Charlie Hodge and *Hockey Night in Canada* viewers how his heavy shot was created. "I've been using a stick with a hook in it for close to three years," explained The Golden Jet. "You become accustomed to where the puck is going with the curved stick. As far as shooting, I think it helps."

The second period was scoreless. Conn Smythe then appeared on the *Hockey Night in Canada* intermission with Lester Pearson, Canada's prime minister, who explained his long-time friendship with the owner of the Toronto Maple Leafs. "We were there [at the University of Toronto] before World War I, when Conn was a star on the Junior OHA hockey team, the Varsity Juniors. I fooled around a bit too and then we went off to war and we've kept in touch since."

Toronto exploded for three goals in the third period. Dave Keon scored at 4:26, explaining, "It ticked in off Sawchuk's glove, hitting the far corner." Just over a minute later, Red Kelly, nursing a bad leg, scored to put Toronto up to a 3–0 lead. The captain, George Armstrong, put the Red Wings away by adding a fourth goal at 15:26 of the third.

As the fans counted down the remaining seconds, Detroit's Larry Jeffrey wrestled the puck into the net, but the red light had already gone on to indicate that time had expired.

The players mobbed Bower. Al Arbour, Kent Douglas and Don Simmons, who weren't dressed for game seven, scrambled out onto the ice to join their teammates. So did Punch Imlach, Harold Ballard, King Clancy and trainer Bob Haggert. Allan Stanley's father, Bill, the Timmins' fire chief, was on the ice to congratulate his son. Stafford Smythe and John Bassett stood on the bench and watched the players embrace.

In a wonderful tradition, adversaries shake hands at the conclusion of each playoff series, and Detroit and Toronto lined up at centre ice to congratulate each other on an excellent, hard-fought series.

The Leafs had won a third consecutive Stanley Cup championship, a feat matched only by the Leafs of 1946–47 to 1948–49 and the Ottawa Senators of 1902–03 to 1904–05, and eclipsed by the Montreal Canadiens' five consecutive Stanley Cup championships, won from 1955–56 to 1959–60.

Red Barber, the public-address announcer, interrupted the celebration by saying, "Ladies and gentlemen, the president of the National Hockey League, Clarence Campbell!" Boos greeted the president as he leaned in to speak into the microphone, only the mic wasn't working. Finally, after feedback mixed into the silence, the Gardens' faithful heard, "Hello! Ladies and gentlemen. As a climax to this magnificently played, record-breaking series, it is my pleasure and responsibility to present to the winners, for the tenth time, the Stanley Cup, emblematic of the world championship! I call on captain George Armstrong to receive the trophy."

The captain graciously accepted the Stanley Cup for the third spring in a row, and with the microphone still live, could be heard saying, "Come on, you guys!" Brewer and Baun were the first to skate over, joined then by the rest of the team. As the Leafs surrounded the Cup, Brewer continued to joke by blowing into the microphone until it was finally turned off.

Armstrong skated with the Cup to the blue line, where *Hockey Night in Canada*'s Ward Cornell interviewed him. "Everybody went all out, and it was a terrific effort by everybody," Armstrong began. "I have to say that the Detroit club is a club that you just don't beat easily. It took everything we had to beat them, and they are a credit to all their fans and to themselves."

After Bob Pulford and David Keon contributed their comments, Detroit's general manager and coach, Sid Abel, strode over to add his praise for the victors. "I want to congratulate Punch and King and, of course, George Armstrong and all the Maple Leafs. It was a terrific series. We gave it everything we had. We wanted to win, I'll tell you that!"

Johnny Bower was then summoned to address the viewers and fans remaining in Maple Leaf Gardens. "I'd like to thank the people of Toronto for having so much patience with us. I know we did have a few bad games. And thanks very much to the CHUM witch tonight by the way also. It certainly is wonderful to win the Stanley Cup, and I certainly give a lot of credit to the Detroit Red Wings, who played so well. The City of Toronto deserves the Stanley Cup more than anybody else!"

On February 13, while commenting on a particularly awful Leafs' loss the night before (4–0 to the Canadiens), a news reader at CHUM Radio in Toronto commented, "The Maple Leafs lost another one last night. Maybe they need a CHUM witch to put a spell on their opponents." And so, Mabel Leaf, the CHUM witch, was born. Dressed in black with a pointed hat and gruesome green makeup, she looked very much like the Wicked Witch of the West as she stirred a steaming cauldron of Imlach punch on Carlton Street outside the Gardens' entrance before the contest on February 15. Just before the opening faceoff, Mabel Leaf (actually, lounge performer Phyllis Shea) sat in the blues (CHUM's corporate seats) and waved her wand as she spat out hexes on the Chicago Black Hawks. That night, Toronto won 4–0.

Toronto tied the next home game, and the CHUM switchboard lit up with fans demanding that Mabel Leaf return. Punch Imlach, as superstitious a man as has ever lived, called the radio station and demanded the CHUM witch attend the next game. She did. They won (Leafs over

Rangers, 5–2). What had been intended as a silly one-off radio stunt had now become a habit!

If the CHUM witch wasn't at a particular game and the Leafs lost, the radio station heard about it for days from the fans, but the worst was Punch Imlach. "Why wasn't the CHUM witch at the game? Listen, I don't accept limp excuses from the players and I sure as hell won't take them from some damn witch. You tell her to be at the next game!" At games attended by Mabel Leaf, the CHUM witch, the Leafs were 11–2–1.

1963-64 Playoff Scoring

RK	NUMBER	PLAYER	POS	AGE	GP	G	A	PTS	PIM
1	27	Frank Mahovlich	LW	26	14	4	11	15	20
2	10	George Armstrong	RW	33	14	5	8	13	10
3	4	Red Kelly	D/C	36	14	4	9	13	4
4	17	Don McKenney	C	29	12	4	8	12	0
5	14	Dave Keon	C	23	14	7	2	9	2
6	9	Andy Bathgate	RW	31	14	5	4	9	25
7	20	Bob Pulford	LW	27	14	5	3	8	20
8	26	Allan Stanley	D	37	14	1	6	7	20
9	21	Bob Baun	D	27	14	2	3	5	42
10	7	Tim Horton	D	34	14	0	4	4	20
11	12	Ron Stewart	RW	31	14	0	4	4	24
12	15	Billy Harris	C	28	9	1	1	2	4
13	8	Gerry Ehman	RW	31	9	1	0	1	4
14	2	Carl Brewer	D	25	12	0	1	1	30
15	23	Eddie Shack	LW	26	13	0	1	1	25
16	3	Al Arbour	D	31	1	0	0	0	0
17	1	Johnny Bower	G	39	14	0	0	0	0
18	22	Larry Hillman	D	26	11	0	0	0	2
19	25	Ed Litzenberger	C/RW	31	1	0	0	0	10
20	18	Jim Pappin	RW	24	11	0	0	0	0
				TEAM TOTALS	14	39	65	104	262

Playoff Netminding

RK	NUMBER	PLAYER	POS	AGE	GP	MIN	W	L	GA	GAA	SO
1	1	Johnny Bower	G	39	14	850	8	6	30	2.12	2

The fans loved the CHUM witch, and soon she was travelling to Madison Square Garden, the Olympia and the Forum to put a hex on the Leafs' opponents. For the playoffs, Flo de Leaf (sales secretary Shirley Hart) was added to perform spells on the Montreal Canadiens in the semi-final and Chicken Wing (Mary McInnes from the CHUM music library) was added for the final against the Detroit Red Wings. The three paraded in front of Maple Leaf Gardens carrying signs: "Mabel Leaf Stabs the Habs," "CHUM Witch Says No to Toe" and "Mabel Leaf — It's Punch Bowl Time."

No wonder Bower publicly thanked the CHUM witch!

It was no surprise that Toe Blake and Billy Reay, guest commentators on *Hockey Night in Canada,* agreed on the evening's first two Stars: Johnny Bower and Bobby Baun. But for the third Star, Reay selected Terry Sawchuk and Blake picked Frank Mahovlich. Frank Selke Jr. added that "Bill Gadsby has been tremendously impressive."

Dave Keon reflected back on the Stanley Cup win, and isolated one specific play in game six that made him realize that the momentum had shifted in the Leafs' favour. "Before we came back and Bobby [Baun] scored that goal, we had been losing by one," recalled Keon. "Norm Ullman and Larry Jeffrey got in all alone on Bower. Norm passed and Larry shot and somehow, Johnny [Bower] reached back and made the save. Right then, I knew we had won the Stanley Cup. We were kind of dead on the bench, everybody tired, but when John made that save, we knew we would come back."

Gordie Howe, 1964's playoff scoring leader, admitted, "I can't remember the last time I was this tired. These playoffs were really tough, especially on an old guy like me." Howe stated that the straw that broke the camel's back was Baun's dramatic overtime goal in game six. "It gave the Leafs the momentum they needed for this game and seemed to take a lot out of us."

"I'm proud of my team," said Sid Abel. "This was the Leafs' best game against us all year, and yet it was 1–0 into the third period. I thought the team that got the next goal would win."

Allan Stanley led the Leafs into the dressing room after their win. Brewer saw Bob Haggert with a cigar in his mouth, went to push it further into the trainer's mouth but burned his hand when he discovered, too late, that the cigar was in fact lit. Brewer then sang "The Maple Leaf Forever," and began throwing people into the shower — first, Stafford Smythe, then Harold Ballard. Reporters were next to feel the sting of the shower's cold water.

For Ed Litzenberger, it was his fourth consecutive Stanley Cup victory — one with the Black Hawks in 1961 and then the three with Toronto. "If I were you, I'd sign me up for life," Litzenberger suggested to Harold Ballard.

Andy Bathgate was thankful to be enjoying his first championship. "It's not only the first time I've ever been on a Stanley Cup winner, it's the first time I've ever been in the final. It's an accomplishment I can't quite realize. It happened so fast — in two months, up from the struggle in the valley to the top of the world."

While lined up on-ice to shake hands, Gordie Howe and Johnny Bower exchanged sticks. Howe had scored four times on Bower during the series. "I should have taken your stick off you seven games ago," said Johnny, laughing. In the dressing room, Howe stopped by to congratulate the victors. Bower grabbed a bottle of champagne and handed it to Howe.

George Armstrong admitted, "We had a lousy year, and we're all part of it. If we blew this, we knew darned well there'd be changes next fall. And we knew who'd get the chop — the old guys. There was a lot more than the Stanley Cup at stake tonight. It was our jobs and our pride we were fighting for."

The age of the roster had been a perennial discussion with the Leafs, even before the three championships. Each year, pundits discussed whether it would be the last hurrah for Bower, Kelly and Stanley, among others. "Stanley was our best defenceman all through the piece," said King Clancy. "Bower's played so well for us that if he wasn't going to get a pension from the NHL, I'd pay him one," laughed Imlach. "I hear age is hurting our club," Carl Brewer said. "And it is. The older guys have played well but age is still our problem. I mean, the age of us younger guys. We're the ones who didn't come through like we can."

It wasn't all joy and frivolity in the Toronto dressing room, as Red Kelly was clearly in great pain, taped from mid-thigh to mid-calf. "I've never had anything that hurt as much," he said. "I couldn't sleep at all last night." He had told his wife and father that he wasn't going to play, but both were stunned to see Red skate out prior to the game. "Kelly really gave a gutty performance," said a member of Toronto's medical team. "I wouldn't have been at all surprised if, after his first turn, he'd quit for the night. To think he could not only go all the way, but play so well is amazing."

While in the shower, the excruciating pain in Kelly's knee caused him to pass out. Horton, Stanley and Stewart carried him from the shower to a makeshift medical area the team doctors set up in the dressing room, and Dr. Hugh Smythe helped Kelly up onto a rubbing table. An ambulance pulled into the Gardens an hour later. Police and employees of the Gardens cleared the dressing room and photographers were prohibited from taking shots of Red being loaded onto the stretcher and being wheeled into the waiting ambulance. He was taken to Toronto General Hospital, where he stayed for the night.

Prime Minister Lester Pearson tramped over soggy equipment, shaking hands with each of the Leafs. "A wonderful game, just wonderful," said the prime minister, who had attended the game with his wife Maryon, daughter Patricia and grandson Paul. Red Kelly, who served as a Liberal member of Parliament for York West in addition to his centre-ice duties for the Leafs, had already been taken to the hospital, and missed seeing his party leader. "If there was such a thing as a medal of merit in hockey, Bob Baun and Red Kelly would deserve one," said the prime minister.

"The Montreal Canadiens parlayed the greatest collection of superstars in hockey history into almost a decade of National Hockey League prominence," wrote *The Globe and Mail*, referring to the Canadiens of the 1950s. "Toronto Maple Leafs rode a different route to Stanley Cup supremacy — balance." The Leafs scored twenty-two goals in the final, divided amongst eleven players. George Armstrong and Dave Keon both scored four goals in the final, while Frank Mahovlich's eight points was a team best. Nine players from that 1964 Stanley Cup squad are now enshrined in the Hockey Hall of Fame. Each of the Maple Leafs earned $500 for finishing third during the regular season, another $1,500 for winning the semi-final and a further $2,000 as Stanley Cup champions.

The team held a party at the Royal York on Saturday, April 25, and then most continued the celebration afterwards at Bob Pulford's home. The team had also committed to go to Hanlan's Point on the Toronto Islands on Sunday the 26th to plant trees in memory of Mayor Don Summerville.

The City of Toronto feted the champions for a third straight spring, holding a Stanley Cup parade for the victors on Monday, April 27. The team left Maple Leaf Gardens at 5:00 p.m., proceeded south on Church to Wellington, west to Bay then north to city hall. However, it was a curious time to hold the parade. That year, it was held in the late afternoon to allow school children to attend, but they missed out on the business people and shoppers who attended when the reception was held at noon in previous years. Besides the scheduling, a chilly, dark day didn't help attendance, which was approximately eight thousand fans who showed up to honour the hockey heroes, easily enforced by five hundred on-duty police officers and a dozen horses.

Several team members missed the parade. Don McKenney, hobbling with torn ligaments that knocked him out of playoff action, had flown home to Boston to meet his newborn baby. Bob Baun, who had suffered a hairline fracture of the fibula in the sixth game of the final, slipped while getting into the convertible for the parade and further injured his leg. While his teammates were being honoured at city hall, Red Kelly was in Ottawa, attending to his political career as member of Parliament for York West. "I felt it was time to come back and see what I could do," he said. "Some of my people had problems." Don Simmons had not attended, although no reason was given.

Philip Givens, the third Toronto mayor in three years, presided over the Stanley Cup reception for the Toronto Maple Leafs, although most of his comments were drowned out by the crowd chanting, "We want Shack! We want Shack!" While Shack contributed but twenty-one points to the team during the regular season, his popularity was unprecedented.

Ed Fitkin was the master of ceremonies at city hall. Coach Punch Imlach and team captain George Armstrong also addressed the crowd from the steps of city hall. Mayor Givens presented each of the players with silver cigarette cases. "I think the council gets a bigger kick out of this than the players," commented Alderman Horace Brown.

Popular conjecture was that Red Kelly would retire and serve full time as Liberal MP for York West. "After Saturday's game, I thought I'd never want to see another skate again. It's been a hectic time. I'm worn out mentally and physically. You know, it's something like an MP going through an election campaign." During a debate on Finance Minister Walter Gordon's amendments to the Income Tax Act, Kelly was welcomed from the floor. Creditiste Gilles Gregoire and Conservative Paul Martineau both congratulated the member from York West.

Kelly had not yet had the opportunity to celebrate with his teammates at that time. Reflecting on that spring of 1964, Kelly remembered, "My wife and I had another baby in '64. Conn [named after former Leafs' owner, Conn Smythe] was born at the end of January. Harold Ballard brought the Cup and a couple bottles of champagne and a photographer out to my house and they took a picture of my family around the Cup. I put Conn in the Cup and they took a picture. And the look on Conn's face — he did the whole load in the Cup! Our family always chuckles when they see guys drinking the champagne out of the Cup."

Through the summer of 1964, pundits questioned how much Imlach would tamper with the lineup. Would Kelly retire? Was the end near for Bower and Stanley? Would Jim Pappin finally find a spot with the team in 1964–65? Could a prospect like Ron Ellis manage to earn a position with the Maple Leafs? And most importantly, could the Toronto Maple Leafs repeat for a fourth straight spring?

SLAPSHOTS AND SNAPSHOTS
GEORGE'S SPAGHETTI HOUSE

While the previous dynasty had made the Old Mill Inn a home away from home, the Leafs of the 1960s found a new refuge.

"We always went to the same place," explained Allan Stanley. "George's Spaghetti House on Dundas." The restaurant was a renowned jazz club in the evenings, but served as an inner sanctum for the Maple Leafs of that era. "It was our main meeting place after practices," recalled Bob Baun. "We'd meet there for lunch and have a couple sandwiches. That team was very much a 'together' team. A lot of things were decided there."

Baun knew one of the owners, Chuck Penstone, who had worked at his father's service station on Kingston Road. Penstone, along with Doug Cole, a police officer, purchased a heritage hotel at the corner of Dundas and Sherbourne in downtown Toronto. The restaurant began offering jazz late on weekend evenings, then in September 1960, provided jazz six evenings a week. "George's" was recognized as the premier jazz facility in Canada. Some of the country's greatest jazz talent performed there on a regular basis. Moe Koffman ("Swinging Shepherd Blues") booked the room, and brought in some of the all-time jazz greats.

"When I heard about the new restaurant, I just couldn't resist checking it out," offered Baun in *Lowering the Boom.* "It quickly became a second home. When it came to food, George's was one of the first places in Toronto to serve pizza, but also stayed true to the spaghetti theme.

Eventually, they took over the second floor, calling it Castle George. Baun served as maitre d' and publicist and, occasionally, bouncer for the room. "This was a great hideout for the players. It's not that we hockey players were anti-social, but as we became more and more successful, the spotlight grew harder and harder to avoid. The Leafs would drop by after every home game, unless we had a flight out that night, and we'd also drop in regularly for lunch. At first, the public wasn't aware we were there, so it was practically a private club. By the time the press let the secret out, the place was so full of hockey players there was little room for anyone else."

George's was also a place where the team could talk, openly and candidly. "We were all one happy family," stated Johnny Bower. "We always got together after practice. George Armstrong would start off by saying what was wrong with him (during the previous game). I might say that I was not playing the way I could be playing and would want to know why. Somebody might say I was fighting the puck or, 'You certainly aren't playing the way you can.' We criticized each other, but in a good way and it worked out fine."

Billy Harris remembered how George's Spaghetti House became a convenient location for the team to congregate to socialize and discuss team concerns away from the glare of the media or the scrutiny of the public. "It was kind of compulsory that fifteen or sixteen of us head down there for lunch, especially on a Monday after practice after a two-game weekend and without a game until the following Thursday or Saturday. On many occasions, several players would leave shortly after lunch and there'd still be players around for supper. It was usually a meeting place where we'd have a couple of bottles of beer and we'd discuss our problems. If we had problems on our defence, Allan Stanley and Tim Horton would want to know why Bob Nevin and Billy Harris weren't backchecking. People got a lot off their chest and we solved a lot of problems — our hockey problems, our team problems — at functions like that. Why it was a popular hangout for us for a long period of time was because Doug Cole was the owner and a friend of all of ours. It was never publicized that it was our hangout."

The players particularly remember one incident. Dick Duff was beating everybody at poker, and made the mistake of taking a swipe at Tim Horton. Baun recalled, "Horton had him hanging out of an office window three storeys up at George's by his heels!"

"George's became a home away from home for Tim and the guys," said Lori Horton in Douglas Hunter's *Open Ice*. "It was a cause for concern for a period of time. You never knew when he [Horton] was coming home. They were either celebrating or drowning their sorrows. It got to the point where there were beginning to be problems."

9

1964–65: The Streak Comes to an End

After sipping champagne from the Stanley Cup for three successive springs, the Maple Leafs vowed to return to hockey supremacy in 1964–65. As usual, pundits questioned whether age was going to play as much of a role in dethroning the reigning champions as would the other five NHL teams, who all had their sights set on a Stanley Cup championship.

With a formula that placed them in first place in 1963–64, the Montreal Canadiens kept their roster virtually intact, inserting Yvan Cournoyer and Ted Harris into their lineup. Boom Boom Geoffrion filed his retirement papers after starring with the Habs for fourteen NHL seasons. One seemingly insignificant trade paid gigantic dividends, but not for several years. The Canadiens traded Guy Allen and Paul Reid to Boston for Alex Campbell and a netminder named Ken Dryden.

Chicago had the nucleus of a great team and added to their foundation by graduating juniors Doug Jarrett and Fred Stanfield to the parent club. The Black Hawks traded popular Reggie Fleming and Ab McDonald, left wing on the Scooter Line, to acquire Doug Mohns, a versatile veteran who played defence or forward, from the

Boston Bruins. Boston sent Matt Ravlich and Jerry Toppazzini to the Black Hawks for Murray Balfour and Mike Draper (Kris's father).

In Detroit, Roger Crozier had been so impressive in goal that the Red Wings rolled the dice and made Terry Sawchuk available in the Intra-League Draft. Despite losing one sure-fire Hall of Famer, they gained another by signing Ted Lindsay, who had been retired for the previous four seasons. Ron Murphy and Aut Erickson arrived in a trade with the Black Hawks. Gary Bergman was chosen from Montreal in the Intra-League Draft, and found an immediate spot on the Detroit blue line. The draft also provided goalie George Gardner from Boston and forward Murray Hall from Chicago.

The New York Rangers got rid of the old and filled in with the new, as defencemen Doug Harvey and Al Langlois were moved out and replaced by Arnie Brown and Rod Seiling, who were the blue-line prospects acquired from Toronto in the Bathgate deal. The Rangers also demoted Jacques Plante to their AHL team in Baltimore, deciding to rely on Marcel Paille in goal. Lou Angotti made the team after arriving with Ed Lawson in a trade that saw Toronto receive Ed Ehrenverth and Duane Rupp.

The Boston Bruins were mired in a horrendous slump that had seen them miss the playoffs in each of the five seasons, beginning with 1959–60, and even worse, finishing last in four of those five campaigns. Yet, the changes to their lineup didn't provide anyone with the confidence that they were turning the franchise around. The Bruins picked up Murray Balfour in a four-player trade with Chicago a day after acquiring Reg Fleming and Ab McDonald from the Hawks. Bob Woytowich was picked up in the draft from New York. Ron Schock found a spot at forward with the Bruins. It was going to be a l-o-n-g season in Boston for the Bruins.

After drafting him from the Canadiens, the Maple Leafs signed Dickie Moore, gambling that the knee injuries that had forced his retirement from Montreal a year earlier had healed sufficiently to see his return to action. "Dickie Moore was the toughest, smartest left winger I ever saw, and I include Ted Lindsay," Carl Brewer later noted. "Moore could do it all, and he was magnificent to watch. The tricks he could do were unbelievable."

Teams were allowed to protect two goaltenders and eighteen skaters in the annual Intra-League Draft. In June 1964, the Red Wings had protected Terry Sawchuk and Roger Crozier, but in the third round, decided to select George Gardner from the Bruins, gambling by electing to drop Sawchuk from their protected list. With Toronto choosing next, the Leafs excitedly plucked Sawchuk from the Wings. "With Terry and Johnny Bower rotating in the nets, we'll be tough to beat," boasted Imlach. "I'm not happy about this, but I'll report," said the disappointed Sawchuk. "I was probably more confused about the drafting of Sawchuk than anyone," Johnny Bower recalled. "Did Imlach think that I was starting to slip? Remember, I was the oldest goalie in the league at the time. At almost forty, it's not safe to take anything for granted."

Imlach's penchant for veterans never became more obvious. Johnny Bower was thirty-nine, Allan Stanley thirty-eight, Red Kelly was thirty-six, Tim Horton thirty-four, George Armstrong thirty-three, Andy Bathgate and Ron Stewart thirty-one. Imlach also claimed veteran Dickie Moore, who was thirty-three years old. "I tell my players to tear up their birth certificates and I'll tell Terry Sawchuk to do the same thing," said Imlach.

Bob Haggert explained how the Leafs' coach shattered the myth that hockey players in their thirties were considered at the end of their NHL careers. "That was a theory that Imlach absolutely destroyed. Imlach gobbled up a lot of guys who were considered finished. He changed the way you manage your hockey team. There is no better product than experience." Larry Hillman was a beneficiary of Imlach's knack for acquiring discarded veterans. "He could pick up hockey players that other teams had given up on and still get good mileage out of them. I think that was his big asset to the organization." Imlach lacked fear in gambling on players who had once performed well but were made available because of their age. "He took a chance on them and they performed for him, not just for one year, but three, four, five or six years," stated Dave Keon. "Whether they did it because they thought this was their last chance or not, I don't know. He put together a blend of ages that served us all very well." At the lower end of the demographic that season for Toronto were rookies Ron Ellis and Peter Stemkowski, introduced to full-time activity after graduating from the Memorial Cup-winning Toronto Marlboros.

Leafs Open Season with Win over Wings
Thursday, October 15, 1964

The season opener for the Toronto Maple Leafs in 1964–65 took place at Detroit's Olympia. Fans looked forward to the returns of two greats — Ted Lindsay and Dickie Moore, both of whom were returning to the NHL wars after retirement. Ted Lindsay earned a two-minute ovation when he first stepped onto the ice, returning to the Red Wings after a four-year retirement. But for Dickie Moore, the planned ovation was premature. "I'm not ready to play yet," he stated. "I would like to get a little better and that might take a week or two. However, it could be mental and what I need is a game to find out."

With Johnny Bower starting in net, the Leafs began the season with a big win, dusting Detroit 5-3. Kent Douglas assisted on four of the five Leafs' goals.

Trouble Brewin' for Boston at Leafs' Home Opener
Saturday, October 17, 1964

"Everything went wrong for the Boston Bruins Saturday night," reported *The Globe and Mail.* "The team that most critics suggest should vacate last place this season was thrashed by the Toronto Maple Leafs 7-2 in Leafs' home opener at the Gardens. Were Leafs that good Saturday night? Or Bruins that bad?" To most in the crowd of 13,958, it appeared to be a combination of both." Red Kelly and Frank Mahovlich both collected two goals and an assist, Dave Keon had a goal and two assists and rookie Ron Ellis scored his first NHL goal. Eddie Shack potted the other Leafs' goal.

If it wasn't for bad luck, the Bruins wouldn't have had any luck at all! Flying home after the game, they ran into poor weather conditions in Boston and were forced to detour to New York. The club spent Saturday overnight in New York, arriving Sunday afternoon, just in time to prepare to play the Montreal Canadiens that night.

Prior to the Leafs' home opener, the 48th Highlanders entertained the Leafs' faithful. Another tradition also took place — Stafford Smythe was booed when he walked the red carpet to centre ice, this time with Ontario's twentieth lieutenant-governor, Earl Rowe. Rowe served the province in that capacity from 1964 to 1968. Prior to that, from 1936 to 1938, he had been the leader of the Conservative Party of Ontario, and was a long-time member of provincial Parliament and member of Parliament. He died in 1984 in Newton Robinson, Ontario, the hamlet in which Bob Pulford was born and which is now part of Bradford/West Gwillimbury. Rowe, who was a special guest at the opening ceremonies, presented Johnny Bower with the J. P. Bickell Award, then conducted the ceremonial faceoff between George Armstrong of the Leafs and Leo Boivin of Boston.

Terry Sawchuk Wins First Game with Maple Leafs
Tuesday, October 27, 1964
Terry Sawchuk stepped in to play goal and in his first game wearing blue and white beat Chicago 3–2. From that point, Imlach began to alternate his two star netminders with some regularity.

Plante Plants Zero on Leafs
Saturday, November 7, 1964
The Leafs hosted the New York Rangers, but with Marcel Paille injured, they recalled Jacques Plante from Baltimore, who promptly stepped into the crease and shut out Toronto, 1–0. Camille Henry scored the only goal of the contest.

Bower Bows Out; Sawchuk Subs in Win
Wednesday, November 11, 1964
With Bower hit by the flu, Sawchuk subbed in goal. "I had a soft night with Carl Brewer, Bobby Baun, Allan Stanley and Tim Horton playing so well on defence," he said after the game. "Man, did they belt those Wings!"

The final score was 3–1 for Toronto, snapping the Red Wings' unbeaten streak at nine games. Jim Pappin, who had been struggling to earn a spot on the talent-heavy Leafs, replaced Dave Keon, who was out with a groin injury, and Pappin proceeded to score his first goal of the season. Dickie Moore continued to struggle on his return to NHL activity.

The Three Stars were Pappin, Mahovlich and Alex Delvecchio, although Delvecchio didn't take his bow as he had been cut for three stitches on his eyebrow from a Red Kelly shot.

Big M Hospitalized as Toronto Injuries Mount
Saturday, November 14, 1964
While members of *Hockey Night in Canada* readied themselves to televise the Leafs/Bruins' game, Frank Mahovlich was hospitalized suffering from fatigue. "I sit beside him in the dressing room and I didn't know there was anything wrong," mentioned George Armstrong. "But then, Frank's like that. He just goes about his business and doesn't bother anybody."

While little information was provided, rumours were rampant. "When the reporters weren't given any information at all, they just speculated," Marie Mahovlich, Frank's wife, recalled in *The Big M*. "I can remember there was a radio broadcaster on CKEY. He gave an editorial piece — he seemed to think that Frank had cancer and was about to die. The Leafs let all these rumours swell up." In fact, it was later determined that Frank had been suffering from acute depression.

By this time, the Leafs' injury list was growing. Not only was Mahovlich out of the lineup, but Bower had the flu, Sawchuk had strained leg muscles, Brewer had taken an elbow to the side of the head and was out, Keon had injured his groin and Don McKenney had a sprained wrist.

Leafs Welcome Back The Big M
Wednesday, December 9, 1964
After missing eleven games, Mahovlich returned to Toronto's lineup with a vengeance. "I bodied Harper to get the feel of the game," said The Big M, who didn't just "body" Harper, he outright flattened him. "That's the best

way to get warmed up to your work." Whether it was dismissive or a reflection of Mahovlich having lost some strength during his time away from the rink, Harper stated, "I could push him off the puck. That seldom happened last season."

Charlie Hodge, Ron Stewart and Henri Richard were the Three Stars in Toronto's 3–2 loss to Montreal. "I thought Frank was more than adequate, considering he's spent most of the last month in bed in the hospital," mentioned Imlach. It didn't take long for Mahovlich to find his stride. In the next game, three nights later, The Big M scored two goals and assisted on two others in a 6–3 win over Boston.

Leafs Blow Lead in Loss to Duff and the Habs
Thursday, December 30, 1964
Toronto blew a two-goal lead for the third time in the previous six games in a 4–3 loss to Montreal. It was the return of former Leafs' star Dick Duff to Maple Leaf Gardens as a member of the Canadiens, having just been traded to Montreal by the New York Rangers. The popular Duff was welcomed warmly. Toronto played without Andy Bathgate and Montreal was missing their captain, Jean Beliveau.

Kelly and Keon put Toronto ahead in the first period, but that lead was erased with second-period goals from Claude Larose and Bobby Rousseau, and then followed by tallies from John Ferguson and Jean-Guy Talbot in the third. Ron Ellis scored a team-best thirteenth goal to make it closer than the 4–3 final score appeared.

Punch Shakes up Leafs; Horton Responds with Move to Forward
Saturday, January 2, 1965
At this time, Punch felt that the team was in a funk. They were winless since December 19, including a 3–0 loss to Boston on New Year's Day. To shake things up, the Leafs' coach tried Tim Horton at forward, and he responded by scoring two goals in a 3–1 victory over the Wings. Horton looked good and was kept on the wing for several games, scoring twice in a 6–0 rout of the Rangers on January 10 and twice more in a 3–1 win over Boston on

January 17. That night, Don McKenney was shipped down to Rochester.

Over the holidays, Montreal's GM, Sam Pollock, offered to strengthen the Bruins by making a trade that would assist Boston, and at the same time, block Toronto in their pursuit of the Stanley Cup. Imlach chuckled, remembering that the last time Montreal came to the aid of the Bruins, they sent Billy Carter in 1960 and Wayne Connelly and Cliff Pennington, separately, in 1961. None of them contributed much to Boston during that talent-fallow period. The rumour was that the Canadiens wanted to pick up Ab McDonald again, before Toronto did, by sending prospects unlikely to crack the Canadiens' roster. For his part, Imlach stated emphatically that McDonald had neither been offered nor was he on Toronto's radar.

Luckless Bruins Lose Game…and Equipment
Saturday, January 30, 1965

The Globe and Mail wrote, "Apparently, things are never so bad for the luckless Boston Bruins that they can't get worse." Boston met Toronto at Maple Leaf Gardens that night, but Ed Johnston, who had played 160 consecutive games in goal for the Bruins, was sick and unable to play. The team called upon Jack Norris from the Los Angeles Blades of the Western Hockey League to start in net. Excited, Norris left his equipment with the bellhop at Toronto's Royal York Hotel on Friday night when the team arrived, but on Saturday when he went to claim his pads and skates so he could head over to the rink, discovered that his equipment was nowhere to be found. Instead, flu and all, Johnston dressed and played. At this point, the bad luck got worse. In the first five minutes, Johnston was slashed on the hand. What he thought was a bruise turned out to be a broken bone. Johnston finished the game, but the Maple Leafs beat the Bruins 6–1. The next night in Boston, Jack Norris was in goal wearing Johnston's equipment when Boston went down in defeat, 4–2.

Ellis Scores Two in Fight-Filled Win over the Habs
Wednesday, February 10, 1965

Ron Ellis scored twice, both assisted by Mahovlich, to beat Montreal 6–2. The rookie's goals were his club-leading fifteenth and sixteenth of the season. Former Hab Dickie Moore also picked up two assists.

While stretching for a shot in the pre-game warm-up, Johnny Bower pulled some groin muscles. Terry Sawchuk stepped in from his perch in the press box.

The game featured fireworks beyond Ellis's scoring exploits. At 5:54 of the second period, a bench-clearing brawl erupted, lasting eighteen minutes and involving every player except four Leafs and the two starting goalies.

Montreal's John Ferguson was signalled for a hooking penalty on Mahovlich, and with Sawchuk out of the goal for an added attacker until the Canadiens gained control of the puck, Mahovlich continued his on-going feud with Terry Harper by taking the defender heavily into the boards. That action drew the attention of Ted Harris, who in barging in to protect his teammate was welcomed with a fist to the face. "If George Chuvalo had possessed a similar weapon, he could have dumped Floyd Patterson," noted *The Globe*. Mahovlich and Harris squared off in a dandy fight. Tim Horton, meanwhile, took Harper in a hold a ranch hand would be proud of and body slammed him to the ice. John Ferguson and Peter Stemkowski tangled, and the Leafs' rookie pulled the sweater of the Habs policeman over his head. Kent Douglas grabbed it and tossed it into the crowd. "Ordinarily, this would have been considered a sweaty souvenir," wrote *The Globe*, "but it was not an ordinary fan who caught the wet garment. This was a Leaf fan, dyed in the blue and white. He refused to be contaminated by the Montreal jersey and threw it back, much disgusted."

The two were pried apart only to engage again in a wild exchange of haymakers. Ellis and Larose paired off, as did Beliveau and Pulford. Jimmy Roberts then led an exodus over the boards, joined immediately by Allan Stanley, who led the Leafs from their bench. Charlie Hodge, who had taken refuge on his team's bench, was the only Hab still there, while

Sawchuk, Bathgate, Brewer, Kelly and Keon remained on the bench for Toronto, to the puzzlement of Leaf fans.

"You see the way I restrained my troops?" boasted Imlach. "Never lost my head at all when the fight started. I controlled most of my people."

Rangers Curb Their Enthusiasm
Saturday, February 27, 1965
Toronto met the New York Rangers, but rather than facing Jacques Plante, the Leafs noted that Marcel Paille was in goal for New York. *Hockey Night in Canada*'s Ward Cornell explained the change in goaltenders. "We got a lot of snow here in Toronto. Jacques Plante and I were walking down Wood Street [the street behind Maple Leaf Gardens] and we stepped off the curb to go across the road. Where I stepped, the snow was packed quite firmly. Where Jacques stepped off, his foot went down about four inches and it tripped him. He fell flat down and twisted his knee, so he limped to the Gardens and is not playing."

The Rangers edged Toronto 4–3. Dave Keon was chosen as the game's first Star. Rod Seiling, with two goals for New York, was second Star and Vic Hadfield was the third Star.

As the Rangers weren't winning with their veterans, they made strategic deals to pick up young talent on which to potentially build a championship team. The Leafs tinkered with their lineup, too. Popular Billy Harris was sent to Rochester and Don McKenney was recalled.

Kelly Counts to Three as Leafs Rout Rangers
Sunday, March 21, 1965
Toronto thrashed the New York Rangers 10–1 as the season was drawing to a close. With Marcel Paille in goal for New York, "The Maple Leafs played like the Stanley Cup defenders they are. Their short passes were gems. Their defence, perhaps the league's roughest, stymied the Rangers," reported the *New York Times*. "Among the players who fattened their statistics were Red Kelly, who scored three goals, and Ron Ellis, who tallied twice. Each wore helmets from some previous misunderstanding. They

could have left the head gear home for all the checking the Rangers were able to muster." Joining Kelly in a four-point game (three goals and an assist) were George Armstrong (two goals and two assists) and former Rangers' captain Andy Bathgate (a goal and three assists). Imlach also employed defenceman Tim Horton at forward on a checking line.

Marcel Paille was in goal for the Rangers, who were playing their third game in three nights. The biggest ovation of the evening came when the public-address announcer called, "One minute to play in the game."

Bower and Sawchuk Lay Claim to Vezina
Saturday, March 27, and Sunday, March 28, 1965
Going into the final weekend of the season, the Maple Leafs faced the Red Wings in an epic home-and-home battle. Detroit had locked up their first regular season championship since 1956–57. While Detroit had clinched first place and the Maple Leafs held fourth, the challenge really boiled down to which team would walk away with the Vezina Trophy, awarded to the goalkeeper who played the most games for the team with the fewest goals-against. Roger Crozier, the Red Wings' rookie sensation, had allowed 170 goals, playing in every one of his team's games. The Toronto tandem of Terry Sawchuk and Johnny Bower had allowed 169 goals. But a dilemma arose.

In an era before goaltending partners were *de rigueur*, the Vezina Trophy was awarded to a single goaltender. An NHL rule stated that the trophy and $1,000 went to the goaltender playing the most games for the team permitting the fewest goals. If a team employed two or more netminders during the season and had the lowest team goals against average, the goalie playing the most games had his name inscribed on the trophy. A situation had reared its head with the Maple Leafs in 1950–51, when Al Rollins of the Maple Leafs won the Vezina Trophy playing thirty-nine games while Turk Broda played thirty-one. But in an era when goaltending tandems were becoming commonplace (in fact, by then, the NHL had ruled that teams had to carry two goaltenders), the Vezina ruling seemed badly outdated.

With two games to play, Terry Sawchuk had played thirty-six games. Johnny Bower had played thirty-two, and even though he was scheduled to play those final two contests, if the Leafs hung onto the Vezina lead, it would be Terry Sawchuk who would be awarded the Vezina Trophy.

But Sawchuk had great respect for his partner, and felt as though he was sharing goaltending duties with an equal partner; one who was also a friend. "If we should win it, I won't accept the trophy unless both our names are on it," he told *The Globe and Mail*. The teammates had already made a pact that, should they win, they'd split the $1,000 awarded to the recipient.

In game sixty-nine, played at Maple Leaf Gardens and broadcast on *Hockey Night in Canada* on March 27, Detroit dumped the Leafs by a 4–1 margin, allowing Crozier to take the lead in the Vezina race. "The swift and dedicated Wings flapped around the agile oldster [Bower] firing shots from all angles as his disorganized teammates stood watching in bewildered admiration," wrote *The Globe*. Detroit's goals were scored by Pit Martin, Ed Joyal, Paul Henderson and Norm Ullman. Ron Ellis scored the lone goal for Toronto.

Game seventy, the final game of the regular season, saw the teams face off again the next day in Detroit.

The Leafs blanketed the Wings throughout the game, while Bower lived up to his nickname "'The China Wall." The Leafs, collecting goals from Don McKenney, Tim Horton, Peter Stemkowski and Dave Keon, earned a 4–0 victory over the Red Wings. "How could a team that looked so ordinary in bowing 4–1 to the Wings in Toronto Saturday be so efficient the next night? The answer is Bower," wrote the *Toronto Daily Star*. "John was phenomenal," exclaimed Bobby Baun. "He robbed them blind, especially Norm Ullman and Gordie Howe."

"I fired three real good shots at him. I got goals on those shots on every other goalkeeper in the league, but not on Bower," said a frustrated Norm Ullman. Gordie Howe, equally vexed, commented, "I said last summer when Sawchuk went to Toronto that he and Bower would win the Vezina. I wish I'd been wrong. We couldn't beat Bower. I should have had at least three in the two games and ended up with a goose egg."

It was the Wings' first loss at home in fifteen games. Toronto didn't do themselves any favours by picking up a string of penalties that left them shorthanded through much of the first and second period, but Keon's penalty-killing, a strong defence and Bower's miraculous netminding kept Detroit at bay.

"I couldn't watch the first two periods," admitted Sawchuk. "I sat in the dressing room. But I was rooting and making every move with him [Bower] in the last twenty minutes. What reflexes! He was like a teenager!"

As Dave Keon slid the puck into an empty net with three seconds remaining on the score clock, both teams realized that Toronto's 4–0 win had allowed the Leaf goaltenders to edge Roger Crozier for the Vezina Trophy. Toronto completed the campaign with 173 goals-against, while Detroit surrendered 174. Chicago, by comparison, had 176 goals-against.

Bower threw his goalstick into the air and Sawchuk, looking on from the bench, raised both arms in victory. With the Vezina race concluded, Bower and Sawchuk embraced in celebration near the Leafs' goal. Toronto's tandem of veteran netminders had been one of the few bright spots in a disappointing season.

Terry Sawchuk's firm stand on sharing the Vezina Trophy with his partner had a sizable impact on the NHL's Board of Governors. At their annual meeting in June 1965, the board amended the rule to allow for co-winners of the Vezina Trophy, provided that both netminders appeared in a minimum of twenty-five games. As such, Terry Sawchuk got his wish, and that summer, the names of Sawchuk and Bower were both engraved on the Vezina Trophy.

At the conclusion of the 1964–65 season, Sawchuk and Bower hosted a party for their teammates at the Conroy Hotel, a hotel owned by former hockey greats Charlie Conacher and Roy Worters. Both goalies contributed $250 from their Vezina win to underwrite the season-ending party. Bower recalled, "In the three years we played together, that's the only time I can ever remember Terry having fun."

1964–65 Regular Season Standings

FINISH	TEAM	GAMES	WINS	LOSSES	TIES	POINTS
1	Detroit Red Wings	70	40	23	7	87
2	Montreal Canadiens	70	36	23	11	83
3	Chicago Black Hawks	70	34	28	8	76
4	Toronto Maple Leafs	70	30	26	14	74
5	New York Rangers	70	20	38	12	52
6	Boston Bruins	70	21	43	6	48

Regular Season Scoring

RK	NUMBER	PLAYER	POS	AGE	GP	G	A	PTS	PIM	ESG	PPG	SHG	GWG
1	27	Frank Mahovlich	LW	27	59	23	28	51	76	16	7	0	4
2	14	Dave Keon	C	24	65	21	29	50	10	14	6	1	2
3	4	Red Kelly	D/C	37	70	18	28	46	8	11	6	1	1
4	9	Andy Bathgate	RW	32	55	16	29	45	34	10	6	0	1
5	11	Ron Ellis	RW	20	62	23	16	39	14	15	7	1	3
6	20	Bob Pulford	LW	28	65	19	20	39	46	13	2	4	4
7	10	George Armstrong	RW	34	59	15	22	37	14	12	3	0	3
8	7	Tim Horton	D	35	70	12	16	28	95	9	2	1	2
9	19	Kent Douglas	D	28	67	5	23	28	129	0	5	0	0
10	12	Ron Stewart	RW	32	65	16	11	27	33	14	2	0	5
11	2	Carl Brewer	D	26	70	4	23	27	177	3	0	1	0
12	25	Peter Stemkowski	C	21	36	5	15	20	33	2	3	0	1
13	17	Don McKenney	C	30	52	6	13	19	6	6	0	0	1
14	18	Jim Pappin	RW	25	44	9	9	18	33	9	0	0	2
15	21	Bob Baun	D	28	70	0	18	18	160	0	0	0	0
16	26	Allan Stanley	D	38	64	2	15	17	30	2	0	0	0
17	23	Eddie Shack	LW	27	67	5	9	14	68	3	2	0	0
18	15	Billy Harris	C	29	48	1	6	7	0	1	0	0	0
19	16	Dickie Moore	LW	34	38	2	4	6	68	2	0	0	0
20	8	Brit Selby	LW	19	3	2	0	2	2	2	0	0	1
21	24	Terry Sawchuk	G	35	36	0	2	2	24	0	0	0	0
22	1	Johnny Bower	G	40	34	0	0	0	6	0	0	0	0
23	22	Larry Hillman	D	27	2	0	0	0	2	0	0	0	0
24	22	Duane Rupp	D	26	2	0	0	0	0	0	0	0	0
		TEAM TOTALS			70	204	336	540	1068	144	51	9	30

Regular Season Netminding												
RK		PLAYER	POS	AGE	GP	MIN	W	L	T/OT	GA	GAA	SO
1	24	Terry Sawchuk	G	35	36	2160	17	13	6	92	2.56	1
2	1	Johnny Bower	G	40	34	2040	13	13	8	81	2.38	3
		TEAM TOTALS			70	4200	30	26	14	173	2.47	4

Roger Crozier, who had just missed out on the Vezina, was awarded the Calder Trophy as rookie of the year.

The Chicago Black Hawks dominated the individual awards in 1964–65. Stan Mikita won the scoring championship with eighty-seven points (twenty-eight goals and fifty-nine assists). Frank Mahovlich was well back with fifty-one points (twenty-three goals and twenty-eight assists) as the leading scorer with the Leafs. Dave Keon, with twenty-one goals and twenty-nine assists, was one point behind his teammate.

Bobby Hull took both the Hart Trophy as the MVP and the Lady Byng as most gentlemanly player. Pierre Pilote received the Norris Trophy as the NHL's premier defenceman for a third consecutive season.

The first-place Detroit Red Wings met the third-place Black Hawks in one semi-final series, while the second-place Montreal Canadiens challenged the fourth-place Maple Leafs in the other series.

Canadiens Edge Leafs in Playoff Opener

Game One, Semi-Final – Thursday, April 1, 1965

The two Canadian teams waged an on-ice war to challenge for the right to compete for the Stanley Cup. There was no love lost between the two teams, whose rivalry dated back to the 1940s.

The playoffs opened at the Montreal Forum, and in the opening contest, Montreal edged Johnny Bower and Toronto 3–2 in a brawl-filled game.

The teams were at full strength for less than two minutes in the first period. Mahovlich's running feud with Terry Harper continued, and the

Habs' defenceman was knocked unconscious by a solid shoulder hit from the Toronto winger. Kent Douglas later chopped down Dave Balon in a stick-swinging duel, and was suspended for a game because of his actions, despite Balon swinging his stick first and missing the target. It marked the first time a player was ejected from a post-season contest since Maurice Richard was tossed following an on-ice incident with Bill Ezinicki in 1947. Ironically, as Douglas was leaving the ice, he was greeted with a punch to the head from The Rocket, who was in the stands watching the contest.

Henri Richard and Ralph Backstrom scored for Montreal in the first period. Toronto rebounded in the third with goals from Carl Brewer and Dickie Moore against Charlie Hodge, but Bobby Rousseau fired the winner in Montreal's opening-night victory.

The Three Stars chosen were Johnny Bower, Henri Richard and Carl Brewer.

Montreal Takes Series Lead with Game Two Victory
Game Two, Semi-Final – Saturday, April 3, 1965
After Johnny Bower accidentally rubbed oil of wintergreen into his eye on the day of game two, Terry Sawchuk was summoned to play for Toronto, but was on the lesser side of the 3–1 score. Charlie Hodge was in goal once again for Montreal.

Claude Provost scored the game's opening goal, with Mahovlich and Horton both sitting in the penalty box. Ron Ellis tied the score in the second period. Later in the period, Jean Beliveau scored what proved to be the winner. In the third, Henri Richard took a shot from sixty-five-feet out that took a crazy bounce and got by Sawchuk for the Canadiens' third goal.

Keon's OT Goal Gives Leafs Game Three Win
Game Three, Semi-Final – Tuesday, April 6, 1965
With the series reverting to Toronto, Johnny Bower was back in net for the Maple Leafs, with Gump Worsley inserted in goal for Montreal.

Montreal's captain, Jean Beliveau, scored in the first. Eddie Shack tied things up with a tally in the second, and then Henri Richard put the Canadiens ahead with a goal in the third period. Andy Bathgate, who through the season had been taunted by boos when he touched the puck, quelled the crowd by scoring the tying goal. At 4:17 of overtime, Dave Keon scored to give the hometown Leafs a 3-2 win.

With the winning goal, Keon was named the game's first Star. Second Star honours went to Gump Worsley, while Eddie Shack was named the third Star of the contest.

Toronto Ties Series on Bower's Dramatic Netminding
Game Four, Semi-Final – Thursday, April 8, 1965

Toronto, backstopped by spectacular goaltending from Johnny Bower, won the fourth game by a 4–2 score. Henri Richard and Bobby Rousseau scored for Montreal within the first six minutes of the game, but Bower slammed the door after that. Red Kelly scored in the second and Ron Ellis and George Armstrong added to the Leafs' count in the third. With Gump Worsley pulled in favour of an extra attacker, Kelly scored an empty-netter to salt away the victory.

Harry Howell of the New York Rangers selected the game's Three Stars and chose Johnny Bower, Ron Ellis and Henri Richard.

Montreal Earns Series Edge With 3–1 Win
Game Five, Semi-Final – Saturday, April 10, 1965

Gump Worsley was solid as a rock in game five, leading his team to a 3–1 victory as the series reverted to La Belle Province. Yvan Cournoyer scored in the first with Toronto two men short. Bob Pulford replied in the second. Bobby Rousseau fired a sixty-foot slapshot that beat Bower at 7:30 of the third. Jean Beliveau scored an empty net goal at 19:16 for a 3–1 win.

With the victory, Montreal led the semi-final series three games to two.

Overtime Tally Ends Leafs' Season
Game Six, Semi-Final – Tuesday, April 13, 1965

The Montreal Canadiens eliminated the Maple Leafs from any further dreams of a fourth Stanley Cup with a 4–1 win in game six.

1964–65 Playoff Scoring

RK	NUMBER	PLAYER	POS	AGE	GP	G	A	PTS	PIM
1	4	Red Kelly	D/C	37	6	3	2	5	2
2	14	Dave Keon	C	24	6	2	2	4	2
3	11	Ron Ellis	RW	20	6	3	0	3	2
4	2	Carl Brewer	D	26	6	1	2	3	12
5	27	Frank Mahovlich	LW	27	6	0	3	3	9
6	25	Peter Stemkowski	C	21	6	0	3	3	7
7	16	Dickie Moore	LW	34	5	1	1	2	6
8	20	Bob Pulford	LW	28	6	1	1	2	16
9	7	Tim Horton	D	35	6	0	2	2	13
10	10	George Armstrong	RW	34	6	1	0	1	4
11	9	Andy Bathgate	RW	32	6	1	0	1	6
12	23	Eddie Shack	LW	27	5	1	0	1	8
13	21	Bob Baun	D	28	6	0	1	1	14
14	19	Kent Douglas	D	28	5	0	1	1	19
15	26	Allan Stanley	D	38	6	0	1	1	12
16	12	Ron Stewart	RW	32	6	0	1	1	2
17	3	Al Arbour	D	32	1	0	0	0	2
18	1	Johnny Bower	G	40	5	0	0	0	0
19	17	Don McKenney	C	30	6	0	0	0	0
20	24	Terry Sawchuk	G	35	1	0	0	0	0
		TEAM TOTALS			6	14	20	34	136

Playoff Netminding

RK	PLAYER		POS	AGE	GP	MIN	W	L	GA	GAA	SO
1	1	Johnny Bower	G	40	5	321	2	3	13	2.43	0
2	24	Terry Sawchuk	G	35	1	60	0	1	3	3.00	0
		TEAM TOTALS			6	381	2	4	16	2.52	0

Toronto had a two-goal lead after one period of play after Dave Keon, Red Kelly and Ronnie Ellis scored for Toronto, with John Ferguson replying for the Canadiens. Jacques Laperriere shaved the lead with a goal in the second, and Bobby Rousseau scored at 6:27 of the third to tie the game.

The game went into overtime, and at 16:33 of extra time, Claude Provost took a swipe at the puck, which eluded Bower to end the season for Toronto and squash the hopes of winning a fourth consecutive Stanley Cup championship. Montreal won the series four games to two, and allowed them to advance to the Stanley Cup final for the first time since their fifth straight Stanley Cup victory in 1960.

"We went down like champs," stated Imlach. "I'd have to say this was our best all-round game in the playoffs."

The Rangers' Red Sullivan selected Gilles Tremblay as the first Star, Bobby Rousseau as the second Star and his third Star choice was defence-man J. C. Tremblay.

The Canadiens went on to meet Chicago in the Stanley Cup final. The series went seven games, but in the deciding contest, Gump Worsley shut out the Black Hawks 4–0 to earn the Stanley Cup for Montreal. Jean Beliveau's goal at the fourteen-second mark of the first period proved to be the Stanley Cup-winning goal. For coach Toe Blake, it was his sixth championship in ten years.

The Maple Leafs' three-season grip on the Stanley Cup had come to an end. The Montreal Canadiens, a developing dynasty (they'd win the Cup in four of five seasons that decade), were going to be difficult to halt, and not just by the Leafs but by anyone!

It was a disappointing conclusion to a disappointing season, one that would have Punch Imlach contemplating changes through the entire summer.

But there was ongoing restlessness with the Maple Leafs. Cracks were beginning to emerge in the facade of the Toronto Maple Leafs Hockey Club. The earlier years of the dynasty had been glorious, but Punch Imlach's dictatorial approach to the game was taking its toll on the team.

While Andy Bathgate had been significantly responsible for the Stanley Cup win in 1964, he was also significantly responsible for Imlach's fall from grace in the eyes of many Maple Leafs' followers. Bathgate never fully adapted to Imlach's restrictive, defensive style, which put him in conflict with his coach and his teammates. His relationship with Imlach came to a head in the spring of 1965, when Montreal eliminated the Maple Leafs in the semi-final.

While Imlach enjoyed virtual autonomy with the Leafs, Bathgate bristled at his methods. "Frankly," Bathgate explained, "I didn't enjoy Punch's methods of training. Punch believed in hard work but geez, there were times when I had no energy at all for the games. He'd wear me out."

A relative newcomer, Bathgate noted that "there was no enthusiasm. We just wanted to get away from the rink and it wasn't fun there. By my second season in Toronto, I just wasn't enjoying playing." Bathgate ran afoul of Imlach's wrath when he went public with his candid feelings that the players were physically and mentally tired to the point that they couldn't get motivated for the playoffs because they had overworked themselves during the season to get there.

Punch was livid that Bathgate went to the press with these comments rather than approaching him face-to-face. Bathgate remembered, "I spoke to Punch and told him, 'Punch, look, I'm still tired, but this article was taken out of context.' The reporter came up and apologized afterwards. The damage was done. It wasn't too long after that I was traded to Detroit."

Bathgate's public criticism actually articulated the sentiments of many of the players, although most were not prepared to speak out against the coach and general manager for fear of exile to Rochester, or worse. In due time, many of the players would divulge their resentment towards Imlach.

Imlach clashed with a number of the players, most notably Carl Brewer, Frank Mahovlich, Mike Walton and Bathgate. Issues ranged from constant contract disputes to being overworked in practices, but the underlying tension was having longer-term ramifications on the team.

Bob Baun recalled how difficult Imlach could be on certain players. "The guys he had trouble with were Mahovlich and Brewer, who were bright, bright guys. But, you're not going to intimidate a guy like Carl, because intimidation is not going to do anything to him. And you're going to intimidate Frank for awhile, but then he's going to do the reverse to you." Larry Hillman's stance was the same. "I don't think he had the right motivation for those two individuals. He might have had problems with those two, but most of the other players, he could get through to them."

While Punch treated all the players equally (some said, equally badly), not every player responded to his methods. "It was an ongoing battle with Punch Imlach," admitted Carl Brewer, whose public feud with the coach resulted in his leaving the team before the start of the next season. "I didn't agree with his methods, I didn't agree with his approach to hockey and I didn't agree with his unnecessary disciplinary measures. He got to me and he got to Frank Mahovlich and Mike Walton. He destroyed our psyches."

While he was no stranger to disciplinary problems himself, Jim McKenny remembered how Brewer was regularly in trouble with the coach. "He was a shit disturber on that team. He was the only one who was really offside. Most of the rest of the team was straight down the middle, 'grind-it-out' guys." Larry Hillman confirmed, "Brewer was going to do whatever he thought should be done. He was too good a hockey player to bench."

Frank Mahovlich's hospital stays had been described as exhaustion, but were later attributed to depression, part of The Big M's ongoing derision from his coach. "Imlach never spoke to Frank Mahovlich or myself for most of the season," Andy Bathgate charged. "When he did, it was to criticize. Frank usually got the worst. We were athletes, not machines!"

Mahovlich admitted, "The first four years with Punch were great and the last four years weren't so great. Things weren't the same after that. He just wasn't the guy I once knew. I later told some of the guys on the Red Wings what he did and they refused to believe me."

It wasn't just pressure from his coach, but the pressure from the media and the fans that crippled Mahovlich. "If there was any such thing as just playing hockey and not worrying about the press, I'd go to heaven," he said.

Dave Keon thought his teammate was misunderstood. "Maybe a little bit too much pressure was placed on him, because he was an enormous talent," while Jim McKenny observed, "Frank was really well-liked by all the players on the team and really respected for his talent." But McKenny believed that The Big M really felt the weight of fan criticism more than most of the other players. "Athletes are like that," he said. "You can say a thousand nice things about them, but you say one bad thing and they'll hate you for life. When you are booed on the road, it's a compliment. When you are booed at home, it kills you. Frank was no different."

McKenny observed that if you didn't deviate from Imlach's demands, you were fine. "If you tried to be an individualist, then they'd just knock you right down. Shakey [Walton] was a real live wire, but he was playing so well at that time they put up with that. After a while, they sort of quelled him down and he was gone because it just got too hard." Carl Brewer saw Mike Walton facing some of the challenges that he, too, had faced. "He had his problems, and I could relate to him over that. But, he was a great hockey player. It was unfortunate that he ran into different problems in the organization, but he was a good guy, and very talented."

Although it wasn't unique to the Toronto Maple Leafs, fear was used by coaches, and Imlach played that emotion to perfection. "There was great fear of, 'You can be sent to the minors,' because there were no restrictions then of sending players up and down, like there are today," explained Bob Haggert.

While Brewer, Mahovlich and Walton were the main whipping boys for the obstinate Imlach, they weren't the only ones. Eddie Shack regularly raised the ire of his coach, and learned that the threat of being sent to the minors was real. "After a game, where something wasn't done properly, he'd say, 'You're going to be sent down.'" The ploy was to strike the fear of God in players who not only would lose the prestige of playing with the Toronto Maple Leafs by being sent to Rochester of the AHL or Tulsa in the WHL, but would also suffer a substantial difference in salary, too. "We always signed two-way contracts, so the money was shittier if you're going down," explained Shack. "[The difference was] probably about $100 to $200 a week, so you didn't want to get sent down."

Jim Pappin also suffered at the hands of Imlach's whims in this manner. Pappin made his debut with Toronto in 1963–64, but found himself regularly boomeranging between the Leafs and Rochester. He started the 1964–65 season with the Leafs but was sent to Rochester in early February and stayed there for the rest of the season. In 1965–66, he played the first seven games of the season with Toronto, then was demoted to Rochester beginning in November, and stayed in the AHL for the rest of the season.

In 1966–67, he was on his way to a twenty-goal season when he was demoted to the Rochester Americans in January 1967. He was brought back to the Leafs, reached the twenty-one-goal mark, and contributed significantly to the Stanley Cup championship. Then, sure enough, he started the season with Toronto in 1967–68, but was again demoted to the AHL in February, returning to the Leafs after briefly quitting the game. That season, Pappin was traded to the Black Hawks.

"I was sent down, up and down, all the time," said Pappin. "In 1964, Punch Imlach and Stafford Smythe bought the Rochester franchise. I don't know if everybody knew that, but we knew it and I can tell you that when they bought the franchise in 1964, we started winning all these championships in the American Hockey League because they stacked the team down there [the Rochester Americans won the Calder Cup in 1965 and in 1966] and that was money in their pockets." Pappin continued, "They would send me down and I would be mad for a little while then I would get over it and start to score goals again."

"He probably caused it himself," said Jim McKenny matter-of-factly. "He would sulk, and Punch didn't go for that shit at all. If you are pissed off, you go harder — that's how you got Punch off your back. Show him that you hate him; just show him he can't put you down, that you're going to be harder than him. Punch loved that. When Pappy got to Chicago and he was happy, boy could he play! He was one of the best right wingers in the league."

Pappin reflected on his tenure with the Maple Leafs in a Leafs' TV interview. After watching himself play, Pappin admitted, "Now I realize why Imlach was so mad at me all the time — not picking up my wing, wandering all over, chasing the puck and making dumb plays up the middle because you are looking to go the other way all the time. I always figured that my job was to score goals, not really supposed to check that hard so that I could save my energy and I was saving a lot of my energy in this game. I wish Punch was here so I could thank him and apologize to him for not trying a lot harder."

Billy Harris observed, "Punch was a very stubborn man, and I think the fact that the first year that he took over, when we snuck into the playoffs on the last game of the year, eliminated Boston in seven games and then gave Montreal a pretty good battle in the finals, I think Punch thought, 'Well, if my methods were successful the first year, then I'm going to use these methods for the rest of my career.'"

Allan Stanley felt that Punch was tough but fair. "He did a great job, but he was a tough bugger. But that's the way that you're going to win. You just had to work hard. You had to be in good shape. But the practices used to be so boring. It was skate, skate, skate. But he always treated me excellent."

Bob Haggert knew the price the team paid if they didn't play up to the coach's expectations. "If you lost a game because you didn't play well, you paid the price the next day in practice. I've seen us lose a 1–0 game versus Montreal with two minutes to go — one of the best hockey games ever played in Maple Leaf Gardens — and the next day, the players skated around in a circle for an hour and a half, never touching a puck. And he sat on centre ice with a coffee, reading *The Globe and Mail*. He ignored them and then said, 'You can go home.'" Billy Harris simply shook his head. "We lose on Saturday, we lose on Sunday, then we have stops and starts for two hours on Monday morning at Maple Leaf Gardens. This is the way that Punch treated our hockey team."

"He tried to exhaust you physically," remarked Keon. "He did it because he was the boss and if you wanted to play, that's what you went through."

Imlach was proud of being the disciplinarian. "I figure if you are going to play a hockey game for an hour, you should probably practise for two hours. It's like a track coach who prepares his runners for a one-mile race by running them five or ten miles. When the time came to work, you worked. After that, as long as you didn't end up in the guardhouse, you were okay. That was the theory. But when I would get mad at them and I would start giving them the tough practices, making them skate without pucks back and forth and up and down the ice, the team's idea was, 'We are not going to let him beat us. Whatever that bastard throws at us, we are going to do it.' They would be swearing at me and everything else. If they would say that to me, you can be sure that when they were playing against another team, they were saying the same thing. 'We are not going to let those SOBs beat us.' So, when you've got that kind of relationship and that kind of player, you've got to win. There is no question about it at all."

But for Punch, it wasn't strictly about attitude and discipline; it also involved conditioning. "The guy who is older is deteriorating, and if you allow it by not forcing yourself to work hard, you can't slow down that deterioration. You can slow it down to the point where a guy can play for maybe one, two or three years more than what he should be able to play."

The "reign of terror" came to an end, for the most part, with the re-formation of the National Hockey League Players' Association in 1967. "As long as there was sponsorship, you could do a lot of things," Keon said. "Once expansion came, you didn't have the leverage to do some of those things, because you just couldn't get away with sending some of the guys to the minors. I think players came in with agents, and agents were asking more questions about what things were happening. I think it was a general evolution, a growing of the game, and the power in the way things were run was restricted a bit more."

In his candid manner, Jim McKenny, who played a handful of games with the Leafs during the dynasty, admitted to surprise at the fear-mongering used by Imlach. "He didn't take any shit from any player. All those guys were terrified of Imlach, but he got their respect and that's the way he got it — by being a hard-ass. If Punch wanted to do something to you, you were gone. I was amazed at how guys that age could be terrified of a man like they were of Punch, but he got every last ounce out of all of them. I don't think any other coach could have got any more out of what that team had."

Threats and fines were the order of the day. Ultimatums were so common that players just began to ignore them. Imlach continued to deal with things in black-and-white terms, when often, especially in dealings with veterans, a subtle grey was often in order. "Imlach was petrified that someone would take his job," stated Eddie Shack. "He was the boss. What he did and what he said, went."

There was a deepening crack in the foundation of the Toronto Maple Leafs during what should have been among their most jubilant of times.

Dave Keon remarked: "I think of what we could have become, and what we did become, in spite of what we were put through."

SLAPSHOTS AND SNAPSHOTS
STARS ON 45S

The 1965–66 season produced its shares of hits and misses, but two Maple Leafs were immortalized through songs. Johnny Bower almost cooked his goose with "Honky" and Eddie Shack was the star of "Clear the Track."

Chip Young, a CBC producer, had written a short Christmas story about a wild goose that ate so much that he couldn't swim or fly, but in the end, saved Santa Claus. Encouraged by *Hockey Night in Canada* broadcaster Ed Fitkin, who was also a prolific hockey author, Young turned the story into a song with the help of composer Orville Hoover. He then approached Toronto's coach Punch Imlach to get permission for one of the Maple Leafs to record the song he had written.

Granted permission to try to recruit a singer, Young went out to the Tam O'Shanter rink in Scarborough where the Leafs practised. "He came into the dressing room and wanted to know if anybody on the team would be interested in singing these songs," recalled Bower. "I've never seen so many guys undress and get into the shower so quickly in my life! I was the only one left sitting there. He said, 'I guess you're the only one left,' and I said, 'Look sir, I can't sing.' I thought he was nuts!"

Bower pointed to the showers and suggested that there were better singers there, noting that Ron Stewart was known for singing in the shower. Young was emphatic. "There's just something about you that seems right for this. Wouldn't you at least try it?" Bower finally agreed. "For my money, he's the friendliest man in Canada; the guy who should sing this [song] regardless of the quality of his pipes," Young told the *Toronto Daily Star*.

Johnny arrived home and told his family about the song. They tried singing "Honky," and his wife, Nancy, smiled. "This is cute," she admitted.

"It's a nice children's song." Then she chuckled and added, "If you only knew how to sing!"

Young was invited over to the Bower home. "He came over with a recorder and the music and the words were all there. He said, 'Work with this for a few days.' So, I started to get to know the words to 'Honky the Christmas Goose.' My wife told me I used to sing the song in my sleep. I would get up at two a.m. and sing 'Honky the Christmas Goose' in bed!"

Johnny recruited his eleven-year-old son, John Jr., as well as five neighbourhood children, to join him for the recording session. For two weeks, they rehearsed until they had the melody and lyrics down cold.

The entourage went into the recording studio on November 9, 1965, to record "Honky" and its B-side, "Banjo Mule." The session was interrupted by the Northeast Blackout, which left twenty-five million people in Ontario and down the eastern seaboard of the United States without power for up to twelve hours. "I nearly died," Johnny told the *Toronto Daily Star*. "I'm no Sinatra but I didn't think my voice would wreck the hydro! I was glad to learn that I hadn't blown all the fuses. We finished by candlelight in a real Christmas atmosphere. It was a lot of fun!"

The group, known as Johnny Bower with Little John and the Rinky Dinks, took just five takes to complete "Honky." John Jr. received $100 for his effort. "We were supposed to be a group of people who are singing songs because we're happy," recalled the netminder. "Nothing professional about it."

Both "Honky the Christmas Goose" and "Banjo Mule" were mixed and pressed within days, and released in a picture sleeve on the Capitol label. Bower was quite prepared for the teasing that was bound to occur. "If I have a bad night in goal, I can just hear those fans shouting, 'Why don't you stick to singing?'"

A CBC-TV show on December 14, 1965, featured the Bower family and helped promote the song. By this time, CHUM Radio, Toronto's powerful Top 40 station, was playing "Honky." To help sell the single, Johnny made a few appearances, including one at Eaton's College Park, in order to sign the picture sleeve. "I was sitting there, selling my records, and there was a big pile of Beatles' records sitting on the table next to me," he remembered. "So I took their pile of records and put them underneath the table, and after that, we were selling all of mine!"

"Honky the Christmas Goose" reached number twenty-nine on the 1050 CHUM Chart, and for a couple of weeks in December 1965, knocked The Beatles' two-sided smash "Day Tripper"/"We Can Work It Out" out of the most-requested spot. On the strength of Bower's name, the single sold forty thousand copies. Seeing the golden goose, Chip Young was elated and planned for Johnny to record an album. "He tells me he's got a whole bunch of new songs to go — 'Jumbo the Elephant,' 'Pelican with the Broken Wing,' another one for a rat. I said, 'Chip, you've got the wrong man.'"

The song has long been unavailable, not through any lack of effort from collectors. Various companies have tried to reissue the recording over the years, with the full blessings of Johnny Bower, but the ownership of the copyright is in dispute, leaving the single a great memory and a much sought-after collectible.

"Shack is rambunctious and barrelling, a right wing, more or less," wrote Dick Beddoes in *The Globe*. "He has fixed himself firmly in a delighted city's heart by what one of the enraptured public calls 'loveable incompetence.'"

So popular was Eddie Shack in Toronto that a song was written about him. "I already had the idea when I approached Shackie, and I remember stopping him near the visiting team bench at Maple Leaf Gardens after a practice," recalled broadcaster Brian McFarlane, co-author of the song, "Clear the Track, Here Comes Shack." "I told him I was thinking about writing this little song and asked if he had any problem with that. He said he didn't and that I should go ahead and do it. So my brother-in-law, Bill McCauley, who had a doctorate in music, wrote the music, and I wrote the words, and in about twenty minutes we had the thing done. It certainly wasn't Eddie's idea. He did give me sanction to do it, but maybe I should have gotten him to sign a release."

With the song completed, McFarlane needed to find performers to record the song. In walked a Toronto group called Douglas Rankine and the Secrets.

"The band was playing at the Toronto Pressman Club," recalled lead singer Doug Rankine. "At the time, we met Brian McFarlane. I forget what the function was, but it was a press gathering of something. He came up to us later in the night and said that he had written a song, and would we listen to it? And he talked about making records. We were very sceptical because lots of people approach bands. Anyway, he came with his brother-in-law to where we were rehearsing. They had the music and asked us to play it. We sang it a couple of times and then he said, "Would you mind coming into the recording studio and recording this?" He offered us a certain amount of money, not a lot. Five hundred dollars. At the time, being seventeen, I needed the money. We jumped on it. We went to RCA to record it. I think it was take two or three and that was the record."

The Secrets were Doug Rankine on vocals and guitar, Bob Mark on lead guitar, Mike Woodruff on bass, Henry S. on electric piano and Rick Felstead on drums.

The song was released with a B-side ("Warming the Bench") in February 1966 on the RCA label. McFarlane had plans for Douglas Rankine and the Secrets to perform the song from the ice surface of Maple Leaf Gardens, wearing Maple Leafs sweaters, and televising it on *Hockey Night in Canada*. The producers vetoed the idea, so instead, the song was launched on *Hockey Night in Canada* between periods, accompanying footage of Shack. The national exposure on Canada's most viewed television program did wonders in launching the record. "Clear the Track" was picked up by CHUM Radio. Eddie Shack remembered the first time he heard the song. "Geez, I'm drivin' down the 401 and I'm listening to 'Clear the Track, Here Comes Shack'! I almost had an accident!"

Rankine, too, was shocked when he heard it. "I was surprised like everybody else! I can still remember [CHUM disc jockey] Bob McAdorey coming on the radio, saying, 'We interrupt this program to bring you this special record.' I was really surprised, and then that it became a hit was even more of a surprise! I thought it was more of a joke. I didn't know it was going to be a 'record' record. Before you know it, people were asking for it and buying it!"

On February 28, 1966, "Clear the Track, Here Comes Shack" displaced Petula Clark's "My Love" as the number one song on the prestigious CHUM Chart, the radio station's weekly list of the city's most popular songs. "Clear the Track" stayed at the coveted number one spot for two weeks before it was replaced by Nancy Sinatra's "These Boots are Made for Walking."

The Secrets often played live, and the song was requested everywhere they went. From time to time, Eddie Shack would show up unannounced and sing a few lines. "I remember one tour through eastern Canada and Ontario at that time," said Rankine. "We never knew when he was going to show up, but I think it was two or three concerts that we did and basically we were on the stage, people were asking for the song and we'd start to play it and sure enough, up he'd come onto the stage and everyone went all crazy for him! I guess he said a few words to people and then he left. He just made an appearance and he was gone."

But the song was an albatross around the neck of the Secrets. "You have to understand that we were trying to be rock 'n' roll stars, and that record kind of got in our way. Subsequently, we ended up changing the name of the band from the Secrets to the Quiet Jungle, to escape that," explained Rankine. The Quiet Jungle recorded a number of singles for the Yorkville label before breaking up.

Both singles, long out of print, are treasured finds at collectors' shows, commanding hundreds of dollars apiece for a piece of vinyl that at the time cost seventy-seven cents. Memories truly are priceless!

10

1965–66: Falling Short Again

The end of Toronto's reign as Stanley Cup champions hadn't come as an entire surprise to most hockey observers, as the Montreal Canadiens usurped Toronto's hold on hockey's most treasured trophy in the spring of 1965. But once you've tasted victory, you want to enjoy it again and again, and Punch and the Leafs vowed they would once again return to supremacy.

Detroit finished the previous season in first place, but had been eliminated by Chicago in the semi-final. They believed they needed to further strengthen their lineup, so they made several pivotal trades. Andy Bathgate, Billy Harris and Gary Jarrett arrived from Toronto, and Don McKenney was chosen from the Leafs through the Intra-League Draft. Bob McCord and Ab McDonald also were picked up by the Wings. A day after being traded from Montreal to Chicago, Bryan Watson was also selected in the draft. Bert Marshall joined the team from their Edmonton farm club.

Although they won the Stanley Cup, the Montreal Canadiens didn't rest on their laurels. In June, they traded excess goaltending in Cesare Maniago, along with Garry Peters, to the New York Rangers for Earl Ingarfield, Gord Labossiere, Dave McComb, Noel

Price and cash. Oddly, the next day, Ingarfield was claimed back by the Rangers in the Intra-League Draft.

The Chicago Black Hawks added Pat Stapleton to an already impressive defence corps, picking him up from Toronto a day after he was traded to the Leafs by Boston. Punch Imlach would later lament losing Stapleton after star defenceman Carl Brewer abruptly quit the Leafs in training camp. The Hawks also added Dick Meissner, Mel Pearson, Tracy Pratt and Dave Richardson. Ken Hodge joined the team as a rookie.

A new era in goaltending for the New York Rangers began with Ed Giacomin arriving, in a trade that sent Aldo Guidolin, Sandy McGregor, Jim Mikol and Marcel Paille to Providence of the AHL. To further shore up the netminding situation, Giacomin was joined by Cesare Maniago, who was obtained from Montreal, and Don Simmons, who was chosen from Tulsa of the CHL in the draft. The Rangers also added forwards Ray Cullen, Earl Ingarfield, Johnny McKenzie and Garry Peters.

Five years in the basement wasn't sitting well with Boston Bruins' executives. Gerry Cheevers was eagerly plucked from Toronto in the Intra-League Draft, giving them a dynamic goaltending threesome of Ed Johnston, Bernie Parent and Cheevers. Gilles Marotte was ready to join the big club on defence. Additions to the Bruins included Bob Dillabough, Ron Harris, Al Langlois and Parker MacDonald, as well as Ron Stewart in a trade with Toronto.

Toronto made some significant changes that they hoped would get them back into Stanley Cup contention. In May, they made a blockbuster swap with Detroit, receiving Aut Erickson, Larry Jeffrey, Ed Joyal, Lowell MacDonald and Marcel Pronovost in return for Andy Bathgate, Billy Harris and Gary Jarrett. "I was very disappointed," stated Pronovost on *Hockey Night in Canada*. "I spent eighteen years with the [Red Wings] organization, and this is more than half my life. Detroit Red Wings were good to me and I don't want to be bitter. This is a nice thing when they tell you, 'You're the guy we were after.'"

Two weeks later, they sent Ron Stewart to the Bruins, receiving Andy Hebenton, Orland Kurtenbach and Pat Stapleton in return. Stapleton and Don McKenney were left unprotected, and both were drafted by other teams. Brit Selby, and later Wally Boyer and Mike Walton, were rookies who cracked the roster that year.

After sitting out the entire 1964–65 season for refusing to report to the AHL Springfield Indians following a trade to Eddie Shore's squad by Boston, Bruce Gamble joined the Maple Leafs in September, in exchange for Larry Johnston and Bill Smith.

The perennial concern of contract holdouts reared its head once again. Veteran Bob Baun was looking for more money, while rookie Brian Conacher was looking for assurances that he'd play for the Leafs and not spend time in Rochester. Veteran Tim Horton was also negotiating a new contract. Horton's wife Lori recalls the back-and-forth Tim went through with Imlach. "Tim would come home and say, 'Well, Punch says this and I'm going to go back and say that tomorrow!' It was always sort of a friendly negotiation. One particular year, Tim had started in the doughnut business and he didn't go to training camp in Peterborough. He and Punch were talking on the phone and not getting very far, so Tim picked up six pieces of dough from the bottom of the fryer and wrapped them up and mailed them to Punch with a note that said, 'With a product like this, who needs hockey!' Punch called up and said, 'Tim, why didn't you send more?' Tim liked Punch Imlach an awful lot, so even in their contract negotiations, even when people thought things were getting pretty tense, they weren't at all. Tim didn't really need training camp anyway. He always said he'd play hockey for nothing. They'd have to pay him for getting there."

But most concerning of all was the saga of Carl Brewer.

Although he appeared at training camp in Peterborough, Brewer decided that had been through enough and quit the Maple Leafs. "It was an ongoing battle with Punch Imlach," he revealed. "I didn't agree with his methods, I didn't agree with his approach to hockey and I didn't agree with his unnecessary disciplinary measures. He got to me and he got to Frank Mahovlich and Mike Walton. He destroyed our psyches."

During an intermission interview on *Hockey Night in Canada*, Bob Baun discussed Carl Brewer's departure. "It's going to be quite a different season, especially after playing eight years together. I wanted him to wait a little while to think it over a bit longer."

The team chemistry had been altered a great deal, and coach Punch Imlach sounded the warning that no one's job was safe. "It's a case of shape up or ship out this year," asserted Imlach. "I have enough talent at Rochester and our other farm clubs to keep the guys on the big club working. If they try to take the easy route, it will mean an air plane ticket to a minor league, and one of our eager beavers will move into the vacated spot. I think Selby has the ability to stick with the team."

Punch wasn't kidding. On September 25, 1965, Jim Proudfoot at the *Toronto Daily Star* editorialized, writing, "If you want my opinion, Eddie Shack is a terrible hockey player. His incompetence irritates me, but not as much as the cheers he draws for doing things incorrectly, but enthusiastically." Shortly afterwards, Shack was sent down to Rochester. Imlach may have had an ulterior motive, since the Rochester team was going to play home games later in the season at Maple Leaf Gardens, and he may have wanted a draw for the Leafs' main farm team.

Leafs Lose to Hull and Hawks in 1965–66 Season Opener
Saturday, October 23, 1965

The season opener took place at home, with the Maple Leafs entertaining the Chicago Black Hawks. Members of the Russian men's and women's volleyball teams were in attendance for the game, as was Bing Crosby, in the company of his long-time friend and former Leafs' great, Charlie Conacher.

Red Barber, who had been the Maple Leafs' public-address announcer since the Gardens opened in 1931, had retired, but just before the home opener, and it was realized that no one had been designated to replace him. Paul Morris, whose father Doug had been the first superintendent of Maple Leaf Gardens, had himself been helping out around the rink for several years, and began working there in the summer of 1958 while he was attending college. He quit school and stayed on at the Gardens. Paul had been the PA announcer at some Marlboros' games, so when they needed a replacement for Barber, Morris was the obvious choice. His distinctive voice announced the goals, penalties and scores for every single Maple Leafs' game until the team moved from Maple Leaf Gardens to the Air Canada Centre. "That streak is a source of pride," he said.

The 48th Highlanders, as per tradition, performed on-ice prior to the game, including the national anthem. Maple Leaf Gardens exhibited the Red Ensign rather than Canada's new flag during the pre-game ceremony. Frederick G. Gardiner, the first chairman of Metropolitan Toronto Council, then strode to centre ice, cane in hand, with Maple Leaf Gardens' president, Stafford Smythe, who was again booed lustily. Gardiner, who had retired from politics and was named commissioner of Toronto Hydro that year, first presented the J. P. Bickell Award to Johnny Bower, who was receiving the award for the third time. Gardiner and Smythe then presented the Vezina Trophy to Bower and Terry Sawchuk, the first time co-winners had ever been named. Finally, Gardiner presided over the ceremonial faceoff between Toronto's captain, George Armstrong, and Chicago's captain, Pierre Pilote.

During the first intermission, Punch Imlach confidently told Ward Cornell on *Hockey Night in Canada*, "We only loaned the Cup to the Canadiens for a year. We'll try to get it back this year."

Bobby Hull scored three goals in a 4–0 loss to the Black Hawks that night. Although the fans booed Hull early on, they gave him a sizable ovation when he scored his third goal. Hull, not surprisingly, was the first Star of the hockey game. "Hockey is really something, but that Hull is something else," said Bing Crosby, shaking his head. The second Star was Glenn Hall with the shutout, and Toronto newcomer Marcel Pronovost was the game's third Star. Pronovost was paired with Bobby Baun in Carl Brewer's former spot.

Toronto Shut Out in Second Straight Game
Sunday, October 24, 1965
Imlach's confidence was being challenged as Toronto was blanked for the second night in a row. Roger Crozier earned the shutout, as Detroit dumped the Leafs 3-0 in just the second game of the young season.

The Globe and Mail pointed out the problem: "Leafs weren't checking, weren't skating and they weren't playing their positions."

"It would have been a cricket score but for Sawchuk," commented Norm Ullman. "He stole us blind and beat us on five breakaways. They won't get better goaltending than that all season." *The Globe* concurred. "If it hadn't been for the brilliant work by goaltender Terry Sawchuk, it would have been much worse." Imlach added, "In the last fifteen seconds, I was even thinking of pulling goalie Terry Sawchuk just to try to prove to them that we had to keep trying."

Frustrated, Punch admitted, "We're not working hard enough and don't have enough bite in our play at either end of the rink. Our guys are letting themselves get pushed around. They don't seem to want to win as much as the other guys."

Leaf Sharpshooters Firing Blanks Early in Season
Sunday, November 7, 1965

"Fortunately, hockey is a game," wrote Paul Rimstead in *The Globe and Mail*. "Otherwise, Maple Leafs' fans would be lined up this morning on the Bloor Street Viaduct, pitching themselves with gay abandon into the smelly Don River. The Leafs didn't play very well again last night."

They certainly didn't. Chicago whipped the Leafs 9–0, the most decisive shutout in Chicago franchise history (on February 25, 1962, the Hawks had buried Boston 8–0). Bobby Hull picked up three goals and three assists to lead the way for the Hawks. His 555 career points with the Black Hawks pushed him past Bill Mosienko as the highest point producer in the club's history.

The Maple Leafs had scored but eleven goals in eight games to that point in the season.

Harold Ballard believed the answer to the Leafs' woes was to have Carl Brewer return to the team. "I don't know whether he's had enough time to sort out the problems that led to his retirement, but I think we have to make a pitch to him. And I'd do it immediately." Ballard liked to offer opinions whenever possible, but he had no say in the hockey department at the time. That domain belonged exclusively to Stafford Smythe. Instead, Ballard looked after non-hockey-related revenue streams.

"I'm at school now and I'm enjoying it and I have an examination this week," Brewer responded when contacted by the *Star*. "No one has approached me."

Imlach sent Jim Pappin to Rochester and called up Eddie Shack. He also stated that he would have sent Kent Douglas packing had Bob Baun not suffered a concussion after blocking a Rod Gilbert slapshot in the Saturday night game against the New York Rangers.

During this time, the Rochester Americans could likely have been dropped into the NHL and been competitive. The combination of veterans and youth was paying huge dividends for the American Hockey League farm club of the Leafs. The Americans won the Calder Cup as AHL champions in both 1965 and 1966, with a roster that included Al Arbour, Don Cherry, Les Duff, Gerry Ehman, Dick Gamble, Bronco Horvath, Ed Litzenberger, Jim Pappin, Duane Rupp and Stan Smrke.

"The bastards put me on a minor-league salary," Shack later recalled. "After two weeks, I told them I wasn't making enough to eat in restaurants, and that I could make more money selling hats, cars or f'#*@in' sausages, that they had another fourteen days, and if I wasn't up with the Leafs, I'd quit hockey."

After eight games in the minors, and with Toronto sitting with just two wins, Eddie was recalled and went on to have a terrific season. "Shack's weakness used to be that he played both wings on the same shift," wrote the *Toronto Star*. "He came pretty close to becoming the first man to rendezvous with himself in orbit."

The Triumphant Return of Eddie the Entertainer
Thursday, November 18, 1965
The Leafs beat Montreal 3–1, but the bigger story was the return of "The Entertainer." "Montreal fans cheered Shack every time he returned to the bench after a shift here last night, even though the man who usually is regarded as public enemy #1 was beating their beloved Canadiens," stated *The Globe*.

The paper hypothesized that being sent to Rochester was the best thing that could have happened to Shack. "He is not getting foolish penalties and is sticking to his wing. He is checking and shooting better and can even pass now." The *Star* agreed: "Shack went to the Leafs' American Hockey League farm club labelled a 'hockey misfit,' a 'clown prince' they could no longer afford. He came back a serious, aggressive, productive player."

The Entertainer had been placed on a new line with Bob Pulford at centre and Red Kelly at left wing. Concentrating on hockey, Shack had a career season in 1965–66, scoring twenty-six goals.

It was Shack's fifth game since being recalled from Rochester, and during that time, he had emerged as the best Leafs' forward. Eddie scored twice against Montreal, including an empty-net goal. He was named the first Star of the contest, followed by Bob Pulford and Ralph Backstrom.

"I'm not worrying any more," said Shack. "I'm giving it my best shot, sticking to business. I've decided that's all I can do. As a result, I'm playing with more confidence and there's no pressure on me."

A Trio of Hat Tricks in Leaf Win over New York
Saturday, December 18, 1965
During an 8–4 thrashing of the Rangers, three players collected hat tricks. Dave Keon recorded his first-ever three-goal game, Bob Pulford compiled his third, and New York's Earl Ingarfield also scored three times.

Toronto's Eddie Shack left wreck and ruin in his wake. On one shift, he left two Rangers unconscious in the Leafs' zone — Phil Goyette was unconscious to Bower's right and Rod Gilbert to his left. Both were helped off the ice, missed a few shifts but returned to play later in the game.

Shack had been hit over the head, and went looking for retribution. "I gave him [Gilbert] an elbow, figured I was gone for a penalty, so I gave him another one, except I hit the wrong guy [Phil Goyette]." After the game, both Gilbert and Goyette could only shake their heads in amazement that no penalty had been called. "He gave me an elbow," stated Gilbert. I'm a bit unsteady." Goyette added, "He cross-checked me on the back of the neck. I can't turn my head."

On the weekly *Sports Hot Seat* program on CFTO Television in Toronto, Rangers' coach and general manager Emile Francis was so dismayed at the Shack escapade that he vowed to hire more muscle for the Rangers, and soon traded Johnny McKenzie to Boston for Shack's arch enemy, Reg Fleming.

Leafs Give Hawks Unexpected Christmas Gift
Saturday, December 25, 1965

On Christmas Eve, the Chicago Black Hawks climbed aboard a train bound for Toronto. Eighty miles out of Chicago, the train ground to a halt due to a wreck on the line. The players woke up Christmas morning believing they were in Toronto, but were surprised to discover they were back in Chicago. They then took a bus to the airport in order to fly to Toronto, but a snowstorm delayed their departure. Finally, arriving mere hours before the opening faceoff, Chicago took to the ice at Maple Leaf Gardens, and in spite of two goals from Bobby Hull, were upset 5–3 by the Leafs. Merry Christmas!

Punch's Kid Dons Dad's Blue and White in NHL Debut
Sunday, January 16, 1966

Toronto had been on a scoring frenzy, pumping six goals past Montreal while shutting out the Canadiens on January 13 and scoring six, including a hat trick from Brit Selby, in a 6–1 shellacking of Boston on the 15th. But it came to a quick end on January 16, when Roger Crozier and his Wings blanked Toronto 4–0 in a game that was most notable by virtue of the NHL debut of Brent Imlach, Punch's son. Nineteen-year-old Brent was a twenty-three-goal scorer for the Leafs' junior squad, the Marlboros, that season, and replaced the injured Wally Boyer.

Injuries Mount, as Does Shack's Goal Count
Thursday, February 3, 1966

Injuries were plaguing the beleaguered Leafs. Marcel Pronovost was placed on the injured list, but fortunately for Toronto, was replaced by Bobby Baun, who had returned for his first game in nine weeks after recuperating from a knee injury. Terry Sawchuk was in goal, backed by Gary Smith, who had been summoned from Rochester while Johnny Bower nursed a groin injury. Coach Imlach feared that Brit Selby might be out of the lineup too, after needing seven stitches to close a gash after receiving the short end of the wishbone in a fight with John Ferguson, which occurred just after a tussle with Terry Harper. According to Selby, it wasn't much of a fight, as he was blindsided by the Montreal policeman while he was entangled with Harper. Leafs' strongman Tim Horton hunted down Ferguson throughout the rest of the game, but Ferguson wisely avoided any confrontation with the enraged Leafs' defenceman.

The altercation wasn't the only battle Toronto lost, as the final score was Montreal 5, Leafs 4. Eddie Shack did provide a temporary bright spot, scoring his eighteenth goal of the season.

NHL Announces End of Original Six Era
Wednesday, February 9, 1966
The NHL's Board of Governors announced that six new teams would be introduced, beginning with the 1967–68 season. Conditional franchises were awarded to Los Angeles, Minneapolis-St. Paul, Philadelphia, Pittsburgh, San Francisco and St. Louis. Shut out in their bid was Vancouver, a franchise that was to be owned by broadcaster Foster Hewitt. In spite of appeals from Prime Minister Lester Pearson and Opposition Leader John Diefenbaker, Vancouver would not join the NHL until 1970.

Can Anyone Stop Bobby Hull's Fifty-Goal Quest?
Wednesday, February 23, 1966
With Bower suffering a pulled hamstring and Sawchuk out with a groin injury, young Gary Smith was called to face Bobby Hull and the Hawks. The Golden Jet needed just three goals to tie Rocket Richard's record of fifty goals in fifty games. And it looked as though Hull had a good chance to tie the record, when Gary Smith went down with an injury and the Leafs were forced to deploy Al Smith, a junior goaltender playing with the Marlboros. But the Leafs' defence created a fortress in front of the youngster, and Toronto won 3–2, with Hull held goalless.

After the game, Imlach sought netminding help from Bruce Gamble, a long-time minor-league goaltender with NHL experience. Gamble had been playing with the Tulsa Oilers of the Central Professional Hockey League and was yet another reclamation project for Imlach. He had already spent time with both the New York Rangers and Boston Bruins, and when he was traded to Eddie Shore's AHL Springfield Indians, chose to sit out the season rather than report to an organization many players tried to avoid playing for.

Gamble would become the fifth goaltender used by the Leafs during the 1965–66 season. His route back to the NHL was circuitous and fortunate, to say the least. After Bower suffered his injury, Gary Smith was called up from the AHL Rochester Americans to be the backup for Sawchuk. But Sawchuk injured his groin on February 16, so Al Smith was called up from the junior Toronto Marlboros to become backup to Gary Smith with the Leafs. Gary Smith played two games when he, too, was injured, and Al Smith then had to take over. Johnny Bower returned from sick bay, so Al Smith was relegated to the backup role. Later, Bower would suffer pulled ligaments in the rib area. Sawchuk was then almost ready to return, but pulled a hamstring and was out of action once again.

Left with only one healthy goalie (Al Smith, a junior with no previous NHL experience), Punch Imlach was forced to look for another goalie within the system. Veteran Bob Perreault had NHL experience, but with Gary Smith injured, he was the only goalie in Rochester, and Rochester was currently on a road trip to the west coast. Imlach was cautious with Rochester, as the team was on a roll towards a second Calder Cup championship, and it would later surface that he had a personal financial investment in the team.

Next in the pecking order for Imlach would be the option of plucking a goalie from the Victoria Maple Leafs of the Western Hockey League. Al Millar, who had played for Imlach in Quebec and had NHL experience (although just six games with the Boston Bruins in 1957–58) would have been a logical selection, but he was under suspension by the Victoria club and his standby, Gary Holland, was still an amateur. So instead, Imlach summoned Bruce Gamble to Toronto from the Tulsa Oilers of the Central Hockey League, where amateur Mike Berridge was the sole substitute. He sent Al Millar to Tulsa from Victoria to replace him, leaving Holland to fend for himself in Victoria.

It was a move of desperation, but the Leafs' coach and GM rolled the dice and came up with a seven.

Toronto-Montreal Rivalry Intensifies

Wednesday, March 2, 1966

The rivalry between Toronto and Montreal was at its most intense during this Centennial year, and the ferocity was most evident in this game, as the score was almost secondary to the number of stitches issued as a result of this grudge match — forty-six. Sixteen stitches closed a cut on the ear of Charlie Hodge after catching a shot from Bob Pulford on the side of the head, four stitches were picked up by Gump Worsley in a collision with Peter Stemkowski after Worsley relieved Hodge in the Montreal goal, Eddie Shack was sewn up with ten stitches after falling on a skate, and it took sixteen stitches to bind cuts over both of Terry Harper's eyes after a second-period brawl with Leafs' tough guy, Orland Kurtenbach.

Bob Baun and John Ferguson were engaged in a bout, with Terry Harper standing just outside the scrum, when Kurtenbach grabbed him before he could step into the fray. Kurtenbach then "destroyed" Terry Harper, according to *The Globe.* "Mr. Harper's always pushing and shoving and coming in late so I decided we better have what we might call a little altercation," smiled Kurtenbach. *The Globe* commented, "The result was a dandy blood-letting, advantage Kurtenbach. Harper required 16 stitches to close wounds over both eyes and his cheeks were swollen as though he had fallen into a hive of bees." Terry Harper's battered face resembled "a sack of doorknobs," wrote the *Star.* The slugfest was so engaging that Baun and Ferguson stopped their brawl to watch. "This guy's got the muscle we need," stated Imlach. "He's the strongest guy in the NHL. I knew he was something after I saw him go in a fight four years ago in the Western league."

Brent Imlach, Punch's son and a member of the Toronto Marlboros junior squad, was at home studying for a high-school exam when his Dad called him and told him to hurry to the Gardens and get dressed, as Brit Selby was unable to play because of the flu. Brent arrived during the second period, dressed, but did not see game action.

The game was also pioneering, as a closed-circuit television set was installed in the penalty-timekeeper's box at Maple Leaf Gardens, and another in the officials' dressing room. "This will give the referee a chance to see an instant playback of their decisions," offered Stafford Smythe, who had the league's permission to experiment with the monitors for a month. "This is another Maple Leafs' first," he said proudly. Referee Frank Udvari was perplexed. "I wasn't told anything about it or why the set was there. There was a TV set in our dressing room as well, but nobody told me why it was there, either."

Also unbeknownst to CTV viewers, this game was telecast in colour without the benefit of the extra lighting traditionally used to broadcast games in colour. This experiment was the prototype for televising games in colour from Maple Leaf Gardens.

The Three Stars of the contest, which ended in a 3–3 tie, were Dave Keon, Jean Beliveau (who scored his 380th goal, passing Ted Lindsay for the third highest goal total in NHL history) and Toronto goaltender Bruce Gamble, subbing for the injured Bower and Sawchuk. But the fans were more interested in Orland Kurtenbach's prowess as a fighter. After the game, the Leafs' dressing room was upbeat about the toughness exhibited during this game, prompting visions of recapturing the Stanley Cup.

Punch's Gamble Pays Dividends
Thursday, March 3, 1966

Ironically, with emotions running high, the very next night, the Leafs and Canadiens were paired again, this time at the Forum in Montreal. Harper and Kurtenbach, the combatants from the previous night, dropped their gloves again on March 3, although with less dramatic results. Brent Imlach centred a line with Kurtenbach and converted forward Tim Horton. To ensure that the slight nineteen-year-old junior wasn't dismembered by aggressive Montreal players, Imlach (wearing both coach and father fedora in this scenario) protected Brent by placing him on a line with Toronto's two toughest players. "You've got two good wing men in Kurtenbach and Horton. There was nobody going to clobber them," Punch said, also remembering, "Beliveau came over to me at the end of the first period and said, 'Are you trying to make me feel old?'"

Through injury misfortune, Leafs' coach Punch Imlach gleefully discovered an untapped vein of success. With Bower and Sawchuk both bothered by nagging injuries, Imlach's faith in Bruce Gamble paid off. Gamble and the Leafs had edged Boston 3–2 on February 26 and skated to back-to-back ties with the Rangers and the Canadiens. But on March 3, Gamble went on an unprecedented tear. Against Montreal on March 3, he earned a 4–0 shutout. Two nights later in Toronto, Gamble blanked Chicago in a 5–0 win. The next night, Toronto beat Boston 5–3, but on March 9, he earned yet another shutout in a 1–0 victory over Detroit. Gamble collected his fourth shutout of March with a 6–0 win over Boston on March 12. "Fill-In Goalie Dazzles NHL," was the headline in *The Hockey News* at the time.

Gamble Thwarts Hull in Shutting Out Chicago
Saturday, March 5, 1966
Bobby Hull had scored his fiftieth goal of the season against Detroit on March 2, and was looking for goal number fifty-one, which would establish the NHL record for goals in a season. His father and nine other family members made the trip to Toronto, hoping to observe Bobby's record-breaking marker. Boom Boom Geoffrion, who held the record of fifty goals in a season with Hull and Maurice Richard, sent a telegram: "Good luck. Hope you get it soon. Couldn't happen to a nicer guy."

It had been a charmed season for the native of Pointe Anne, Ontario, not far from Belleville. During the first intermission of *Hockey Night in Canada*, Hull was presented with the key to the City of Belleville by Mayor Jack Ellis.

Leafs' goalie Bruce Gamble was asked by Ward Cornell how it felt facing Hull as he attempted to break the record. "If it's going to happen to anybody, it's going to happen," he shrugged.

The broadcast was highly anticipated, and with the eyes of the hockey world focused on Bobby Hull and his burgeoning goal-scoring record, "Hardly anybody paid heed to the beefy individual with the Paladin sideburns who waddled out to play goal [for the Maple Leafs]," commented the *Toronto Daily Star.* The contest featured fast up-and-down hockey, with the Golden Jet leading numerous end-to-end rushes. Hull totalled just over thirty-one minutes of ice time that night, but came up empty as Gamble earned another shutout and first Star selection in the 5–0 victory over Chicago. The second Star, Dave Keon, "with a deft d'Artagnan flourish of his blade," deflected shots by Bobby Baun, Kent Douglas and Larry Hillman past a startled Glenn Hall. Bob Pulford was the game's third Star.

Dick Gamble had been called up from the Rochester Americans to fill in for Brit Selby, who was injured and suffering from the flu. It was the first of only three games Gamble would play with the Leafs. The veteran, who had played for Imlach in Quebec City, had been with the Montreal Canadiens when they won the Stanley Cup in 1953. A lesser-known fact is that Gamble was the model for table-hockey-game players during that era. Viewers were perplexed why this unknown player was awarded the alternate captaincy for the game. The veteran winger had simply been given Andy Bathgate's number 9 jersey with the "A" on the chest from the previous season.

Did Douglas Deck D'Amico?
Saturday, March 19, 1966
The Leafs downed Chicago 4–2, but the bigger battle took place between Kent Douglas and NHL officials. During a bout with Doug Mohns in the third period, linesman John D'Amico grabbed Douglas, while Neil Armstrong held Mohns. But the Chicago forward wrestled himself out of Armstrong's grip and landed a couple of punches on Douglas, whose arms were being held. As Douglas tried to extricate himself to get at Mohns, D'Amico pulled the sweater of the Leafs' defenceman over his head. Douglas was finally able to shed his sweater and turned to D'Amico in frustration. He appeared to rush at D'Amico on two occasions, and some claimed he tried to strike the official, although no contact was made. Mahovlich broke away from a clinch and ended the altercation by tackling his teammate.

"I haven't got a f&%$in' thing to say," he told *The Globe*. Imlach defended his defenceman. "The movies did not show Douglas hitting D'Amico." Nonetheless, Douglas was assessed a major for fighting and a game misconduct. NHL president Clarence Campbell later added a two-game suspension.

Earlier in the game, Douglas had ripped the replay monitor out of the penalty box in frustration after being assessed a misconduct.

Conn Smythe Resigns following Boxing Match
Tuesday, March 29, 1966

While the event wasn't hockey, this date reverberates through the hockey world to this day. It marked the end of an era.

With 13,919 fans shoehorned into Maple Leaf Gardens, Cassius Clay and George Chuvalo slugged it out in a monumental heavyweight boxing match. The battle had come under immense scrutiny because Clay, the world heavyweight champion, refused to be drafted into the United States Army. "I ain't got no quarrel with the Viet Cong," he stated. And as a result, many boxing commissions refused to approve any defence of his belt. But Harold Ballard managed to have the Ontario minister of labour, who controlled boxing in the province, approve the match, and he booked it into Maple Leaf Gardens.

"All the disinfectant in the world will never make the Gardens clean again," declared the *Toronto Telegram*. *The Globe and Mail* concurred: "Now we are infested with the gladiators and their assorted leeches, avaricious characters looking to make a buck from the pain of two manipulated pugs."

While the match went the distance, one man was seething in the background. Conn Smythe, who served in both World Wars, detested the fact that Ballard had allowed a draft dodger to use the Gardens' stage to ply his trade. "Cash before class," he spat. While Cassius Clay (later to be known as Muhammad Ali) retained the Heavyweight Championship, Smythe resigned his positions as a director of Maple Leaf Gardens and, in disgust, sold the last of his shares in the building and team he had built. "The Gardens was founded by men — sportsmen — who fought for their country," he stated in his autobiography. "It is no place for those who want to evade conscription."

The boxing match of March 29, 1966, severed the last official connection to the Toronto Maple Leafs and Maple Leaf Gardens by Smythe, who had purchased the franchise in 1927, renamed it the Toronto Maple Leafs and miraculously, in the depth of the Great Depression, orchestrated the construction of Maple Leaf Gardens in 1931.

Trio of Goaltenders Guard Goal to Conclude Regular Season
Thursday, March 31, 1966

It was a horrific sight.

Eddie Shack wound up for a slapshot, but his stick snapped and the jagged end flew out, catching Boston defenceman Gilles Marotte in the throat. There was an eerie hush over the crowd as Marotte skated to the Bruins' bench clutching his throat with a large splinter dangling there. Prompt attention from the trainer stemmed the flow of blood, which spilled from a wound that was not as deep as initially believed.

With the season all but over, Imlach experimented with his goalies. In the 3–1 loss to Boston on March 31, the Leafs' coach alternated Bower and Sawchuk repeatedly through the game. Two nights later, facing the Rangers, it was Sawchuk and Gamble who rotated back and forth every five minutes as the teams skated to a 3–3 tie.

On April 3, the final game of the regular season, the Leafs used three netminders against the Wings in Detroit. Johnny Bower played the first period, but came down with the "flu" after the first period, which allowed a third goaltender to dress.

Terry Sawchuk played the second period and Bruce Gamble played the third. Johnny Bower, miraculously feeling much better, coached from behind the bench while Imlach observed the game from the stands. "Coaching added a headache to my flu," said Bower, laughing.

League rules stated that a third goaltender cannot be used unless both other goaltenders are unfit to play. Imlach explained away the situation. "Bower's sick. He's got the flu. Sawchuk felt a little pull in his groin and we don't want to take any chances so I declared an emergency situation."

Wings' coach Sid Abel was furious. "[Imlach] pulled a fast one. I brought it to referee John Ashley's attention, but we have no intention of making an official protest." Referee-In-Chief Scotty Morrison stated, "Imlach was within his rights to dress and play the third goalkeeper when the other two became incapacitated."

On the third of April, with Toronto using three goaltenders, it seems only appropriate that the final score would be 3–3.

"The Leafs came up with a real clinker in their final home game of the NHL schedule," wrote the *Toronto Daily Star*. "Sure they were lousy," admitted Imlach, who had watched his club squander a 3–0 lead after the first period. "How can you blame them? It didn't mean anything. Their main concern is to be healthy for the playoffs." Eddie Shack scored his career-best twenty-sixth goal in the game.

Two weeks prior, the Maple Leafs had been competing for first place, but after a serious slump, finished the season in third. Montreal finished first, Chicago was second, Toronto third, and the final playoff spot went to Detroit. The Boston Bruins and New York Rangers sat out the postseason for a fourth consecutive year.

Bobby Hull won the Art Ross Trophy with ninety-seven points, including fifty-four goals, and also was named recipient of the Hart Trophy. Montreal netminders Gump Worsley and Charlie Hodge took the Vezina Trophy, while teammate Jacques Laperriere was named the Norris Trophy winner as the NHL's best defenceman. Detroit's Alex Delvecchio was winner of the Lady Byng.

1965–66 Regular Season Standings						
FINISH	TEAM	GAMES	WINS	LOSSES	TIES	POINTS
1	Montreal Canadiens	70	41	21	8	90
2	Chicago Black Hawks	70	37	25	8	82
3	Toronto Maple Leafs	70	34	25	11	79
4	Detroit Red Wings	70	31	27	12	74
5	Boston Bruins	70	21	43	6	48
6	New York Rangers	70	18	41	11	47

1965–66 Regular Season Scoring

RK	NUMBER	PLAYER	POS	AGE	GP	G	A	PTS	PIM	ESG	PPG	SHG	GWG
1	27	Frank Mahovlich	LW	28	68	32	24	56	68	22	10	0	6
2	20	Bob Pulford	LW	29	70	28	28	56	51	15	11	2	2
3	14	Dave Keon	C	25	69	24	30	54	4	18	6	0	5
4	10	George Armstrong	RW	35	70	16	35	51	12	11	3	2	3
5	23	Eddie Shack	LW	28	63	26	17	43	88	24	2	0	6
6	8	Ron Ellis	RW	21	70	19	23	42	24	16	3	0	1
7	4	Red Kelly	D/C	38	63	8	24	32	12	8	0	0	2
8	7	Tim Horton	D	36	70	6	22	28	76	3	3	0	2
9	16	Larry Hillman	D	28	48	3	25	28	34	0	3	0	0
10	11	Brit Selby	LW	20	61	14	13	27	26	13	1	0	2
11	15	Wally Boyer	C	28	46	4	17	21	23	2	1	1	0
12	19	Kent Douglas	D	29	64	6	14	20	97	1	5	0	0
13	26	Allan Stanley	D	39	59	4	14	18	35	3	1	0	0
14	12	Peter Stemkowski	C	22	56	4	12	16	55	4	0	0	1
15	25	Orland Kurtenbach	C	29	70	9	6	15	54	6	2	1	3
16	3	Marcel Pronovost	D	35	54	2	8	10	34	2	0	0	0
17	21	Bob Baun	D	29	44	0	6	6	68	0	0	0	0
18	15	Mike Walton	C	21	6	1	3	4	0	1	0	0	0
19	17	Jim Pappin	RW	26	7	0	3	3	8	0	0	0	0
20	22	Larry Jeffrey	LW	25	20	1	1	2	22	1	0	0	1
21	24	Ed Joyal	C	25	14	0	2	2	2	0	0	0	0
22	9	Dick Gamble	LW	37	2	1	0	1	0	0	1	0	0
23	18	Al Arbour	D	33	4	0	1	1	2	0	0	0	0
24	1	Johnny Bower	G	41	35	0	1	1	0	0	0	0	0
25	25	Wayne Carleton	LW	19	2	0	1	1	0	0	0	0	0
26	17	Duane Rupp	D	27	2	0	1	1	0	0	0	0	0
27	30	Terry Sawchuk	G	36	27	0	1	1	12	0	0	0	0
28	18	Brian Conacher	LW	24	2	0	0	0	2	0	0	0	0
29	30	Bruce Gamble	G	27	10	0	0	0	0	0	0	0	0
30	24	Brent Imlach	F	19	2	0	0	0	0	0	0	0	0
31	25	Jim McKenny	D	19	2	0	0	0	2	0	0	0	0
32	21	Darryl Sly	D	26	2	0	0	0	0	0	0	0	0
33	30	Al Smith	G	20	2	0	0	0	0	0	0	0	0
34	1	Gary Smith	G	21	3	0	0	0	0	0	0	0	0
		TEAM TOTALS			70	208	332	540	811	150	52	6	34

Regular Season Netminding													
RK		PLAYER	POS	AGE	GP	MIN	W	L	T	GA	GAA	SO
1	1	Johnny Bower	G	41	35	1998	18	10	5	75	2.25	3
2	30	Terry Sawchuk	G	36	27	1521	10	11	3	80	3.16	1
3	30	Bruce Gamble	G	27	10	501	5	2	3	21	2.51	4
4	30	Al Smith	G	20	2	62	1	0	0	2	1.94	0
5	1	Gary Smith	G	21	3	118	0	2	0	7	3.56	0
		TEAM TOTALS			70	4200	34	25	11	185	2.64	8

Frank Mahovlich and Bob Pulford tied for the Leafs' scoring leaders, each with fifty-six points. The Big M's thirty-two goals was the team-best. Brit Selby, with fourteen goals and thirteen assists, was the league's rookie of the year, winning the Calder Trophy.

Montreal Opens Semi-Final with 4–3 Win
Game One, Semi-Final – Thursday, April 7, 1966
The underdog Maple Leafs met the first-place Canadiens in the semifinal, which opened at the Forum in Montreal.

At the end of the first period, Toronto was ahead 2–1 on goals from Shack and Mahovlich, with J. C. Tremblay countering for the Habs. Montreal led the game after second-period goals from John Ferguson and Bobby Rousseau, but a Bob Pulford tally for Toronto in the third tied the game. Jean Beliveau scored the winning goal at 17:48 to give Montreal a 4–3 victory.

"It was a game of mistakes," stated Montreal coach Toe Blake. "We gave the puck away twenty times and the Leafs a little more. A win like that is a bonus, believe me!"

Allan Stanley played briefly in this game but would not see further post-season action due to a knee injury.

Canadiens Blank Leafs to Take a Two-Game Lead

Game Two, Semi-Final – Saturday, April 9, 1966

Toronto had King Clancy behind the bench for game two in place of an ailing Punch Imlach. Several of the players also felt the effects of the flu as the series went on. Nevertheless, the Leafs' game plan differed not an iota, and Toronto came out banging and crashing. The rivalry blossomed further with a scoreless, penalty-filled first period that took almost an hour to complete, as thirteen penalties were called.

Toronto's strategy was one of intimidation. At one point, Bob Pulford charged at Terry Harper from behind, and the Habs' blue liner had to be helped off the ice after suffering a sore back, sore knee and a bruise below his eye. There was no penalty call on the play. Bob Baun, and later Larry Hillman, took runs at Henri Richard. The Pocket Rocket was injured on the Hillman hit.

All the scoring took place in the third as Terry Sawchuk surrendered two goals, one each to Claude Provost and Bobby Rousseau. Provost, whose principle role was to shadow Frank Mahovlich, scored the game winner when he took a pass from Gilles Tremblay and caught Sawchuk off guard. Gump Worsley earned his third career shutout.

"They [the Leafs] should know by now that they're not going to chase us out of the rink," Toe Blake said. "We haven't been manhandled the past three years and that stuff doesn't work against the Canadiens any more."

Punch Brings in Bower but Leafs Fall

Game Three, Semi-Final – Tuesday, April 12, 1966

After two straight losses, Imlach substituted Bower for Sawchuk in goal for game three, played at Maple Leaf Gardens. The Leafs came out flying, taking a 2–0 lead on goals from Eddie Shack and Tim Horton in the first period.

In the second period, Montreal roared back, collecting goals from Ralph Backstrom and Bobby Rousseau. Twenty-six seconds after Montreal's tying goal, Terry Harper scored on a low drive from the point to put the Canadiens ahead 3–2.

Sixteen seconds into the third period, John Ferguson fired a laser from thirty feet out that caught the top corner behind Bower. While the goal took the wind out of Toronto's sails, a comeback was envisioned right to the end. Imlach pulled Bower for an added attacker around the nineteen-minute mark, but Jean Beliveau scored an empty-netter to cap the game.

With the 5–2 win, Montreal had a stranglehold on the series, up three games to none and already prepared for the Stanley Cup final against the eventual winner of the Chicago/Detroit semi-final.

Montreal Ends Toronto's Season by Sweeping Leafs
Game Four, Semi-Final – Thursday, April 14, 1966
The Toronto Maple Leafs' season ended with a thud at Maple Leaf Gardens on April 14, although they didn't go down without a fight — literally.

At 3:37 of the first period, a twelve-minute melee took place, with Eddie Shack, Orland Kurtenbach, John Ferguson and Ted Harris all earning majors as the main combatants. The brawl started when Toronto centre Peter Stemkowski plastered John Ferguson into the boards, and the gloves were off between the two antagonists, who engaged in a dandy fight during the regular season. The other main event was the much anticipated tilt between the heavyweight champions of the rivals — Ted Harris for Montreal and Orland Kurtenbach of the Leafs. The two squared off, but Kurtenbach slipped and Harris landed on top of him, only to have the positions reversed moments later.

Montreal's Dave Balon then took a turn with Eddie Shack, and while he held down the big Leafs' winger, Claude Larose planted punches on the defenceless Shack. Larry Hillman was able to come to his teammate's rescue, and he and Shack then briefly double-teamed Larose.

Eight penalty records were established in the free-for-all, and the teams were forced to play shorthanded for thirty-two minutes. Incensed, Imlach pulled on a pair of skates, intent on chasing down referee Art Skov, but while he stood in the gateway threatening to come out onto the ice, he did not do so. "I was going out after the referee," Imlach said. "We had sixty-four minutes in penalties and Montreal had sixty-six when [Skov] told us we would be shorthanded. I just wouldn't go for it!"

This bitter donnybrook was only viewed by those in attendance at Maple Leaf Gardens that night, as the *Hockey Night in Canada* broadcast began a half hour after the opening faceoff. It was the greatest brawl "never seen," until Leafs TV uncovered the kinescope reel and presented the entire game on a "Leaf Classic" show.

The game was delayed twenty-five minutes, but once resumed, Toronto briefly glimpsed hope in the form of a goal from Larry Hillman. It was for nought, though, as Gilles Tremblay scored twice in the second period and Jimmy Roberts and Dick Duff buried the Leafs in the final frame for a 4–1 victory that eliminated Toronto from Stanley Cup contention.

Gilles Tremblay earned the nod as the game's first Star, with Bobby Rousseau chosen second and J. C. Tremblay third.

1965–66 Playoff Scoring									
RK	NUMBER	PLAYER	POS	AGE	GP	G	A	PTS	PIM
1	23	Eddie Shack	LW	28	4	2	1	3	33
2	16	Larry Hillman	D	28	4	1	1	2	6
3	20	Bob Pulford	LW	29	4	1	1	2	12
4	4	Red Kelly	D/C	38	4	0	2	2	0
5	14	Dave Keon	C	25	4	0	2	2	0
6	7	Tim Horton	D	36	4	1	0	1	12
7	27	Frank Mahovlich	LW	28	4	1	0	1	10
8	10	George Armstrong	RW	35	4	0	1	1	4
9	21	Bob Baun	D	29	4	0	1	1	8
10	15	Wally Boyer	C	28	4	0	1	1	0
11	19	Kent Douglas	D	29	4	0	1	1	12
12	1	Johnny Bower	G	41	2	0	0	0	0
13	8	Ron Ellis	RW	21	4	0	0	0	2
14	25	Orland Kurtenbach	C	29	4	0	0	0	20
15	3	Marcel Pronovost	D	35	4	0	0	0	6
16	30	Terry Sawchuk	G	36	2	0	0	0	0
17	11	Brit Selby	LW	20	4	0	0	0	0
18	26	Allan Stanley	D	39	1	0	0	0	0
19	12	Peter Stemkowski	C	22	4	0	0	0	26
		TEAM TOTALS			4	6	11	17	151

Playoff Netminding												
RK	NUMBER	PLAYER	POS	AGE	GP	MIN	W	L	GA	GAA	SO
1	1	Johnny Bower	G	41	2	120	0	2	8	4.00	0
2	30	Terry Sawchuk	G	36	2	120	0	2	6	3.00	0
				TEAM TOTALS	4	240	0	4	14	3.50	0

The Montreal Canadiens went on to defeat the Detroit Red Wings in six games, in spite of Roger Crozier's acrobatics, to claim the Stanley Cup. It was the second straight Stanley Cup championship for the Canadiens. Crozier was so sensational in defeat that he was awarded the Conn Smythe Trophy as the most valuable performer in the playoffs.

At the conclusion of the season, Allan Stanley was selected as the most valuable Leaf, and was awarded the J. P. Bickell Trophy. "That's a very prestigious trophy," stated Stanley. "I really hold that right beside the Stanley Cup as one of my proudest achievements." The forty-year-old Stanley, who had completed his eighteenth NHL season, was also selected to the NHL's Second All-Star Team. "You can say anything good that you want to about the guy," remarked Punch Imlach. King Clancy added, "He's amazing. His play has been fantastic."

Punch Imlach reflected on the peculiar season he had just endured. "I've never been through a season like this one. We've had troubles before but not all to the defensive team. We lost Carl Brewer for the entire season, which we didn't expect, Bob Baun and Marcel Pronovost for two months each and both goalies have been hurt on three different occasions. Even Gary Smith got into the act."

The Montreal Canadiens had usurped the Stanley Cup that Imlach and his troops should rightfully return to Toronto. The Leafs had experience, they had skill, they had toughness and they had goaltending. There was just one thing they didn't have — the Stanley Cup.

SLAPSHOTS AND SNAPSHOTS
HOCKEY NIGHT IN CANADA PERSONALITIES

While there were a number of highly recognizable *Hockey Night in Canada* personalities through the dynasty decade, not the least of which included play-by-play announcer Bill Hewitt and his father Foster, who contributed the game's Three Stars and analysis at the conclusion of each broadcast, few were as well-remembered as Murray Westgate and Ward Cornell.

For sixteen years, Toronto Maple Leafs' fans warmly welcomed Murray Westgate into their homes on Saturday nights. The friendly Esso dealer with the friendly approach and dulcet tones was included in each broadcast to inform us of the best deals at Imperial Oil on tires, oil, maps and movie cameras.

Born in Regina, Saskatchewan, in 1918, Westgate served with the Canadian Navy during the Second World War before joining a repertory theatre company in Vancouver. This led him to join the acclaimed radio drama department at CBC Vancouver.

In 1949, Westgate moved to Toronto, stating, "If you want to grow strawberries, you go where they grow them." In Toronto, Murray worked radio and did some acting and modelling. But the break that led to the role that would forever identify him was being hired by Imperial Oil to act in some promotional films. "I played a smiling, nicely dressed gas station dealer," he recalled. "They showed this film to gas station dealers at conventions."

In anticipation of *Hockey Night in Canada* making its television debut in 1952, principal sponsor Imperial Oil decided to use a genial actor as a dealer to promote its various products on the fledgling broadcasts. "Someone at Imperial Oil said, 'Why don't you use this bird we've been using in our films?' And that's how I got the job," Murray said.

For the first several years, the commercials were performed live, and Westgate would spend hours rehearsing to ensure that he didn't stumble over his words. "What I used to do was write out the script and paste it on the back of an oil can, and if anything went wrong, I just glanced at it and the words were there," he told *Marketing Magazine* in January 2008.

The actor was so believable that most viewers were convinced that he was indeed a gas station attendant. "I can't tell you how many times a stranger asked me to have a look at their car," he laughed.

But it wasn't all positive. Murray was so closely identified with the Imperial Oil role that he was passed over for other roles. "I was having trouble, because of my identity, getting parts in plays," he admitted later. His acting resume during the *Hockey Night in Canada* years contains a number of roles in long-forgotten television series: *First Performance, A Dangerous Age, R.C.M.P., Junior Round-up"* and *The Forest Rangers.*

Then, in 1968, Westgate's sixteen-year career as the Imperial Oil dealer on *Hockey Night in Canada* came to an abrupt end. "I knew it had to end sometime," he lamented. "I just wish it had ended with a little more courtesy."

Murray Westgate continued to act, including an occasional role in CBC's *Seeing Things*, which ran from 1980 to 1986. In 1991, the kindly gas station attendant was brought back by Imperial Oil to help market Esso in a "then and now" commercial. But it was his ever-present smile and his comforting salutation, "Happy motoring," that earned Murray Westgate a secure place in the most pleasant of memories of the Toronto Maple Leafs' glory years.

From 1960 until 1971, Ward Cornell was the ubiquitous host for millions of *Hockey Night in Canada* viewers, providing intermission content during Saturday, and later Wednesday, broadcasts.

A native of London, Ontario, Cornell had an interest in broadcasting that was nurtured as a student at the University of Western Ontario, where he was the radio voice of the school's football and basketball games on CFPL Radio. Following his graduation in 1949, Cornell appeared doing sports on the fledgling television station, CFPL-TV. Through the next five years, he taught English literature, geography and history at Pickering College in Newmarket, Ontario, and then returned to London as general manager of CFPL Radio.

While remaining with the station until 1967, in 1960, Cornell was hired as the host of *Hockey Night in Canada*'s' between-period intermissions, and became a fixture on the broadcasts during the Toronto Maple Leafs' dynasty years. His *Hockey Night in Canada* career began with a January 23, 1960, interview with Bronco Horvath, conducted in black and white when the show had a single intermission, and concluded with an interview with Ken Dryden following the Montreal Canadiens' Stanley Cup win on May 18, 1971.

After departing from *Hockey Night in Canada* in 1971, replaced by Dave Hodge, Ward Cornell was Ontario's agent-general in London, England, until 1978. He returned to Canada in 1980 and was Ontario's deputy minister for culture and recreation, and later, the province's deputy housing minister.

Ward MacLaurin Cornell, born May 4, 1924, died in Uxbridge, Ontario on February 5, 2000, but will forever be remembered by hockey fans of a certain vintage for bringing our hockey heroes to life during the 1960s.

Through the Maple Leafs' dynasty years of the late 1950s and into the 1960s, Murray Westgate and Ward Cornell would arguably have been every bit as identifiable to *Hockey Night in Canada* viewers as Bill or Foster Hewitt.

11

1966–67: The Cup Returns to Toronto

The Original Six Era would come to an abrupt halt with the Stanley Cup presentation that concluded this 1966–67 season. Although a misnomer (the National Hockey League actually debuted in 1917 with four teams), the era had existed with the same six teams for twenty-five seasons, beginning in 1942–43.

The New York Rangers had finished last in 1965–66, allowing the Boston Bruins a reprieve after five years of cellar dwelling. The Rangers promoted Emile Francis to coach the team, and gave him firepower in the guise of Boom Boom Geoffrion, secured on waivers from Montreal after having been retired for two seasons. "Red" Berenson joined the Rangers from Montreal, Orland Kurtenbach came over from Toronto, and the Rangers received Al MacNeil from Montreal in the same draft.

Boston, which had escaped last place by a single point, also changed coaches. Harry Sinden was hired to replace Milt Schmidt, who would concentrate on his role as general manager. The Bruins pinned much of their hope on the shoulders of Bobby Orr, an eighteen-year-old phenom who leapt to the NHL from the junior ranks of the Oshawa Generals. Joe Watson also joined the Bruins' lineup.

In 1965–66, Detroit finished fourth, and had an unfortunate situation on the blue line that needed to be addressed. In a game against Chicago on January 30, 1966, Doug Barkley lost the vision in his right eye when clipped by the stick of Doug Mohns, and his young career came to a sudden conclusion. In desperation, the Wings reacquired the volatile and unpredictable Howie Young for their blue line.

Chicago's defence was weakened by the retirement of Elmer "Moose" Vasko, while Al MacNeil was picked up by Rangers. Ed Van Impe was promoted to fill one of the blue-line vacancies. Chicago received Wally Boyer from Montreal in the Intra-League Draft. In addition, Denis DeJordy replaced Dave Dryden as the backup goalie to Glenn Hall.

After a disappointing season, Punch Imlach vowed to make changes, but few actually transpired. The Leafs lost Wally Boyer and Orland Kurtenbach in the Intra-League Draft, while they picked up John Brenneman from the Rangers and Don Blackburn from Montreal. Brian Conacher, who had already enjoyed a cup of coffee with Toronto, was the sole rookie to crack the lineup.

The *Toronto Star* stated what most in the league believed: "The closest thing to a cinch: Habs." Toronto's Kent Douglas stated, "I think this club [the Leafs] will finish no worse than second to the Canadiens. Right now, they have the most solid club." King Clancy predicted, "It's Canadiens and then you can flip a coin." Montreal's GM Sam Pollock added, "If we work, we should be good enough to finish on top."

The Habs picked up several players in that summer's Intra-League Draft, including Wally Boyer from Toronto, Mike McMahon from the Rangers, Al MacNeil from Chicago and Pat Quinn from Detroit. Rogatien Vachon and Carol Vadnais made their debuts with Montreal during this season.

Maple Leaf Gardens went through a dramatic metamorphosis during the summer, completed in time for the first game of the 1966–67 season.

When Stafford Smythe and his partners took control of Maple Leaf Gardens in 1961, seating capacity was 12,583. By opening night of the 1966–67 season, the seating capacity had been increased to 15,481, as well as standing room for another 450.

The additional seats came at the expense of several beloved features. The flag-draped photograph of Queen Elizabeth II was removed from the south end wall in order to add extra seats. Several aisles and exits were removed in order to accommodate more seats. Some of the previous standing room was also converted to seating. Leg space between rows in the reds was reduced to incorporate more seating. Mezzanines were installed at the north and south ends, with more seating added in the corners.

A new score clock, constructed by Gardens' staff at a cost of $50,000, weighed seven thousand pounds and hung above centre ice. The elapsed time of the on-ice action was prominent on the new clock, although the penalty times would continue to be shown on clocks on the north wall. The score clock was not ready for the opening game of the season. In addition, the large flags had also been removed, replaced by two small flags lowered from the bottom of the new clock.

Another link to the past was also changed. Painted on the wall of the Maple Leafs' dressing room, the motto, installed by Conn Smythe when the Gardens was built in 1931 — "Defeat Does Not Rest Lightly On Their Shoulders" — was changed to "The Price of Success is Hard Work."

Leafs Earn a Tie in 1966–67 Season Opener
Saturday, October 22, 1966
Contract disputes were ongoing right up to the day of the season opener. Dave Keon signed that morning, leaving Hillman, Shack and Mahovlich unsigned. Mahovlich was looking for $30,000 per year plus bonuses, an increase of $5,000 from his last contract. While sitting out during training camp, The Big M purchased a travel agency. "I'm going into business with

two other chaps," Mahovlich announced. "I'll spend a lot of time on the job during the off-season."

Mike Walton walked away from Toronto's AHL affiliate, the Rochester Americans, in protest over being sent down to the minors again, after earning accolades as that league's most valuable player in 1965–66. But, equally galling to Walton, was the reduction in salary. Walton was reported to have asked for $13,000 plus bonuses while the Leafs were offering $11,000 plus bonuses. Instead, Walton would earn $9,000 in the AHL. Although considered brash by the Maple Leafs' management, complicating the matter was Walton's engagement to Candy Hoult, granddaughter of Conn Smythe.

Between contract disputes and injuries, the Maple Leafs were badly under-manned going into the regular season. Bob Baun, Red Kelly, Marcel Pronovost, Bob Pulford and Allan Stanley were all nursing injuries.

Carl Brewer, meantime, who had quit the Leafs a year earlier, was seeking reinstatement as an amateur in order to join the Canadian National Team.

Hockey Night in Canada also began regularly broadcasting in colour that evening. Peter Gzowski, writing for the *Toronto Star*, remarked, "The most spectacular sports show I've ever seen on TV — in the true sense of spectacular. As bright as ballet, almost more brilliant than life. A whole new lease on hockey's pleasures."

While there were only an estimated seventy thousand colour televisions in all of Canada, clearly, the broadcasting of the game in colour was a major advancement. But several adjustments were required in order to televise in colour. The terrible condition of the ice was attributed to the extra-bright lights used for colour television. Viewers also noted that the ice had a blue tinge, dyed as such to lessen the glare of the extra lighting.

Several players used burnt cork under their eyes to negate the glare from the bright lights. Defenceman Allan Stanley, just back from a knee injury suffered during training camp, "could have qualified as a panda bear in the Ice Capades," according to *The Globe*. In place of burnt cork, Bob Haggert brought in a jar of theatrical anti-glare grease paint, which

Johnny Bower used and thought was effective. Kent Douglas insisted it gave off a shine and continued using the cork. Even more peculiar was Terry Sawchuk, watching the game from the end of the Leafs' bench wearing sunglasses.

John Robarts, the premier of Ontario, dropped the puck between George Armstrong of the Leafs and Harry Howell of the New York Rangers to signal the start of the new season.

Brian Conacher scored the first of his two goals against Cesare Maniago in the Rangers' goal at the fifty-eight-second mark of the first period. Conacher had played a single game for the Leafs in 1961–62, and two more in 1965–66, but finally cracked the Leafs' lineup in 1966–67. He came from one of hockey's most storied families. His father, three uncles and two cousins all enjoyed NHL careers. His Dad, Lionel, is an Honoured Member of the Hockey Hall of Fame. So, too, are his uncles Charlie and Roy Conacher. Harold Cotton, married to his mother's sister, was an NHL star and later served as a scout for the Boston Bruins. Cousins Pete Conacher (son of Charlie) and Murray Henderson (son of his Aunt Dolly, one of Lionel, Charlie and Roy's sisters) also played in the NHL.

Another rookie, Wayne Carleton, scored five minutes later for Toronto. Red Kelly scored at 11:15 to make it 3–0 in the first. Later in that period, a deflected Toronto shot caught Maniago in the mouth, breaking his upper plate. In the second, a stray stick from Toronto's John Brenneman cut Maniago from his lower lip to his chin. He exited the ice surface to be stitched up, and backup Ed Giacomin took his place for the rest of the game.

Rod Gilbert scored three times and assisted on a fourth by Wayne Hillman for the Rangers. Conacher's second goal resulted in a 4–4 opening-night tie. "This kid's got the family aggressiveness," stated King Clancy, who played with Charlie Conacher on the Maple Leafs' first Stanley Cup championship squad. "Brian skated strongly, checked diligently and worked resolutely without let-up," wrote the *Star*. "His positional play was letter perfect."

The next night, with both teams playing at Madison Square Garden, the Rangers blanked the Leafs 1–0. Wayne Hillman, who had scored but eight goals in his career, scored for a second night in a row. Giacomin earned his first career shutout.

"I have reason to stand up and cheer," said Rangers' coach Emile Francis. "We came from behind in the other guy's building [the Gardens] Saturday to tie it [4–4] and then dumped them here to get three big points."

Mahovlich Signs in Time to Face Brother
Wednesday, October 26, 1966
Frank Mahovlich missed both weekend games after being suspended for rejecting the latest contract offer from Punch Imlach, but came to terms with the Leafs before that night's contest against the Red Wings back at Maple Leaf Gardens. "Funny thing, but the more I talked to him, the more respect I got for him as a man," stated King Clancy, who was conducting some of the stalled contract negotiations with The Big M. "I'm happy, Clancy is happy, Frank is happy — we're all happy," said a relieved Imlach.

That night, The Big M contributed to a 3–2 Toronto win over Detroit, playing on a line with Dave Keon and Jim Pappin and competing against his brother Peter for the first time in NHL action. Frank also suffered a five-stitch cut to the elbow during the game.

John Brenneman scored his first goal as a Maple Leaf. Imlach admitted that he had drafted Brenneman from the Rangers in order to play for Rochester, as well as for protection against the upcoming expansion draft, but the twenty-three-year-old forward, playing for his third NHL team, earned a spot on the Leafs through his hard work during the pre-season.

Although he allowed two third-period goals, Terry Sawchuk was awarded the first Star selection. He discovered after the game that his mother-in-law was gravely ill.

Tie with Bruins Features Bobby Orr's MLG Debut
Saturday, October 29, 1966
Bruce Gamble started in goal for Toronto's game against Boston. Terry Sawchuk had returned to Detroit to deal with his mother-in-law's death. Johnny Bower was struggling with a back ailment, although dressed as the

backup netminder for this game. Bob Pulford returned to the team for the first time in 1966–67 after returning from injury bay.

This contest, a 3–3 tie, was Bobby Orr's first game at the Gardens as an NHLer. In the third period, he missed one scoring opportunity on a two-on-none breakaway with Johnny McKenzie. "I goofed," said Orr. "When Mac [McKenzie] got in the clear, I was sure he'd shoot, so I turned away and wasn't in position to take his return pass." But Orr nearly won the game for Boston when his drive from the point clanged off the crossbar. "The teenager made moves that suckered veteran Leafs out of position. He promises to be quite an asset to the Bruins," stated the *Toronto Star*.

Foster Hewitt chose Red Kelly, Johnny Bucyk and Dave Keon as his Three Stars.

Keon earned two assists, Bucyk had a goal and an assist and Kelly had a goal and two assists. Earlier that day, Red Kelly announced to the team that he had resigned from his position as a member of Parliament, a role in which he earned $18,000 a year, in order to concentrate solely on hockey.

Leafs Settle for Tie after Bad Goal
Wednesday, November 2, 1966

Frank Mahovlich "went around Bobby Rousseau as if he were frozen into the ice, shredded the defence of J. C. Tremblay and Ted Harris and then, after goalie Charlie Hodge had made a great stop on his first shot, he came back to wrap in his own rebound," described the *Toronto Daily Star* of The Big M's goal that gave Toronto a 2–0 lead over Montreal. "I'd like to have a film clip of that play just to show our fans a truly sensational solo goal," said Red Sullivan, former coach of the New York Rangers.

The Leafs led 2–0, but had to settle for a tie. "I blew it," shrugged Terry Sawchuk, commenting on J. C. Tremblay's power play blooper late in the second period that provided the tying goal. "The darn thing [puck] bounced up through my legs just above the top of my goal pads. It was an ordinary bouncer and I'd have made the save if I had stayed on my feet instead of dropping to my knees. That's what happens when you are overcautious."

Foster Hewitt selected Henri Richard, John Brenneman and Bobby Rousseau as the Three Stars of this game.

Wholesale Changes, but Leafs Blanked by Bruins
Thursday, November 10, 1966

Earlier in the week, Punch Imlach made modest changes to the complexion of the team. Acknowledging that he preferred to go with veterans, he sent two of his young prospects to the minors for additional seasoning.

Brit Selby was sent to the Vancouver Canucks of the Western League to work on his confidence under Bert Olmstead. While Vancouver was not a Leafs' affiliate (Victoria was the WHL affiliate), Imlach owed the Canucks three players in return for Billy McNeill, who was observed during Toronto's training camp. "I was lousy at training camp," admitted the Calder Trophy winner. "I came in about fifteen pounds overweight and I never could get started." Imlach responded, "[Selby] will get lots of ice time to get himself straightened out. Here, he'd sit on the bench and it would only get worse." Vancouver also received Bob Cook and Barry Watson, son of Hall of Famer Harry Watson, as compensation for McNeill, who briefly retired after being cut by the Leafs but later re-joined the Canucks.

In addition, Wayne Carleton was moved to Tulsa of the Central Hockey League. He had exhausted the five-game trial he was allowed to play with the Maple Leafs as an amateur. "I can't learn anything sitting on the bench, so I was happy to agree to the transfer to the Oilers," he admitted.

That night, Gerry Cheevers was in goal for the Boston Bruins, facing the team with which he turned professional. "I got as big a drive out of that 4–0 shutout as I did the day Northern Dancer won the Kentucky Derby," joked Cheevers, a great fan of the ponies. "This was my first shutout in this league and it came against a club that had gone seven games without a defeat. Maybe I get a bigger boot out of beating the Leafs, but there's no revenge motive."

The Leafs, who started with Sawchuk and finished with Gamble, surrendered goals to Murray Oliver, Pit Martin, Johnny Bucyk and Wayne Connelly.

The only Leaf to show any passion was Eddie Shack, who was blamed for injuries to Joe Watson, Johnny McKenzie and Johnny Bucyk. McKenzie suffered battered ribs, Bucyk had a charley horse and Watson lost three teeth and was cut for three stitches inside his mouth and another three outside his upper lip when he charged Shack, who braced and met Watson with a stick across the chest, but the lumber slid up and caught Watson in the mouth.

King Predicts Stanley Cup Appearance for Leafs
Saturday, November 12, 1966
After being sidelined with a back injury for more than three weeks, Johnny Bower was able to don his skates to ready himself for game action. "It was tougher to watch the games on television and listen to them on the radio than it is to stop shots from Bobby Hull and Gordie Howe," he joked. "I've been doing exercises and riding the bicycle. My back stiffens and is 'ouchy' for awhile after I exercise, but there is no pull on the muscles."

For the first time since *Hockey Night in Canada* began broadcasting as a Saturday night radio staple, the Toronto Maple Leafs played a road game on a Saturday night. The Leafs faced off against the Red Wings at the Olympia in Detroit, tying 3–3. The game was not televised, CBC-TV deciding to broadcast the Montreal Canadiens/New York Rangers contest instead.

After the game, King Clancy predicted that the Maple Leafs would go to the Stanley Cup final. "I can't pinpoint it, but there's a new kind of spirit on this club," said Clancy, who was overseeing the team while Imlach took advantage of a six-day break in the schedule to scout the Leafs' affiliates in western Canada. "We can go all the way on desire alone."

Bower Back after Month on Shelf
Saturday, November 19, 1966
The last-place Montreal Canadiens arrived in Toronto for their Saturday *Hockey Night in Canada* foray and were handed their fifth consecutive loss when the Maple Leafs outscored the Habs 5–1. The line of Red Kelly, Ron Ellis and Larry Jeffrey dominated the scoring for Toronto, each

collecting three points. Ellis scored twice, and Kelly and Jeffrey added one each. Jim Pappin scored the other Leafs' goal, while Dave Balon beat Terry Sawchuk for the Canadiens' sole goal. the Toronto *Daily Star* called the game "a deplorably dull contest in which you had to look twice to believe that those really were the Canadiens."

The next day, on a short-lived television show called *The Umbrella*, the CBC aired a segment titled "Eddie Shack's Nightmare." Described as a surrealistic fantasy, the feature included the Leafs' winger, a jazz band, a modern dancer, a brass bed, custard pies and a soda syphon. Also on the program that afternoon were novelist Margaret Laurence and Morton Shulman. The announcer on the long-forgotten show was Lloyd Robertson, and *The Umbrella* also featured a bikini-clad Barbara Amiel, now Mrs. Conrad Black.

The Maple Leafs were unable to watch *The Umbrella*, as they were in Chicago tying the Black Hawks 2–2. Johnny Bower was in goal for the first time in twenty-eight days and looked sharp for Toronto.

Big M Scores Penalty Shot Goal, but Hawks Double Leafs
Wednesday, November 23, 1966
Eddie Shack was his rambunctious self during a 6–3 win over the Hawks. "The Entertainer, at his best, gave the 15,688 cash customers and thousands of television viewers a little of everything," reported the *Star*. Shack hit everything that moved, scored two goals, collected two minors and clowned enough to keep the fans thoroughly entertained, earning a first Star selection from Foster Hewitt.

Down 2–0 to Chicago after the first period, Pat Stapleton smothered the puck in the crease, and referee Bill Friday immediately signalled for a penalty shot. Frank Mahovlich had just stepped onto the ice, so Imlach pointed to The Big M to take the shot. Chicago coach Billy Reay pulled Denis DeJordy in favour of the more experienced Glenn Hall, drawing howls of protest from the Leafs' bench. Mahovlich swooped in and deposited a sizzling shot past Hall's outstretched glove hand to score Toronto's opening goal at 5:35. Before the puck was again faced off,

DeJordy was re-inserted into the Hawks' net. Glenn Hall had surrendered a goal in a game in which he was not credited with any playing time. The penalty shot was only the second called in the NHL in two years, and both took place at Maple Leaf Gardens. Mahovlich also scored the Leafs' sixth goal with seconds remaining in the game. With two goals, The Big M was awarded the game's second Star.

With Bower still nursing a back injury, Terry Sawchuk played goal that night. The Leafs' third goalie, Bruce Gamble, was sent to Rochester to cover injuries to Americans' netminders Gary Smith and Bob Perreault. Bob Baun, perhaps the unluckiest Leaf of 1966–67, broke his toe blocking a Bobby Hull slapshot. "It couldn't have been more dead-on," said Baun, exhibiting the smashed toe of his skate. Baun broke his thumb during training camp, and had broken his nose earlier in the season.

Rookie Reminds Smythe of Conachers
Wednesday, November 30, 1966
Brian Conacher scored the winning goal in a 3–2 win over Montreal. "That Conacher is much like his father [Lionel] and his uncle [Charlie] when they broke into the NHL," stated Conn Smythe, who had watched them all during their prime.

Orr Damages Knee in Dominant Leaf Win
Sunday, December 4, 1966
The Boston Bruins were humiliated by the Maple Leafs 8–3 at the Garden in Boston, but more importantly, rookie star Bobby Orr was assisted off the ice with the first of several serious knee injuries that would eventually curtail his extraordinary NHL career. Early in the second period, Orr was carrying the puck down the boards when he was jolted to the ice by Marcel Pronovost. "I caught him with his head down and hit him low with my hip," said the veteran blue liner. Orr left the rink on crutches and was diagnosed as having a strained internal ligament of the left knee. Boston's team physician, Dr. Ron Adams, stated, "If he keeps his weight off the knee and we're lucky, we may have him back in three weeks."

It was a massive weekend for Toronto, who dumped Detroit 5–2 on the Saturday night and followed it with a thrashing of the Bruins the next night. "That was a nightmare for us," said Ron Stewart. "I have never seen the Leafs play better since I moved here."

The back-to-back wins pushed Toronto into first place.

Injuries Dominate Leaf Loss
Wednesday, December 7, 1966

After spending time in the NHL cellar, Montreal began to look like the defending Stanley Cup champions, and took out their bitterness on Toronto by doubling the Maple Leafs 6–3 in Montreal.

Eddie Shack was cut badly over the eye in a third-period collision with defenceman Ted Harris. While Shack was heading to the infirmary for fifteen stitches over his right eye, and later, a trip to the hospital with a suspected concussion, Harris was assessed a major for elbowing. Gump Worsley had to leave the game with a knee injury, and was replaced by Charlie Hodge. "Some guy fell on me in a pile-up," said The Gumper.

With the score 5–3 at 8:01 of the third period, Imlach replaced Terry Sawchuk with Johnny Bower. "We figured Terry had had enough," Imlach said. "It just wasn't his night." Indeed it wasn't. Sawchuk collapsed after the game with a back injury. During the summer, he had undergone spinal surgery to repair two damaged discs, and this was a recurring effect of that operation. "He's had more than his share of injuries already," said Imlach. "Best goalie in the league until [that game]."

Leafs Dropped Out of First by Detroit
Sunday, December 11, 1966

Detroit knocked Toronto out of first place with a 4–1 win. The Red Wings employed a rookie goaltender, George Gardner, and the youngster stood on his head to earn the game's first Star. "I'm just too weary to cheer," he said, having played his third game in as many nights. On the Friday, he was in goal for a Pittsburgh Hornets' win over the Baltimore Clippers in AHL action. After that game, he flew to Montreal and was on the losing end of a 5–1 Saturday night game. He arrived in

Toronto and backstopped his Wings to a victory on Sunday evening. "I was never so glad to hear anything as I was the final buzzer," he smiled through bloodshot eyes.

Also new to the Red Wings was Howie Young, who re-joined them after playing himself out of the league several years earlier. "I'm a changed man," claimed Young, whose often irrational behaviour was explained by his admission that he had been a member in good standing of Alcoholics Anonymous since May 4, 1965, a day after finding himself in a Los Angeles jail. "I'm delighted to get a second chance in the NHL. I'd been fighting myself and circumstances and people since I was sixteen [he had been playing for the Leafs' junior affiliate, St. Michael's College, at the time]. Now I've got a set of principles that govern the way I handle all affairs. I face things one day at a time."

With three minutes left in regulation and Detroit up 3–1, Imlach pulled Bower in order to ice an extra skater. Gordie Howe scored an empty net goal with twelve seconds remaining. "We only had a dozen guys going, and I thought the move might result in a quick goal and wake the others up for a last-ditch dive," remarked Imlach. "At least I found out how to beat Bower," said Howe. "Shoot while he's sitting on the bench!"

Goaltenders Galore as Leafs Parade to Sick Bay
Saturday, December 17, 1966
It wasn't the Christmas gift Imlach was hoping to get. With *Hockey Night in Canada* ready to go to air with the Rangers/Leafs' contest, Imlach announced that Johnny Bower had suffered a shoulder injury stumbling over Marcel Pronovost's stick during a 2–1 win over Boston on December 14. During a practice on December 16, Bruce Gamble had taken a Jim Pappin shot to the throat. While Gamble played against first-place New York, he had difficulty swallowing. Gary Smith, summoned from Rochester, was ready to sub for Gamble if necessary.

On this night, the Rangers got goals from Earl Ingarfield, Rod Gilbert and Boom Boom Geoffrion. Frank Mahovlich scored for the Leafs. The Three Stars were Orland Kurtenbach, Ed Giacomin and George Armstrong.

Fists Fly in Loss to Habs

Wednesday, December 21, 1966

A first-period brawl involving virtually every player on both teams took almost an hour to quell, as the Montreal Canadiens dumped the Maple Leafs in a dominant 6–2 victory.

Larry Jeffrey opened the scoring at the thirty-nine-second mark, but the Canadiens quickly rebounded and earned goals from Yvan Cournoyer at 1:57 and Ralph Backstrom at 5:23.

Montreal's John Ferguson engaged Eddie Shack in a fight by high-sticking the Leafs' winger before passing the puck to Backstrom for the goal. As Ferguson completed the play, Eddie speared the Habs' enforcer, setting off the fireworks between the rivals. Ferguson admitted, "I high-sticked Shack but it wasn't called. After Shack speared me, I waited until the goal light went on and went after him." Ferguson had earlier incensed Toronto by waving his stick in Shack's face early in the game. While the Canadiens were celebrating their go-ahead goal, Ferguson dropped his gloves and chased Shack. While winning a decision over Eddie, Kent Douglas stepped up to protect his teammate and was also beaten by the Canadiens' winger until the linesmen pulled the two sparring partners apart. Shack then grabbed Ralph Backstrom and the two tugged at each others' sweaters. John Brenneman grappled with J. C. Tremblay, and Bob Baun took on Jacques Laperriere, then tangled with Claude Larose, who had just finished wrestling with Bob Pulford.

Imlach started Bruce Gamble in goal, but switched to Gary Smith after the brawl that followed the second goal. Smith was at his daring best, at one point stick-handling to centre ice before shooting the puck away. But J. C. Tremblay corralled the puck and fired a long shot at the open goal. Smith was only at his own blue line when Tremblay's shot was taken, but Marcel Pronovost scrambled back to block what otherwise would have been a sure goal.

Yvan Cournoyer scored three goals, all on power plays. Backstrom connected twice, and Jimmy Roberts scored the final Montreal goal. Jeffrey and Kent Douglas scored for Toronto. "Our guys enjoyed their Christmas turkey early," noted Canadiens coach Toe Blake.

Twin Wins Give Leafs a Merry Christmas
Saturday and Sunday, December 24 and 25, 1966

The Maple Leafs blanked Boston 3–0 in Toronto on Christmas Eve, with Johnny Bower earning the shutout on *Hockey Night in Canada*. After planes were grounded due to the blustery weather, both teams took buses to Buffalo and flew from there to Boston, arriving at 2:30 Christmas afternoon. That night, Toronto doubled the Bruins 4–2. Punch Imlach dressed his son, Brent, a junior with the Toronto-affiliated London Nationals, for the contest in Boston. Bobby Orr returned to the Bruins' lineup following his knee injury, and was played at both defence and centre.

The Leafs were off until New Year's Eve, but Dominion Stores in the Greater Toronto Area awarded a crowd of nine thousand the chance to watch a Leafs' scrimmage at Maple Leaf Gardens on December 28. The beleaguered Leafs were gobsmacked when Johnny Bower stopped a blistering shot from Frank Mahovlich and left the ice surface for X-rays on his right hand. It turned out to be broken, and Bower was out of action for approximately three weeks. "It was just one of those things," commented Bower, who endured his fifth injury of the season. "Frank's job is to shoot them and mine to stop them. I knew the hand was broken the minute that puck landed."

During the same exhibition contest, Kent Douglas landed a body-check on Larry Jeffrey that left him groggy in his wake. The check resulted in a concussion for Jeffrey, who vowed to begin wearing protection for his head. "This is about the sixth time I've had a concussion," he said. "One thing is certain. From now on, I'll wear a helmet."

Crowded Crease as Imlach Looks for Goaltender
Wednesday, January 4, 1967

The Maple Leafs began Canada's centennial year with a 2–1 victory over the Rangers in New York on New Year's Day. Frank Mahovlich, who seemed to have a bounty on goaltenders, rang a shot off Ed Giacomin's head, forcing the acrobatic netminder to leave the New York goal. Bruce Gamble, in the Leafs' goal, banged his head on the goal post. Both netminders were attended to, but remained in the game.

With Bower and Sawchuk out with injuries, Gamble carried the load for Toronto. The Leafs had several netminders in their chain, including Gary Smith and thirty-six-year-old Bob Perreault in Rochester with the AHL Americans, Al Smith with the Victoria Maple Leafs of the WHL, thirty-seven-year-old Al Millar in Tulsa with the Oilers of the CHL, Dave Kelly with the Los Angeles Blades of the WHL and Ken Broderick with Canada's National Team. Pundits believed that Perreault and Millar were unlikely to be summoned due to their age, that Millar had fallen out of favour with the organization, and that Kelly and Broderick were long shots at best. "The kid looked very sharp," said Imlach in praise of Al Smith after watching him in practice.

Leafs Start Bleak Streak
Sunday, January 15, 1967
Denis DeJordy and the Chicago Black Hawks blanked the Maple Leafs 4–0. This Sunday evening game in the Windy City marked the first of ten straight losses for Toronto.

Imlach Calls Out Stars as Team Flounders
Wednesday, February 1, 1967
Panicked in the midst of a monumental skid, Imlach's threat of making changes came to fruition prior to the contest against the Canadiens in Montreal. Toronto had lost seven straight games and scored just eleven goals over that period. In his rant, Imlach claimed that with Red Kelly out, there was no leadership, and blamed Keon, Mahovlich, Pulford and Shack for not earning their large pay cheques.

With Terry Sawchuk injured and Bruce Gamble attending the funeral of his father-in-law, the coach promoted netminder Gary Smith from the AHL's Rochester Americans as an emergency backup to Johnny Bower. Dick Gamble was also promoted from Rochester to replace Mahovlich, who had injured his leg. Shack was benched in favour of Jim Pappin, while Kent Douglas was demoted to Tulsa of the CPHL, in order to make room for Larry Hillman. Douglas threatened to quit rather than report to the minors, but did report. "He'll get lots of ice time there and will be back if he regains his top form," replied the Leafs' coach.

That evening's game saw Toronto hit rock bottom. "They were so inept in the last few minutes while having a man advantage that the Forum crowd laughed as they foundered to a 7–1 humiliation at the hands of the fired-up Montreal Canadiens," reported the *Toronto Star*.

Eddie Shack and John Brenneman did not make the trip to Montreal. In their places, Jim Pappin played well but thirty-eight-year-old Dick Gamble was unable to keep up and was deemed inadequate. Larry Hillman was solid in the losing cause. As the game went on, Imlach benched Pulford and Stemkowski, allowing Mike Walton to get more ice time. "Marcel Pronovost had a terrible night after the first period. He and Baun were on for five goals," claimed Punch. "And the fact that our left wingers weren't moving back fast enough didn't help. Our fellows have got to stop standing around after they lose the puck. That's the time to put your head down, dig in and get back to help the defence."

Yvan Cournoyer scored twice, both power-play tallies. The Road-runner was feasting on Toronto in 1966–67, scoring ten of his eighteen goals against the Leafs. And nine of his ten goals against Toronto were with a man advantage.

"I'm going to keep making changes," affirmed Imlach when pondering what was next for his squad. He suggested that Jim McKenny would be promoted from Tulsa as one of several changes.

Leafs Shake Losing Streak against Streaking Chicago
Saturday, February 11, 1967

"Eleven has always been lucky for me," admitted the superstitious coach. "I've never lost ten in a row before, not even in cribbage. Maybe we'll win against Chicago on Saturday."

As a soothsayer, Punch Imlach did all right. The Leafs didn't win against the first-place Black Hawks, but the best news was that they didn't lose, either.

The Maple Leafs and Hawks skated to a 4–4 tie, giving Toronto their first point in eleven starts.

Dave Keon scored just eleven seconds into the game. Larry Hillman, Peter Stemkowski and Red Kelly also scored for Toronto, while Stan Mikita scored once and Bobby Hull notched three for the Hawks. "That guy looks like a limousine tangling with compacts," said King Clancy. Bruce Gamble was in goal for the Leafs and took a beating from the Hawks' sharpshooters. Ken Wharram hit him in the head with a shot, Bobby Hull caught him on the shoulder and Dennis Hull was the cause of a bruised elbow after a deadly slapshot. The *Toronto Star* wrote, "Gamble skated slowly and humbly toward his hideaway beneath the stands, like a man who had just been given a reprieve by the firing squad."

Frank Mahovlich returned to the lineup after missing six games with a leg injury, and Terry Sawchuk's recurring back ailment, which kept him out of the Leafs' lineup for two months, had healed enough to return the veteran goaltender to the roster. "It's the first time all season that I've had the whole team on the ice," complained Imlach.

"The Leafs were in a free fall, with nothing on the horizon that would indicate they were going be able to stop it," recalled Brian Conacher. "We lost ten games, and three of them were to Chicago. No one was going to stop Chicago that year. They had a very powerful offensive team, they had good goaltending, they were legitimately in first place and we were slipping right out of the playoff picture. The harder Punch would push, the worse the reaction was. A coach can only push so far, and if the chemistry isn't right, the harder they push, it just seems to come apart. But this was a pivotal game. We had to put it together. Punch was trying anything to get us going. The lines were all shuffled around, and there were huge expectations that this would be the turnaround game, but in hindsight, it was.

"At this stage of the game, I don't even know that we were thinking that we were a playoff contender," analyzed Conacher. "We saw ourselves slipping right out of it, with no ability to stop the free fall. On a night like this, with Bobby Hull getting geared up, skating on a few rushes going end-to-end, this was going to be a tough place to come out of a slump. The objective was simply to have a good solid game and to start building towards winning a game. The margin between winning and losing is so fine, it's not always a physical thing but a mental thing."

Ward Cornell and Foster Hewitt discussed the losing streak with Punch Imlach during the first intermission on *Hockey Night in Canada*. Hewitt suggested that a slump early in the year was not unusual for Toronto hockey teams. "I can't remember a slump as bad as this, but it seems to me they always have a slump every year. It's only the length that has been different this year. I remember Hap Day, year in and year out, always had a slump in January. He called it the 'January thaw.'"

Imlach responded by describing his plan of attack. "You don't sleep at night. You are always thinking about it, even when driving a car going along the road, you are thinking about who you should be playing and what is wrong with this player and the next thing you know, you are going through a stoplight. But we'll have to make some changes. We'll have to bring up some young players to give them a chance or we'll have to make some trades. I think the players realize that the pressure is on. They have to do everything the hard way."

Ward Cornell posed an interesting question of Imlach, asking, "As general manager of the Leafs, have you ever considered replacing Punch Imlach as coach?" Imlach replied, "Don't think I haven't thought about it. I don't run from anything and we'll try and work it out, the best we can, that's for sure."

Brian Conacher later discussed this horrific month for the Maple Leafs. "Punch, at the best of times, wasn't an easy guy to work for, and the veterans were 'conditioned' to tolerate Punch. They knew that he was a winner, and that he had the ability to get you to the Stanley Cup. I think a lot of the veteran players on our team realized that this was their last opportunity."

Conacher, a rookie in 1966–67, described playing for Imlach and suggested what may have gone wrong during the early weeks of 1967. "Punch used the 'f' word with great frequency," Conacher said. "We used to sit in the dressing room when he would rant and rave and I think was literally pulling his hair out — and he didn't have a lot left to pull out. He was beside himself because he wasn't able to get the team to react to all this ranting and raving. The team just quit on him. There used to be a lottery in the dressing room about how many times he would use the 'f' word in his motivational speeches."

It's a Sign of the Apocalypse — The Leafs Win!
Sunday, February 12, 1967

The Maple Leafs earned their first win in a month as they rolled into Boston and beat the hometown Bruins 2–1. Peter Stemkowski deflected a pass from Jim Pappin past Ed Johnston to score the winning goal at 4:32 of the third period. "The kid has been carrying us for the last couple of weeks," mentioned Imlach.

Johnny Bower was a last-minute roster announcement for Toronto. Bruce Gamble had been pencilled in to start, but reported to his coach that he could barely grip his goalie stick after he took a Dennis Hull shot on the elbow in the game on Saturday night. "He fires as hard as the other guy [his brother, Bobby]," Gamble told a *Toronto Star* reporter. "Not as accurately, but as hard." While Sawchuk was practising, he was not deemed ready to play.

"The old man wasn't great; rather out of this world," stated the *Star* in describing Bower's role in the victory. "It's a wonder I wasn't too stiff to move," Bower said, laughing. "Army [roommate George Armstrong] insisted on opening a window last night and it was so cold two oranges on the sill froze solid!"

Imlach Hospitalized; Clancy Takes Over Bench
Saturday, February 18, 1967

With the accumulation of three out of four possible points over the weekend, the mood in the Leafs' dressing room changed substantially. The dark cloud that had hung over the team through thirty days of hell had made way for a lighthearted return to the game, with the players enjoying themselves once again. "Amazing, isn't it?" said Imlach incredulously.

After losing ten in a row, the Leafs tied Chicago on the eleventh and then followed with a win over Boston on the twelfth. Relieved, the Leafs then pounded the second-place New York Rangers by a lopsided score of 6–0. Frank Mahovlich was dominant, first giving Ed Giacomin fits, and then, when the Rangers' first-stringer was replaced, pressuring Cesare Maniago. He finished the night with a goal and an assist and plenty of chances.

Injuries continued to haunt the Leafs. On that Saturday, Jim McKenny was called up from the Tulsa Oilers to replace Bobby Baun, who had a badly bruised shoulder. Meantime, on that same date, Tulsa lost netminder Al Millar to injury, so the Maple Leafs sent Bruce Gamble to the Oilers in order to keep Tulsa competitive. But that roster move meant that Gamble could not be recalled to the parent Leafs for at least fourteen days in a ruling put in place to protect minor-league teams from being decimated by their parent NHL clubs. Gamble had played twenty-one of Toronto's forty-nine games to that point.

But with a season of woe due to repeated injuries, no one expected that the next person to go down was going to be the coach. Imlach held his regular Saturday morning practice, but afterwards, sat down beside his colleague, King Clancy, and admitted he felt ill. "Got a congested feeling here," he said, indicating his chest, then pointed to his left arm and added, "And a lot of pain here." Clancy suggested he see a doctor, but Imlach brushed him off, reminding him that the Leafs played the Bruins that night. But while the two were having lunch, Imlach saw Dr. Tate McPhedran and mentioned his condition. Dr. McPhedran insisted that the coach meet him in his office at Toronto General Hospital, and Clancy dropped him off there at 2:30.

McPhedran ran Imlach through a few tests and immediately told the Leafs' coach that he was to be admitted to the hospital that afternoon, game or no game. "There's no. . . way I'll miss it," lashed out Imlach, but after calming down, he realized the doctors knew best. He called Clancy and asked him to handle the bench against the Boston Bruins.

Electrocardiographs confirmed that the coach had not had a heart attack. "There doesn't seem to be any heart damage," reported his doctor. "We plan to keep him a few more days to do some tests but there is nothing worrisome."

"He bleeds inwards," said King Clancy. "Losing ten games in a row really frazzled him up. He wants me to run the hockey team, and anything he asks is okay as far as I'm concerned."

Clancy was assigned the coaching role until Stafford Smythe could decipher how long Imlach would be out of action and what options might be available should the coach's hospital stay be more than a few days in length. The players were very comfortable with King as coach. Clancy had coached the team from 1953–54 to 1955–56, had filled in for Imlach on two previous occasions and was always kibitzing with the players. "King's always been around," suggested Red Kelly. "It would be different if he were a new man brought in for the job. Then it would be upsetting to the club. We have a lot of experienced players who know what we're supposed to do."

The differences between Clancy and Imlach were in fact stark. While Clancy was described by *The Globe and Mail* as "the original Good Humour man with the built-in public relations of a Francis of Assisi," the same newspaper called Imlach "perverse, profane, loyal and demanding, refusing to accept less from any player than his absolute best every day."

In spite of the injuries and illnesses, the Maple Leafs beat Boston 5–3. Rumours swirled that Imlach had suffered a heart attack. The coach was not allowed to watch the game, but Clancy visited him afterwards. "He was full of dope and pills, but he knew the score," reported King.

Clancy didn't slavishly follow Imlach's coaching template. He placed Mike Walton, often in Imlach's doghouse, with Bob Pulford, and the two responded with their best efforts of the season. Walton scored one of Toronto's goals. Clancy played Mahovlich twenty-three minutes of the game, more than any other game that season. Horton was on the ice for thirty-five minutes, and scored Toronto's final goal. Jim McKenny played his first game of the season, replacing Baun.

Clancy Confirmed as Coach; the Return of Terry Sawchuk
Sunday, February 23, 1967

Stafford Smythe was faced with a decision: should he keep King Clancy behind the bench for the duration of Imlach's absence, promote Joe Crozier from Rochester, move Jim Gregory in from the Marlboros or tap Bert Olmstead for the role?

Crozier was certain that he would be heading to Toronto. "Stafford Smythe has told me that, under no circumstances, will King Clancy be running the club after Monday. He tells me that all along, I've been groomed as the likely replacement for Punch." Meantime, Harold Ballard indicated he knew nothing of Crozier being considered to replace Imlach.

Clancy continued behind the bench and was able to accomplish something that Imlach had not in almost two years — a defeat of the Red Wings in Detroit. The Clancy-led Leafs, with former Red Wing Terry Sawchuk in goal playing his first game since December 7, beat Detroit 4–2. Sawchuk reported, "I feel so good, it scares me. Five weeks ago, I wondered if I'd ever play again."

Down 2–1 in the second period, the Maple Leafs got goals from Walton and Ellis just eighteen seconds apart in the second period to take the lead. It was Ellis's seventeenth goal of the season, six of which were game winners.

In his biography, *Over the Boards,* Ellis stated, "Punch got things straightened out after our losing streak and King kept it going. He would get so enthusiastic in the dressing room that it rubbed off on the guys. He injected his own enthusiasm into us."

Leafs Steal a Tie; Thieves Rob Leafs' Coach
March 1, 1967
While Henri Richard scored deep into the first period, both goaltenders — Johnny Bower for Toronto and rookie Rogatien Vachon, up from Houston of the CPHL for Montreal — were superb through a tight, tough battle. With 1:12 to play in the third, King Clancy called Bower to the bench for an added attacker. Bower balked, arguing, "King, the faceoff isn't deep enough in the Canadiens' zone to take me out," to which Clancy replied, "John, it's deep enough for me. Take a seat." The desperation gamble paid off. Mahovlich fed Jim Pappin a perfect pass and he scored with just forty-nine seconds remaining to give the Leafs and Canadiens a 1–1 tie. "When Frank gave me the pass, I was in the clear. I cut to the kid's left, then brought the puck back and slipped it past him."

Unshackled from Imlach's rule, The Big M seemed to have a new lease on life, playing with great enthusiasm. "The Big M was all over the ice as he zigged and zagged, lugging the puck out of the Leafs zone," reported *The Globe.*

Bower was twice struck by John Ferguson, and Tim Horton had seen enough and leapt onto the winger's back. Larry Hillman also poked at Ferguson, standing up for his netminder. "Bower was the game's superstar," said Howie Meeker, in town from Newfoundland. "He made a dozen big saves; impossible saves."

Doctors at Toronto General said Imlach's overall health was improving. He had several electrocardiographs done, and none were abnormal during his two-week stay in the hospital.

Sawchuk Hits One Hundred

Saturday, March 4, 1967

Hockey Night in Canada viewers settled in to watch Toronto face Chicago, and ended up watching history. On that evening, Terry Sawchuk earned his hundredth regular season NHL shutout when Toronto blanked Bobby Hull and the Hawks 3–0.

Punch Imlach was released from the hospital that afternoon, but like most hockey fans across Canada, he too watched the game on *Hockey Night in Canada* while resting at home. Doctors told him he'd be able to return to coaching on March 12.

Peter Stemkowski stripped Pat Stapleton of the puck and fired it past Denis DeJordy at 1:52 of the first period to put the Leafs up 1–0. In the third, Dave Keon fed a pass to George Armstrong, who scored his 250th career goal at the fifty-second mark. "Davey did all the work," the captain humbly offered. All I had to do was snap his pass out home. My 250-goal feat is nothing alongside Terry's NHL record. His 100 shutouts are like a forward scoring 500 goals. I don't think any other goalkeeper will ever reach that plateau."

Later in the period, Bob Pulford stole the puck from Ken Hodge, deked Ed Van Impe and beat DeJordy to complete the scoring.

The Hawks were held scoreless as the Leafs checked, poked loose pucks away and furiously back-pedalled into their own end to prevent a Hawk from getting a good scoring opportunity. "Man, they were coming back tonight," Sawchuk later said with a broad smile. "They were really checking for me." The first teammate back to congratulate his goaltender was Marcel Pronovost, who, as a long-time teammate of Sawchuk's in both Detroit and Toronto, had seen most of his friend's shutouts. "He's the greatest goalie I've ever seen, and certainly the greatest competitor," said Pronovost.

The Hall of Fame netminder got emotional as Foster Hewitt announced his name as first Star of the game. After the contest, Sawchuk walked around the dressing room, thanking each of his teammates for helping him achieve such a landmark plateau. "The ovation from the Toronto fans is something I'll never forget," he said. Punch Imlach walked into the dressing room and first congratulated Clancy, saying, "Way to go, Shorty." Laughing, he then shook hands with each of the players, stopping for an extended visit with both Sawchuk and Armstrong.

Terry Sawchuk earned his first NHL shutout while playing with the Red Wings, defeating the Bruins 2–0 on January 15, 1950. He broke George Hainsworth's NHL record of ninety-four shutouts on January 18, 1964, when he and the Wings blanked Montreal 2–0.

Clancy's Streak Stopped
Sunday, March 5, 1967

After losing ten in a row earlier in the year, the Maple Leafs went undefeated in ten, but that streak concluded with a 5–2 loss in Chicago on March 5 during the second game of a home-and-home series.

Chicago coach Billy Reay said. "We started the Maple Leafs on their ten-game unbeaten streak, and it's only right that we finish it." Stan Mikita admitted, "We had to play hockey for our fans after turning in such a stinker in Toronto."

The Leafs lost Larry Jeffrey within the first three minutes of play when Eric Nesterenko left him woozy with a hard check into the boards. Shortly afterwards, Johnny Bower pulled a hamstring in his left leg, making a spectacular save on Nesterenko. Although Bower stayed in the game at that time, he left after Bobby Hull scored at the fifty-eight-second mark of the second period. While Johnny insisted he was fine to finish the game,

Coach Clancy noted that his goaltender was hampered in trying to reach the puck, and insisted he leave the game.

Hull scored two goals, giving him forty-six on the season, and Mikita added to his NHL scoring lead with three assists. Pierre Pilote also picked up three assists.

The Leafs were encumbered with more injury woes. Bobby Baun left the game early in the third when his bum shoulder gave out on him. Dave Keon sprained an ankle when he tumbled into the boards in the third period. This was certainly not good news, as the Leafs looked towards their playoff run.

Team Gives Clancy a Tie as a Parting Gift
Saturday, March 11, 1967
King Clancy knew that this tenth game behind the bench would be his final match before the return of Punch Imlach, and he had hoped to turn the team over to the coach with the Leafs sitting in second place. Although he didn't quite achieve that feat, Clancy left the Maple Leafs in terrific shape.

While *The Globe and Mail* claimed that the 2–2 tie against the Rangers was "a misleading indicator, because the Leafs weren't fit to be tied," the point gave King a record of seven wins, one loss and two ties during his ten games as interim coach, helping dramatically alter the team's fortunes and ensuring a berth in the Stanley Cup playoffs.

Rod Gilbert and Ken Schinkel scored for New York and Dave Keon and Jim Pappin for Toronto.

The superstitious Clancy wore the same fedora, the same socks and the same blue-striped shirt during his entire time behind the Leafs' bench. In fact, he refused to have his fedora cleaned after a pigeon left a present on it on his way to his first game as acting coach, although he said, "It's not the hat or a shirt that is doing it, it's those guys on the ice. They're working, and things are starting to bounce a little better for us now."

The self-effacing Clancy shrugged off his contribution. "I haven't done a damned thing," he stated modestly yet emphatically. "Our goaltending got good when Bower and Sawchuk got healthy and everything began to click. This is Imlach's team. It'd gone three games without losing when I took over, and I'm certain it'd have gone right on winning, regardless. I don't take any credit at all for what's been happening."

"King's been doing a great job, don't get me wrong, but Punch had us straightened out before his health gave out," said Tim Horton, who was occasionally shuffled from defence to wing under Clancy's command. "Instead of criticizing, [Punch] went out of his way to try and build up our confidence and kept impressing on us that we had too much ability to keep skidding. It took patience and courage on his part to wait out the slump."

Bob Pulford sang from the same songbook. "Don't forget, we were beginning to win again before Punch got sick. That stuff about us playing better for one coach than another was overplayed."

Larry Hillman, however, believed that King Clancy played an important role in the 1966–67 season. "Clancy was the spark plug, the funny guy, where Imlach was serious. Everybody just wanted to play for King. I don't think he coached any better than Imlach. It was just a change, and it was a welcome change."

But a few others felt that Imlach's illness allowed Clancy to experiment, which helped change the complexion of the team's spirit. He improvised impressively, putting Frank Mahovlich on the point on power plays, something The Big M hadn't done previously during the 1966–67 season, which gave the big winger added ice time. Clancy also showed added confidence in rookie Mike Walton. "King gave me lots of ice time," Walton said. "That's all I wanted to prove myself." Walton had been rookie of the year in both the Central Hockey League and the American Hockey League, and was quite vocal in his desire to stay with the Leafs and not be demoted to Rochester.

Jim Pappin, a frequent traveller between Toronto and Rochester, found stability under Clancy. "The big break I got was being put on a line with Peter Stemkowski and Bob Pulford. We were in that ten-game losing streak. It looked like Pete and I were bound for Rochester again and they had Bobby up for trade bait. Putting us together made us realize that we were the third line and we had to prove ourselves. We had to produce or else." Imlach also acknowledged the improved play of the trio. "Pappin's really been scoring lately and Pully is playing like the fine left winger he was before I converted him to centre. Stemmer is the most improved centre in the league. I'm delighted at the progress he's made in the past fifteen games."

While King Clancy had helped alter the mood around the team and arguably contributed to turning the Leafs' fortunes around in the process, his greatest contribution may arguably have been creating the line of Bob Pulford, Jim Pappin and Peter Stemkowski. The line proved to be the most productive for the Leafs through the conclusion of the regular season, and their effectiveness extended into the playoffs.

Punch Imlach discovered something else during his time off, which was attributed to a hiatus hernia. "I found out I can get just as mad watching the games on TV as I do behind the bench."

The Return of Punch
Sunday, March 12, 1967
The Chicago Black Hawks clinched first place by blanking Toronto 5–0 in Punch Imlach's return behind the bench. It was the franchise's initial first-place finish in its forty-year history, breaking the so-called "curse of Muldoon."

Pete Muldoon was the franchise's first coach when the Black Hawks made their NHL debut in 1926–27. He was fired by owner Frederick McLaughlin after one season on the job and, according to hockey lore, took revenge on the franchise by swearing that they would never finish in first place. The legend was perpetuated by the fact that through thirty-nine years, Chicago blew insurmountable leads on a few occasions and missed out on first place by a single point in 1963 and 1964. With the win, the curse was shattered and the champagne enjoyed immensely

Bobby Hull collected his forty-eighth goal of the season, and Ken Hodge and Lou Angotti both scored twice for Chicago. Angotti didn't even touch the puck on his first goal, scored when Dave Keon backhanded the puck into the net past Sawchuk on a faceoff. "Davey beat me cleanly," Angotti stated excitedly. "I guess he got too much wood on it."

Hull Victimizes Leafs for Fiftieth Goal

Saturday, March 18, 1967

After two losses since his return, including a 5–0 debacle six days earlier, Punch Imlach finally got to enjoy a victory, and did so in convincing fashion with a 9–5 trouncing of the Black Hawks.

While Chicago had little to prove as a team, having already earned a first-place finish, there was more than pride on the line. Bobby Hull was on a trajectory to break the single-season goal-scoring record of fifty-four, which he established in 1965–66; Stan Mikita was attempting to break the single-season point record of ninety-seven, set by Hull in 1965–66; and net-minders Glenn Hall and Denis DeJordy were gunning to claim the Vezina Trophy, awarded to the team allowing the fewest goals during the regular season.

Toronto jumped into a 3–0 lead within the first six minutes of the contest, but Chicago roared back to tie the game before the end of the period. In the second period, the Leafs fired five unanswered goals. Chicago made a valiant attempt to even things up in the third, scoring twice while Toronto countered with one, but when the buzzer sounded, the final score was 9–5.

"Those were nine important goals for us," Imlach said. "Some of our guys who haven't been scoring too often found their touch." Maple Leafs' goal scorers were Keon and Kelly with two each with, singles going to George Armstrong, Ron Ellis, Frank Mahovlich, Eddie Shack and Peter Stemkowski.

Bobby Hull scored his fiftieth goal of the season, the third time he had reached that plateau. In fact, for a few minutes, he was credited with his fifty-first after a Doug Jarrett slapshot was deflected past Bruce Gamble into the net. Hull was announced by Paul Morris as the goal scorer, but he quickly took referee Art Skov aside. "The puck didn't deflect in off me," he told the *Toronto Star*. "I don't want something for nothing. I asked the referee to change it." Hull also picked up three assists in the contest.

Stan Mikita, meanwhile, picked up a goal to give him ninety points on the season, seven shy of Hull's record.

Skov threatened to quit during the game, after he was struck by a program tossed by Stafford Smythe at the penalty box while recording a minor to Eddie Shack. Referee-In-Chief Scotty Morrison recounted the incident. "At the second intermission, he dangled his whistle on the end of one finger and told me to take it, that he was all through and that he didn't have to put up with that kind of treatment." No further action was taken, although NHL president Clarence Campbell stated that Skov erred by not immediately assessing a bench minor to Toronto.

Before the game, the Black Hawks entered their dressing room at Maple Leaf Gardens greeted by a large crate that contained the Prince of Wales Trophy, earned by finishing first during the regular season. Excited, they went to hoist their reward only to discover that the case was locked, and no one had the key.

Leafs Win Battle for Third Place
Saturday, April 1, 1967
After being dumped 4–0 by the Rangers the previous Sunday, the Leafs faced New York again on April 1 and avenged the shutout in fine fashion. Johnny Bower had not been impressive in the prior meeting but played as though he was in the thick of the playoffs on April 1.

Jim Pappin scored twice, with Walton, Mahovlich and Horton picking up the other goals. But it was Bower who made the difference. Emile Francis, Rangers' assistant GM, said, "I don't think they were much better than we were, but what can you do when that old guy plays like that?" Vic Hadfield spoiled Bower's shutout bid with a shot that bounced off Horton's shoulder, bounced off the ice and into the net at 14:31 of the third period, with Johnny frantically attempting to corral the elusive puck.

In the second period, Bower was cut above his right eye by the stick of Rod Gilbert and replaced by Terry Sawchuk, but he returned, stitches and all, after the very next whistle.

When the puck was faced off, the Maple Leafs, Rangers and Canadiens all had the opportunity to finish second, with just two games remaining in the regular season. But a Montreal win (5–4 over the league-leading Black Hawks) gave them seventy-five points, the Leafs' win put them at seventy-four and New York's loss left the Rangers with seventy-two points and the fourth and final playoff spot.

Regular Season Concludes
Sunday, April 2, 1967
The Leafs concluded the regular season with a 5–2 whipping of the injury-depleted Bruins. Boston was without Johnny Bucyk, Ted Green, Skip Krake, Ron Schock, Ron Stewart and Bob Woytowich. Injury woes again beset the Leafs during this contest. Armstrong's groin injury acted up, and he left the game midway through the first period. Larry Jeffrey slid into the boards that same period and separated his shoulder. Marcel Pronovost blocked a Joe Watson shot in the second and left the game with a bruised instep. Frank Mahovlich caught his skate in a rut in the third period and was helped off the ice with a sprained knee.

The Bruins faithful applauded Johnny Bower heartily when he left the game at the 10:35 mark of the third, replaced by Terry Sawchuk. Bower had been miraculous in goal up that point.

Bob Pulford scored twice for Toronto, his sixteenth and seventeenth of the season, Dave Keon potted his nineteenth, Mahovlich collected his eighteenth before leaving the game, and Ron Ellis scored his team-best twenty-second.

As the teams left the ice at the conclusion of the game, Boston fans chanted, "We're number six! Next season number twelve!" With the brilliant introduction of Bobby Orr in 1966–67, Boston would soon have few reasons to be so pessimistic.

The final season of the so-called Original Six Era concluded with Chicago in first place with a dominant ninety-four points. Montreal finished second, Toronto just behind in third place and the Rangers finished fourth. Detroit and Boston were excluded from post-season play.

Chicago's Stan Mikita won the Art Ross Trophy as the scoring champion with ninety-seven points, equalling teammate Bobby Hull's record-breaking total from the previous season. Mikita was also awarded the Hart Trophy as the league's most valuable player, and the Lady Byng as the NHL's most gentlemanly player. Dave Keon led all Maple Leaf point-getters with fifty-two points.

While the Maurice Richard Trophy was decades away from being introduced, Bobby Hull led all NHL goal scorers with fifty-two.

Bobby Orr was an easy choice for the Calder Trophy as the NHL's best first-year player. Harry Howell was awarded the Norris Trophy and acknowledged the Bruins' defenceman. "I'm glad I won it now because it's going to belong to Orr from here on." It did — for the next eight years.

The Chicago duo of Glenn Hall and Denis DeJordy earned the Vezina Trophy for allowing the fewest number of goals during the 1966–67 season.

The New York Rangers and Montreal Canadiens faced off in one semi-final series, while Toronto was faced with the task of trying to upset the heavily favoured Chicago Black Hawks. The gargantuan task could only be accomplished if each member of the Maple Leafs played beyond his ability.

The Leafs had failed to win on the ice at Chicago Stadium all season, and had only been able to muster a November tie against the powerful Black Hawks. "The past few seasons, experts have labelled Billy Reay's men the 'choke-up brigade,' as they faded, first in the league race and then in the playoffs," the *Toronto Star* reminded readers. It seemed that this spring, Reay had his troops healthy (although Bobby Hull was hampered by a sore knee) and chomping at the bit to earn another Stanley Cup championship.

1966–67 Regular Season Standings						
FINISH	TEAM	GAMES	WINS	LOSSES	TIES	POINTS
1	Chicago Black Hawks	70	41	17	12	94
2	Montreal Canadiens	70	32	25	13	77
3	Toronto Maple Leafs	70	32	27	11	75
4	New York Rangers	70	30	28	12	72
5	Detroit Red Wings	70	27	39	4	58
6	Boston Bruins	70	17	43	10	44

RK	NUMBER	PLAYER	POS	AGE	GP	G	A	PTS	PIM	ESG	PPG	SHG	GWG
1	14	Dave Keon	C	26	66	19	33	52	2	13	5	1	2
2	27	Frank Mahovlich	LW	29	63	18	28	46	44	14	4	0	3
3	8	Ron Ellis	RW	22	67	22	23	45	14	16	4	2	7
4	20	Bob Pulford	LW	30	67	17	28	45	28	15	1	1	1
5	4	Red Kelly	D/C	39	61	14	24	38	4	12	2	0	0
6	12	Peter Stemkowski	C	23	68	13	22	35	75	12	1	0	4
7	10	George Armstrong	RW	36	70	9	24	33	26	6	3	0	3
8	18	Jim Pappin	RW	27	64	21	11	32	89	15	6	0	7
9	15	Larry Jeffrey	LW	26	56	11	17	28	27	9	1	1	1
10	22	Brian Conacher	LW	25	66	14	13	27	47	13	1	0	1
11	23	Eddie Shack	LW	29	63	11	14	25	58	11	0	0	2
12	7	Tim Horton	D	37	70	8	17	25	70	5	3	0	1
13	2	Larry Hillman	D	29	55	4	19	23	40	4	0	0	0
14	16	Mike Walton	C	22	31	7	10	17	13	3	4	0	0
15	19	Kent Douglas	D	30	39	2	12	14	48	1	1	0	0
16	3	Marcel Pronovost	D	36	58	2	12	14	28	2	0	0	0
17	26	Allan Stanley	D	40	53	1	12	13	20	1	0	0	0
18	24	John Brenneman	LW	24	41	6	4	10	4	5	0	1	0
19	21	Bob Baun	D	30	54	2	8	10	83	2	0	0	0
20	11	Brit Selby	LW	21	6	1	1	2	0	1	0	0	0
21	25	Wayne Carleton	LW	20	5	1	0	1	14	0	1	0	0
22	25	Jim McKenny	D	20	6	1	0	1	0	1	0	0	0
23	1	Johnny Bower	G	42	27	0	0	0	0	0	0	0	0
24	1	Bruce Gamble	G	28	23	0	0	0	0	0	0	0	0
25	9	Dick Gamble	LW	38	1	0	0	0	0	0	0	0	0
26	11	Brent Imlach	F	20	1	0	0	0	0	0	0	0	0
27	17	Duane Rupp	D	28	3	0	0	0	0	0	0	0	0
28	30	Terry Sawchuk	G	37	28	0	0	0	2	0	0	0	0
29	30	Al Smith	G	21	1	0	0	0	0	0	0	0	0
30	1	Gary Smith	G	22	2	0	0	0	0	0	0	0	0
		TEAM TOTALS			70	204	332	536	736	161	37	6	32

In order to prepare for the playoffs and to cover for injured players, Punch Imlach brought up Aut Erickson and Milan Marcetta from the Victoria Maple Leafs of the Western Hockey League. Erickson was an

NHL veteran who had played with both Boston and Chicago, but the defenceman's only NHL playoff experience was limited to six games with the Black Hawks in 1963–64. The thirty-year-old Marcetta, a centre, had yet to play a single game in the NHL, although he had earned the opportunity by leading the WHL's Victoria Maple Leafs in both goals (forty) and points (seventy-five) that season.

The Leafs were sequestered in Peterborough as they prepared for the opening faceoff of the 1966–67 Stanley Cup playoffs. Although Imlach held the title of coach, by the 1966–67 season, George Armstrong, Tim Horton and Red Kelly were especially relevant in plotting strategy regarding how opponents should be handled.

"We had a team meeting before the Chicago series and asked ourselves how we were going to win this thing," recalled Allan Stanley. "The consensus was that whoever was closest to Mikita and Hull, don't let them carry the puck. Let them give it to anybody else. Let the other guys try to beat you." Red Kelly recalled another strategy employed by the Leafs in the series against Chicago. "Those guys with the curved sticks (Mikita, Wharram and the Brothers Hull) got beat because of those curved sticks. We tried to keep them on their backhands whenever possible. They had trouble on those backhands, but they sure could blast that forehand."

While in Peterborough, Johnny Bower injured the baby finger on his right hand, but true to form, no one on the team would discuss Bower's bandaged pinky. It was later learned that a bullet from the stick of Peter Stemkowski had done the damage.

Regular Season Netminding												
RK		PLAYER	POS	AGE	GP	MIN	W	L	T	GA	GAA	SO
1	30	Terry Sawchuk	G	37	28	1409	15	5	4	66	2.81	2
2	1	Johnny Bower	G	42	27	1431	12	9	3	63	2.64	2
3	1	Bruce Gamble	G	28	23	1185	5	10	4	67	3.39	0
4	30	Al Smith	G	21	1	60	0	1	0	5	5	0
5	1	Gary Smith	G	22	2	115	0	2	0	7	3.65	0
		TEAM TOTALS			70	4200	32	27	11	208	2.97	4

But more drama also unfolded in Peterborough before the commencement of the playoffs. Bob Baun and Punch Imlach jousted verbally and publicly, likely contributing to his lack of ice time during the spring of 1967, and almost certainly expediting his exit from Toronto during the following expansion draft. "We used to go out of town to practise before the playoffs started. I wasn't playing. Larry Hillman and Marcel Pronovost were one pair, Allan Stanley and Timmy Horton were the other partners and I was the extra guy. So, I'd stay out on the ice, working out longer to keep in shape. Punch came out and told me to get off 'the friggin' ice.' He didn't say 'friggin', by the way. He had all these reporters around him when he was telling me this, so I told him to stick the team in his backside. At that particular time, my job was to stay in shape in case you need me. I wanted to be in the best shape that I could possibly be in to help the team, and with that we parted. So after we won the Cup that year, they had all the celebrations, which I didn't participate in, and Punch really got quite mad at that."

Chicago Toys with Toronto in Playoff Opener
Game One, Semi-Final – Thursday, April 6, 1967

The series began with two games played at venerable old Chicago Stadium, and those without tickets had a choice of watching the contest in one of five movie theatres showing the game on the silver screen via closed-circuit TV.

After huddling with Glenn Hall, Billy Reay played a hunch and started backup netminder Denis DeJordy, who had shut out the New York Rangers in his last game, but had all of one-and-two-thirds games of Stanley Cup experience. Nonetheless, DeJordy was outstanding. "Can't recall when I enjoyed a playoff game as much," said Hall. "DeJordy was terrific."

The start of the semi-final opener was delayed fifteen minutes when a connection to the goal lights came loose and some wiring had to be replaced. But something else almost jeopardized the game, too. The ice at Chicago Stadium was horrific. The Ice Capades had completed a two-week stand, and a new sheet of ice was required for the semi-final opener. "It normally takes a week for the ice to age properly and reach the right degree of hardness, a fact of which the Hawks' management was aware of before it scheduled the ice show," reported the *Chicago Tribune*. The ice was filled with ruts and holes, and the Zamboni inadvertently dumped a large amount of muddy water in one corner of the rink.

Frank Mahovlich and Ken Wharram swapped power-play goals in the first period, but the powerful Hawks busted out in the second, with Stan Mikita and Bobby Hull scoring. Pierre Pilote and Lou Angotti added to the carnage in the third. Toronto salvaged some semblance of respect when Jim Pappin scored with the man advantage with eight seconds to play.

Punch Imlach was no stranger to unorthodox coaching strategies. In a game against the Black Hawks on December 18, the Leafs' coach started the contest with Peter Stemkowski at centre, flanked by four defencemen — Bobby Baun, Kent Douglas, Tim Horton and Marcel Pronovost. While Hawks' coach Billy Reay was more perplexed than startled, his Scooter Line of Stan Mikita, Ken Wharram and Doug Mohns shook off the strange configuration and the game proceeded normally. But in this game, Imlach bettered his best example of unorthodox coaching strategy. With the game seemingly out of reach, Imlach pulled Terry Sawchuk from the crease with 8:40 remaining in the third period, and added an extra skater to the attack. The bewildered Hawks stared at the yawning cage, but had the Leafs potted a goal (or two) at that junction, the momentum in the game would have changed, and a series-opening victory would have given a further advantage to Toronto. Alas, the game concluded with the Hawks taking game one.

"We just took advantage of our opportunities, finished our plays better and were aided by superior goaltending," explained Coach Reay. Punch Imlach countered, "I don't think we were as bad as the score indicated."

Pierre Pilote, goalie Denis DeJordy and Stan Mikita were the first, second and third stars in a 5–2 victory for the Black Hawks.

Sawchuk Sensational as Leafs Tie Series
Game Two, Semi-Final – Sunday, April 9, 1967
A bomb scare late in the afternoon threatened the start of semi-final game two, but police scanned the stands prior to the game and indicated that it would be fine to go ahead with the game.

Terry Sawchuk was brilliant in the Toronto goal in this contest, leading the Leafs to a 3–1 win. "They took the play away from us right at the opening faceoff and we didn't catch up to them until the third, and by then it was too late," said Bobby Hull.

Peter Stemkowski opened the scoring on a backhand that eluded De-Jordy in the first period. Dave Keon's shorthanded marker late in the period gave Toronto a 2–0 lead. "I wasn't out there to score a goal," said Keon. "I was out to kill the penalty and the goal was just a bonus."

George Armstrong scored the third Toronto goal on a power play at 8:24 of the second. Later that period, Armstrong was steamrolled to the ice and twisted his knee. Brian Conacher, normally a left winger, stepped into the captain's spot on the right wing. "He was moving faster, shooting with more accuracy and checking with authority from the unfamiliar right side of the rink," wrote the *Star*.

Stan Mikita spoiled Sawchuk's shutout bid with a goal at 8:45 of the third. Mikita tapped in a pass from the corner courtesy of Doug Mohns.

"That was the best game this team has played in two seasons," boasted King Clancy. Dave Keon suggested, "We did in this game for sixty minutes what we only did for four minutes in the opener — checked."

Keon, Sawchuk and Eric Nesterenko were the Three Stars, as selected by Foster Hewitt.

No Place Like Home for Leafs
Game Three, Semi-Final – Tuesday, April 11, 1967
The series moved to Maple Leaf Gardens for games three and four, which was a relief for most players, as the Chicago ice had been slushy, hampering skaters on both sides.

Chicago changed netminders for game three, choosing veteran Glenn Hall to start. Terry Sawchuk was in goal once again for Toronto.

Ron Ellis opened the scoring with a goal midway through the first period. "That was a hell of a goal he got," admitted Billy Reay. He only had about six inches to put it in, and he did." Frank Mahovlich scored at 10:22 of the second and Jim Pappin put Toronto up 3–0 with a goal at 19:15 that same period. For a second straight game, Chicago again foiled Sawchuk in his quest for a shutout when Bobby Hull scored at 16:30 of the third. The *Chicago Tribune* reported, "Tonight, the Hawks averted a shutout with less than four minutes to play. Bobby Hull snapped Lou Angotti's rebound behind Terry Sawchuk, the only one of thirty-six shots to evade the Methuselah of the mesh."

Imlach commented, "We had to get a super effort from every man to beat them. I've never been prouder of this team than tonight!"

The best shot of the day may very well have been taken before the game. Bobby Hull rifled a shot that cleared the end glass and caught Leafs' owner Harold Ballard right between the eyes, sending him flying backwards from his chair in his bunker and breaking his nose and glasses. Milt Dunnell of the *Toronto Daily Star* joked that Ballard was hit so hard "that doctors picked an eyebrow from the back of his neck."

Hawks Tie Series with Win in Toronto

Game Four, Semi-Final – Thursday, April 13, 1967

The Black Hawks evened the series by edging Toronto 4–3 in what the *Toronto Star* termed "a bruising, battering cliffhanger" at Maple Leaf Gardens.

Ken Wharram tied an NHL Stanley Cup record set by Gordie Howe against Toronto in 1954 by beating Terry Sawchuk just nine seconds after the opening faceoff. The Leafs rebounded, and after the first period, had tied Chicago at two apiece. Pierre Pilote scored the second Chicago goal with Keon, and then Horton, countering for Toronto. After a scoreless second, Eric Nesterenko and Bobby Hull, on a wicked blast from fifty-feet out, put the Hawks ahead by two.

At 16:41 of the third period, Jim Pappin felled Glenn Hall with a blast that removed a tooth, his first such loss in thirteen seasons, and required twenty-five stitches to close. Denis DeJordy skated out in relief as his mentor was patched up.

Punch Imlach again gambled by pulling his netminder earlier than tradition (and common sense) dictated. Sawchuk bolted to the bench in favour of a sixth attacker at 17:28 of the third, and the hunch paid off.

Mike Walton victimized DeJordy just nine seconds later to reduce Chicago's lead to 4–3. At 18:28, Sawchuk again was pulled for the extra skater, but while the Leafs shot at DeJordy like a carnival arcade, they were not able to add an equalizer.

"That was our best effort of the series," crowed Billy Reay.

Hawks captain Pierre Pilote earned the first Star, Bobby Hull took the second Star and Davey Keon was the game's third Star.

Substitute Sawchuk Stones Hawk Stars
Game Five, Semi-Final – Saturday, April 15, 1967
Stanley Cup viewers watched this afternoon's contest between Toronto and Chicago, and had their choice of watching it on CBC or on the U.S. network, CBS. Although the American Federation of Television and Radio Artists (AFTRA) was on strike in the States, CBS still carried the game as promised.

Terry Sawchuk was so battered and bruised from the four semi-final games played to that point that he asked Imlach to start Bower instead. "I'm just one great big aching bruise and had to bandage both legs before the game," Sawchuk admitted. Johnny opened in goal for Toronto in game five, played in Chicago, but after surrendering goals to Lou Angotti and Bobby Hull, was deemed "shaky" and replaced by Sawchuk to start the second. The score was tied at two after the first period, with Walton and Mahovlich both scoring on power plays for the Maple Leafs.

Sawchuk was flawless the rest of the way. "He proceeded to do everything but eat pucks to humble the league's greatest galaxy of scoring stars," commented the *Toronto Star*. Bobby Hull simply shook his head. "I saw him make those saves, but I still can't believe it. That was the most frustrating experience of my career." The Leafs got goals from Pappin and Stemkowski in the third, giving the Maple Leafs a 4–2 win and a three-game-to-two lead in the semi-final series.

Early in the second period, fans gasped when a Bobby Hull blast hit the Leafs' goaltender in the neck and knocked him down, "as if he had been poleaxed," to use a phrase employed by Foster Hewitt. Trainer Bob

Haggert asked Sawchuk if he was okay and got the response, "I stopped the f&@%ing puck, didn't I?" Brian Conacher claims that the shot, the save, the injury and Sawchuk's rebounding from the incident provided a wake-up call for the team, and the Maple Leafs played with more determination in order to win the game.

Terry Sawchuk was appropriately named the first Star. Bob Goldham on *Hockey Night in Canada* said of the netminder he once played with, "That's the way he played goal when we won those Stanley Cups with the Red Wings." Larry Hillman, who played most of the second period with a cut on the top of the head that required five stitches to close, was the game's second Star. Pierre Pilote was the final Star of the contest.

Sawchuk had regularly spoken of retirement through the season. After the game, the wisp of a smile finally creasing his craggy features, he said quietly, "I guess I'm going to leave it in good style, eh?"

Conacher the Conquering Hero as Leafs Eliminate Hawks
Game Six, Semi-Final – Tuesday, April 18, 1967

Back in Toronto, both teams were super-charged for game six, and it was the unlikely Brian Conacher who played hero. "I still can't believe I got two playoff goals in one game," he later said. His uncle, Charlie Conacher, the hero of the Toronto Maple Leafs' first Stanley Cup championship in 1932, had undergone surgery for throat cancer earlier that day.

Frank Mahovlich did much of the work on Conacher's first goal, which occurred just past the five-minute mark of the first period. The Big M beat blue liner Ed Van Impe and sent a perfect pass over to Conacher, who made no mistake in firing the puck past Hall. Later in that period, Pat Stapleton scored to tie the game at one apiece.

On the game-winning goal, which took place in the third, Conacher flattened Van Impe, picked up the puck and found himself in a two-on-one facing Pat Stapleton. "Dave [Keon] yelled, and this forced Stapleton to hold his ground and allowed me to move in closer for my shot," explained the rookie. "I didn't aim or try to pick a spot. I just fired and I think it went in off Hall's pad."

George Armstrong was very pleased for the man who filled his spot after being injured. "I'm for Brian and he's for me. That's the way it is for this team — one for all and all for one. It doesn't matter who scores the goals as long as they are in the other team's net and we win the game."

Stemkowski described his insurance goal, saying, "I had Pappy [Pappin] on my right and figured if I missed, he'd have a chance on the rebound. I just hammered the puck at the goal and didn't even know it was in until the crowd let out a roar!"

The 3–1 game six win eliminated the much-heralded Black Hawks, with Toronto winning the semi-final series four games to two. Brian Conacher, Terry Sawchuk and Glenn Hall were the Three Stars.

"This was farewell to a dream," rhapsodized the *Chicago Tribune.* "It was goodbye to the Black Hawks, the team that destiny forgot. If ever a team appeared to be destiny's darling, it was this one. For 40 years had this team wandered, an outcast, through hockey's nether regions. Never, not once in all those 40 years, had it won a National Hockey League championship. Rarely had it won the Stanley Cup. But this was destiny's team, and it was going to do both. It did win the league title. There was no weeping that day when the Black Hawks clinched the title. There was laughing and shouting in the triumphant locker room. Saturday, in the same room deep in the belly of Chicago Stadium, there was only silence. It was the silence of the tomb and the few reporters who came to pay their last respects walked softly and spoke reluctantly to the grieving men who had lived a dream."

Coach Billy Reay wanted nothing more than revenge on the club that unceremoniously dethroned him in 1958, but acknowledged Terry Sawchuk's brilliant goaltending in the fifth game as the turning point of the series. "Had we won it, there was no tomorrow for them."

While his teammates were celebrating their victory, Larry Jeffrey was on his way to the hospital with a torn ligament in his right knee, injured in the process of checking Stan Mikita. It had been a tough season for the winger. He missed fifteen games with a concussion and another ten with low blood count and another concussion. "He was really playing well and tough when we were shorthanded," said George Armstrong.

King Clancy ran through the dressing room glad handing the troops. "This is one of the gamest clubs I've ever been associated with," he said. "And the man chiefly responsible for its success is Punch. He stuck with the guys when they lost ten straight. He kept faith and finally convinced the kids and veterans that they belonged in this league and could do the job."

Pierre Pilote, the captain of the Black Hawks, congratulated Toronto, and said, "They had a hot hand. We didn't. If they keep on playing the way they did against us, it won't surprise me if they knock off the Canadiens."

It was a significant victory for Toronto, as Ron Ellis indicated. "Chicago was the class of the league that year. Getting by Chicago made us all believe that maybe we had a chance to win it all. When you knock off the first-place team, that's big. That was when it started to sink in that we could win the Stanley Cup."

It was a particularly emotional Stanley Cup final in 1967. For one thing, it drew a close to the Original Six Era. For another, it was the first all-Canadian final since 1960; all the more poignant since 1967 signalled Canada's one hundredth birthday as a nation.

Both teams, clearly, were eager to lay claim to the Stanley Cup. Jean Beliveau, the captain of the Canadiens, spoke passionately to his team-mates about what a Stanley Cup victory would mean for Montreal. "We feel we are representing French Canada when we play hockey, and the Cup is the main objective. I tell them what the Stanley Cup means; the sad story of men like Bill Gadsby, who played his whole career without winning the most important championship."

Coach Toe Blake didn't mince words about his optimism that the Canadiens would win a third straight Stanley Cup championship. He commented, "We're as strong as we've been in quite some time. Stronger, actually. Everybody is healthy and everybody is working hard."

The City of Montreal was hosting the World's Fair at a celebration called Expo '67, which coincided with the celebration of the country's

Centennial. They announced that a special spot to exhibit the Stanley Cup had already been selected in the Quebec pavilion. Punch Imlach was riled when he read this, and used it as ammunition to fuel his troops, who already were anxious to topple the team that most were ready to anoint as the next Stanley Cup champion.

Toronto had a not-so-secret weapon going for them. The words that needn't be spoken were that this was the last shot at a championship for the aged team. Dubbed by journalists as the "Over the Hill Gang," the core of the Leafs was comprised of Johnny Bower, who was forty-two; Allan Stanley, forty-one; Red Kelly, thirty-nine; Tim Horton and Terry Sawchuk, both thirty-seven; and Marcel Pronovost, thirty-six. All were nearing the end of their glorious careers (although only Red Kelly would retire following the 1966–67 season). The players knew that while retirement wasn't necessarily imminent, each of them could see it on the horizon, and with expansion just around the corner, there was no certainty that they would still be wearing blue and white when the next season began.

Since the Original Six Era dawned in 1942, only four teams finishing lower than second place had won the Stanley Cup — Toronto finished third in 1945, fourth in 1949 and third in 1964 and went on to claim the Cup, while Chicago finished third in 1961 and proceeded to collect Lord Stanley's legacy. The Maple Leafs of 1967 had every intention of adding to that total.

"It seemed like every year back then that it was Montreal and Toronto in the playoffs," remarked Red Kelly. "If we wanted to win the Cup, sooner or later we had to beat Montreal. I guess they probably felt the same way, meaning they knew they'd have to beat us."

Terry Harper agreed, quoting from Stephen Cole's *The Last Hurrah:* "On the Canadiens, we felt that we played everyone else just so we could play Toronto. That was the series. Those were the games. Boy oh boy, one half the country against the other, with everybody watching!"

While Montreal planned to shadow Mahovlich with Claude Provost, they made no special adjustments to their game, which had successfully carried them to a second-place finish and a sweep of the New York Rangers in the semi-final.

In a players' meeting, Dave Keon devised the plan that would topple the heavily favoured Habs. "The way we have to play, it's got to be a maximum team effort. There isn't a guy on the club who isn't playing excellent hockey right now. We can't go in and score a lot of goals. We have to check steadily. If our wings come back, their wings are tied up at our blue line. That means their centre comes to our blue line with no one to pass the puck to. If you backcheck, their forwards can't break across our line in full stride. That way, our defencemen can meet the opposition and kill off all the traffic before it gets into our zone, and not retreat into our zone. When the whole team is playing well enough to make all this work, then we win. It's as simple as that."

Montreal would employ rookie Rogatien Vachon in goal. Vachon had an interesting history, having exploded onto the NHL scene after being buried deep within the Canadiens' goaltending depth chart. Vachon was just a year out of junior and was playing with the Houston Apollos of the Central Professional Hockey League when he was promoted to the Canadiens in February 1967. "When I went down to our top farm club [in Houston], I saw three games," said Sam Pollock, in *The Last Hurrah*. "Our young goalie, Rogatien Vachon, was sensational all three nights. Vachon was the guy who looked like he could help most. We made the decision and up he came."

Gump Worsley had been injured on February 11, and backup netminder Charlie Hodge took his place, with Vachon serving as Hodge's backup. But when Hodge faltered, Vachon usurped the Montreal veteran and found a regular spot in goal. Worsley returned from his injury on March 11, only to suffer a concussion after being struck by an egg thrown from the crowd. Vachon supplanted Hodge in goal, first as a backup and then as the principal goalkeeper.

Montreal bypassed more experienced netminders in Garry Baumann, Ernie Wakely, Jean-Guy Morissette and Gerry Desjardins in favour of the diminutive goalie, and Vachon didn't disappoint. Down the stretch, he played nineteen games, winning eleven, losing three and tying four. "There were games in those final weeks we had to win, and the kid didn't let it bother him a bit," proclaimed Coach Blake. Vachon played, and won, all four of the semi-final games against the Rangers. "I'm not worrying about going into the finals with a kid in the nets. He's not likely to have any more pressure on him in the finals than he had in the last few weeks of the schedule."

Imlach was reminded that Vachon had been quoted as saying he hoped Toronto would beat Chicago in the semi-final because he thought the Leafs would be an easier opponent to face. In a calculated war of words, Imlach ridiculed Blake's use of Vachon in goal. "Tell that cocky Junior 'B' goaltender that he won't be facing New York Ranger peashooters when he plays against the Leafs," snapped Imlach. "I just hope he doesn't disappoint me by putting somebody else in besides Vachon."

The comment has gone down through hockey history as one of Imlach's finest quotes.

Junior 'B' Netminder Upsets Imlach and Leafs
Game One, Stanley Cup Final – Thursday, April 20, 1967
Punch Imlach choked on his Junior 'B' quote when Rogatien Vachon backstopped the Canadiens to a 6–2 opening-game win. Early in the contest, he robbed Tim Horton on a breakaway, which set the tone for the night. "I know Punch planted that story to upset the kid, so I kept it away from him," admitted Blake.

The Canadiens, who stayed out of the spotlight by preparing for the final at a Laurentian mountain resort, bussed to the Forum in time for the game.

Yvan Cournoyer scored the opening goal of the game, whipping a backhander past Terry Sawchuk on the power play at 6:25 of the first. He had feasted on Toronto during the regular season, scoring eleven of his twenty-five goals against the Leafs. Fifteen seconds later, Larry Hillman fired a shot from the blue line that hit a stick along the way and deflected into the upper corner of the net behind Vachon. Henri Richard had a Leon Rochefort shot glance in off his skate to put Montreal ahead 2–1 at 11:19 of the first period.

Cournoyer scored another power play goal at 5:03 of the second period when he quickly grabbed the rebound on a shot by Bobby Rousseau and caught Sawchuk out of position. At 6:06, Jean Beliveau scored after Gilles Tremblay blocked a Tim Horton shot at the blue line and took off down the ice with the puck. With Allan Stanley in pursuit, Tremblay passed over to Beliveau, who flipped the puck past Sawchuk. At 12:54 of the second, Jim Pappin fired a power-play rocket into the far corner to bring the score to 4–2.

Richard nabbed a clearing attempt by Sawchuk and passed it to Leon Rochefort, who fired a bullet that was stopped by the Leafs' netminder, but the rebound came out to the Pocket Rocket, who tucked it into the empty cage at 4:52 of the third for his second goal of the game.

"Sawchuk, who has been complaining of fatigue, looked and played like a tired goaltender last night," reported *The Globe*. He skated to the Toronto bench after Richard's second goal, and Johnny Bower skated out to take his place. Sawchuk was banged up — a bruised ankle, a bump on the head and a banged nose — so was taken out of the game to be saved from further punishment. "I took Sawchuk out simply to conserve his energy," Imlach stated after the game. "Terry doesn't have a lot of it, so when the game is gone, we've got to save what energy he has."

"Some days you stop 'em and some days you don't," sighed Sawchuk.

Johnny Bower replaced his partner in net and played well, but surrendered another goal to Henri Richard on a deflection, giving the Pocket Rocket his hat trick at 8:21. Imlach decided to play Baun, Erickson, Shack and Walton more in the third period. "I'm not going to take any chances on my big guns getting hurt when the score is out of reach," said Imlach.

For Aut Erickson, it was his sole appearance with the Maple Leafs during his NHL career. Baun had been a victim of numbers. "The four guys I've been using — Horton, Stanley, Hillman and Pronovost — have been doing such a great job that I can't change them," said Imlach. "I've been a pro long enough to know it isn't what you did yesterday that counts. It's what you do today," mentioned Baun. "I feel I can do a good job if I get the chance." As for Eddie Shack, the *Star* remarked, "His favourite music is the roar of the crowd."

The Maple Leafs simply couldn't get untracked. The tight checking of Claude Provost ensured that Frank Mahovlich was rendered ineffective. Horton and Stanley had a tough game, and were on the ice for the first four Montreal goals.

"I thought they would come out hitting, but they didn't," shrugged Henri Richard. "For me, it was just one of those nights when everything seemed to go right."

At that early junction in his career, Yvan Cournoyer was simply a power-play specialist, usually only seeing ice time when the Leafs earned a penalty. With Beliveau at centre and Gilles Tremblay and Cournoyer on the wings, joined by J. C. Tremblay and Bobby Rousseau on the points, the Canadiens had a lethal offence. "When the team wins, I'm satisfied," said Cournoyer. "It is better to be on the power play and getting some goals than playing regularly and not scoring."

Jean-Guy Talbot admitted, "Most of us would sooner beat Toronto than any other team in the National Hockey League. I guess there is a natural rivalry between the two Canadian cities."

"This was one we let the Canadiens win by default," suggested Stafford Smythe. "We just didn't play well. That's all there is to it," said Imlach dismissively.

The final score, Montreal 6, Toronto 2. The Three Stars, chosen by former Canadien and Leaf Dickie Moore, were Henri Richard, J. C. Tremblay and Jim Pappin.

When Imlach was reminded of his quote about Montreal using a Junior 'B' goalie, he replied, "Vachon's still Junior 'B,' but he's the best Junior 'B' in the country."

Bower Slams Door on Canadiens
Game Two, Stanley Cup Final – Saturday, April 24, 1967
Clearly, the opening salvo of the series had shocked the Leafs into action. It was a different team that showed up at the Forum for game two.

Peter Stemkowski clanged a shot off the post behind Vachon just fifteen seconds after the opening faceoff, and it was all Leafs from then on. With Terry Harper in the penalty box, Stemkowski batted in Pulford's goalmouth pass to open the scoring at 12:14 of the first. On the second goal, Frank Mahovlich sped down the right wing on the Leafs' power play. He was stopped by Jean-Guy Talbot, but Pappin picked up the puck and quickly fed it to Mike Walton, who scored on a bullet from forty-feet out to put Toronto up 2–0 at 9:12 of the second period. The Leafs added a third goal, as Brian Conacher was aggressively forechecking the Canadiens and pried the puck loose, slipping it over to Stemkowski, who passed it back to Horton on the blue line. As Ted Harris speared Stemkowski in the stomach, Horton wired a shot past Vachon for the Leafs' third goal at 16:57 of the second. Referee Vern Buffey didn't call a penalty on the play. "He didn't see it, but when you're winning, you can put up with it," Imlach said after the game. Stemkowski was left prone on the ice for five minutes, administered to by Bob Haggert.

"That 3–0 win over the Canadiens doesn't mean a thing unless we can add three more victories and regain the Stanley Cup as our Centennial project," blurted Imlach after game two, a matinee contest. "There's no champagne for finishing second, just sour grapes!"

Bower was sensational in goal, and Imlach pointed out one pivotal play that defined the game. "His stop on Claude Larose in the final seconds of the second period was the key," pointed out the coach. "I thought that puck was in, but Johnny's toe came from nowhere and kicked it clear. A goal there might have fired them up, but John's save broke their hearts for the umpteenth time."

John Ferguson wreaked havoc on Bower through the game. "He charged me three times," Johnny recalled, annoyed. "The first time, he got me on the forehead. The second, Larry Hillman lifted his stick and it took the bark off my nose. The third time, he caught me on the collarbone." Deflecting his actions, Ferguson complimented the Leafs' netminder. "Bower was the key to what happened today."

After the game, Johnny claimed that he would be wearing a mask in 1967–68, something he had done in practice since his days in the American Hockey League. "I used an old, clear welder's mask," he said. "Most of the injuries occurred in practice, when you had guys coming into the league trying to make their mark. As a goalie, practice is when you'd let up a bit and maybe not feel as sharp. But I never used it in games until near the end because it got in the way." While Bower vowed to don a mask due to the scrambles and curved sticks that had become fashionable in the NHL, he didn't use one in games until his second-last NHL season, 1968–69.

Bower had deduced that Sawchuk would start, as he had been strong in the playoffs to date and Johnny had played but thirty-five minutes in the seven playoff games to that point, but was surprised and pleased to be tagged by Imlach to start in goal.

Of particular note in game two was the strong work of defence pairings Tim Horton and Allan Stanley, as well as Larry Hillman and Marcel Pronovost. "Playing with Marce was a big break for me. I never saw him play better than he did in those playoffs," recalled Hillman, who had made an excruciating number of trips between the Leafs and their Rochester farm team since 1960. Punch Imlach called Hillman "the most underrated player in the league," and added, "Nobody has worked harder to improve himself."

In losing, the Canadiens had a sixteen-game undefeated streak come to a crashing halt. The Leafs had demonstrated the same determination that earned them the semi-final victory over Chicago.

Pulford Scores in Double-Overtime to Give Leafs Thrilling Victory
Game Three, Stanley Cup Final – Tuesday, April 25, 1967
"For 88 minutes and 26 seconds, two of the world's great shinny teams had traded every trick of their skilled profession," wrote the *Toronto Daily Star*. "The result was a standoff, mostly because a pair of weary warriors — Johnny Bower and Rogatien Vachon — were too stubborn to accept defeat."

Jean Beliveau had endured his worst season in hockey. A broken thumb began his streak of miseries, then just as he had recovered, he caught Stan Mikita's stick in his eye, keeping him out of action for five more weeks. "After returning, I lost my confidence," he admitted. "I couldn't help thinking something might happen to my eyes." Beliveau finished the season with a disappointing total of twelve goals. Yet, he had come alive in the post-season, and opened the scoring at 2:27 with his fourth playoff tally.

The Pappin-Pulford-Stemkowski line would produce all three Leafs' goals on this night. With John Ferguson fuming in the penalty box, Stemkowski scored his fifth goal of the playoffs at 8:39 of the first. Jim Pappin also scored his fifth playoff marker, putting the Leafs ahead 2–1 at 10:34 of the second period. Ferguson made retribution for his earlier sin at 19:10 of the second frame. The second period also featured some fisticuffs, with Montreal's Claude Larose facing Brian Conacher of the Leafs. "I was sick and tired of him always swinging his stick from behind at you," said Conacher. "He's been doing it all season long." The two duelled and the Canadiens' forward skated away with a cut on the forehead that took seven stitches to close.

Both teams were held scoreless in the third, sending the game into sudden-death overtime.

In the first extra frame, Habs' defenceman J. C. Tremblay led the rush, spotting Jean Beliveau on the centre red line and placing a perfect pass onto the captain's blade. The pass stranded Marcel Pronovost up the ice. Beliveau caught Cournoyer breaking for the net and got the puck to "The Roadrunner," who cut inside of Dave Keon and around Larry Hillman, who stumbled on the play. Bower readied himself, and as Cournoyer cut across the net, Johnny expertly poke checked him and knocked the puck off the Montreal forward's stick. Bower's artfully executed move, one he seemingly patented while playing for Toronto, was the turning point of the game. "I knew if I missed, he would go right by me and have an open net for the game-winning goal," said Bower. "I would look terribly foolish." After the game, Cournoyer shrugged, "I knew he was going to beat me and there wasn't a thing I could do about it."

Early in the second overtime period at Maple Leaf Gardens, Allan Stanley's dramatic open-ice hit on Henri Richard knocked the Habs' skilled centre out of the game. Right winger Bobby Rousseau, playing in Richard's place, lost a crucial faceoff to Stemkowski. Bob Pulford cruised behind the Montreal net, glancing at the play in hopes of swooping in to grab a stray puck. "I came around to the right side of their net, then shifted to the opposite side," he explained. "It wasn't intuition or anything. In fact, I was ready to race back in the event the puck was cleared back toward our end." Pappin got possession of the puck and slid it across the front of the net where it eluded several sticks and skates and landed on Pulford's stick. With Vachon on the other side of the net, Pulford was able to nudge the puck into the wide open side of the net at 8:26 of the second overtime period for the Leafs' victory.

"That's probably the most thrilling goal I've scored. It's the first overtime one I've ever had," said Pulford.

The Pulford-Pappin-Stemkowski line had been red hot through the latter half of the regular season and carried that momentum into the playoffs. Pappin (thirteen points) and Stemkowski (ten) were one-two in playoff scoring at that point.

"That was a line that was probably put together because they didn't know what else to do with the three of us," suggested Pulford. None of the three were particular favourites of Imlach. Bob Pulford was a friend of Alan Eagleson, the lawyer and agent despised by the Toronto coach, and Pulford was a union agitator, much to Imlach's chagrin. Jim Pappin had a chip on his shoulder, having been recalled and returned to the Leafs' AHL farm team so often that he had all but worn a path between Rochester and Toronto. Pete Stemkowski, the hulking Winnipeg forward, never felt that he fit in with the Leafs. "The team didn't make me feel all that welcome," he recalled. During Imlach's reign, few rookies cracked the veteran-laden lineup, but Stemkowski was one of the few that did. "No wonder we didn't click, we were a generation apart," he mentioned in '67 by Damien Cox and Bob Stellick. But it was his support of the union that caused Imlach to harbour resentment towards Stemkowski. Nevertheless, the trio clicked. Pulford was a strong, experienced two-way forward. Pappin was a finisher; a forward with a deft scoring touch. And Stemkowski was a punishing hitter and an indefatigable forechecker. "We just seemed to complement each other so well," said Stemkowski.

In spite of the heroics of the trio, Imlach proclaimed that goaltending had been the key to this victory. "Johnny was great. He made six big saves in overtime and a dozen in regular play. But that kid [Vachon] was nearly as good."

The Three Stars of the contest were Bower, Vachon and Davey Keon.

Sawchuk Last-Second Substitute for Bower in Debacle
Game Four, Stanley Cup Final – Thursday, April 27, 1967

Johnny Bower was injured in the pre-game warm-up, stretching to block a Larry Hillman shot. The injury forced Terry Sawchuk to enter the game cold. "I'm not worried about goaltending," admitted Imlach. "Sawchuk stopped the Black Hawks, didn't he? They're tougher shooters than the Canadiens."

Gossip has perennially insisted that Sawchuk was not in game shape when he was forced to step in for Bower, who had pulled his left hamstring. "Sawchuk was so hung over, his hair hurt, his vision blurred and his body felt like lead," wrote Jack Batten in *The Leafs*.

Al Smith was summoned to Maple Leaf Gardens to be Toronto's backup goalie that evening and didn't arrive until the start of the second period. By then, Bower had changed into his street clothes and was watching the game unfold on a small television set in a room across from the team's dressing room. He left for home before the end of the game.

"I was fighting the puck a little bit," Sawchuk told reporters. "I've had better nights and I've had worse nights, but real early, I found out what kind of night I was going to have. The first of Backstrom's goals [scored at 12:25 of the first period] changed direction. The first one by Beliveau [forty-three seconds later] hit the back of my leg and squirted into the goal. On the third, by Richard [at 2:26 of the second period], I got a piece of it with my glove but wasn't fast enough. That's the way it was all night."

Toronto fans jeered Sawchuk every time he touched the puck in the second and third periods.

Mike Walton scored a power play tally at 2:09 of the second, fifteen seconds before Richard's goal. The Leafs got a brief glimmer of hope when Tim Horton added a goal at 12:16, but at 13:41, Jean Beliveau scored his second of the night, then Backstrom earned his second at 15:58. Jimmy Roberts bounced a shot in off Sawchuk's shoulder at 15:17 of the third period to complete the scoring in Toronto's 6–2 loss.

"What is this?" blurted King Clancy on entering a subdued Leafs' dressing room. "You'd think it was a wake. It's not the end of the world, for God's sake. We just didn't play good."

After Punch Imlach quickly exited the building, Clancy was left to face reporters. "Look, it was Terry who got us here," he insisted. "I won't say he played his best game, but just about everybody we had was bad."

"Let's put it this way," began Ralph Backstrom. "In the previous two games, we had ninety-four shots on Bower. Out of all that, we got two goals, so you wouldn't expect us to shed a tear when we saw he [Bower] wasn't in the net."

Gump Worsley, who was pushed out of his role as the Canadiens' starting netminder by Vachon, said, "You look at this 6–2 score and figure it was easy, but if the kid didn't rob Stemkowski and Walton twice while Jacques Laperriere served that penalty in the first three minutes, it could have been a different story. The Leafs came out flying, and a goal then would have ignited them. Hell, our fellows didn't get untracked until the eight-minute mark."

The Three Stars of the game were Jean Beliveau, Ralph Backstrom and Rogie Vachon.

The worst-kept secret in hockey emerged on game day. It was revealed that Red Kelly intended on retiring after the current season to take on the role of head coach with the expansion team in Los Angeles. Kelly was, in fact, the third choice of Jack Kent Cooke, the Canadian who owned the franchise that would become the Los Angeles Kings in 1967–68. Bert Olmstead, coach of the WHL's Vancouver Canucks, declined the offer and would later turn up with the Oakland Seals. Allan Stanley was the second to reject the offer, deciding he wanted to continue playing.

Sawchuk Rebounds with Sensational Effort in Leafs' Win

Game Five, Stanley Cup Final – Saturday, April 29, 1967

After a pair of games in both cities, the series reverted to the Montreal Forum for game five. With the series tied at two games apiece, this was a pivotal contest.

After a poor showing in the previous game, the Maple Leafs were on edge. Imlach did not name his starting goaltender until the afternoon, although later admitted that he intended to come back with Sawchuk all along. Bower was still nursing a hamstring injury, and the coach was not prepared to use the untried Al Smith.

Dick Duff stripped Allan Stanley of the puck in the corner, then passed it out front of the Leafs' net, where Leon Rochefort slapped a shot that deflected off Tim Horton and eluded Sawchuk at 6:03 into the first period. But Sawchuk then stopped each of the following shots, finishing with thirty-seven saves.

At 15:06, Toronto scored its first goal of the night when Jim Pappin picked up a pass from Frank Mahovlich and fired a long shot past Vachon while Montreal was shorthanded.

At 3:07 of the second period, Brian Conacher picked up a greasy rebound from a Red Kelly attempt and lifted it over Vachon for the Leafs' second goal. Then at 12:02, with Red Kelly serving a rare penalty, which he claimed was the result of a dive from Bobby Rousseau, Marcel Pronovost lugged the puck up the left boards and fired a shot from the blue line that seemed to change direction before catching the far side of the net behind Vachon. With Ellis and Duff serving matched minors, Dave Keon scored the Leafs' fourth goal on an outstanding individual effort at 19:27 of the period.

Vachon had surrendered four goals on nineteen shots, and when the teams skated out for the third period, Gump Worsley was in goal for the Canadiens, although he hadn't seen game action since March 12. "I felt nervous until I got the first shot and then I was okay," Gump said. "After all, I haven't played for quite some time." There was no scoring in the third period.

A stunned Forum crowd watched its team skate off the ice on the short end of a 4–1 score, which gave the Toronto Maple Leafs a 3–2 lead in the Stanley Cup derby. Sawchuk's netminding and Keon's relentless skating had made all the difference for the victors.

"I'm not blaming Vachon for the loss," stated Toe Blake. "The defence-men were standing around admiring those Leaf passes and shots most of the second period." Guesting on *Hockey Night in Canada*, Jacques Plante said of Vachon, "He was not sharp. Two of the Toronto goals were from forty feet out and on the ice. You shouldn't get beaten on those kind."

At the other end of the ice, the Leafs' netminder was named the game's first Star.

"Sawchuk played a terrific game, but I wasn't surprised. I expected it," said Imlach. Marcel Pronovost was the second Star and Tim Horton the third.

Leafs' captain, George Armstrong, commented, "Let's say we made a hell of a down payment on the Cup by winning that game on their ice. But we're still that big win away and I've found it the toughest victory to earn."

Maple Leafs Win Fourth Stanley Cup of Decade!
Game Six, Stanley Cup Final – Tuesday, May 2, 1967

Viewers warmed up their television sets and were ready, anxiously waiting for the beginning of game six of the Stanley Cup final. "From Maple Leaf Gardens in Toronto, the Stanley Cup playoffs between the Toronto Maple Leafs and Montreal Canadiens, brought to you by Molsons," began the *Hockey Night in Canada* announcer, and hockey fans settled in for a night guaranteed to be exciting.

While there was no doubt that Terry Sawchuk would start in goal for Toronto, curiously, the Leafs had three netminders skating in that familiar clockwise oval — Sawchuk, Bower and Al Smith. Meanwhile, Montreal coach Toe Blake had a decision to make: in what could be the most important game of the season, would he ride on the back of the goalie who had carried the team to the final, or go with the vast experience of the netminder who had helped them win back-to-back Stanley

Cup championships in 1965 and 1966? Then, the Montreal goalkeeping speculation ended. "It's Gump Worsley in the net," announced Frank Selke Jr.

Commentator Bob Goldham expounded on the decision, saying, "The real pressure is on The Gumper. Being an old pro, I don't think we should worry too much about his performance." Selke agreed, stating, "Bob, that show he put on in Montreal on in the third period on Saturday night, do you think that will get him up for this hockey game tonight?" Goldham responded, "If he hadn't been in, I would have been more concerned for him, but he'll be all right." When Frank Selke asked Goldham about Terry Sawchuk starting for Toronto, he simply said, "We got two of the best." And that was borne out over the next sixty minutes of action.

With the game being played in Toronto in front of an audience that included Prime Minister Lester B. Pearson, Punch Imlach showed such confidence in a Maple Leafs' win that he made neither travel nor hotel arrangements in Montreal for a possible game seven.

Prior to the contest, sports writers congregated around the Leafs' coach for a comment. "After ninety-six games, I'm all talked out," he said, laughing. "The team will have to do the talking in this one."

But Imlach did address his team in the dressing room, discarding hell-fire and brimstone for a surprisingly sentimental talk. "Some of you have been with me for nine years," he said. "It has been said that I stuck with the old men so long we couldn't possibly win the Stanley Cup. For some of you, it's a farewell. Go out there and put that puck down their throats!"

While Terry Sawchuk skated to his sentry post in the Toronto goal, Gump Worsley, to the surprise of few, ventured into the Montreal crease. Although he had only played one complete game and portions of two others in three months, his experience made the decision for the Canadiens' coach.

The first period went scoreless in what was becoming a classic nail-biter of a contest. Then, in the second period, Jacques Laperriere took a slapshot from the left point that hit Allan Stanley and cleared the Leafs' zone. Bill Hewitt described the action. "A race for it. Kelly goes after it.

Going over the line with Ellis. Kelly shoots. Ellis shoots. He scores! Ellis got the rebound!" Red Kelly, playing what would be his final NHL game, corralled the puck, and with Ron Ellis accompanying him, had only Terry Harper of the Canadiens back to defend Worsley. "The Montreal defenceman hesitated, then started to back up," recalled Kelly. "I got the puck and saw Ronnie coming down on my left side. I tried to pull the defenceman over so I could get the puck to Ronnie, but he stayed between us. I had to shoot. Worsley made the save but couldn't control the puck, and Ronnie barged in and scored on the rebound."

The opening goal, scored at 6:25, was a big goal for Toronto. "It gave us our start and got the fans behind us," said Ellis. "I thought we controlled the game from that point on. The team realized they were a period and a half away from the Cup. Everybody just reached down and played their hearts out."

Later in the period, Hewitt described the second Leafs' goal. "Larose brings it back with Ferguson. Over the line. Pulford is there to get the rebound. Up to Pappin with Stemkowski, they are over the line. To Pappin, closing in. Pappin goes to the wing, centred it. He scores! Stemkowski! Pappin shot it and hit Stemkowski." With Harper and Stemkowski fencing in front of Worsley, Jim

Pappin put the puck in the back of the Montreal net at 19:24. "I was trying to backhand a pass to Pete Stemkowski in the goalmouth," he later explained. "The puck hit [Jacques] Laperriere's skate and caromed into the net. Pete told the referee right away that it was my goal, but they gave him credit for it. Later, they corrected it and I wound up with lucky seven for the playoffs."

During the second intermission of the radio broadcast, Dan Kelly and Jim Chorley hosted a discussion about possible candidates for the Conn Smythe Trophy as the most valuable playoff performer. It was the third spring that the trophy was to be awarded. Guests on the panel were Rudy Pilous, former Chicago coach and recently named general manager of the expansion Oakland Seals, and Emile Francis, the coach and general manager of the New York Rangers.

Before the game, the National Hockey League announced that the 1967 recipient of the Conn Smythe Trophy would not be announced or presented until two days after the Stanley Cup presentation. The league's board of governors believed that two presentations in one evening were too much.

Pilous stated that Sawchuk and Bower were deserving, but he believed that either Peter Stemkowski or Dave Keon should win it — Stemkowski for his punishing bodychecks and scoring and Keon for his all-round play.

Emile Francis decreed that he would vote for Keon because he had done it all for Toronto — backcheck, forecheck, winning faceoffs, goals and defence.

Dan Kelly said that if it hadn't been for Sawchuk, the Leafs wouldn't even be in the finals, and added that Bower had been strong in replacing Sawchuk. He believed there should be co-recipients, with both Toronto goalkeepers sharing the trophy.

Pilous disagreed, stating that the Smythe Trophy should not be awarded to a goalie who only played half the games, and again put forward that Keon should win, having extended himself in every game of the playoffs while doing everything to help his team win.

Francis then said that the Leafs could win with either Sawchuk or Bower, but they couldn't win the Cup without Keon. "He is one of the finest centres in the National Hockey League because he can do so many things for you. Being as quick as he is, he is a fellow who is back in your end, he's getting that pass, he's carrying the play out of it. On many occasions throughout the playoffs you see this guy killing penalties, taking his regular turn and coming up winning those big faceoffs."

Back into the action, with Sawchuk performing miracles in goal, his teammates played a solid positional game that held the Canadiens at bay throughout the contest. The game became increasingly more intense for Leafs' fans when Dick Duff showed the Leafs some of his best moves, dancing past Tim Horton and Allan Stanley and then throwing a backhand shot past Sawchuk at 5:28 of the third period. "Horton, over the line," Bill Hewitt told viewers in describing the play. "Takes a shot and Worsley caught it. Harris, a pass up to Duff. Duff coming up over the line, right around Horton. Gets right in front. A shot; he scores! Dick Duff has scored for the Canadiens." Brian McFarlane commented, "A beautiful play by Dick Duff. A real solo effort."

The contest had evolved into a gripping duel as Toronto hung on by playing a stubborn defensive game. Montreal was unable to penetrate the Maple Leafs' zone with any authority.

At 19:05, Larry Hillman fired the puck the length of the ice, and the Maple Leafs were called for icing. As the players retreated to the Toronto zone, Montreal coach Toe Blake waved Worsley over to the bench for a sixth attacker.

Imlach met the challenge by putting his old guard out on the ice: George Armstrong, Red Kelly and Bob Pulford at forward and Tim Horton and Allan Stanley on defence. Each one had played a key role in all three previous Stanley Cup championships. "I think I knew at that moment that that was our swan song," remembered Pulford. "That was the swan song of his dynasty."

Defenceman Allan Stanley was assigned to take the faceoff. While contemporary thought would question a defenceman taking a crucial faceoff, it was a strategy that Imlach used regularly through the decade when the faceoff was in the defensive zone. The coach expected his defenceman to tie up the centreman in the faceoff circle, at which time a forward would dart in and pick up the puck. In game six alone, Imlach always employed Hillman, Horton, Pronovost and Stanley to take defensive zone faceoffs. Hillman took ten draws, Stanley eight, Horton seven and Marcel Pronovost took four faceoffs. Stanley, in fact, was the team's best faceoff man that night, winning five of his eight draws, losing just two and tying the other, so there was no question that the veteran Leafs' defenceman would line up against Jean Beliveau in one of the most memorable faceoffs in Maple Leafs' history.

Bill Hewitt described the action for *Hockey Night in Canada* viewers. "So, it's six attackers for Montreal, trailing the Leafs two to one. They've got Cournoyer, Beliveau, Roberts, Ferguson, Henri Richard and Jacques Laperriere. Now then, Backstrom comes out." The players focus, some gliding, others poised and ready to play as workers scrape an egg off the ice. "All set for the faceoff now, Canadiens using six attackers. The net is empty; fifty-five seconds left. Armstrong goes over to the bench, and it's electrifying here at Maple Leaf Gardens at the moment."

Stanley coasted into the faceoff circle to the left of Sawchuk in the Toronto crease and looked across to see Jean Beliveau, Montreal's finest centre. "Beliveau is standing out there in the faceoff circle waiting for our faceoff guy," recalled Stanley. John Ferguson skated in to Beliveau and said something, while the fans booed. "So, here I come," Stanley remembered. "On the way out, I skated out very slowly. You know, Beliveau is an expert. I got out there and [Red] Kelly was standing over to the right of the circle. I think everybody has to put on a little show, so I asked Red to move to the right side of the faceoff circle instead of the left. I think I was just trying to waste a little time to figure out what the hell I was going to do." Horton moved back in front of Sawchuk, Armstrong is behind Kelly and Pulford is on the left at the boards with Cournoyer.

Stanley recalled his strategy. "I determined that I was going to take one half-swipe at the puck, play [Beliveau's] stick and then run the son of a gun right out of there. I was pretty good at anticipating the drop, which I did. I just took one swipe. I got his stick and then I ran him right between the legs and ran him out of there. So, the puck came back a little bit, which meant I got the draw."

With Beliveau hollering "faceoff interference" to referee John Ashley, Bill Hewitt described the play for *Hockey Night in Canada* viewers. "The puck is dropped. Kelly, up to Pulford. Pulford gets it up to Armstrong. Armstrong waits, takes a shot...he scores!"

While Bill Hewitt was doing the play-by-play on TV, his father, Foster, described the play to his radio audience. "The puck is dropped. It rolls to Kelly, who tipped it to Pulford. Pulford gets it over to Armstrong. Armstrong gets a shot at the empty net....scores! Armstrong has scored what will be the deciding goal. Armstrong, the captain, scores the third goal for the Maple Leafs and that makes it three to one, so that strategy by Toe Blake has boomeranged. And the Leafs have just about salted away the Stanley Cup with that shot by Armstrong from Pulford when the Leafs got the draw. "

Brian McFarlane described the activity on the ice for the TV audience. "A wild finish! The players jump on the ice. Everybody is up and standing and cheering. All the Leafs' fans here at the Gardens go wild — programs on the ice. The players swarmed over the boards. This game is not finished, but that would appear to be the insurance goal the Leafs were looking for. Very, very important faceoff. Sawchuk at the far end of the rink with his head way down, over his goal stick, as he feels that relief of tension and pressure."

The Maple Leafs held off the Canadiens as the seconds evaporated, and the Toronto Maple Leafs' faithful helped the Hewitts count down the time remaining: "Seven, six, five, four, three, two, one. The game is over and the Leafs have won the Stanley Cup! They are mobbing each other."

While Armstrong's goal was not the Stanley Cup-winning tally, it is the goal remembered by fans of the Leafs' dynasty. The goal, though crucial and conclusive, was, like its shooter, more solid than spectacular. That insurance marker enabled the man who shot the puck to bask in the limelight of the most satisfying Stanley Cup triumph of his long, unselfish career.

Johnny Bower was the first one off the Leafs' bench to congratulate Sawchuk, followed immediately by Pappin and Walton. As the final buzzer sounded, a teenaged boy grabbed the stick from J. C. Tremblay and skidded across the ice. Tremblay skated after the boy, knocked him down and retrieved his stick. "That is the first time Tremblay hit anybody this season," joked a Montreal sportswriter.

When Punch Imlach joined the embracing players, Peter Stemkowski grabbed the coach's fedora and flung it in celebration.

The teams lined up near centre ice and in one of the great time-honoured traditions of playoff hockey, shook hands. Pronovost, Bower and Kelly led the way for Toronto.

The Stanley Cup was carried to a table at centre, and NHL president Clarence Campbell gripped the microphone and began the presentation. "Ladies and gentlemen, it is now my very pleasant duty and responsibility to present the Stanley Cup to the Maple Leaf Hockey Club for the eleventh time." George Armstrong skated in, joined by his son Brian, and accepted hockey's most prestigious trophy. The captain smiled, tipped the Cup and then held it over his head. Armstrong then waved his teammates over to enjoy their victory.

Neither Bob Baun nor Terry Sawchuk waited for Campbell's Stanley Cup presentation, retiring to the dressing room instead. But the two had distinctly different reasons for their actions. "I just didn't feel part of the team or the organization at that particular time," admitted Baun. "I think that was probably my competitive spirit or might have been an immaturity, I'm not sure." For Sawchuk, it was the end of a glorious season marred by injury and thoughts of retirement. "It may sound corny, but this has to be the greatest thrill of my life," he stated. "I've had a lot of wonderful moments in hockey and other Stanley Cups, but nothing to equal this." He reminisced about the season. "First, I had that back operation. Then, Punch had to talk me out of walking out of training camp and quitting hockey. Next, there was my physical collapse in the Montreal Forum shower in mid-season. I wondered if I'd ever play again. And it wound up in a Stanley Cup win, so I guess it was all worthwhile. It'd be nice to bow out a winner, the first star in a Cup-winning game. I have a wife, six kids and another on the way and I miss them very much during the hockey season."

As George Armstrong exited the ice surface, he stumbled on a cord and almost fumbled the Stanley Cup. Looking on, Jim Pappin helped his captain secure his grip.

The Leafs' dressing room was bedlam. Beer and champagne flowed readily, and Jim Pappin and Mike Walton carried their coach, suit and all, into the shower. Right behind, Ron Ellis hustled King Clancy in for his soaking. "I think there was maybe less antics than the previous times we won," recalled Allan Stanley. "More than anything else, we were just so satisfied, especially us old guys. Everybody told us we were at the end, that hockey was changing and that we were too old, but we proved them wrong. We won the thing one more time. I never got more satisfaction out of anything in my career. I still think about those games today."

Upstairs in the gondola, Foster Hewitt and Don Chevrier announced the game's Three Stars for their radio audience: Sawchuk, Keon and Beliveau. Foster claimed that when Toe Blake pulled Worsley for a sixth attacker, it was "curtains for the Montreal Canadiens for the Stanley Cup."

Tim Horton was interviewed by Ward Cornell for *Hockey Night in Canada*. "I think it was one of the happiest moments I can remember in hockey," Horton said. "When Army scored that goal, I actually thought I was going to start crying, there were tears starting to go down my cheeks, and it's never happened that way before."

Punch Imlach noted the importance Horton had played in the success of the Maple Leafs during the sixties. "I would say that Horton, a little more than any other player, was the key to the success we had. He was always there, always the same, always giving the effort, the best he had, every night."

Imlach also commended his "over-the-hill" squad. "They're the best bunch of players I've ever had," he said. "And great guys too. We won it with the old guys." He quickly added, "Don't forget the Canadiens. They played a hell of a game, too. They didn't quit, not for one second."

The coach took a moment to take in the magnitude of the team's achievement, savouring the moment. "This is the sweetest of my four Stanley Cup wins as manager-coach," he beamed. "A lot of wise guys said this team wasn't good enough, that we couldn't beat Chicago or the Canadiens. Well, we shoved it right down their throats." He added, "We beat two great teams, so we have to be a great team. What's more, it's the guttiest gang I've ever been associated with. Look what we overcame — a shaky start while youngsters were blending with the veterans, a ten-game losing streak, injuries to our goalkeepers, my trip to the hospital and injuries to Larry Jeffrey and Bower in the playoffs. But we sure as hell ruined the Canadiens' plans to display the Cup at Expo 67 and completed a successful Centennial project of our own."

RK	NUMBER	PLAYER	POS	AGE	GP	G	A	PTS	PIM
		1966–67 Playoff Scoring							
1	18	Jim Pappin	RW	27	12	7	8	15	12
2	12	Peter Stemkowski	C	23	12	5	7	12	20
3	20	Bob Pulford	LW	30	12	1	10	11	12
4	27	Frank Mahovlich	LW	29	12	3	7	10	8
5	7	Tim Horton	D	37	12	3	5	8	25
6	14	Dave Keon	C	26	12	3	5	8	0
7	16	Mike Walton	C	22	12	4	3	7	2
8	22	Brian Conacher	LW	25	12	3	2	5	21
9	4	Red Kelly	D/C	39	12	0	5	5	2
10	10	George Armstrong	RW	36	9	2	1	3	6
11	8	Ron Ellis	RW	22	12	2	1	3	4
12	2	Larry Hillman	D	29	12	1	2	3	0
13	26	Allan Stanley	D	40	12	0	2	2	10
14	3	Marcel Pronovost	D	36	12	1	0	1	8
15	18	Larry Jeffrey	LW	26	6	0	1	1	4
16	21	Bob Baun	D	30	10	0	0	0	4
17	1	Johnny Bower	G	42	4	0	0	0	2
18	24	Aut Erickson	D	29	1	0	0	0	2
19	25	Milan Marcetta	C	30	3	0	0	0	0
20	30	Terry Sawchuk	G	37	10	0	0	0	0
21	23	Eddie Shack	LW	29	8	0	0	0	8
		TEAM TOTALS			12	35	59	94	150

In defeat, Montreal captain Jean Beliveau heaped praise on the Leafs, specifically Sawchuk. "He came up with the key saves and gave them the time to get ahead." Henri Richard noted, "My biggest disappointment in hockey."

Toe Blake also acknowledged the role played by Sawchuk and Bower. "Leafs' goalies won this series for them," confirmed the Montreal coach. "I'm not going to beef. There was a time this season when it looked as though we wouldn't even make the playoffs!"

Through a toothless grin, Dave Keon said, "We beat the Canadiens the only way we can — playing tough hockey."

Playoff Netminding											
RK	NUMBER	PLAYER	POS	AGE	GP	MIN	W	L	GA	GAA	SO
1	30	Terry Sawchuk	G	37	10	565	6	4	25	2.65	0
2	1	Johnny Bower	G	42	4	183	2	0	5	1.64	1
		TEAM TOTALS			12	748	8	4	30	2.41	1

Leafs' captain George Armstrong suggested, "In past years, we've maybe had teams with more ability, but certainly we've never had a team that had more fight, more desire or determination."

Jim Pappin, who had scored the Stanley Cup-winning goal, led all playoff performers in scoring with fifteen points — seven goals and eight assists. Pappin, who had finally been given a chance to show his considerable NHL-level skills, hosted a party for the team at his home after the game.

Pappin's linemates were second and third in playoff scoring. Peter Stemkowski collected twelve points (five goals and seven assists) while Bob Pulford contributed one goal and ten assists for eleven points, tied with Montreal's Jean Beliveau.

The line of Pulford/Stemkowski/Pappin had been superb. "That was our strong line," said Ron Ellis. "That line got a lot of big goals for us that year." Yet, in the summer prior to this season, Imlach almost let Stemkowski get away. "It had to be between Stemkowski and Orland Kurtenbach," he remembered. "We had to give it a lot of thought. We decided to keep Stemkowski and let Kurt go." During the Stanley Cup final, Imlach revealed that he saw Stemkowski emerging as a leader. "He could become as important to the Leafs as Ted Kennedy was when he played for Hap Day and King Clancy. Teeder was a great one."

Although the NHL vowed to keep the winner of the Conn Smythe under wraps until 5:30 the next day, it was learned during the celebration that Dave Keon had been selected as recipient of the award. Voting was done by NHL governors or their representatives before they left the arena. Foster Hewitt wasn't surprised. "I think he was the top player in the playoffs this season."

For several players, it was their fourth Stanley Cup win: George Armstrong, Bobby Baun, Johnny Bower, Larry Hillman, Tim Horton, Red Kelly, David Keon, Frank Mahovlich, Bob Pulford, Eddie Shack and Allan Stanley. Also enjoying a fourth championship were owners Stafford Smythe, Harold Ballard and John Bassett; coach and general manager Punch Imlach; assistant general manager King Clancy; head scout Bob Davidson; trainer Bob Haggert and assistant trainer Tommy Nayler. It was the first Stanley Cup win for Brian Conacher, Ron Ellis, Aut Erickson, Larry Jeffrey, Milan Marcetta, Peter Stemkowski and Mike Walton.

Most members of that Stanley Cup championship regard the spring of 1967 as the zenith of their NHL careers.

Allan Stanley proudly announced his career highlight. "The most satisfying was, of course, the last one, 1967, because we were a third-place team and there were two teams that had a better team than we did — Chicago and Montreal. Nobody expected us to do anything except us. That's the finest example of team play that I've ever experienced in all my career. Everybody got honest with themselves, to say what they had to do to win the game. Talking about team play. That's the finest example I ever saw."

Frank Mahovlich echoed his teammate's comment. "1967 was a highlight. That was a big one because Montreal had won the two previous years, and that was Expo '67, so it was quite a surprise."

Any number of players could have been regarded as instrumental for the Maple Leafs' Cinderella season. Bob Haggert, the team's trainer during the decade, had his own thoughts. "The biggest asset in '67 was Terry Sawchuk. Sawchuk and Bower were unbeatable in that playoff; the best two-goalie system in the history of the league. When we needed goaltending, we got it. That's what made it happen.

Larry Hillman and Marcel Pronovost had been superb on defence for the Leafs during the spring of 1967. The tandem was on the ice for just one even-strength goal throughout the entire playoffs. "Pronovost, who had played on some great Detroit teams, probably had the best playoff he ever had in his life," recalled Bob Haggert. Hillman, always a solid performer, had spent the better part of the 1960s trying to crack a Leafs' defence corps comprised of Baun, Brewer, Horton and Stanley. "He was a good, hard-working kid and he was kind of a fringe NHLer," mentioned Imlach. "The best games he ever played were in sixty-seven, and it was with Pronovost. He and Pronovost played better than Stanley and Horton in those two series."

Pronovost, who had won four championships with the Red Wings, was enjoying his first Stanley Cup win in blue and white. "The big thing on that hockey club was that it was a self-taught hockey club, in the sense that Imlach didn't do any teaching," he explained. "He motivated and disciplined and it was a combination of experience, veterans and some few youngsters that reached a peak because of associating with these veterans. We would play one game at a time and not look any further and not worry any more than that. The easiest game to play is when you have the puck. With the puck, it's a pleasure. Without the puck, it's work, because you have to pick up the guy and you have to react, constantly, to the situation."

George Armstrong cut right to the point in describing why the Leafs won the Stanley Cup in 1967. "It was a fine blend of old and young, plus superb goaltending. We might not have outplayed them, but we outscored them and that's what counts."

Ron Ellis was subdued in spite of enjoying his first Stanley Cup celebration. "At the time, I didn't allow myself to really experience that moment the way I should have. My personality, my makeup, had me worrying about making the team the next year. That's where my mind was."

Red Kelly was thirty-nine years old and in the twilight of his career during the 1966–67 season. Like Ellis, while the champagne and cheering were transpiring around him, his mind was also elsewhere. "That was the fourth Cup for us and my eighth," he stated proudly. "We were the 'over-the-hill-gang.' Toronto offered me a four-year contract to stay and play for the Leafs, but I realized I couldn't do what I used to do. I used to be able to overpower guys just by my skating. If I had to beat a guy, I could beat a guy. I found that I wasn't able to do that anymore.

They said, 'You could be a ticket taker or this or that,' but I thought, 'No, I'd rather go out on top. We had just won and I wanted to go out when I wanted to go out rather [than] when someone tells you you can't cut it anymore." The rumours were soon confirmed. Red Kelly retired and was headed to Los Angeles to coach the fledgling Kings. "What we had there will always be something we won't ever forget because those were really good times for the Toronto Maple Leafs and for all the players. They were the best of times. There were trials and tribulations that the players went through together beginning in 1958. I was not yet there, to go through that. I just came when it was all gelling. I think that what we went through is something that we'll always treasure."

Dave Keon, who had excelled during the playoffs and would soon be rewarded for his efforts, also commented on the Leafs' victorious season. "In '67, we played well, then we didn't play very well. There was a great deal of turmoil during the year. We had a team that was fairly old, and I think that everybody seemed to peak at the same time. We had some injuries, but everyone contributed. But in the playoffs, we were the best team for about a month at the end of the year, and that's really what it boiled down to."

"It was the end of the run," added Bob Haggert wistfully. "Players got older, players got traded, players would go through expansion. In my opinion, it was the end of the glory years for the Toronto Maple Leafs."

There were few secrets in the nitty gritty city, and the name of the player who would be awarded the Conn Smythe Trophy was the worst-kept secret of all.

In a reception held Wednesday, May 3, in the Hot Stove Lounge of Maple Leaf Gardens, Don Ruck, the newly named publicity director for the National Hockey League, was on hand to deliver the Conn Smythe

Trophy to the most valuable player in the 1967 playoffs. Ruck's boss, Clarence Campbell, was consumed with league business in Montreal and was unable to attend.

Six league governors or representatives cast ballots for the MVP after the Stanley Cup championship contest. NHL president Clarence Campbell took the sealed envelopes to Montreal, where they were counted. One ballot indicated Terry Sawchuk as the most valuable playoff performer, but five selected Dave Keon, the sprightly centre of the Stanley Cup champion Toronto Maple Leafs, as recipient of the prestigious Conn Smythe Trophy.

Looking on in support of their teammate were Punch Imlach, Harold Ballard, King Clancy, George Armstrong, Johnny Bower, Aut Erickson, Tim Horton, Red Kelly, Jim Pappin and Allan Stanley. Stafford Smythe was delayed in arriving, as he had been at the airport meeting his daughter on a flight from England, but showed up in support after the presentation.

Humbly, Keon commented, "This is a great honour for me, but there are eighteen players on this hockey team. They deserve to have their name on it along with mine."

"It was certainly a wise choice," said Punch Imlach. "He's on our power play, he kills penalties and takes a regular shift. Keon is a competitor who wants to win. He gives one hundred per cent all the time. He plays with a bulldog tenacity. That's the only way he knows how to play the game. What more can you ask?" Keon scored three goals and had five assists during the post-season.

Dave Keon earned $1,500 as the Smythe award winner. In addition, he received $500 as runner-up to Stan Mikita for the Lady Byng Trophy as the league's most gentlemanly player. The bonus payday continued as, like each of his teammates, Keon earned $5,250 as Stanley Cup champion and $750 for the team's third-place finish during the regular season.

Team owner Stafford Smythe and his wife Dorothea hosted a team party at their Etobicoke home the night after the Cup win. The Smythes always staged outstanding Stanley Cup parties, where the music was live and loud, the food was excellent and the beverages flowed freely.

Ron Ellis allowed himself the opportunity to celebrate. "We went to Stafford Smythe's house for a party. It was fantastic, just to be with your teammates and experience such an accomplishment." Bob Baun attended, but more out of his affection for the Smythe family than to revel in the team's win. It would be the only team celebration in which he would participate that year.

The party had its share of hijinks. "Horton and Pully were carrying Stafford, pretending they were going to throw him into the pool — clothes, wallet, watch — the f*%kin' works," laughed Shack. "So while they're making a big show for everybody, I came runnin' up behind and pushed all three of them in. Uh-oh! I don't give a shit about Smythe — serves him right for sending me to Rochester. And Pully, who cares? But Timmy was a handful. When he drank, everybody drank. When he told a joke, everybody laughed. The best thing to do when he got pissed was to stay out of his way. Now I'm lookin' over my shoulder for goddamned days right, knowin' Horton's gonna get me. But he never got the chance. I got traded."

Less than two weeks later, on May 15, 1967, Shack was peddled to the Bruins for Murray Oliver and $100,000.

The City of Toronto feted their championship hockey team for the fourth time that decade with a celebration on Friday, May 5. Municipal leaders decided to stage the parade and civic ceremony later in the afternoon in order to attract more school children, although this plan didn't work as well as had been hoped. Earlier ceremonies had taken place at noon, a perfect time for the downtown business core to witness the event on their lunch hour.

The three previous Stanley Cup parades had culminated on the steps of what is now known as Old City Hall, a magnificent edifice built in 1899 that stood conveniently for civic parades at the north end of Bay Street at

Queen. But in 1961, a new city hall was being constructed across the street on the northwest corner of Queen and Bay. The distinctive landmark was opened in 1965, so the Toronto Maple Leafs' Stanley Cup parade ended this time at the impressive new city hall.

Each of the three prior Stanley Cup parades for the Maple Leafs had been presided over by a different mayor. In 1962, it was Mayor Nathan Phillips. In 1963, Mayor Donald Summerville was the host. In 1964, it was Mayor Phil Givens, and in 1967, Mayor William Dennison welcomed the Stanley Cup champions to city hall.

The victory cavalcade commenced from Maple Leaf Gardens at 4:00 p.m., proceeded south on Church Street to Wellington, west to Bay Street and then, amidst tickertape and cheering, north on Bay Street to city hall.

The parade was led by a phalanx of mounted police constables, followed by the 48th Highlanders. The pipe-and-drum troupe have been intrinsically tied to the Maple Leafs for decades, and to this day, perform on-ice at each season's home opener.

While an estimated twenty-five-thousand fans attended the civic reception, and with Nathan Phillips Square all but full three hours before the parade began, it was still the smallest crowd to attend a Stanley Cup celebration in Toronto.

Each Maple Leafs' player rode in an open convertible with their name attached to the side of the car. The players wore blue and white carnations on their lapels. Peter Stemkowski added a yellow lei to his ensemble.

Captain George Armstrong, clutching the Stanley Cup, rode in the lead car along with Stafford Smythe and Harold Ballard. All the team members were out in force to enjoy the adulation. All but one. Played sparingly, Bobby Baun dressed for every game against Montreal but appeared in just one of the six games. He felt he had not contributed to the championship, and steered clear of the parade, instead choosing to take his sons fishing at Charleston Lake, north of Brockville. Many of his teammates had tried to persuade him to attend, but he refused. "You know what great pride Bob has," explained his wife, Sallie. "And that pride has been hurt."

After driving up Bay Street with the sidewalks lined with fans and tickertape swirling between the columns of office buildings, the players were officially greeted by Mayor William Dennison and Metro Chairman William Allen.

Mayor Dennison began by saying, "Such receptions have become a tradition, and we are proud to honour this team." He casually mentioned that he had, at one time, been a pretty fair hockey player while growing up in Pembroke.

Dennison continued, "It's a great win for Toronto. Never have they deserved such a reception as they do today in this, Canada's Centennial year."

After a short ceremony on a platform in front of city hall, Mayor Dennison presented Toronto's captain with a gold watch, engraved with his name and the inscription: "In honour of winning the Stanley Cup, the world championship of hockey. City Hall. May 5, 1967. William Dennison, Mayor." The mayor also announced that the rest of the team members would receive their watches at a later date, as they were out being engraved.

George Armstrong stepped up to the microphone and said, "We're especially proud to win this year. All of the experts said we couldn't win. They said Chicago had too much scoring and Montreal had too much skating. But they forgot the most important ability of all — the ability to work and dig in when it counted."

Those assembled in the civic square cheered animatedly as the Canadian flag, created in blue and white rather than the standard red and white, was hoisted up the flagpole in Nathan Phillips Square, while fireworks exploded all around.

Wives, girlfriends and family members had watched the proceedings from an overhead ramp, but joined the team in the council chambers as the players and coach signed Toronto's Centennial register. Short speeches were made by Punch Imlach and Stafford Smythe.

Afterwards, the team and their guests were driven to Maple Leaf Gardens for a staff celebration. Each staff member, and his or her family, had their picture taken with the Stanley Cup and was given an extra week's paid vacation courtesy of Stafford Smythe.

At the Gardens, players and team officials were told plans for their Stanley Cup rings. First-time Leafs' winners would receive a Stanley Cup ring, while repeat winners would have the diamond in their existing ring enlarged.

A surprise also unfolded at Maple Leaf Gardens. Terry Sawchuk was awarded the Air Canada Trophy for "outstanding team work in the Stanley Cup playoffs," and with it, a flight for two. Why a Toronto MVP trophy was presented to Sawchuk while the Conn Smythe Trophy was awarded to Dave Keon is curious, but a bigger mystery is, whatever became of this award? Maple Leaf Sports and Entertainment has never heard of it and Air Canada could find nothing in their files. The Hockey Hall of Fame has no record of it. The Sawchuk family is aware that Terry won the award and believes that the Leafs players themselves voted on the recipient of the award. On closer inspection, the Air Canada Trophy is actually engraved as the Trans-Canada Airlines Trophy, leading historians to believe that the trophy might have been awarded prior to January 1965, when Trans-Canada changed its name to Air Canada, and yet newspapers for earlier years make no mention of either a Trans-Canada Airlines Trophy or an Air Canada Trophy. After Sawchuk was awarded the trophy in 1967, it was never presented again.

The players soaked up the fun and congratulations received through the day. Most had made plans to head back to their homes, where jobs that helped pay household bills awaited.

After the parade, Ron Ellis left his teammates and joined his family at Sandhurst Vacationland, a tourist resort they owned just north of Huntsville, Ontario. "The Stanley Cup victory only happened once for me, and I should have taken the time to really enjoy the moment with my wife and my teammates. I left the Stanley Cup celebration to cut grass amongst the blackflies."

At a dinner for the 1966 Stanley Cup champion Montreal Canadiens, coach Toe Blake vowed that the Stanley Cup would return to Montreal in

1967, specifically to be placed prominently in the Quebec pavilion at Expo 67. "We were very disappointed," admitted Jean Beliveau. "We knew that Toe had made that promise to Mayor Drapeau. But honestly, he had said both their goalies, Bower and Terry Sawchuk, beat us."

"[The Canadiens] were so sure they were going to win that they had the Stanley Cup in the Quebec pavilion at Expo 67," smirked Punch Imlach. "They had to take it out and put it in the Ontario one. And of course I loved that."

The Stanley Cup, won by the Toronto Maple Leafs, was publicly displayed at Expo 67, in the Ontario exhibit, during July of that year.

SLAPSHOTS AND SNAPSHOTS
STANLEY CUP CAPER

Most of us dream about enjoying the fifteen minutes of fame espoused by Andy Warhol. For one young man, that fifteen minutes of fame came in Maple Leaf Gardens on May 2, 1967.

"I was on my way to Montreal for a summer job at Expo '67," began the twenty-year-old, who'd left his home in Prince Albert, Saskatchewan. With a coveted ticket in hand to game six of the Stanley Cup final between Toronto and Montreal, he watched as the Maple Leafs toppled the Canadiens, 3–1.

"I had told the people back home, 'I'm going to try to get on TV!'" As the period wound down, the young man formulated a plan that would allow him to say hi to his pals back in Saskatchewan. He fidgeted as the crowd counted down the final seconds to the Leafs' fourth Stanley Cup championship that decade. "At the end of the game, I had my father's business card for CKBI Radio, so I went down [to ice level] and showed it to the guy and said, 'I'm here,' and he said, 'Yeah, go ahead.'"

Clarence Campbell, the NHL's president, stood at centre ice, the Stanley Cup placed on a table to his right. He called for Toronto's captain, George Armstrong, to proceed to centre ice to accept Lord Stanley's legacy. The Chief skated over, his son in tow shuffling alongside. Armstrong tipped the Cup slightly and held it aloft, sharing the glory with his son, the fans in the arena and those watching on television from coast to coast. The captain then waved over his teammates to join him at centre ice.

"In those days, they didn't parade around with the Stanley Cup. They all just gathered around it, and as they did that, I just went in there," said the young man, reflecting on his daring intrusion. As the crowd roared, the Maple Leafs huddled around the Stanley Cup for the photographers. The bespectacled young man, looking dapper, was living a dream as he jostled in amongst the victors. Standing just behind the kneeling captain, who was cradling the Stanley Cup, the pride of Prince Albert stood shoulder to shoulder with Milan Marcetta on his right and Larry Jeffrey, dressed in civilian clothes and hobbling on crutches, to his left. "I could hear the odd player say, 'Who is this?' but I just stood there."

As the flashes turned the cavernous Gardens into an explosion of light, the mystery man stared straight into the television cameras and beamed. Allan Stanley gripped the trophy to the young man's right, with Tim Horton directly behind and goalkeeper Al Smith craning his neck to get a glimpse of the Stanley Cup. The blond-haired fan took a moment to wave to the crowd as several members of the team began to leave the ice. Pete Stemkowski and George Armstrong collaborated on lifting the Cup and prepared to carry it to their dressing room, which was prepared to host a celebration. Armstrong then took control and skated towards the exit, when Jim Pappin reached over to embrace the Cup. As he did, and as the ice was clearing of Leafs, our young fan turned towards the camera and gave one final wave to his friends back home in Prince Albert.

"There were many calls to my folks back in Prince Albert," laughed the mystery fan. "My father said that he spent more than two hours with his hand on the phone and he would lift it up and say, 'We saw him. Thanks a lot.' He wouldn't even take his hand off the phone because as soon as he put it down, it would ring again. People kept calling, saying, 'We saw your son on the ice with the Stanley Cup!'"

Today, Gordon Rawlinson, that fan who became part of history by talking his way onto the ice for the Stanley Cup celebration in 1967, is the president of Rawlco Radio, one of Canada's larger media companies, based in Saskatchewan.

Among his other successes, Gordon Rawlinson looked back with great pride at this escapade. "It didn't last very long, maybe thirty seconds," he said, grinning, "It was quite fun."

12

REFLECTIONS

There is an indestructible bond that forever ties together teammates on championship squads. Repeated success only strengthens the enduring relationships. While cliched, analogies to soldiers at war are fitting. No one can understand the experience other than those that went through it. The undertaking — inexplicable. The images — unshakeable. The resolve — unwavering.

While most of the players who wore the blue and white during the dynasty do not see each other often, there is no doubt that these teammates are lifelong brothers.

"To live with eighteen guys like that for ten years is an experience that one should have in a lifetime," said Bob Baun. "Very few people have that kind of emotional experience." Comparing the experience to war, he noted, "It's like the old war movies, where you have a bomber crew that lived through that whole experience. They bring tears to your eyes just talking about them; about one another. All I can say is that I love them all."

Bob Pulford maintains a great sense of accomplishment as he looks back at the Maple Leafs of that era. "We reached the top of our profession. That's something that a lot of people have never done. You look back on those years and remember the time with pride. You wear the ring and you know that you've won the Stanley Cup. There are a lot of people who didn't win it."

Brotherhood comes into play in Pulford's memories, too. "When we get together, it's like a bunch of guys you grew up with. You don't see them for a long period of time, but when you do, you're close friends again. There was a great feeling of friendship and respect between those players on those teams. You might get mad at a guy in practice but you'd live and die with them."

Dick Duff also remembered the kinship between Leafs teammates. "Players on Stanley Cup teams share a special bond because the nature of the game is to win, and you really have to be a solid team to do that. To go against guys like [Gordie] Howe and [Red] Kelly on Detroit, or the Richards and [Jean] Beliveau on Montreal takes a united group. We couldn't afford to have some guys not getting along."

Duff chuckled, remembering the dressing room teasing. "We bent over backwards so it would be fun within our own group. We made fun of people's size or their features. We would remind a guy that he was bald or had a big nose, or his legs were like a cowboy or something. But the kidding only went to a certain point and then it stopped. We knew that there were barriers that you couldn't pass with certain people."

Duff won the Stanley Cup twice with Toronto, but it broke his heart to be traded away. First he went to New York, but ended up in Montreal, where he played with four more Stanley Cup-winning teams. "Winning the Stanley Cup was probably every person's dream. It was the thing that got them involved in hockey. Making the NHL is great, but it doesn't mean anything until you can win a championship. Then you can say, 'Not only did I make it, but our team was the best team.'"

Dave Keon, one of the lynchpins of the dynasty, reflected on it: "We had very skilled personnel on the first three that we won. Everyone worked well together and there was unity. We played for each other and won it as a team. And at that time, we probably had the best talent. In sixty-seven, our talent wasn't expected to carry us, but players came through in other ways and played very well. Our goaltenders played extremely well, and everyone just picked it up from there. Everyone got the feeling that, 'yes, we could do it,' and once we got that feeling, we were very difficult to beat."

Pulford agreed that the 1967 Leafs' team had something special. "There was a tremendous mixture of veterans and young players. You had Armstrong, Horton, Stanley, Kelly and Bower mixed in with some pretty good young hockey players. It was the camaraderie that existed that made that championship team, not ability, but a bunch of guys coming together to play who really wanted it."

In Pulford's opinion, one shared by most members of the teams that played in Toronto during the sixties, there was one key to the success. "In my own opinion, George Armstrong was the key to it all. He was the one ingredient that was responsible for those teams winning because he had great leadership qualities."

Another player integral to the success of the Leafs was Tim Horton. "He was really the heart of the Leafs," noted Jim McKenny. "There was a real bond amongst those old guys. They were real tight together like a family. It was like a war unit, and they had a hell of a lot of respect for each other."

Punch Imlach must be given credit for the role he played in constructing and motivating the team, but there is a stirring debate about how much credit he should receive. Bob Pulford suggested, "A good coach doesn't win hockey games but a bad coach can lose hockey games. Imlach was obviously a good coach because he won with a good team. He was loyal. When he had the right mix of people, he knew how to get the most out of them. He was good at that."

Discussion revolving around Punch Imlach generated comments on whether the Toronto Maple Leafs could have won further championships during that era. Billy Harris recalled, "Bob Baun was interviewed on CFRB and he said he would kid Punch by saying, 'Okay, four Stanley Cups in the sixties, but if you had any knowledge about coaching, we should have won ten or eleven!' Baun said this in jest, but what is scary is, I don't think the Toronto fans ever saw Carl Brewer or Frank Mahovlich at their best. They were two of the most talented hockey players that ever played the game, but Punch never came close to getting the potential out of those two guys. They were two people who required a one-on-one relationship with the boss, but Punch treated the team as a regiment."

Harris mused whether it mattered who coached the team during those glory years. "I don't know if Punch was lucky. We could discuss whether we would have won the Stanley Cups without Imlach for the next hundred years. I feel there is a good argument for that because of the quality of people we had on that hockey team. The guys were just starting to mature, and with the leadership that Bert Olmstead provided, we might have won some Stanley Cups with anybody as a coach. Maybe we could have won more Stanley Cups. Maybe we should have won ten."

"Imlach was there for eleven years," commented Carl Brewer, who was at odds with Imlach through much of his tenure with the Leafs. "People said [Imlach] was great because he won four Stanley Cups in eleven years. A lot of us felt that he should have had eight."

Imlach himself believed that the Maple Leafs should have won more than four Stanley Cup championships during that decade. "We could have won in 1961," he claimed. "If we had gotten by Detroit, we would certainly have knocked Chicago out. What happened to us was injuries. Olmstead and Kelly were hurt and Bower got hurt. I remember Howie Young charged Bower in the crease and put him out."

Johnny Bower was proud to be a part of the dynasty that was awarded the Stanley Cup on four occasions. "We were certainly happy we won as many as we did, particularly me, because when you are at the stage when you are playing at thirty-five, thirty-six, thirty-seven, you are getting old, and not too many goalies last that long. So I always considered myself pretty lucky and happy that I was on four Stanley Cups."

The simple fact is that the Toronto Maple Leafs, winners of the Stanley Cup in 1962, 1963, 1964 and 1967, have left an indelible legacy on fans; one that resonates all these decades later. As Allan Stanley concluded, "It was continuous excitement, and I'm just happy that I was a part of it."

13

Epilogue

So then, why has "Canada's team," as iconic a franchise as exists anywhere in sports, had the Stanley Cup elude them since 1967?

The answer is complex.

The 1967 Expansion Draft certainly played a role in demoting the defending Stanley Cup champions to a team that missed the playoffs in the very next season. Father Time finally caught up to the core of the team, and poor management decisions certainly played a critical role through the years

The complexion of the league was entirely different from the first puck drop of the 1967–68 season. What had been a six-team league since 1942–43 had now doubled in size, and the league introduced the Los Angeles Kings, Minnesota North Stars, Oakland Seals, Philadelphia Flyers, Pittsburgh Penguins and St. Louis Blues. All six cities had housed minor-league teams through the years, while Philadelphia (Quakers), Pittsburgh (Pirates) and St. Louis (Eagles) had each briefly existed as NHL franchises.

In preparation for the NHL Expansion Draft, each of the six existing NHL franchises was able to protect one goaltender and eleven skaters. Also excluded from the draft were players still of junior age (born on or after June 1, 1946), whether they were still playing junior or had turned professional.

The Maple Leafs protected Johnny Bower in goal and skaters Brian Conacher, Ron Ellis, Larry Hillman, Tim Horton, Dave Keon, Frank Mahovlich, Jim Pappin, Bob Pulford, Marcel Pronovost, Peter Stemkowski and Mike Walton. *The Globe and Mail* compared the draft to a rummage sale. For the most part, players made available were ageing veterans nearing retirement, career minor leaguers and youngsters who had dubious NHL futures. Nevertheless, the draft created a substantial upheaval to the Original Six franchises.

The draft was held on June 6, 1967, at the Queen Elizabeth Hotel in Montreal. The first two rounds were specific to goaltenders, and with the very first selection, the Los Angeles Kings chose Toronto's Terry Sawchuk. The Maple Leafs would also lose Gary Smith to the Oakland Seals.

Through twenty rounds, each of the six expansion franchises stocked up their rosters. Toronto was hit hard, losing twenty players. The Los Angeles Kings picked Terry Sawchuk, Mike Corrigan, Bill Flett, Ed Joyal and Lowell MacDonald from the Leafs. The Minnesota North Stars did not select any players from Toronto's unprotected list. The Oakland Seals chose Gary Smith, Bob Baun, Terry Clancy, Kent Douglas, Aut Erickson and Mike Laughton. The Pittsburgh Penguins' sole choice from the Leafs was Larry Jeffrey. The Philadelphia Flyers selected Don Blackburn and Brit Selby from Toronto. The St. Louis Blues plucked Al Arbour, John Brenneman, Darryl Edestrand, Fred Hucul, Larry Keenan and Gary Veneruzzo from the Maple Leafs. Of those players chosen, only Sawchuk, Baun, Douglas and Jeffrey could be deemed regulars with the Leafs in 1966–67.

Through the process, as players were selected from the list of one of the existing teams, unprotected players were able to be added to the protected list, and Toronto was able to re-add netminder Al Smith and skaters George Armstrong, Murray Oliver, Duane Rupp and Allan Stanley in this manner.

Certainly Toronto was not the only team hurt by the Expansion Draft, as the rules were common to all six existing NHL teams. It can be argued that the Leafs had greater depth, so that losing as many as twenty players wouldn't hurt the Maple Leafs as much, but in fact, the depth was no longer there. A farm system that through the decade had provided a wealth of talent ready to step into any hole, permanent or temporary, within the Leafs' roster, had been gutted. The short-sighted Leafs compromised their depth by selling their AHL team, the Rochester Americans, the previous summer, and their WHL affiliate, the Victoria Maple Leafs, just after the Expansion Draft. The Rochester Americans were sold to Vancouver purchasers for $400,000 in 1967 and the Victoria Maple Leafs were sold to a group from Phoenix for $500,000. But there were problems with that sale, and after a lawsuit ensued, it is doubtful that the Leafs' ownership ended up with much of anything. Through the sale of these two affiliates, the Maple Leafs lost forty-five players, many of whom had NHL potential. Some could have been exposed in the Expansion Draft to ensure that Toronto did not lose roster players.

Father Time certainly was finally able to catch up to the Toronto Maple Leafs. The age of the team had been questioned as early as 1962's Stanley Cup win. Journalists debated whether Allan Stanley was through, whether Johnny Bower was done, how much more hockey life still existed in George Armstrong. Imlach defied logic and rode his veterans, adding more along the way. His madness was, in fact, genius at the time. The addition of core players like Red Kelly paid substantial dividends, as did short-term role players like Gerry Ehman and Larry Regan. Later acquisitions such as Terry Sawchuk and Marcel Pronovost may have seemed hare-brained to some, but Imlach was able to squeeze every bit of pride and talent they had left out of them. While the Leafs had enjoyed amazing success with ageing veterans, the Dickie Moore comeback was unsuccessful.

Perhaps the superstitious Imlach was lucky in 1967. By then, the Over-the-Hill Gang truly was running on fumes. Bower was forty-two, Stanley forty, Kelly was thirty-nine, Horton and Sawchuk were thirty-seven, Armstrong and Pronovost thirty-six. "We went with a veteran team and won the Cup in sixty-seven," said Ron Ellis, just twenty-two himself at the time. "Within a year or two, a number of those players retired. We had a lot of holes to fill, but no farmhands were available. Management certainly knew that we were going to have six or eight guys retire, and they certainly had to be aware our farm system was going to be hit the hardest. I don't think the Leafs' management gave it much thought — a little arrogance, perhaps. We ended up more like an expansion team than the expansion teams were. That's how sad it was."

After winning the Stanley Cup in 1967, Imlach began dismantling the Toronto Maple Leafs. In part, it was done to update an aged squad, but there was more than a hint of spite and vindictiveness. The face of hockey was changing, and Punch was unwilling — and unable — to change with it.

Soon, most of that last championship squad was gone. Kelly retired at the conclusion of the 1966–67 season, and it was no surprise that he was hired to coach the L.A. Kings (although Imlach pulled a fast one by adding Kelly to the protected list as a fill during the Expansion Draft, simply to spite both the Kings and Kelly. Los Angeles was required to send a player to the Leafs in order to secure their coach). Not long afterwards, Pronovost went, too. But Imlach peddled most of his stars, many in questionable deals. Mahovlich and Stemkowski were packaged off to Detroit, Pappin to Chicago and Shack to Boston. By the fall of 1969, only six of the key members of Toronto's last championship remained: George Armstrong, Ron Ellis, Tim Horton, Dave Keon, Bob Pulford and Mike Walton.

The National Hockey League Players' Association was revived in 1967, and Imlach fought tooth and nail to rid his team of anything that would wrestle control out of the hands of the team management. He banned agents, especially the hated Alan Eagleson, from playing any role in contract negotiations.

There is little doubt that Imlach's arrogance contributed to the demise of the dynasty. Riding the miraculous finish in 1958–59, it seemed that Imlach did indeed have a crystal ball. A repeat visit to the Stanley Cup final in 1959–60 seemed to confirm that. But as the Maple Leafs enjoyed Stanley Cup success, Imlach, who was referred to behind closed doors as "the Big I," took on a facade of being bigger than the team. His coaching methods seem to work, but did they really? In fact, the notable battles with All-Stars Carl Brewer and Frank Mahovlich eroded the team and its spirit.

Some might argue that the Leafs began to go into decline following the Stanley Cup victory in 1964. Carl Brewer left the team a year later after a series of ongoing disputes. After being named to the NHL's First All-Star Team in 1962–63, he believed he deserved more money. When Imlach refused, Brewer retired and began attending classes at McMaster University in Hamilton. When Imlach realized that the tactic was not a bluff, he revisited the contract, and Brewer returned. But in 1963, Brewer broke his arm in the playoffs and felt that he should be compensated by the Maple Leafs because he was not able to work during that summer. Again, it was back to school for Carl, and again, a settlement was reached. But Imlach's penchant for motivation through intimidation finally drove Carl Brewer to leave the team for good while still in his prime. He was twenty-seven years old.

Frank Mahovlich was tortured by Imlach's methods. He became withdrawn, and his play was adversely affected. The fans booed him. He was forced to take two separate leaves from the team; both during the regular season play. During his final two seasons as a Maple Leaf, his productivity fell off to such a level that Mahovlich only scored eighteen and nineteen goals respectively. "I wasn't getting along with Imlach. The outcome was that they had to get rid of me," Mahovlich admitted. "I wasn't going to perform up to my ability."

In 1968, he was traded to Detroit and scored forty-nine goals. He scored forty-three with the Montreal Canadiens. "As soon as I left, my production went sky high," responded The Big M. "It was as if a piano had been lifted off my back."

There is a rebuttal to both of those arguments. Imlach admitted, "I had my battles with Frank Mahovlich, who sometimes couldn't stand what I asked of everybody on the Leafs team then; and with Carl Brewer, who quit the Leafs after our first three Stanley Cups. Sometimes, I think those cases are allowed to obscure the fact that with players like Johnny

Bower, Terry Sawchuk, George Armstrong, Allan Stanley, Tim Horton, Davey Keon and many others I had a good rapport that lasted well beyond my time with the Leafs." Punch was right. In fact, in the ultimate of ironies, after a long sojourn away, Carl Brewer actually returned to play for Imlach and the Maple Leafs in 1979–80.

"The one war I could not win was with Stafford Smythe," stated Imlach. "I could win battles, but not the war. Stafford and I did not get along. He found it galling that it was my team, not his."

Imlach walked out of Maple Leaf Gardens after eleven seasons and four Stanley Cup championships on April 6, 1969. Shortly after he arrived at his Scarborough home, friends began to congregate — King Clancy, *Toronto Telegram* sportswriter George Gross, former Leaf and long-time friend "Windy" O'Neill. "In each of my four Stanley Cups in the 1960s, champagne had flowed, and each time, I had put a bottle aside, taken it home and saved it. It seemed a good time to open the four bottles of champagne and toast not only what had been good about the last ten-and-a-half years, but what was going to happen next, whatever it was."

And so ended the Imlach era.

Finally, poor management decisions helped end the Maple Leafs' dynasty. The Leafs had squandered an outstanding core of prospects, some through the Expansion Draft, others in trades and some in waiver drafts. In 1972, with the onset of the fledgling World Hockey Association, belligerence took several other players out of the grip of the Maple Leafs, including Bernie Parent. Dave Keon, most regrettably, fled his beloved Leafs in a money squabble that left the player regarded as one of the finest ever to pull on a blue-and-white sweater with such animosity that, to this day, he refuses to involve himself in activities associated with the Toronto Maple Leafs, with the notable exception of an on-ice reunion for the 1967 Stanley Cup champions on February 7, 2007.

The NHL Entry Draft, an equitable opportunity for all NHL teams set up in part by Stafford Smythe, replaced sponsorship, but Toronto has not been particularly adept at drafting star players. While other teams landed franchise players, the Leafs' record is littered with names like Ernie

Moser (1969), who failed to make the grade after huge expectations. Toronto did, of course, hit the jackpot in 1970 with the selection of Darryl Sittler from the OHA's London Nationals.

As long as the Toronto Maple Leafs play hockey, the fans will continue to hold on to that dream that one day, soon, the team will return to Stanley Cup glory. But until that day arrives, we gaze back with eternal fondness at the Maple Leafs Forever, the dynastic team that captured the country's heart by capturing the Stanley Cup four times during the glory years.

BIBLIOGRAPHY

Batten, Jack. *Hockey Dynasty*. Toronto: Pagurian Press, 1969.

Batten, Jack. *The Leafs: An Anecdotal History of the Toronto Maple Leafs*. Toronto: Key Porter Books, 1994.

Baun, Bobby. *Lowering the Boom: The Bobby Baun Story*. Toronto: Stoddart Publishing, 2000.

Berger, Howard. *Maple Leaf Moments*. Toronto: Warwick Publishing, 1994.

Brewitt, Ross. *Clear the Track: The Eddie Shack Story*. Toronto: Stoddart Publishing, 1997.

Cole, Stephen. *The Last Hurrah: A Celebration of Hockey's Greatest Season '66-'67*. Toronto: Viking Books, 1995.

Coleman, Charles. *The Trail of the Stanley Cup, Volume 3, 1947-1967*. Sherbrooke, QC: Progressive Publications, 1976.

Conacher, Brian. *Hockey in Canada: The Way It Is*. Toronto: Gateway Press, 1970.

Conacher, Brian. *As the Puck Turns: A Personal Journey Through the World of Hockey*. Toronto: John Wiley and Sons, 2007.

Cox, Damien and Gord Stellick. *'67*. Toronto: John Wiley and Sons, 2004.

Duff, Bob with Johnny Bower. *The China Wall: The Timeless Legend of Johnny Bower*. Bolton, ON: Fenn Publishing, 2008.

Duplacey, James and Joseph Romain. *Toronto Maple Leafs: Images of Glory*. Scarborough, ON: McGraw-Hill Ryerson Ltd., 1990.

Ellis, Ron and Kevin Shea. *Over the Boards: The Ron Ellis Story*. Bolton, ON: Fenn Publishing, 2002.

Feschuk, Dave and Michael Grange. *Leafs Abomination*. Toronto: Random House Canada, 2009.

Fischler, Stan. *The Rivalry: Canadiens vs. Leafs*. Toronto: McGraw-Hill Ryerson Ltd., 1991.

Foster, Susan with Carl Brewer. *The Power of Two*. Bolton, ON: Fenn Publishing, 2006.

Gaston, Tom with Kevin Shea. *A Fan For All Seasons*. Bolton, ON: Fenn Publishing, 2001.

Harris, Billy. *The Glory Years*. Scarborough, ON: Prentice-Hall Canada, 1989.

Hodge, Charlie. *Golly Gee, It's Me: The Howie Meeker Story*. Toronto: Stoddart Publishing, 1996.

Horton, Lori and Tim Griggs. *In Loving Memory: A Tribute to Tim Horton*. Toronto: ECW Press, 1997.

Houston, William. *Inside Maple Leaf Gardens: The Rise and Fall of the Toronto Maple Leafs*. Scarborough, ON: McGraw-Hill Ryerson, 1989.

Hunter, Douglas. *Champions: The Illustrated History of Hockey's Greatest Dynasties*. Toronto: Penguin Books Canada, 1997.

Hunter, Douglas. *Open Ice: The Tim Horton Story*. Toronto: Viking Books, 1994.

Imlach, Punch with Scott Young. *Heaven and Hell in the NHL*. Toronto: McClelland and Stewart, 1982.

Imlach, Punch with Scott Young. *Hockey Is a Battle*. Toronto: Macmillan Company of Canada, 1969.

Leonetti, Mike. *Cold War: A Decade of Hockey's Greatest Rivalry*. Toronto: HarperCollins Canada, 2001.

Mahovlich, Ted. *The Big M: The Frank Mahovlich Story*. Toronto: HarperCollins Canada, 1999.

McFarlane, Brian. *Clancy: The King's Story*. Toronto: ECW Press, 1997.

Obodiac, Stan, editor. *The Leafs: The First 50 Years*. Toronto: McClelland and Stewart Ltd., 1977.

Obodiac, Stan. *Maple Leaf Gardens: Fifty Years of History*. Toronto: Van Nostrand Reinhold Ltd., 1981.

Podnieks, Andrew. *The Essential Blue & White Book*. Vancouver: Greystone Books, 2001.

Podnieks, Andrew. *Lord Stanley's Cup*. Bolton, ON: Fenn Publishing, 2004.

Shea, Kevin. *Barilko: Without A Trace*. Bolton, ON: Fenn Publishing, 2004.

Smythe, Conn with Scott Young. *Conn Smythe: If You Can't Beat 'Em in the Alley*. Toronto: McClelland and Stewart Limited, 1981.

Smythe, Thomas with Kevin Shea. *Centre Ice: The Smythe Family, the Gardens and the Toronto Maple Leafs Hockey Club*. Bolton, ON: Fenn Publishing, 2000.

Young, Scott. *The Leafs I Knew*. Toronto: Ryerson Press, 1966.

Zweig, Eric et al. *Maple Leaf Gardens: Memories and Dreams, 1931-1999*. Toronto: Dan Diamond and Associates, 1999.

NEWSPAPERS AND PERIODICALS

Boston Globe

Chicago Tribune

Globe and Mail

Montreal Gazette

New York Times

Toronto (Daily) Star

Toronto Telegram

The Hockey News

ELECTRONIC MEDIA

www.hhof.com Hockey Hall of Fame

www.sihrhockey.org Society for International Hockey Research (SIHR)

Hockey Night in Canada

Leafs TV "Classic Games"

ORAL REPORTS

George Armstrong
Andy Bathgate
Bob Baun
Johnny Bower
Carl Brewer
King Clancy
Brian Conacher
Dick Duff
Karl Elieff
Ron Ellis
Bob Haggert
Billy Harris
Larry Hillman
Gerri Horton
Lori Horton
Punch Imlach
Red Kelly
David Keon
Jim McKenny
Bert Olmstead
Jim Pappin
Marcel Pronovost
Bob Pulford
Frank Mahovlich
Eddie Shack

ACKNOWLEDGEMENTS

Creating this book has been a monumental task that required significant efforts from four passionate Maple Leafs' fans who share credit as co-authors.

KEVIN SHEA

The idea for this book tapped into some of my most cherished childhood memories. Like my co-authors, I must thank my father for nurturing my love of the Toronto Maple Leafs. We lost Dad in 1991, but he left us with a lifetime of memories and an unwavering passion for the blue and white. Today, that passion continues with my brother, Dale, and my Mom, Margaret England. While Dale now lives in Vancouver and professes to enjoying the Canucks, deep down he will always be a Leafs' fan. And my mother wouldn't miss a Maple Leafs' broadcast, and wears her Leafs' sweater while watching the games on TV. I come from good blue-and-white stock!

My love and thanks to Nancy, who has barely seen me for the past two years while I hunkered down to research and write this book. Her encouragement, patience and frequent forays to Tim Hortons are appreciated more than she will ever know.

A few more thank yous to those who have steadfastly provided encouragement: Maureen and Tim Burgess, Steve Waxman, Kim Cooke, Andrea

Orlick and Betty Shea. My thanks, too, to the team at the Hockey Hall of Fame, as well as Cathy Kinast and Kevin Vautour for providing additional research assistance.

And then there are my partners, each of whom contributed in unique and significant ways. My heartfelt appreciation to Paul Patskou, Roly Harris and Paul Bruno, who made the journey enjoyable and the realization of this dream possible.

PAUL PATSKOU

My first recollection of watching hockey was during the magical 1958–59 season. Each Saturday night, my father and I would anxiously wait for 9 p.m. to arrive to watch the Leafs on *Hockey Night in Canada.* What a season that was! The Leafs spent most of the season in last place and made the playoffs on the final night of the season. An inspirational Cup run ensued, and I fell in love with both hockey and the Leafs. A few months later, my father passed away, and those Saturday nights of the '58–59 season have since become more special to me.

This love of the game led me to a career as a hockey historian, video archivist and author. I always thought it would be fun to relate the story of those great Toronto teams of the sixties to other Leaf fans. And what better way for readers to relive that era than the way it was experienced back then — through the eyes of *Hockey Night in Canada.*

It was a thrill for me to be the associate producer of the Maple Leafs' "Classic Games" on *Leafs TV.* I was fortunate to be able to watch many of the televised games played by the Leafs from 1957 to 1967. Besides analyzing these vintage games, which gave me great insight into the era, the conversations with Leafs' alumni both on and off-camera were enlightening. I have used all of this experience and information to help provide the best possible account of the Leafs of the 1960s in this book.

I would like to thank a few people who were instrumental in my career. Brian McFarlane not only opened doors for me, but allowed me to pick his brain about anything to do with HNIC and the Leafs. I would also like to thank Mark Askin for his tremendous help through the years.

My gratitude also goes to John Shannon for giving me the opportunity to be the historical consultant on *Leafs TV*. I am grateful to Joe Bowen, Natalie Tedesco, Jeff Marek and Craig Campbell and the staff at the HHOF for their continued support. And thanks to my uncles, who took me to Leafs' games, and to my mother, who through trying times in the 1960s, always persevered to make things better, for putting up with my obsession for my Toronto Maple Leafs.

ROLY HARRIS

In 1956, when I was a nine-year-old growing up in Toronto, I lost my Dad, Charlie, who was a sports-lover. My mother, Muriel, was a rock, but I pretty well had the run of the city. This circumstance led to a 250-home *Globe and Mail* paper route and subway rides to $2 standing-room tickets at Leafs' games at my second home — Maple Leaf Gardens

I was fortunate enough to witness the Punch Imlach era in its entirety. Imlach was fired, unceremoniously, in 1969. I went on to other things, including family and a legal career. As time passed, I couldn't understand why no one had adequately recorded and published the recollections of the players and staff of those special Toronto Stanley Cup teams of the 1960s

On April 21, 1985, Leafs' broadcaster Foster Hewitt died at age eighty-two, providing the impetus for me, a thirty-seven-year-old assistant crown attorney with no journalistic background but a passion for the project, to begin interviews before the subjects lost their lives or memories (King Clancy died in 1986, Punch Imlach in 1987). I'd been conducting audio interviews with my elderly mother and Aunt Isobel before Alzheimers and the effects of an auto-pedestrian collision, respectively, took them away, and didn't realize the enormity of this larger undertaking or the time involved.

I owe a special debt to Gord Stellick, who was working for the Leafs at that time. Stellick, physiotherapist Karl Elieff and Billy Harris were invaluable in linking me to others — for example, Imlach via Elieff, whom I would not have been able to interview otherwise. I am still amazed and touched, almost a quarter century later, by how generous the Leafs' players and staff were in sharing their time, reminiscences, insights into teammates, and often their homes, with a stranger with a tape recorder.

Friends Gwen Grubb, Joni Glover and Ann Stokes helped by typing transcripts, and author Jack Batten took time to read them. My in-laws, Jim and Marion Moyes, visited Bert Olmstead in Calgary to take pictures.

Closer to home, our children, Summer, Christian and Stuart, tolerated my absences and distraction, and my wife, Janie, not only typed interviews, but in this enterprise, as in all things, provided the faith and encouragement which kept me going.

PAUL BRUNO

The first game I ever attended was the 1962 All-Star Game as a three-year-old. I still have the program from that game. Ever since then, I, like many members of the burgeoning Leaf Nation, lived for each television or radio broadcast of the next Leafs' game. That's still the case today.

I always dreamed of having an impact on this great sport, and establish a rapport with my favourite team, the Toronto Maple Leafs. In 1991, I found that opportunity by approaching Pat Park in the Maple Leafs' Media Relations department with my idea to track a wider range of in-game statistics than had ever previously been attempted. Soon after that, General Manager Cliff Fletcher saw the end product and helped to introduce it to his peers in the NHL. This process evolved as the prototype of the current Real Time Scoring System, used by the NHL and all major hockey leagues throughout the world.

That experience, and this one, where we have recounted the success of the Toronto Maple Leafs of the 1960s, have been labours of love, for a true blue and white fanatic.

I would like to send my love and thanks to my wife Cathy and children Daniel and Valerie, my own championship team. I would also never have dreamed of something like this without the inspiration of my late parents, Mario and Lina. Best of all, it gives me a chance to relive this time that I shared with my brother, Silvano. All of us are Leafs' fans, forever.

INDEX

Page numbers in *italics* refer to photographs.